Language
and Thinking
in School

Language and Thinking in School

A Whole-Language Curriculum

Kenneth S. Goodman
University of Arizona

E. Brooks Smith
Wayne State University

Robert Meredith
Wheelock College

Yetta M. Goodman
University of Arizona

RICHARD C. OWEN PUBLISHERS, INC.
New York

Library of Congress Cataloging in Publication Data

Language and thinking in school.

   Rev. ed. of: Language and thinking in school /
E. Brooks Smith, Kenneth S. Goodman, Robert Meredith.
2nd ed. c1976.
   Includes bibliographies and index.
   1. Language arts.   2. Thought and thinking.
3. English language—Study and teaching.   4. Children—
language.   I. Goodman, Kenneth S.   II. Smith, E.
Brooks, 1917–   .   Language and thinking in school.
LB1576.L294 1986   372.6   86–28601
ISBN 0–913461–81–4

RICHARD C. OWEN PUBLISHERS, INC.
Rockefeller Center
Box 819
New York, New York 10185

Printed in the United States of America

Preface

In this, the third edition of this book, the major purpose remains what it was in the first two editions: to synthesize some modern views of language and linguistics, of literature and semiotics, and of thinking and knowing that are pertinent to education. The third edition is much changed because there has been so much development in all these areas in the period between editions. We think the earlier editions may have played a role in the growing recognition that since language, in a broad sense, is the medium of instruction and learning, a language-thought centered view of teaching and learning is indispensible to planning curricular strategies and instructional tactics for all subject areas. Our goal has always been to focus on the nature of language and thinking so that we could bring new significance to some older ideas of the child-centered era and lend support of more modern approaches in open inquiry education and whole language. This has made it possible to suggest new views of the teaching of reading, writing and the language arts rooted in the best intuitions of the past and strongly based on modern scholarship and research.

We have drawn heavily on many historical and contemporary resources but the basic thesis is the authors'. This is a thematic book exploring many possible relationships among language, thought processes, and education. It is not an eclectic summary. Rather it develops theoretical positions and proposes practical applications for the consideration of both beginning and experienced teachers who have seen the power of language and thinking in their classrooms and would like to investigate these phenomena further in relation to their work. We believe school administrators, curriculum leaders, and teacher educators will find here a rationale by which they can assess the soundness of present programs and the potential of new proposals. Practical means for building and assessing curriculum and instruction centered around the development of language and thinking are presented throughout the book.

The development of the three successive editions of the book reflects development and events in education and the foundational disciplines but it also reflects the development of the authors. We've learned much over the 20-year period since the book was first conceived. We've learned from colleagues, from teachers and from children. The comments of readers and reviewers have encouraged us to maintain the style and voice of the original and avoid slipping toward those of a conventional methods text. We are grateful for their suggestions for improving and updating the content of this book.

In the period of this book's existence a battle has been sharpening in contemporary education between a behavioristic-mechanistic view of education that sees teachers as technicians to be trained to "deliver" prepackaged technology-based curricula and a humanistic-scientific view that sees teachers as intelligent professionals who need a base of knowledge and theory for the decisions they must make in helping their pupils to grow. We're pleased that readers of our previous editions have recognized and appreciated our commitment throughout the book to this latter view. We regard our potential audience as committed educators who want access to the best knowledge so that they may be highly effective teachers.

Over the three editions, the book has broadened its focus in several directions. Originally, it had an elementary school focus. It has broadened to include the full range of use and development of language and thought in teaching learning situations that range from preschool to adult education. It also has become a more international book, partly by the intention of the authors and partly by adoption. Since the book was first published, it has been well received outside the United States, especially in Canada, England, Australia, and New Zealand. The non-North American examples that we include come to us from our readers and our broadening experience outside the United States. Still, the authors are Americans and we hope our non-American readers will forgive our tendency towards preoccupation with the peculiarities of late twentieth-century American education and culture.

In the third edition our view of a dual curriculum based on language and thinking has matured and is more completely explicated throughout the book. The psycholinguistically based view of reading has developed into a transactional view of written language, reading, and writing. The book reflects new theoretical understanding of how and why both written and oral language develop. Yetta Goodman, who joins us as the fourth author, has added greatly to our discussion of preschool growth into literacy. A new chapter on the teaching of writing reflects the movements toward more writing at all levels of education. With Fred Burton's help, we give more concern to literature for young people.

The current edition also reflects the exciting developments in classroom practices and school policies in English-speaking countries. The grass-roots movement in Canada and in the United States, which teachers call whole-language teaching, has created a reality consistent with concepts of the authors and has provided us with rich examples and practical concerns. In many places school, local authority, state or provincial—and even national decisions—have made the holistic language-thought views we advocate official policy. Where this is true the major concern becomes how to turn theory and belief into practice and reality. In the final chapter we consider implementation. If this book has been successful in synthesizing the knowledge base for this movement and these policies, then it may help to assure that this is not simply another fad but a major step forward in education.

The authors hope that the book may contribute to the maximal educational use of the full, versatile resources of language and of the thinking potential of young people.

K.S.G., E.B.S., R.M., and Y.M.G

Acknowledgments

The authors are indebted to the scholarship of the late Lawrence V. Frank for his able synthesis of a number of key modern ideas from psychology and philosophy and from cognitive and linguistic studies as they relate to education. Edward Chittenden reviewed the original Piaget formulations and ideas on "open" education. Many people contributed to the book: John Camp on mathematics literacy; Thomas Davidson on the analysis and evaluation of communication in teaching; Lawrence Gagnon on questioning; and Dwayne Huebner on the arts of teaching. We drew on the ideas of Joseph Grannis in curriculum design. Carolyn Burke, Dorothy Menosky, P. David Allen, Barbara Greene, William Page, Rudine Sims, Dorothy Watson, Mervin Thornton, Patricia Rigg, Hughes Moir, and Peter Rousch shared their research studies in applied linguistics. William Curtis and Ruth Moline contributed to the earlier editions on children's literature. Fred Burton provided the major redrafting of that section for the current edition.

Robert Williams, Gene Yax, and Richard Snell provided classroom activity suggestions in language arts and social studies. Peter Dow, Ruth MacDonald, Costa Leodas, Lansing Wagner, Gary Kilarr, Gred Davenport, Paul Jacobs, Bill Greenwood, A. J. Light, Joseph Sales, David Wallace, Patrick Johnson, and Pierce McLeod all shared ideas. Haig Derderian, Harry Woods, Ann Crile, Norine Donaldson, Marion Riseborough, and Jean Fuqua are teachers who contributed examples of their planning and practices. Special appreciation is given to Jonathan Smith, Debra Goodman, Karen Goodman Castro, and Wendy Goodman Hood for sharing their stories and experiences. Allan Priore provided careful and insightful editing.

In the third edition, special thanks are due to Kristine Jilbert, and Yvonne and David Freeman. Bryan Taylor supplied more UK examples and insights. David Wallace was helpful to Brooks Smith in the original editing.

This third edition is dedicated to the memory of Elizabeth K. Smith, who gave so much support on the earlier editions.

Contents

1

Language, Thinking, and Learning:
Focal Points of a
Dual Curriculum

Even if the thing is there to represent the meaning, the word may be produced so as to evoke the meaning. Since intellectual life depends on possession of a store of meanings, the importance of language as a tool of preserving meanings cannot be overstated.

. . . Without words as vehicles . . . no cumulative growth of intelligence could occur. Experience might form habits of physical adaptation but it would not teach anything; for we should not be able to use old experience consciously to anticipate and regulate a new experience.

(John Dewey, 1933)

Anthropologists named our species "Homo sapiens," wise human, in honor of our ability to think in ways no other species, living or dead, has achieved. They might just as well have called us "Homo linguisticus," language-using human, because it is our ability to develop and use language which makes it possible to pool our wisdom, to share learning with others, and to manipulate our thoughts. And our ability to create and use language is just as unique among all species.

In this book we start from a simple premise: the basic responsibility of schools is to cultivate language and thinking and the knowledge which is acquired through their use. We see language and thinking as developing through the content of the curriculum and we see the development of knowledge in every area of the curriculum as always necessarily involving language and thinking.

In recent years curriculum planning has been dominated by industrial systems models which tend to fractionate the curriculum into separate highly structured bits and pieces to be taught and evaluated separately. In these narrow curricula, language and thinking have been separated from the subject matter content. Language has been treated as an object of instruction, not the basic medium of learning. And thinking has been neglected altogether since it can not be seen or evaluated directly. At the same time the curriculum has been straightjacketed by back-to-basics movements linked to mastery-learning systems in the "skills" of reading, writing, and arithmetic.

This latter trend has caused the curriculum to be further disconnected from the substance of language and thinking in education—ideas that are developed through the interplay of experience, language, and knowledge. The focus on development of language and thinking in this book brings back continuity, substance, and drive to curriculum making by putting to work new insights from theory and studies on language and thinking and their development.

In the schools John Goodlad studied, he found that the focus in the first nine grades and in lower tracks beyond that was on language arts and mathematics but only treating them as facts and skills. In these basic subjects, the schools were not "developing all those qualities listed under "intellectual development": the ability to think rationally, the ability to use, evaluate, and accumulate knowledge, a desire for further learning." (Goodlad, 1984, p. 236)

Our view puts language and thinking back at the center of the curriculum. It offers an approach to teaching and learning based in modern scientific theory and research, and offers a humanistic, holistic alternative to the sterilized, atomistic approaches that Goodlad found so dominant in American schools.

Rationale

Language and thinking develop together as children confront new problematic situations. Children respond to them, try to figure out what is happening, and finally come to terms with the problems by modifying their own schemes of things by incorporating into them the resultant impressions, attitudes, and ideas. Even before children begin to speak, they are responding to speech in situations involving parents and other speakers while they pick up impressions through all their senses. Even before children sense the communicative functions of language, they sense its social function—they know that people interact through language before they know why. All parents sense that children understand others more completely than they can express themselves, particularly in concrete observable situations.

Although both language and thought seem to arise from children's universal innate human potential, they develop and are nurtured through social situations that require language and thought. Language is both personal and social. So, as language develops it moves toward the dialect of the community, and as thought develops it also reflects the way the community organizes meaning: the categories, values, and life views. The home and neighborhood are rich in opportunities to learn.

The school environment must also be rich in opportunities to meet new situations requiring new language and thought. When children are deprived of such situations, the development of these two essentials for effectively coping with life is retarded or diverted. The devastating impact of such deprivation is dramatically illustrated in Herzog's fllm, *Land of Silence and Darkness* (1971). In the film, a child born deaf and blind has been incarcerated in a prison-like room for 21 years.

In the real world language is extended, enriched, restructured, and self-corrected as people move into new situations confronting new people, new problems that must be solved, or new ideas that must be met, understood, and used. The present everyday level of language is challenged; when it does not suffice, new language is developed. This can mean expanding the first language, the mother tongue, or it can mean learning a second dialect or a second language.

When people are placed in a new area of life space, facing new people, problems, and experiences, they are likely to find that their language and conceptual schemas are inadequate and so a striving for expanded expression becomes an educating life force. But experience that is supported by intellectual reflection and/or dialogue through speech and writing with knowledgeable persons will be much more likely to produce growth. That's why school is so important.

Language development follows and is facilitated by cognitive development and in turn facilitates such development. Both language and thought expand through this interaction, and it is this expansion that becomes the key objective of the school curriculum. Expansion on the preexisting base of language, thinking, and knowledge will be a theme throughout this book.

In *Children's Minds,* Margaret Donaldson summarizes recent research in both language and thinking that shows that young children build thought and language structures of some sophistication, provided they are developed in life situations within the experience of the children. (Donaldson, 1978) Many children can succeed in tasks requiring a "decentering" or "conservation" process, for example, when the tasks are set in familiar situations and if familiar language is used to let the children know what is expected.

This research extends the overall significance of the concepts of Jean Piaget. (Piaget and Inhelder, 1969) Thinking, like language, is developmental. Very young children are not capable of complex, abstract, and objective thinking, but they can make sense of the world around them by observing, listening, and making inferences, testing them out at the same time that they develop the language to express their insights. Indeed, it seems that they can find new language if there are familiar situations where the concepts will develop and the language will be needed.

But situations in school may not be so familiar for children. Often many abstractions are introduced, including decontextualized letters and numerals. Teachers and organizers of schools need to encourage learners to bring real life and real life problems into the school or take the children out of school to observe real life so they can think, talk, and write about significant, relevant life situations. At the same time, social studies, sciences, and the humanities can provide the context for situations in which language-thought structures can be expanded and deepened. Making school experiences relevant and functional will be another major theme of this book.

The Curricular Tradition

This is a book about curriculum as well as about development and use of language and thinking. Our plea for real life learning situations is not new. It draws on the philosophy of progressivism with its "life experience" oriented curriculum. In the era of progressive education, John Dewey's idea of intellectualized experience became the organizing concept, with thematic, integrated units built around the project method developed by William Heard Kilpatrick. (1925) Groups of children worked on theme-based projects and learned language, science, social science, and the arts in the process. Florence Stratemeyer stressed the need for intellectualizing experience by using "persistent life situations" as the thematic spiraling core of the curriculum. (Stratemeyer, Forker, and McKim, 1947)

All of these leaders stressed the progressive notion of "learning by doing." What was not well developed is the concept that thought and language are part of doing things and in turn are the media of turning experiences into knowledge and concepts. Teachers can confront their learners with situations, choosing those which will be more relevant to the learners and most likely to produce growth in thought and language as well as knowledge.

Bruner inspired the conceptual theme process for curriculum construction. (1966) Such curricula were developed in the 1960s for the physical and social sciences. These curricula used the processes and themes of each field of science as central constructs. They emphasized scientific inquiry. They should now be recreated in view of contemporary life situations in relation to changing times and attitudes. They must be tailored to local interests and concerns.

Current Needs for a Language and Thought Core

Teachers, administrators, and school boards need to call a halt to the industrializing, dehumanizing, and anti-intellectual approaches to curriculum building. What is needed is a unified, holistic curriculum for the concluding decades of the twentieth century to serve the ever-evolving social, political, and economic needs of democratic societies.

A literate citizen who has little ability for dealing with the analysis of ideas is a danger to a democratic society. A skills curriculum detached from situational activities that require thought and language of a substantive and analytical nature not only excludes students from real problem solving but is a danger to the survival of schooling for democracy.

In Great Britain, the Department of Education and Science sponsored an "11-16 Curriculum Project" that stresses an innovative secondary school curriculum. In a paper entitled "Language in the Whole Curriculum: English and a Linguistic Education," they proposed a linguistic education for which the responsibility lies in the school as a community. They point out that language experiences in school are all too frequently limited to superficial uses of language, such as direct and simple questions and answers, as the deeper and more significant language becomes alien to pupils. The authors see school language as a vital core to the whole educational process, with the teacher in the pivotal role of monitoring, supporting, modeling, and expanding. (Schools Council, 1976, p. 30)

Moira McKenzie, from the Inner London Education Authority, has developed a set of videotapes that show teachers integrating, conceptualizing, analyzing, and generalizing with reading, speaking, and writing. (McKenzie, 1977) Middle-grade children are shown working individually, in pairs, and in groups on science, social studies, and humanities under the teacher's interactive guidance. The tapes illustrate well a curriculum built around language and thinking.

In this chapter we'll focus on some specifics of this thought and language centered curricula. In the rest of the book we'll build the knowledge base for teachers to develop and facilitate such a curriculum. In the closing chapter we'll discuss whole language programs for putting these ideas into action.

A Thought and Language-centered Curriculum

Essentially what we propose is a double agenda for schools. From the general perspective this is a thought and language-centered curriculum, but it is two curricula in one. It is a curriculum for the development of language and thinking, and it is a curriculum for learning through language and thinking. Our view is that each serves the other and that both have to be planned and monitored for either to be successful. We need to be concerned for the thought and language structures that should be developing and then consider the kinds of life situations that rely on knowledge from the arts, sciences, mathematics, or social studies that should become the matrix for their development.

The curriculum is integrated, holistic, and naturalistic. It integrates traditional disciplines and subject areas around life situations and problem solving. It emphasizes language, whole and undivided, in use in the context of real speech events and literacy events rather than fragmented into skill exercises. And it is naturalistic in that it treats learning in school as much the same as it is outside of school: human beings are constantly trying to make sense of their world.

Throughout this book we will be utilizing a concept articulated by Halliday. (1979) There are three types of learning that involve language:

Learning language
Learning through language
Learning about language

But these three kinds of learning are interdependent; they happen simultaneously in the course of real speech events and literacy events. These are instances of the use of oral or written language by real people with real purposes, needs, and intentions, in the context of real events. We learn about language as we learn language, and we learn through language. Teachers and curricula cannot usefully sequence these. They cannot teach *about* language in order to facilitate *learning* language. They cannot teach language apart from its use as a prerequisite to learning *through* language. When children are involved in the functional use of language, then opportunities for all three kinds of learning are present. Thus, the dual school curriculum develops language through learning and learning through language, and, in the process of doing both, children develop a keen interest in language itself and learn about language.

The Whole-Language Curriculum

We use the term *whole-language curriculum* for our dual curriculum because that is becoming the most popular term among teachers for curricula that keep language whole and in the context of its thoughtful use in real situations. In this chapter we provide an overview of such a curriculum. The rest of the book cycles back on all the ideas presented here to expand, provide more examples, and provide additional rationale for their use.

Partly to defend themselves and their pupils against isolated and arbitrary skill drills and mastery learning schemes, teachers have become increasingly interested in such activities as having young readers predict what will happen in stories rather than in having them answer multiple-answer questions and fill-in workbook pages. They are involving children in writing rather than drilling them on spelling words. They are seeing, once again, the values of integrating studies around central themes that encourage thought and language development. They are using new questioning strategies to lift the levels of classroom thinking and language use.

The whole-language curriculum involves learners in expanding cycles of the thinking processes at advancing levels of language complexity and sophistication in tune with the needs of modern growing young people. At any point in time these processes are expressed through intensive functional and relevant use of talking, listening, reading, and writing that emerges from real and simulated life situations motivated, planned, and monitored by the teachers and learners.

The Content Curriculum

In our curriculum, knowledge, attitudes, and competence are being built within and across subjects and disciplines through the use of language and thinking processes. But our concern is not with isolated strings of facts. Rather, we are concerned with learning how to learn—with use of scientific method, logic, and reason—with solving problems efficiently and effectively—with a love of learning and a zest for problem solving. We want to create learning situations in which risk-taking is encouraged, time is allowed for thinking, and mistakes and mis-understandings are accepted as essential to human growth and development.

At the elementary level, the dual curricula are usually taught by one teacher in self-contained classrooms or by a team in a school using nongraded or family grouping. At the secondary level, English teachers are responsible for the whole-language curriculum, but their efforts must be coordinated with the other teachers whose focus is on content.

Implementing the Whole-Language Curriculum

The whole-language curriculum recognizes an essential of language learning: people learn to talk by talking, comprehend oral language by listening, write by writing, and read by reading. And they learn to think by thinking. The school program is built around stimulating the expansion of language and thinking in the context of their functional use. It uses every opportunity to expand on the existing base of language and thinking to provide rich opportunities for their functional use and to encourage refinement, flexibility, and variety within these uses.

Hermine Sinclair-de-Zwart, a psycholinguist who worked with Piaget, has demonstrated that language follows rather than precedes conceptual development. (Sinclair-de-Zwart, 1969) In studying children who did and did not have the concept of conservation she found that those that did conserve used more relational terms (for example, "more than") and more varied terms rather than polar opposites like "big" and "small." They also used more coordinated terms to describe ("He has more marbles, but they are smaller."). Her research suggests that there is little merit in trying to get children to use more complex and advanced language before they have developed the cognitive structures and patterns of thinking that require such language.

Children learn language because they need to describe their universe and communicate with those around them. They learn by wholes and eventually induce from these learned wholes the underlying structures of the language. If the school works with children toward expanded efficiency and effectiveness in the use of language, eventually, as their language grows more effective, it will also fall within the general norms of society. Language and its structure are interwoven with cultural values and cultural perceptions. Expansion in language must closely parallel the learners' expanding views, perceptions, and cognitive schemes of the world around them.

In developing language effectiveness in a pragmatic way, communication of meaning should be the guide to decisions about usage. Is meaning enhanced or diminished by a certain expression? A phrase may have low status in certain social settings, but it still may be the most effective way to state the idea in communicating with certain audiences. On the other hand, a localism may be less effective than a more widely used expression in communicating to a general audience.

Language is constantly changing, but social attitudes toward change lag behind. At appropriate ages children need to learn about this social dimension of language; then they will understand why certain expressions are useful in one context but not in another. *If the teacher concentrates on expanding their language, children with varying dialect backgrounds can eventually achieve a flexibility that meets the demands of society for situationally appropriate English.*

Priorities and Objectives

In this section we'll briefly show how a whole-language curriculum would incorporate major aspects of a school's language arts program. A key decision in planning any language arts program is what it will include. Some programs are narrow, confining themselves to presenting isolated reading and writing "skills" and a system of grammatical descriptions and selected aspects of language etiquette labeled "usage." But an effective language arts or English program must be much broader. The time and energy devoted to any single aspect must be keyed to purposes based on a point of view of the role of the school in language development—a school language policy.

A modern policy is based on two premises: (1) all children have achieved a high degree of language competence in at least one dialect of one language by the time they come to school and (2) this language is at the same time their means of expression and communication, their medium of thought, and the central tool of their learning.

The vital role of the school is to build on the existing competence. In exercising this role, teachers and curriculum planners must keep in mind that all aspects of oral and written language are developmental. Growth in effectiveness, not perfection, must be stressed.

Oral language is learned in the context of real speech events, real communicative transactions with people where the characteristics of the participants, their purposes, the context of the situation, what is being communicated, and the language used all are important. The counterparts of speech events for written language are literacy events—real, purposeful uses of written language in which people are participants as writers, readers, or both.

Since within any speech event or literacy event there are, as Halliday says, simultaneous possibilities for three kinds of learning (learning language, learning about language, and learning through language), then a whole-language curriculum must be designed to further all three.

In a whole-language program there is little use for instruction designed to present knowledge about language directly. Knowledge about language and how it works is important, but it develops best and most usefully in the context of real speech events or literacy events.

No language curriculum could or should effectively isolate reading, writing, and literature or any aspect of them from the rest of the language program. Oral and written language activities can draw heavily on literature and lead outward to literature. The reading program, integrated with the whole-language curriculum, can help to develop taste, interest, and critical insight into literature. An effective written composition program will also support development of spelling and handwriting. In a whole-language curriculum they become part of development toward effective writing, not ends in themselves.

The common division of the English curriculum in colleges and secondary schools into language, composition, and literature is not a useful framework. A more appropriate division would be into language processes: reading, writing, speaking, and listening. This would, however, unnecessarily separate oral and written language and productive and receptive language.

Our whole-language curriculum picks up on the three types of learning cited above but translates them into focuses of instruction. There are thus three focal concerns: (1) concerns for language development, which can be subdivided into (a) increasing language effectiveness and (b) changing language; (2) learning about language; and (3) learning through language, which is the basis for the content curriculum.

1. *Language development*
   a. *Increasing language effectiveness.* If we "start where the learner is," then the objectives of increasing language effectiveness must include the following:
      (i) *Listening.* This deserves far fuller and more sophisticated treatment than it gets in most programs. It's not a matter of developing listening comprehension exercises. Rather, it's a matter of teachers involving pupils in real speech events, helping pupils be aware of their roles as listeners in speech events, providing them opportunities to discuss what they understand from what they hear, and demonstrating that a value is placed on effective listening.

(ii) *Informal language.* There needs to be concern for language in its most basic and fundamental uses: conversation, discussion, argument, persuasion, questioning, answering, problem solving, and narrating personal experiences.

(iii) *Narrative composition.* This includes all imaginative uses of language to achieve aesthetic as well as communicative effects. Oral composition should be stressed as well as written composition.

(iv) *Expository composition.* Schools should value list making; letter and note writing; journals and diaries; reporting; describing and communicating complex ideas, instructions, and directions in effective ways, research and study skills; and essays.

(v) *Reading.* Since reading, like writing, extends language competence into a new medium, it may be considered as part of the general objective of increasing language effectiveness in all areas of the curriculum.

(vi) *Literature.* Literature is also an extension of the students' language effectiveness, because through it they expand their effectiveness in dealing with aesthetic uses of language. Students develop a sense of story, they develop a feeling for the macrostructure of different kinds of texts, and they develop their personal taste and responses to literature. All this builds their ability to comprehend a widening range of written language.

b. *Changing language.* School language curriculum traditionally has made a major effort, while teaching language, to try to change the way pupils use language. Even grammar has been taught for the purpose of changing the grammar of the language that pupils use. Such programs are not based on an understanding of the role of grammar in language or on how people develop grammar. If attempts to change language are seen as helping pupils grow in flexibility and effectiveness, then they support natural growth and development. Too often pressure for change has been at cross purposes to the pupils' development and attempts to push them into the narrow constraints of "standard" language. In many cases, the instruction has treated the pupils' language as wrong and used isolated drill to teach "correct" or "proper" forms. Such exercises are misguided in two respects. They treat the pupils' language as defective and they assume that language can be taught and learned a piece at a time. Neither premise is true.

Schools face the issue of how to deal with the range of dialects pupils speak and their social status. Do schools have the mission of changing pupils' language? No. But do they have the mission of helping pupils comprehend high-status dialects and even switch to them in some speaking and writing? In this book we'll argue that true language change is a response to personal language need and that instruction can support change, but it can't force or control it.

2. *Learning about language.* We learn about language as we use it. Children at very young ages will comment about language or begin asking what particular words mean. Schools can help pupils to sort out what they have learned intuitively about language. Furthermore, language is an important aspect of

culture and of each person. So it's certainly worthy of study. And learning linguistic terminology can provide a means for talking about language.

a. *Grammar*. Language has structure and a set of rules by which that structure is built. Everyone who uses language has developed control over these rules and their use. Grammar isn't studied then as a way of improving one's language. However, pupils will find it interesting to examine the rules they use to understand how language works.

b. *Other language aspects*. In learning about language there are many aspects that are worthy of attention: the history of language, semantics, pragmatics, word derivations, the relationships between languages, dialectology, linguistic geography, linguistic logic, and language games. British schools in the last few years have introduced "language awareness" courses and units, which are designed to help students become aware of language, its functions, forms, and components in the context of the students' own language uses and encounters.

If real speech events and literacy events comprise the substance of the pupils' school language experiences, then all these objectives will be served at the same time. But there are times when the teacher will help pupils to focus on one or another of the objectives.

We visualize a curriculum built on the base of the existing linguistic and cognitive development of the pupils. There is an unfortunate history of building curriculum from the top down, starting with college entrance requirements and orienting the secondary school curriculum to these, then gearing the elementary curriculum to demands of the secondary school. Such an approach ignores the opportunities to expand on the preexisting competence of the learners at each stage.

Several national groups in the United States using the banner of education for excellence have strongly advocated this dominance of the curriculum from above. Here's one such statement:

> The curriculum in the crucial eight grades leading to the high school years should be specifically designed to provide a sound base for study in those and later years in such areas as English-language development and writing. (National Commission on Excellence in Education, 1983)

Sequence: From Preschool to High School

In our view children have the right to be children. They have the right to grow, to develop, to think and to inquire like children, to learn through play, and to take the time to explore their world. The goal of each successive level of schooling is not to prepare pupils to succeed in the next level but rather to build a growing foundation of language, thought, knowledge, and experience that will lead outward as well as upward.

So we assume a focus, in early childhood and kindergarten education, on informal, functional oral and written language, with much experience with listening to and reading a wide range of language including literature. This literature will be in the form of stories told and read by teachers, as well as rhymes, songs, and plays. It will be found in books, but it also may be found in films, records, tapes, television, and other media. There needs to be plenty of time for conversing, discussing, and sharing experiences and a wide range of opportunities and materials for speaking and writing.

Children are already making strong beginnings in awareness of uses of print in their environment as well as books before they start school. They have also begun to be aware of and to learn writing. Preschool and early school grades should expand on this base.

In the early grades there continues to be a stress on informal, functional language. Speaking and listening are still stressed. But there is an increase in the use of reading and writing and an expansion to include a wider range of language functions. Composition, both oral and written, assumes increased importance. Much of this is based on personal experience and is often more writer centered than reader centered, in keeping with the egocentrism of young children. Grammar and other aspects of language are dealt with incidentally, as useful opportunities occur.

In the upper elementary years there is a continuation of expansion to a broader and more sophisticated range of language functions and forms as thought becomes more sophisticated and as the base of knowledge that children have built expands and becomes more complex. But there are no sudden shifts in this curriculum and no sudden terminations of concern for oral language or informal, mundane language functions.

In a strong sense the curriculum follows and tracks the development of the pupils, supporting and encouraging their growth in effectiveness and efficiency. Teachers and curriculum planners need to understand how both thought and language develop, not so they can push pupils more quickly into the next stage but so that they can support development and provide the rich, relevant learning experiences and opportunities that will nurture the pupils' growth. We believe teaching can never force learning, but it can powerfully support it.

Implementing Learning Through Language and Thinking

Here is an example of an activity that helps to develop language while developing thinking and conceptualizing, since pupils are encouraged to express their impressions in discussion and in writing:

A primary teacher is holding an object that will be used in a classroom cooking project. It is unknown to the children, but its design and look offer some clues that relate to familiarities of the youngsters. The learners are asked to form small groups, are given a large piece of butcher paper, and are then asked to choose someone to write down ways to describe it. They can view it closely, smell it, touch it, even taste it if they can do so hygienically. Then the descriptions are shared, and only after this is done is the question asked, "What is it?" A game can be played in which the kids use their clues until they agree on what the object is and what it is used for.

In this example, pupils are using language to express their developing schemas for the object, its traits and uses. They explore cognitive strategies and react to their own and each other's impressions and hunches. They defend their logic and consider the logic of alternatives.

Such experiences provide opportunities to learn about language. The teacher may, as needed, introduce terms such as *statement, sentence,* or *question.* Some words may be identified as *nouns* and others, which add description, may be identified as *adjectives.* List forms may be explored and a composite list created. Subsequently, pupils may be encouraged to develop their own lists of the features of familiar objects to see whether classmates can guess them from the listed descriptions.

A similar activity relating to a social studies unit on the local community could involve the pupils getting from parents and grandparents old-fashioned tools, utensils, pictures, or other artifacts once common in the community. Eventually the class could develop a museum of their discoveries with displays showing the uses of each item and charts listing important features and providing historical information.

In science the categorization and classification of objects is an essential process. What is alike about these things and what is different? This thinking process requires clear, referential ways of using language. It is facilitated by use of written tables and charts that compare things on a series of important traits. So collecting leaves in the autumn and examining their features, particularly their structures, is a good science activity, but it also develops the thought and language processes of naming, categorizing, labeling, and comparing and contrasting.

Such activities are particularly good for group activities, because some children will be more advanced in observation, some in related knowledge and concepts and some in the language needed for the group to complete the tasks and answer their questions. All will learn as they express what they are coming to understand. When young minds are seeing similarities and differences in leaves, birds, rocks, or clouds they expand their language in a number of ways. The most basic is the use of metaphors and similes: language is created by abduction, by seeing analogous traits in very different things and then transferring the language. The grape leaf skeletonized by army worms may be "like a lace tablecloth"; another leaf may have a "saw-tooth edge"; a third needs a shave because it's "hairy all over." Leaves of some grass have such sharp edges that they're called "razor grass." There are, of course, precise, even scientific names for things, and pupils eventually need to understand the value of having common terms in scientific classification, but they also need to appreciate their own ability to use metaphors and similes to create useful language and they need to appreciate the power of analogy as a thought process to cope with new experience.

The metaphoric mode of thinking is rooted in the humanities, but it is also used extensively in the sciences and social studies. As investigators try to envision a new concept they have to compare it to something that they already know about. Many scientific concepts now are simply accepted metaphors. The pecking order in sociology or business comes from someone's comparison of people and chickens. "Game plans" may have started in sports, but they now describe any overall strategy for any human activity. Even this book has a "game plan," a macrostructure for its development.

Life experiences don't just involve things; more commonly they involve learners in dynamic processes of transaction with the world. Discussing and describing actions and processes necessarily involve verbs, adverbs, and clausal relationships. There may be value in naming parts of speech for the convenience of discussing them but facility in their use comes from using them in situations that require them.

Conditional Thinking and Language

A key concern in our dual curriculum is problem solving. In the course of solving real problems, learners must identify their questions and seek answers:

What are the questions?
What is the evidence?
How can you find out?
What happens?
What makes it happen?
What if there were other circumstances?
What can you guess?
Can you be more exact?
Is it worth it?

All these questions take learners to higher levels of thinking and to the more complex language structures that go with them: differentiating, predicting,analyzing, inferring, hypothesizing, theorizing, assessing, valuing, and making choices.

One way to move toward conditional thinking—the "what if" question—is the mystery story: trying to figure out what happened from clues in the environment and situation. There are some popular commercial games that involve using clues to figure out "whodunit." One teacher created a western tracking mystery. She set up a campsite in the room in such a way that there were clues to who the campers were, where they came from, and where they were going. This, together with reading a Sherlock Holmes story, stimulated a lot of mystery writing for several weeks among her pupils.

The framing of good questions and the formulation of causal statements are essential in these life-related experiences. In science the open-ended approach to experimentation is very common in building conditional thinking. Some examples are: What are the conditions under which water will become water vapor? What conditions keep the planets in place? How are those like artificial satellites? What happens when the conditions change? In social studies we can ask questions such as how history might have been changed or what would have happened if the events that brought our ancestors to where we live now hadn't taken place.

All this requires a curriculum that values language and thinking, not just facts. It requires teachers who value risk taking on the part of their pupils and who are willing to take risks too. In school, teachers can provide situations that confront students with real problems that will provoke them to take some risks in both language and thinking. The teachers will focus the pupils' attention on the problems but they also will be continuously monitoring the language and thinking that the pupils use to solve the problems.

Expressive and Process Objectives

The strong push toward use of explicit, preplanned, behavioral objectives cannot provide the kind of integrated experiences needed to develop concepts and language and thinking strategies. In the curriculum we are advocating, the teacher needs to start from life situations, which have the potential for bringing forward the desired risk taking. Then the educational double agenda needs to be considered. There are ideas, concepts, generalizations, and attitudes that become the content of what teachers want the learners to be able to express. These become *expressive objectives*. Teachers also must be monitoring the thinking and language processes and structures used. These are *process objectives*.

Instructional methods should fit the objectives by using teaching and learning processes that support and amplify the objectives. The major process objective of our whole-language curriculum is:

> To expand the language of pupils through a process of generative thinking and to expand expression of the ideas generated in speech, writing, and other symbolic representational systems.

Open Inquiry

An open inquiry method is required to stimulate productive thinking, speaking, and writing, as well as reflective listening. The method must also encourage pupils to take risks as they approach novel situations and come to terms with them. The following construction has proven helpful to curriculum workers as a way to help teachers remember the phases students go through in coming to know about some happening or event. These phases are perceiving, deating, and presenting. These, in turn, suggest teaching strategies (confronting, dialoguing, rehearsing) appropriate to each phase for encouraging the expansion of language and thinking. Later chapters will develop these concepts in considerable detail.

Phases of symbolic transformation of experience into knowledge	Pedagogical strategies for meeting and extending these phases
Perceiving	*Confronting*
Making initial impressions and reactions; using descriptive language	Bringing awareness, labeling, describing, comparing perceptions with peers and teacher, using open and direct questions
Ideating	*Dialoguing*
Categorizing, conceptualizing, hypothesizing, analyzing and generalizing; thinking conditionally	Problem finding, questioning, informing, experimenting, using inquiry questions, using increasingly economical and complex language

Presenting

Organizing and summarizing ideas and feelings in symbolic forms for presentation to self and others; using an increasing array of language and other forms to express ideas and feelings

Rehearsing

Problem solving and reporting, making applications of ideas in new contexts, arguing, debating, performing, producing cohesive and coherent language forms

Teaching, a Language Art

Suppose that a word count of a teacher's day were taken at any level of school. It would be overwhelming: multiply one day's words by 180 school days and the count would be astronomical. But the number of words cannot equate with the amount of learning that takes place. To make words count in teaching, artful language strategies have to be composed that will engage learners in equally artful language and thinking strategies. The thinking teacher, who uses language effectively to solicit thinking from others, to help learners organize ideas, and to encourage them to analyze, summarize, and theorize, understands both the capabilities of language and its limitations.

Teaching requires a theoretical base, a view of how language and thinking work, how they are learned and how they facilitate the learning and formulation of concepts and schemas. Teaching requires a prethinking process as well as an active on-the-job thinking process. The prethinking stage is called curriculum development, unit and activity planning, while the active aspect of teaching might be called instruction, the give and take of the classroom dialogue. The teacher begins planning with a theoretically based idea formulated in an imagining process of what would involve and excite learners to become engaged in the thoughts to be developed. The artful teaching plan is a composition of demonstration, argument, and persuasion. The art of teaching is not unlike persuasive drama in which thematic ideas are developed in dialogue.

Language and thinking permeate the teaching-learning process. Children are surely at the center of the learning process, for they will only learn what they can incorporate into their knowing. Teachers are certainly at the center of what will be taught, for they alone can prepare the environment and set the stage for instruction. But language and thinking must be central to the interaction of teaching and learning if education is to take place.

The succeeding chapters of this book focus on what teachers need to know about language and thinking, how they develop, and how teaching can support and promote their development. Throughout the book we seek to move from such knowledge to application in curriculum building and instruction. Our goal is to help our readers to become whole-language teachers capable of promoting the development of thought and language and the development of knowledge through thought and language.

References

Jerome Bruner, *Toward a Theory of Instruction* (Cambridge, MA: Harvard University Press, 1966).

John Dewey, *How We Think* (Boston: D. C. Heath, 1933).

Margaret Donaldson, *Children's Minds* (London: Fontana, 1978).

John Goodlad, *A Place Called School* (New York: McGraw-Hill, 1984).

Michael Halliday, "Three Aspects of Children's Language Development: Learning Language, Learning Through Language, Learning About Language," in Y. Goodman, M. Haussler, and D. Strickland (Eds.), *Oral and Written Language Development Research: Impact on the Schools* (Urbana, IL: National Council of Teachers of English, 1979).

William Heard Kilpatrick, *Foundations of Method* (New York: Macmillan, 1925).

Nancy Martin, Patricia D'Arcy, B. Newton, and Robert Parker, *Writing and Learning Across the Curriculum: 11-16* (London: Ward Lock Educational, 1976).

Moira McKenzie, *Becoming a Reader, Programme Notes* (London: Inner London Education Authority, 1977).

National Commission on Excellence in Education, *A Nation at Risk. The Imperative for Educational Reform,* reprinted in *Education Week,* April 27, 1983.

Jean Piaget and Barbel Inhelder, *The Psychology of the Child* (New York: Basic Books, 1969).

Schools Council, *Language in the Whole Curriculum: English and a Linguistic Education* (London: HMSO, 1976).

Hermine Sinclair-de-Swart, "Developmental Psycholinguistics," in D. Elkind and D. Flavell, *Studies in Cognitive Development* (New York: Oxford University Press, 1969).

Florence Stratemeyer, Hamden Forker, and Margaret McKim, *Developing a Curriculum for Modern Living* (New York: Teachers' College Press, 1947).

2

Language:
Why and How

The Animals

They do not live in the world,
Are not in time and space.
From birth to death hurled
No word do they have, not one
To plant a foot upon,
Were never in any place.

For with names the world was called
Out of the empty air,
With names was built and walled,
Line and circle and square,
Dust and emerald;
Snatched from deceiving death
By the articulate breath.

But these have never trod
Twice the familiar track,
Never never turned back
Into the memoried day.
All is new and near
In the unchanging Here
Of the fifth great day of God,
That shall remain the same,
Never shall pass away.

On the sixth day we came.

(Edwin Muir, 1960)

Creating One's World through Language

Until children assume language they cannot separate themselves from the all-consuming moment. Like the other animals, they are in the world without knowing they are in the world. Language makes it possible for them to objectify and to conceptualize their world and themselves and to share the responsibility for their destiny.

Children come into the world with the physical and mental potential for language and find themselves immersed in a ready made symbolic structure, the end product of thousands of years of social development awaiting their personal development of it. In their personal development of language they race along, retracing swiftly the trails built socially over the centuries. They cannot simply start where the previous generation left off; the whole development must be recreated in them. It is this legacy of a continuously developed language and human capacity as heir that set humans apart from all the other animals.

A primary personal function of language is to represent reality, to be a symbolic carrier, a semiotic, of world images. Children see a tree, hear it called a tree, chant "tree, tree, tree," and go around forever after with a tree in their heads, which they can conjure up in the dark, in the middle of the desert, or multiply into a forest at will. This first freshness of symbolic embodiment is polished by the transactions with many other speakers of the language and by endless experiences with other trees. The landscape of word symbols that looms in children's minds forms the scene in which every act is laid. What they do with the world, how they make relationships within it, and the impact of the sensuous awareness of it go far beyond that. However, this aspect of social-personal recognition should never be forgotten, for it remains central to language at all levels.

Finding Reality through Language

A reality that exists within the limits of language may not be reality in some absolute sense, but it is as much a reality as the individual and the language community will ever know. Eskimos reflect their own environment and their interest by their many classifications of snow unknown to inhabitants of the temperate zone. Arabs may distinguish endlessly among camels, and some Brazilian Indians have hundreds of words for different birds without a generic term for bird. Inner city children have many colorful words for police officers. The fact that people from other language

20

communities can learn Eskimo or Brazilian distinctions does not destroy the validity of these as examples of language culture delimitation. It is possible to learn other languages, including nuances and refinements, but one still only knows about them. Without the psychological depth and sensuous involvement that grow out of extended transactions of individuals with their environment through the medium of language, something will always be lacking to some degree when one learns another language. One's particular grasp of reality is determined by the structure of the language as well as by its references.

Everyone and every language community starts with the same physical world, but each sees it from a slightly shifted perspective. Our common humanity pre-determines what we shall find in reality, but our common humanity also allows ample room for community and individual differences. Although we have begun to find ways of radically shifting our perspectives to those of other persons or cultures, ultimately all will be qualified by the final individual perspective. All world views, no matter how wide the horizons, turn on the axial "I"; that is, they are egocentric.

Using Language in the Particular and in the Universal

Language scholars speak of individual language (idiolect) at one end of a scale and the speech of a community (dialect) at the other, and there are many gradations in between. Within a broad dialect there are many subdialects that generate particular words and expressions peculiar to a family causing the family's total language, a famiolect, to differ somewhat from that of the community. The language of a region such as the southeastern United States or Lancashire, England—or even a city neighborhood—will have its differences. The language area might be extended to larger areas, such as major languages, families of languages, and the final category, human language. In going from the smallest unit to the next largest, something is lost and something is gained. The broader groupings broaden communication; the smaller areas exclude more and more of humanity for the sake of socially more intimate, psychologically deeper particularity. Literary language tries to preserve a dynamic tension between the richly particular language of a person and the broadly representational language of a culture. The ultimate in literature is achieved when the universal is realized through the smallest particular, as in Blake's

> To see a world in a grain of sand,
> And a heaven in a wild flower.

Language cannot exist in a vacuum. It depends on the sensuous particulars of experience as a firm foundation for the ladder of abstraction. The physical grasp of the senses is extended into the world by means of the symbolic process of language, much of which, in its roots, leads back metaphorically to the parts of the body, figuratively extended into the world, from the face of the cliff to the foot of the hills, from the mouth of the river to an arm of the sea.

Language gains life and strength through the psychological and aesthetic grasp of reality centered in the individual. Though it is the codification of centuries of human experience, transformed by creative intelligence and preserved and changed from generation to generation by the means it itself supplies, language still must be recreated in the individual. It binds us to the earth as well as separates us from it. As an ideational means, language separates us from total immersion in the particulars of life by making objectification possible, while at the same time it permits us to express immediate relations to the world around us, thus preventing our alienation from it.

Projecting Language into the World

Humanity speaks and a resonant world responds. We feel that when we project our voices, like sonar the echo seems to give us the contour of what is out there. A danger for modern people has been the prevalent concept that nature is unresponsive, made up of dead matter, that even other people are objects spoken at. Persons who deny the living world are speaking to the crevices and craters of the blighted landscape of a dead planet, killed by their own hands. Language is projected into the world, and if we listen carefully we know what world this is and who we are in relationship to it. The preservation of this constant and ever comforting relatedness prevents our alienation from our environment.

Definition: For Jane

I am, I shout.
Hop-hoppers in the grass
hop round me as I pass
through the sunlit scene,
pulsing yellow on green,
flower opening all day long
to a whirring song,
I, mid arcing petals,
bright enameled metals
of summer. Fields lie still
before, behind. At will,
like poets ringed in rhyme
that beats and meets in time,
I move my circle round
me anywhere. No sound
can be beyond my ear,
a silent world until I hear,
no sight beyond my seeing,
O worlds await my being.
Through the fields of choice,
called to life by my voice,
I sing from morning to night,
then darkness dims my sight.
A light goes on ahead
to light my way to bed
and after, out. (Meredith, 1959)

Shaping Reactions to the World in Words

Part of a new experience is naming, describing, and classifying it. Anxiety about the unknown collapses in the presence of experience organized into concepts and schemas and expressed in language. Roman troops panicked when first faced with war elephants. In the next encounter, the troops perhaps said something like, "Well, here come those war elephants again," opened their ranks to let them pass through, and then closed their ranks again. When the first satellite went into orbit, we witnessed a widespread attempt to make the awesome feat tolerable by saying just what it was and how it worked. We could not let it fly around up there undescribed. Curiosity required that it be put safely within the controlling lines of language.

We all speak to ourselves as well as to the world. We carry on a dialogue with ourselves, rehearsing our being constantly. Adults often misread the changing pattern of child language. They see the discontinuance of monologue and the gradual diminution of egocentric language as putting away childish things and developing a more mature and social language use. Desirable as the development of the social use of language is, it should not supersede the egocentered grasp of reality that takes place in language, which should be continued and extended rather than supplanted. It should not kill the animistic grasp of nature but should put it in perspective.

Language, from beginning to end, is shot through with sensuous elements that are basic and necessary to scientific and rational language. A prosaic approach to language tends to kill its psychologically and aesthetically satisfying aspects and in the end even defeats the purpose of prose. A narrow, "correct" language dries up the wellspring of language.

Growing children learn to submerge their dialogue with themselves, their dramatization of their roles in the world; but substantially the same process goes on beneath the surface. In mature people the quality of thought and decision making depends on inner representation of opposing sides and in the judicial hearing of causes and actions. Even unrehearsed actions are based on precedents established in past rehearsals.

Developing Language

The development of language is not a passive process. A dynamic transaction takes place between the individual and the preexisting language pattern. Children racing along the well-worn path of language are not just being initiated into the dialect of the tribe or the neighborhood; they acquire an idiolect, a personal language that interacts in an intricate way with the dialect.

Individuals have the potential for extremely rapid and widespread language extension, but this is not to say the growth cannot be blocked, slowed, inhibited, or distorted. Whether individuals have a rich, sensuously rewarding world with wide horizons and dynamic and stimulating interrelationships within it or a colorless,

dwarfed world depends to a large degree on whether language growth is confirmed, enriched, and encouraged, and whether the individuals are able to reach
out and extend themselves into the world through language. Independence depends on whether people use their own language as the instrument of their own
will in creating personally authenticated worlds or whether they use others'
language and through it accept someone else's fixed and safe world. Language
must, in any case, be both personal and social, but whether it is richly personal or
atrophied and weak depends on the formative language experience.

If the expansion of their world through language is discouraged in the
classroom and the home, children will take it to the playground and the street. To
inhibit children in their assumption of language and the world is to limit their
lifespace and to take some of the life out of what remains. Language is the carrier of
experience insofar as we are aware of experience, and any effort by society,
parents, or teachers to restrict it or deny it to young people can only make them
lesser people and can only lead to the very chaos which the shaper may fear.
Children's language development can be stunted whether they live in a restricted
ghetto, in a protected suburb, or in an isolated farm community. Young people
should no more be excluded from the rich range of personal language than they
should have all evil and threatening representations removed from their literature.
They must be given all of their world. All teachers assume this mission.

Understanding the Child Learning Language

> Every language is a vast pattern system, different from others, in which are cultur-
> ally ordained the forms and categories by which the personality not only com-
> municates, but also analyzes nature, notices or neglects types of relationship and
> phenomena, channels his reasoning, and builds the house of his consciousness.
> (Whorf, 1956)

Language is the most useful and marvelous human invention, and it is
amazing that virtually all children achieve near mastery of at least one dialect of one
language by the time they are 5 or 6 years old. Studies have confirmed that by
school age most children's speech is a close approximation of adult speech in their
communities. (Cazden, 1972) Adults tend to overlook the immensity of this
achievement. Because virtually every child learns to talk, adults presume it is a part
of the natural growth of children. They also tend to pay more attention to the
relatively few signs of immaturity in the speech of children than to the high level of
control over the conventions of the language they display. Adults may notice the
one or two sounds a 5-year-old cannot yet produce and not the fact that she has
mastered all the other phonemes (sound units) of the language as well as an
extensive vocabulary.

Many adults find it hard to believe the studies of the vocabulary of school
beginners that have indicated that the average child knows at least 8000 words and
may know over 20,000. If we assume that the average child knows 10,000 words at

age 5, this would mean that the child has learned an average of 5½ words a day from *birth*.

Adults are aware of the sentences that children produce that are not grammatical by adult standards, but often they do not realize that the bulk of children's speech is entirely grammatical. Children can produce sentences that they have never heard before but that nevertheless are grammatical. Even their errors tend to be overgeneralizations of common language patterns. For example, they may say "he bringed it" rather than "he brought it." They could not make such an error unless they had well-established notions of how past-tense verb forms are usually produced.

Studies by Ruth Strickland and Walter Loban (1963) have established that kindergarten and first-grade children use all the basic sentence patterns of English in their speech. Language development after school begins is largely a matter of expansion, refinement, and embellishment. (Chomsky, 1970)

Adults who are closely associated with infants and small children during the period when they are learning to control language are vaguely aware that there is a learning process involved. The popular view is that children move from babbling, through first words, through a phase of immature speech commonly labeled baby talk, to speech that falls within the language norms of the community. But even parents focus more on the cute, the quaint, and the charming than on the process. In fact, parents tend to be unaware of the vital role they play as responsive language users who want very much to understand everything the child tries to communicate. Sometimes parents are startled to hear their own remarks, complete with intonational detail, coming back at them from the mouths of their children.

All children invent a system for expressing their needs, wishes, desires, and thoughts to persons around them. This personal communication system eventually coincides with the language of their family and subculture. They develop the sounds and units of this language, and the structure of the language becomes part of their minds and personalities. This internalization of the structure of language not only influences the way children express their reactions to the world but also helps structure their perceptions as their world and language expand. As they learn language, they learn to mean things to other people that reflect the way their culture views the world.

Why Children Learn Language

Before we can consider how children learn language, we must consider an even more basic question: *Why do children learn language?*

Children who grow up isolated from human society do not develop language. Human beings have the capacity to produce a great variety of sounds. The use of phonemes, significant variations in sounds, as the unitary symbols of the language is a social invention of human society. The choice of which features of sound variation will be significant in a particular language is entirely arbitrary. Some languages utilize clicks, which are almost totally ignored in English. Some languages (Chinese, for example) make much more significant use of pitch or tone variation than does English.

Complex languages can be built that do not use sounds at all but rather utilize systems of visual symbols—signs made with fingers or other body parts, puffs of smoke, pictures, or abstract graphic designs such as letters.

Language systems utilizing symbols based on other sensory stimuli could also be constructed. Some tactile stimuli, for example, have the symbolic quality of a rudimentary language: a squeezed hand, a pat on the head, a slap on the shoulder, or a kick in the shins under the table are all symbols that convey simple messages. Braille, of course, utilizes tactile symbols.

However, human beings can produce and discern an almost unlimited variety of sounds, whereas our control over production and discrimination of other sensory stimuli is more limited.

All known human societies develop languages that utilize sounds as symbols. Other animals (parrots, for example) have a similar ability to produce a range of sounds but have not developed a spoken language; a few primates have been taught to use rudimentary signs. Two human qualities explain the development of language:

1. The capacity of the human mind to imagine and think symbolically, that is, to assign meaning to something that has no intrinsic meaning of its own, to let something stand for something else
2. The human need for complex and varied communication. So universal is this need for communication that people invented language not once but perhaps many times, wherever, in fact, they congregated.

The ability of children to think symbolically and to produce sound symbols makes it *possible* for children to learn oral/aural language; the need to communicate makes it *necessary* for children to learn language. Children learn a particular language not just because it is the only one available but because it is the one that makes communication possible with the people around them. In fact, if they need to learn two or more languages to communicate effectively, they will do so, as has been amply demonstrated by children who grow up in bilingual homes. Ursula Bellugi has studied language learning in deaf children of deaf parents. She finds that such children learn sign as a first language as easily, as early, and as well as children acquire speech. (Bellugi, 1971)

Studies in language development have given disproportionate attention to physical development in children. Physically and mentally normal children do develop control over the speech apparatus, but the ability of children eventually to produce exactly the sounds that are the symbols of the language of their society is determined by their need for effective communication. Because almost all children are born into societies that have oral language, it is the oral language that is learned first and that becomes primary to all hearing children. The need to communicate is ever present; the choice of language is personal and social.

Communicative Need Expands Language and Thinking

As language develops, it becomes a tool for children striving to derive meaning from their world. In turn, language is expanded by this striving. There must be purpose in learning, and communication (at least in a general sense) is the immediate reason for language learning.

From this axiom of communicative need in language learning several corollaries follow:

The closer the language of children comes to the language norms of the adult community, the more effective becomes communication.

There is a continuous tendency, therefore, for children's language to move toward adult norms.

Involvement in a range of life situations with language-using family members is sufficient to produce language development in infants.

The more opportunities children have to communicate, the more effective they will become in using language and the more acceptable will be their language by adult standards. They need to be spoken to, listened to, responded to. They need to see and hear people using language.

In literate societies, communicative need will play the same prime motivational role in children's learning to read and write as it does in their learning to speak and listen with understanding.

Halliday argues for a functional-interactional approach to language development, which explains how language develops and the form language takes in terms of why it is developed. (Halliday, 1975) At the same time that the language is developing, a conceptual framework is also developing and the child is using language to develop a "functional potential." Children use language to serve a range of developing language functions, and at the same time this leads to using language to develop conceptual schemas for organizing their thoughts and responses to the world. This implies also that language development is sociolinguistic as well as psycholinguistic: "learning the mother tongue is interpreted as a process of interaction between the child and other human beings." (pp. 5–6) Halliday argues persuasively that language development can only be understood in the context of asking the question, "What has the child learned to do by means of language?" (p. 6)

Language, Experience, and Situation

Most people tend to think of language as a series of words that stand in close relationship to objects they name. But language does not confine itself to naming the things in the world. Language must be capable of conveying the most abstract feelings and relationships as well as conveying concise, concrete descriptions. Actually, language development in children moves from vague associations between utterances and their referents to precise ones, from general meanings to particular meanings, from large language units to small units. At the same time it moves from being very specific to particular contexts or experiences to being applicable to recurrent aspects of a wide range of contexts.

"From the functional point of view," Halliday says, "as soon as there are meaningful expressions there is language." (p. 6) Shoshana at 14 months began to say "owow" when she saw a certain dog. Soon she was saying it for all dogs and then for pictures and toy dogs. But she was also saying it when she saw horses, cows, and other animals. Not until much later had she sufficiently organized her world that she was showing control of the concept, *DOG*. Her "owow" is a meaningful expression, but it is not a word in the sense that a word is a constituent of language that represents a concept consistently.

These processes operate in the constant language encounters human infants have with language. For instance consider this episode:

A 5-month-old boy is lying in his crib. An adult appears. The child feels discomfort and begins to express it through his body movements. He starts to cry. The adult changes the baby's diaper, lifts him, holds him, pats his back and bottom, all the time saying: "Oh, your diaper's wet. Well, Mommy will fix that." Other persons are present. "Karen, hand me the powder. Here, Daddy, hold the baby while I get his food ready." The child is carried into another room. The talking continues amid other sounds. Other voices are heard: the high-pitched voice of a 5-year-old sister, the deep voice of the father, the dimly heard voices of a television program in an adjacent room, his own voice as he babbles in response to what he hears.

The child feels himself placed in a reclining seat. The feeling is a familiar one. He has experienced it many times before. His mother begins to feed him. The taste is new and unexpected yet pleasant (a new fruit), but the spoon and the process are familiar. And all the time, the language continues. Some is directed to the baby, "I have something new for you, Tommy. Open your mouth. That's a good boy. Aren't the peaches good? Yes, Tommy likes peaches."

This episode is not a particularly complex or unusual one. The child experiences repeated variations of it. The episode takes place in the context of a situation. Everything that happens to children is experienced in a situational context. They can focus their attention on one aspect of a situation, but the particular aspect cannot be isolated from the context. Some aspects of the situation are closely related—the dish and spoon, for example. Some aspects of the situation are experienced simultaneously, such as the feel of the spoon and the food. Others occur sequentially: the sight of the spoon and the dish usually precedes the taste of the food. In the situation, speech acts occur. This baby cannot yet assume the role of speaker or fully comprehending listener and yet he still is a participant in each speech act. Very young babies show the early beginnings of turn taking, a crucial aspect of human conversation. Each time something is said to the baby, the baby responds. Soon the baby babbles and then waits for the expected response before babbling again.

Language is always experienced by children in the context of the situation. The children associate the whole language utterance with the whole situation or at least with the aspects of the situation that they experience at the same time that they hear the language. To acquire effective control of language, children must sort out recurrent relationships between language and particular aspects of the situation in which the language is heard. They must be aware, for instance, that when the language includes the recurrent element *mommy,* the situation almost always includes the presence of a particular person.

Sometimes adults simplify the situation, the language, and the focusing problem. The mother will point to the father while repeatedly uttering, "Daddy, Daddy, Daddy." Still, children must sort out of the situation that it is the person pointed to rather than the speaker to which the term refers. They must also delimit the term; they may, for instance, apply it to all adults or all male adults. Gradually, different language functions are added. *Daddy* has an interpersonal function at first, a way of interacting with a familiar other. But they then become aware that by producing a recognizable approximation of *daddy* they can summon adult aid, get picked up, get changed or fed or hugged or kissed. Soon, also, children are using *daddy* as a comment meaning, "that person is daddy."

Children's reaction to the situation is also a part of the language-learning process. Their emotions and their developing ability to think, to process perceptions, and to begin forming concepts actually become part of the situation as children experience it.

One of the earliest language insights many children seem to develop is that language has a social function. They may not know what it does, but they know that language happens when people are together, so they participate too. They make noises like the other people are making; they take turns listening intently when people talk to them and babble in response. Babies want to be part of the interpersonal transactions around them. That may explain why *bye-bye, hi,* and *peek-a-boo,* which are basically interpersonal forms with no communicative meaning, are often among the first things babies say.

The sounds that compose the speech children hear have many variable dimensions. They must learn which of these variables are the significant ones. They must learn that recognizing the difference in voices is useful only because it tells them which person is speaking. In some Chinese-language communities they would need to learn to attend to many different pitch levels, because the same sounds said at different pitch levels are different phonemes. Babies begin to specialize in the sounds of their language community very early. As babies grow, for example, Spanish babbling begins to sound very different from English babbling.

Children learn to use different intonation patterns too for different functions. One intonation pattern comes to represent a question or a demand and another a comment. Halliday found this differentiation of intonation very early in his son's development. (Halliday, 1975, p. 56)

Holophrastic Language

Essentially, the early language of infants is made up of whole, indivisible, language utterances *(holophrastic units)* that they use for generalized purposes in repetitious situations. When language becomes purposeful, the purpose is a generalized one also. A child says *daddy* in a certain tone that is conveying a message that is a general "I need help!" or "Please pick me up; I want to be carried."

Adults tend to think that children learn words as individual units, which are then joined in longer and longer sentences. This misconception is partly due to the limited ability of young children to produce long utterances in speech, even though they may have the whole idea in mind. Children are limited to uttering short sound sequences by their lack of physical coordination and by other factors. Their ability to perform lags behind and limits their ability to show their developing underlying language competence.

Children don't know which aspects of the speech they hear are most significant or contribute most to the meaning, so they use the most salient features in their own language production. They fix on the most prominent characteristics because they cannot produce everything. Roger Brown (1973) reports that the children they studied tended to repeat the most heavily stressed words in an utterance. Often, intonation contours appear before the actual phonemes. A child playing peek-a-boo may use the "I see you" intonation at the right point in the game without any of the English phonemes.

Children do not begin to speak in words, then, but in brief utterances. To an adult it appears to be a kind of telegraphic language. One dimension of the way language develops is that these utterances appear to expand until they eventually are complete in virtually every detail.

There is a play aspect to the language development of children. Babbling, experimenting with sounds, getting control of the apparatus for producing sound variations are all part of this play. These phases of language development are only vaguely and broadly communicative and rational. But the close relationship between language and experience in the context of recurrent situations brings about an important interplay between the language and thought of children. Bits of language become closely related in children's minds with bits of experience. Recurrence of an experience brings to children's minds the language that they have come to relate to it. Hearing familiar language, even their own speech, recalls the experience.

Rational Speech and Verbal Thought

Children's early utterances are often quite appropriate to the situation, because a schema, or thought pattern, is formed in which the utterance is an integral part of the situation as it is experienced. The language is a reaction to the situation, to the role the child plays in the situation, and to other aspects (being changed, fed, carried, and so on). The language becomes a means of recreating the situation. There is thus always a sense of function that becomes more sharply defined in the child's mind. This in turn leads to more definite purposes and the need for more control over the language forms to serve these purposes. As adults and other children respond to their early speech, children begin to use it consciously and communicatively.

As language becomes a means of expression, it becomes rational. Lev Vygotsky believed that speech and thought have separate roots: "Up to a certain point in time, the two follow different lines independently of each other. At a certain point these lines meet, whereupon thought becomes verbal and speech rational." (Vygotsky, 1962)

When speech becomes rational, not only do children begin to use it to express their needs but also they begin to manipulate their perceptions of the world by mentally manipulating language. Thus, thought becomes verbal. It is not that they cannot think without language but that language becomes a convenient symbolic medium for thought. In the process, the perceptions themselves are sorted into categories that are available in the language. Thus, the language to some extent structures the children's developing life view. The categories of the language, of course, are those of the culture into which the children have been born. They begin to see things the way others in their society see them. Their ability to communicate with others is thereby increased; they not only speak the same language but also see things their way.

Language Errors and Misconceptions
What appear to adults as language errors and misconceptions of children have the same genesis as their language which appears correct by adult language norms. These miscues are very important in the development of thought and language in children. They represent essential aspects of development. Children must be able to compare situations in which their language is effective or ineffective, in which concepts work or do not work.

Suppose, for example, a little boy wants to be picked up and he says to his mother, "Up, up." When she picks him up their communication has been effective. Suppose, however, that she is holding him and he wants to be put down, but he says "Up, up." The mother may do nothing; the language then will be ineffective. Or she may guess from his body movements that he wants to be put down. As she does put him down, she will very likely use appropriate language: "Oh, you want to go down." Children learn language in a number of situations and use subsequent situations to verify their language and to refine and limit it. In doing so they have to deal with considerable linguistic complexity and even more conceptual complexity. So they will make mistakes. *Up* and *down* seem to contrast sharply until we start talking about going "down the road" or "up the road," which can often be used interchangeably. An 18-month-old baby is told to "Climb up on the bed and lie down."

Or consider how the concept of *brother* might be developed by a child. It may be associated with situations in which children are present, then siblings are present, and, finally, male siblings are present. His understanding begins to acquire the status of a concept when the child generalizes that other children also have brothers—that, in fact, *brother* is a category of relationship between people, that he is his brother's brother. Later he may be aware that in his culture people address male friends as "brother," that the male members of his family's church are called "Brother ____," that his father walks a picket line with his union "brothers."

In each new context the limits of the concept and its metaphoric extensions are shaped. The eventual meanings that any term has for any person are not precise dictionary definitions; they are ranges of meaning that depend on the context of a situation and the pragmatics (practical, cultural aspects) of particular speech acts or literacy events for their meaning. Through many experiences in many situations the concept develops, takes on subtlety, acquires emotional overlays. As the boy grows older, the concept becomes more abstract, and he is able to describe a brother-like relationship. Eventually, he may grasp the significance of *brotherhood.* Only then can he deal rationally with the question, "Am I my brother's keeper?" The misconceptions and early concepts that he abandons along the way are as much a part of the process of conceptualization as the final concept. And this process of thought and language development is a life-long process, not one that is over in the first few years of life.

Views of How Children Learn Language

Studies of child language development have provided much new information about how children learn language. Still, there is no general agreement on the total process and sequence involved.

Nature-Nurture Views

One simple but important explanation of the development of language in children that has recently gained considerable acceptance among linguists and psycholinguists is that the human brain is uniquely equipped for the development of language. In this view, a language acquisition device is supplied to all human brains just as the procedure for pecking is preprogrammed in the brain of a newborn chick. Language is, therefore, an innate human attribute, not an acquired one. It's instinctive. All that is required for its development is exposure to a natural language. Under such exposure, human infants adapt their universal grammatical system to the particular surface structure of the language they hear. In this view, learning to walk and learning to talk are much alike; both are inevitable when given the characteristics of the human organism unless physical or mental impairment intervenes. (Lenneberg and Lenneberg, 1975)

Perhaps the strongest argument in favor of this view is the research evidence that children's language development far outstrips their other intellectual achievements, notably concept development. Language in all its complexity is learned with such ease and at so early an age that it does seem possible that instinct (albeit a complex one) may be at play. (McNeil, 1966) However, the "innate" theory leaves much still to be explained. The innate theory does not sufficiently explain the errors that both learners and adults make in language (here an "error" is something that is outside the system of the language).

The theory does not account for or concern itself sufficiently with language change, a universal characteristic of language. The result is that significant differences between dialects are treated as unimportant.

What has been missed is that, as complex as language is, it is far less complex than the whole of life experience to which children must bring some kind of schematic order. Once children have control over the rules by which language is governed, they can generate new language to meet any new experience; language that they can reasonably assume will be understood by other speakers of the language. But life is constantly confronting them with new experience and confounding old ideas with conflicting evidence, so cognitive development must seem to move more slowly than linguistic development.

One reason why many linguists accept a view of language as innate is that they are strongly rejecting the view of B. F. Skinner and other behavioral learning theorists that language learning is simply an example of operant conditioning in which stimulus imitation and conditioned response play the major roles. It could not explain, the linguists argue, the learning of the rules by which language is produced, which are not present in what children hear. So the argument becomes an extension of the old nature-nurture argument. Behaviorists say language is a learned behavior, and those who reject that view say language is part of human nature and innate. (Skinner, 1966; Chomsky, 1966)

The innate theory so minimizes the development of language as a learning process that it is, at best, counterproductive. If all children learn to talk, why be concerned about the process? Why study something that is innate and happens universally anyway? At worst, the innate view leads to the neglect of the social and personal functions, circumstances, and contexts within which human language develops. If language is innate, the most that social and physical environmental factors can do is to inhibit innate development.

For educators, this lack of interest is unfortunate. Understanding the processes of language acquisition is important for understanding the acquisition of literacy, reading, and writing, which are also language processes.

A Social-Personal View
It is not necessary to accept either the behaviorists' or the nativists' views of language development, if language is understood as part of the culture, a human social invention. Only human beings are capable of the level of interaction they achieve because only human beings are capable of creating and learning language, and language is necessary for the full sharing of feelings, needs, wants, experiences, and insights. Language becomes the social medium for the sharing of thoughts; it creates a social mind from individual minds and thus greatly magnifies the learning ability of any one person. But it also becomes the medium of individual thinking and learning. Through language, people may link their minds, pool their experiences, learn together and from each other, and form a social base for a shared life view. Thus language is both the product of a culture and the principal means by which culture is created and transmitted. As children develop language, they also become participants in the culture; as they become participants in the culture, they learn language; as they learn language they learn conceptual schemas shared in the society for assigning meaning to life's experiences.

So language is social as well as personal. It is a personal invention, but it is also a social invention, because the process by which children develop language is much the same as the process by which society has developed it. The ability to create language is still present in every human infant and in every human congregation. Each child personally and each generation in each society continues the creation of language. This explains many things. It explains why the language every child develops moves rapidly toward the language of the community, but it also explains the ways that each child's developing language differs from the adult language as it develops. It explains why language is so stable over many generations and vast geographic areas, but it also explains why language changes and why dialect differences develop and continue to exist.

Centrifugal and Centripetal Forces.   Two opposing forces shape the development of language in individuals and in communities. They can be compared to the centrifugal and centripetal forces of physics. If a ball is twirled on a string, there is a centrifugal force pulling it away from the center. If the twirler lets go, the ball flies off in a straight line. The string is an opposing, centripetal force pulling it back toward the middle. As long as these are in balance, the ball will orbit the center. Placing a satellite in orbit is largely a matter of creating enough thrust to create a centrifugal force to counter the earth's gravitational centripetal force.

In language the centrifugal force is the ability of people individually and collectively to create new language to deal with new experience. This force produces change and makes it possible for language continuously to meet the developing and changing needs of its users. If language were static and unchanging it would quickly inhibit its users in learning and in communicating their responses to new experiences. But if this force were unchecked, language would expand so rapidly that it would lose its social utility. People would soon be unable to understand each other at all.

The centripetal force that provides the counterbalance and relative stability is the social nature of language. Change may be initiated by individuals, but it must be understood and accepted by others in order for language to be affected temporarily or permanently. To serve its functions it must be comprehensible by others, not just by the speaker or the writer. When language changes there is always balance between the creative force and the need to communicate. Every language must have within it devices for change, but innovators must use the devices for change the language provides or risk not being understood.

Language development in children, then, can be understood as being shaped by these two forces. There is an almost explosive force from within the children that propels them to express themselves, and at the same time there is a strong need to communicate that pushes the direction of growth and development toward the language of the family and community. This shaping is accomplished through the myriad language transactions that involve children with others. The language is generated by the child, but it is changed in transactions with others by their comprehension or lack of comprehension and by their responses. Thus parents, care-givers, siblings, peers, and significant others with whom developing infants interact play vital roles in their language development. They are less teachers than essential communicative partners, less role models than respondents, less to be imitated than to be understood and understanding.

The concept of the opposing forces shaping language can also explain both similarities and differences across languages. Supporters of nativistic views of language have cited linguistic universals, common features or structures across otherwise unrelated languages. Take, for example, the issue of syntactic sequence of subject, verb, and object (SVO). English tends to use a SVO fixed sequence with little variation. Other languages use SOV, while others use the sequence of verb, subject, object (VSO). Some permit more than one pattern, differentiating subject from object by inflectional endings rather than position in fixed patterns. But every language has some way for a speaker to let a listener know which is subject and which is object when nouns are used. There are even languages with no formal pattern whose context determines subject and object.

What's universal is not the language structures but the fact that the language must provide some means of differentiating subject from object for the listener as well as the speaker, since both must know this for the communication to be successful. Furthermore, this means must be structured and relatively consistent over many speech acts; that is, there must be rules shared by speakers and listeners for communication to succeed. Linguistic rules develop in the first place because language is social. They take the particular forms they do because there are only limited ways that language can vary and still meet social constraints. Within these variations particular languages make arbitrary choices.

References

Ursula Bellugi, *"The Language of Signs and the Signs of Language,"* paper presented at the Michigan Conference on Applied Linguistics, January 1971.

Roger Brown, *First Language: The Early Stages* (Cambridge: Harvard University Press, 1973).

Courtney B. Cazden, *Child Language and Education* (New York: Holt, Rinehart and Winston, 1972).

Carol Chomsky, "Language Development After Six," *Harvard Graduate School of Education Association Bulletin,* vol. 14, no. 3 (Spring 1970), pp. 14–16.

Noam Chomsky, Review of *Verbal Learning,* in F. Smith and G. Miller, *The Genesis of Language: A Psycholinguistic View* (Cambridge, MA: M.I.T. Press, 1966).

Michael Halliday, *Learning How to Mean: Explorations in the Development of Language* (London: Edward Arnold, 1975).

Eric Lenneberg and E. H. Lenneberg, *Foundations of Language Development: A Multidisciplinary Approach* (New York: Basic Books, 1975).

Walter Loban, *Language Development: Kindergarten through Grade 12* (Urbana: NCTE, 1976).

David McNeil, "Developmental Psycholinguistics," in F. Smith and G. A. Miller (Eds.), *The Genesis of Language* (Cambridge, MA: M.I.T. Press, 1966).

Robert Meredith, "Definition: For Jane," from *Quicksilver,* 1959, by permission of the author.

Edwin Muir, *Collected Poems 1921–1958* (Oxford: Oxford University Press, 1960). Copyright 1960 by Willa Muir. Reprinted by permission of Oxford University Press, Inc., and Faber and Faber Ltd.

B. F. Skinner, *Verbal Behavior* (New York: Appleton-Century-Crofts, 1957).

Ruth Strickland, *The Language of Elementary School Children: Its Relationship to the Language of Reading,* Bulletin (Bloomington: Indiana University, 1962).

Lev S. Vygotsky, Thought and Language (Cambridge, MA: M.I.T. Press, 1962), p. 44.

Benjamin Lee Whorf, *Language, Thought, and Reality* (New York: Wiley, 1956), p. 252.

3

Language Development

There will. . . . be conflicts and tensions between the various different realities; this is where learning takes place, when there is some kind of tension between the child's world and that of the adults, or between different aspects of the child's own world, and the child's attempt to resolve it. There may also be tension between the language and the reality it is being used to encode.

(Halliday, 1975)

Outside of School

Throughout Chapter 2 we talked about language *development* rather than language *acquisition,* because *acquisition* implies that there is something outside the children to be acquired, like shoes or clothes; rather, the process must be seen as personal *development* in the context of social use.

In this process of language development, there are four continuing cycles: increasing experience, increasing conceptualization, increasing communicative need, and increasing effectiveness in communication. The last can be considered synonymous with increased control over the language or languages of the family and the community.

Language development is greatly facilitated by the fact that the others with whom infants are transacting want very much to understand and to be understood by the children. So children are successful in their attempts at language use far out of proportion to the degree to which that developing language fits adult language norms. Adults in the family are likely to be so thrilled at anything that approaches meaningful utterances that they will do everything they can to make the transaction successful. Aaron's grandfather was sure he heard him say *grandpa* long before any other family members agreed, and when, over time, Aaron's utterances became more discernibly *bapy* and then *bapa,* and eventually *drampa,* they never failed to evoke responses from his grandfather.

Function in a Social Theory of Language Development

Michael Halliday, in his study of his son's language development, concludes that in the beginning a child's functional-linguistic system consists of a series of independent functions served by unitary utterances. Then there is a transitional period in which utterances become able to serve multiple functions, and finally the functions merge into a small number of abstract language functions able to serve a myriad of language uses in adult language (1975, p. 7).

In the beginning, the only elements of language are content (meaning) and expression (sound or gesture). However, in order for what children produce to qualify as language, there must be a constant relationship between the form and the meaning, which Halliday calls *systematicity.* And it must also be *functional,* that is, it must serve some generalized purpose of the user. (p. 15)

Halliday explains this requirement for system and function:

The child is learning to be and to do, to act and to interact in meaningful ways. He is learning a system of meaningful behaviour; in other words, he is learning a semiotic system. Part of his meaningful action is linguistic. But none of it takes place in isolation; it is always within some social context. So the content of the utterance is the meaning that it has with respect to a given function, to one or other of the things that the child is making language do for him. It is a semiotic act which is interpretable by reference to the total range of semiotic options, the total meaning potential that the child has accessible to him at that moment. (p. 15)

Very simply this means that language only develops in the service of meaning and that it is meaningful only in terms of some broad purpose or function. Halliday sees the child's development of function as movement toward three abstract functions of adult language:

1. *Ideational—the observer function.* Language as a means of talking about the world.
2. *Interpersonal—the intruder function.* The speaker assumes and assigns roles in speech situations. Buber's "I-Thou" corresponds to this function.
3. *Textual—the enabling function.* This function makes it possible to so operationalize the others through the creation of language texts that it "breathes life into the language." It carries language beyond pointing, naming, and citing to the full expression of ideas, emotions, values, and feelings. (p. 17)

These functions are often present simultaneously in adult language use and are complexly interwoven, but children start with a collection of rather specific functions, which, at least in the beginning, are served separately by specific language utterances. In Halliday's study of his son he found these specific functions emerging in approximately the order listed:

1. *Instrumental—the "I want" functon.* Children use this language function to serve their material needs—to get things.
2. *Regulatory—*this involves controlling what people do.
3. *Interactional—*With this function the child interacts socially with others. It includes the use of greetings and names (to get someone's attention). The child uses language as a major form of socializing with others. (p. 19)
4. *Personal—*Halliday calls this the self-discovery, "Here I come" language function. It includes expressions showing emotional response.
5. *Heuristic—*children are using language to explore and establish the environment (What's that? Why?).
6. *Imaginative—*this is the use of language for story, make-believe, and pretending. Children use language to go beyond discovery of the universe and create new realities. (p. 20)
7. *Informative—*This is an important language function that happens later than the others. Whereas the others are probably a prerequisite to the development of adult language, this last may actually accompany that development as children begin to review, evaluate, and remember experience and present their developing schemas to others. Halliday calls this the "I've got something to tell you" function. (p. 37)

The early language development is almost all the result of what we have called the centrifugal force in language development: language is quite individualistic and is created by children to serve their developing functional needs. Their success largely stems from the joyful willingness of parents, siblings, and others to comprehend and respond, but these very social acts of response begin the centripetal pressures that will shape the language development toward the language of the family and the community. The child's language is perceived by other language users as attempts at using the community language. In their responses, reactions, and comments they tend to provide rich, repetitious, and highly articulated selections from the language. They take their lead from the child's language and effectively support its growth as they also begin to affect the directions of that growth.

Form and Function

Halliday's son began at about 18 months to develop an important new aspect of language that was part of a transition in his language. Besides *content* (meaning) and *expression* (utterance) there is now linguistic *form* or *grammar*. Utterances are no longer free-standing units. Groups of utterances have parallel structures. This third system is what makes the difference between a language and a set of utterances. It is what ultimately makes it possible for people to express new ideas about new experiences with novel language to each other and be reasonably assured of being understood.

Another important change occurs. The utterances are now made up of recognizably English words and phrases (or approximations to them), although, at least at the beginning of this phase, the utterances are holophrastic, complete, and indivisible in themselves. (p. 41) Halliday sees the expansion of the vocabulary as serving two purposes: expanding the child's capacity to exercise existing functions and at the same time making it possible to combine functions in single utterances; that is, to do more than one thing with language at a time.

The heuristic function, using language to organize the world, seems to be a driving force behind the rapid expansion of vocabulary. But this is combined with the personal function—not only naming but showing emotional response to what is experienced. (p. 43)

Dialogue also begins, according to Halliday, during this transitional phase. What this means is that the child begins to be able to take a role in a speech act: to respond to questions, commands, statements and even initiate a conversation. As dialogue emerges, the two forces on language development, centrifugal and centripetal, begin to come into some balance as language takes on more and more of the personal-social characteristic of mature language use. Halliday puts it this way:

> The child learns to participate linguistically, and to intrude his own angle, his individuality and his personal involvement in the linguistic structure. In this way language becomes for him an effective channel of social learning, a means of participating in and receiving the culture. Meanings are expressed as verbal interaction in social contexts; this is the essential condition for the transmission of culture, and makes it possible for certain types of context to play a critical part in the socialization process (p. 50)

The two forces we have described relate closely to the two-way functional distinction of adult language Halliday calls *ideational* and *interpersonal.* But in adult language every utterance is both ideational and interpersonal; from our perspective the forces are in relative balance, embodied in existing language and interacting in the creation of new language.

Phonological Development

Children's early babbling and experimenting with the sounds they can produce are not yet language by the criteria discussed above. Phonology begins as children vary the way that they use their tongue, mouth, lips, and so on, much as they kick their arms and legs and flex their fingers and toes.

But humans are social animals, and whatever babies do is in the context of their increasing interpersonal needs. They continue phonological development by producing sound as part of their reaction to discomfort: they cry when they are hungry, dirty, wet, in pain, too hot, too cold, or frightened. Because adults around them respond to the noise they make, they develop a generalized ability to use sound purposefully as an attention-getting signal. They learn that gestures can provoke responses and that sounds can produce responses from people at a distance who cannot respond to their body movements and other visual signals.

Studies of Russian, German, and American babies all confirm that at early ages physically normal children produce all the sounds that are significant in the language of their societies, as well as sounds that have significance in other languages. (Tischler, 1957) More recent studies have shown children beginning to specialize in the sounds of their own language communities.

The sounds babies produce are usually pleasant to them, although they may occasionally startle themselves. They play for long periods at noise making. Often their babbling is composed of consonant-vowel links such as "ma-ma-ma-ma, goo-goo-goo, da-da-da." The peak of babbling is between 8–10 months of age. (Tischler, 1957)

Eventually, in situational contexts, children are engaging in some intentional, selective sound making and begin to achieve the control over the sounds they make so that they are able to produce particular sounds at will. Thus, their development of the physical coordination necessary for speech begins before speech, but language development does not wait for physical maturation and coordination. The two processes—language development and physical maturation—go on simultaneously. To some extent, the actual quality of early speech is limited by the level of physical development, but development of language seems to leap ahead, particularly receptive language, so that it can stimulate the physical development and control necessary for further development. This is another example of the centripetal and centrifugal forces shaping language.

The development of phonology in infants begins independently of the development of language functions, syntax, and semantics. To speak a language requires control over the phonology, but control over the phonology, though it has this independent beginning, is not a prerequisite for language development. In fact, it would never become so refined or highly controlled as it eventually does if it did not become a system of language.

Ironically, imitation of language requires both a high level of physical coordination and a considerable control over systems of the language. When children are able to imitate with reasonable accuracy, they are showing considerable development. Thus, imitation cannot play much of a role in language development. Some infants do appear to become fascinated with the language sounds they hear and seem to work at them to the point where they respond to a limited repertoire of adult words and phrases by repeating them. This has a social function and may perhaps even appear briefly to the child to be what language is about. What it lacks is a meaning to which the form systematically relates.

At 7–8 months of age, infants begin to show preference for vocal sounds over other sounds. They soon show that they can learn to respond to verbal signals much more quickly than to other sounds. They know their names, and they look at familiar people as their names are called. (Ervin and Miller, 1963)

Now children begin to produce sounds to serve a function and to express a need or a desire. This sense of function stimulates the development of the form of language. Sometimes babbling stops when this phase begins, but it often continues.

At this point, children develop utterances, short units of language used with more or less stable meanings. These are the "first words," but they are not simply words. We must not be misled by the general shortness of each utterance, often limited to a single syllable. The length of each utterance is a function of their level of physical development and control over the sound-producing apparatus. But children have generalized needs and feelings to express; their language has its referents in their developing conceptual schemas for the total situation in which it is uttered. And the particular syllables used will be their approximations of features of language that they associate with a situation, such as feeding time.

Brown and Bellugi report that in their study of a boy and a girl learning to talk, the children, whom they labeled Adam and Eve, used statements that seemed like a kind of telegraphic language composed of utterances two to four *morphemes* long. A morpheme is a minimal meaningful language unit. These morphemes were the most heavily stressed words or parts of words in the utterances children were hearing. Adam, for example, said "He go out" when he heard his mother say "He's going out." (Brown and Bellugi, 1966, p. 7)

In English the words that get the greatest stress are the ones that carry the most meaning, so that children's abbreviations carry enough meaning for an adult to construct a total utterance and respond to it. Studies by Paula Menyuk and N. Bernholz have shown that the one-word utterance of an 18-month-old child may have several meanings, depending on the situational context and the intonation. *Door,* for example, may mean "That's a door"; "Is that a door?"; "Shut the door!" (Menyuk and Bernholz, 1969)

The telegraphic abbreviations of Adam and Eve almost always preserved English word order. This would seem to be evidence that the early sentences of children are not lists of words put together but rather are holistic utterances, each an independent unit of language. Because word order is an important signal of contextual meaning, children's retention of word order incidentally makes their communication more effective. Their speech gives adults a feeling of grammatical consistency, although it is devoid, for the most part, of inflectional endings and function words.

In this phase of children's language, the *phonemes* (the significant sound units) of their language do not coincide with the phonemes of adult speech. They have fewer phonemes, each of which may function in place of several adult phonemes. This is partly because of limited control over the organs used in speech and partly because of limited ability to discriminate fine differences in sounds. Roman Jakobson and Morris Halle have suggested that there is a certain economy in developing a stock of phonemes. Children may possess four consonant phonemes. When they have divided one of these phonemes into two, a voiced and an unvoiced form, for example, they may suddenly have eight consonant phonemes, because the physical process that they now control can be used in the case of their other three original consonants to make each a pair: voiced and unvoiced. (Jakobson and Halle, 1956; Jakobson, 1968)

In this process, as in all language processes, children hear differences some time before they can produce them. In fact, even babies as young as 1–4 months old can distinguish adult phonemes. (Eimas, et al., 1971)

At a certain point, then, child language is largely a collection of utterances, each an independent unit, each serving a single function. The utterances are abbreviated. They are limited in length to a few highly stressed morphemes (idea units), and they are composed of a more limited number of phonemes than adult speech. There are notable giant steps toward sounding more like adult speech as children gain control over their speech apparatus. The word order of adult speech is maintained in children's abbreviations.

Expansion and Delimitation

Language now moves in two directions at the same time. The utterances are both expanded and delimited as the centripetal and centrifugal forces are at work. The expansion is from the one- or two-syllable utterances to fuller and fuller approximations of adult speech. This is not a process of combining words to make sentences; it is an expansion of the nucleus so that minor features are included. *Eat* may become "wanna eat" and then become "I want to eat." This shows children's language moving toward the norms of adult language. As rules are tried out there is some building up or generating of language, but at this point most of the children's more complete utterances are not built up; they are filled out. They come to correspond closely to adult utterances, but they are still mostly independent wholes.

At the same time that children are filling out and expanding their utterances, they are delimiting their use. The utterances come to mean what they mean to adults. They become more and more precise in expressing more and more particular needs, wishes, or feelings. The situations in which each utterance is used become increasingly more narrow. In the process of striving for more effective communication, children learn the approximate limits within which adults will accept each utterance as appropriate. If they say something in a situation in which the utterance is not appropriate, the result is either unsatisfactory or unexpected. Children will tend not to repeat the utterances in similar situations. When they use utterances in appropriate situations, the responses are the desired ones, and they will tend to use them again in similar circumstances. Their need to communicate is the centripetal force pulling the developing language toward the adult language.

Brown and Bellugi report that in their study the mothers of Adam and Eve tend to repeat and expand the utterances of children to complete simple utterances appropriate to the situations. When the children say, "Baby high chair," the mother says, "Baby is in the high chair." (Brown and Bellugi, p. 12.) The mother, when she does this, indicates to the children that their utterances are appropriate. What she adds as language elements is not only grammatical by her standards but also expresses what to the mother is significant in the situation. Not only are children being aided in developing language, but they are being guided toward the expression of a view that is meaningful to the adult. This view is likely to be one shared by the culture in which the family lives. Thus, as adults respond to children, the children's perceptions of the world are also shaped to the cultural norms.

Because children's utterances are abbreviations for more complete utterances, it sometimes appears to adults that their language explodes overnight. Joan Velten reports that her daughter developed prepositions, demonstratives, auxiliaries, articles, conjunctions, possessives, personal pronouns, and suffixes for past tense, plurals, and possessives all in the brief period between 27–30 months of age. (Velten, 1943) All these were implicit in the utterances that her daughter had used in abbreviated forms, but as her speech expanded toward complete utterances, they began for the first time to appear in her speech.

By 36 months of age most children whose mother tongue is English are using all varieties of complete simple English sentences. These may be up to 10 or 11 words long. By the fourth year children's phonological systems, with one or two minor exceptions, are within the norms of adult speech. Their speech is composed of complete utterances that preserve the word order and inflectional suffixes of adult speech. (Ervin and Miller, 1963)

Through the processes of expanding expression and delimiting use, children have come to speak a language remarkably like adult speech. Because much of this language is composed of discrete wholes, it will have all the features of adult speech and sound like adult speech, and because the utterances are usually used in acceptable situations, this language is very effective. But at the same time another process is well underway. It is the process of rule development and will, ironically, make the child's speech seem less mature and adult-like.

Developing Rules: Generating Language

A key understanding that transformational-generative linguistics, based on the work of Noam Chomsky, has contributed to our understanding of language development in children is that there is a limited set of these rules by which every language is generated and comprehended. More than anything else after the development of functions, language development is a matter of coming to control this set of rules. With the rules, children become capable of generating language they have never heard, which will be comprehensible by other speakers of the language. With the rules, children are able to channel their ability to create language into the means by which a particular language is generated. This channeling is not inhibiting; rather it is liberating because it makes children full participants in language communities, able to share their needs and experiences, and able to use language to learn from and with others.

Children develop control over these rules in much the same way that society developed them. They try to communicate, experiment with a range of forms within their attempts to communicate, and eventually establish order, that is rules, for accomplishing their purposes. In this, language learning is much the same as all learning, as Jean Piaget has described it. Children are operating on the premise that there is order in the world. By attempting to impose order, they reach a functional equilibrium between their knowledge of the order in the physical world and the actual rules by which things work.

An advantage children have in language development is that they are transacting with people who are already using rule-governed language. The young language learners move toward the rules of the language community because those work best for communication with people in that community. On the way children will try out many alternatives. Some will be incomplete and inadequate as rules as the child's horizons expand. Some will be useful rules that unfortunately are not those used by others with whom the children are transacting in generating and comprehending language. And some will be overextensions of adult rules to include instances in which they don't work. An example of the latter is the overgeneralization of the common English past tense rule. Consider this conversation between Reuben (age 2) and his mother:

Reuben: I broked it.
Mother: Did you break it?
Reuben: No, I breaked it.

In his first attempt he attaches the *ed* to *broke,* which he may know but which doesn't fit his new past-tense rule. In response to his mother, he shifts to adding *ed* to the simple, present tense form, producing *breaked.* He is using his rules to generate language and then in the transactions with his mother and others testing out his rules.

Language cannot continue to develop a unit at a time. Children have learned to cope with the recurring situations of their lives, but their language functions and needs become more complex and they need to be able to respond to new experiences and to express the more complex ways of thinking their minds are now capable of. They have questions to ask, emotions to express, and observations to make.

Fortunately, they are developing the ability to generalize. They seek order in their linguistic experience. They hypothesize about how language works, noticing the common elements in similar utterances. They may notice that *no* or *not* occurs in many utterances that have a common negative attribute, so they will try to generate their own negatives. Because these are not the wholes they have used before, their early attempts will not be quite like anything they have ever heard. They might say, "No, I want to eat," grafting their negative to a positive utterance but not sure of the means. Eventually, they induce a rule for negation, which then makes it possible to generate new negative statements. David McNeil cites an example of a child who developed a double negative rule, "Nobody don't like me." This rule was so strong that the child kept saying, "Nobody don't like me," when she was asked to repeat, "Nobody likes me." (McNeil, 1966, p. 61)

As in everything they encounter, children operate with language as if they expect it to be orderly and predictable. They seem to be searching for rules and regularities. Children will begin to notice parallel elements in utterances that are otherwise the same. They generalize a pattern in which certain elements can be interchanged. An example of such a pattern that could appear quite early is one in which a series of things or people are inserted in the object slot, such as: "I want milk," "I want apple," "I want cereal," "I want Mommy" "I want chair," and so on.

Ruth Weir reports that her 2 1/2-year-old son actually engaged in linguistic play that revealed his pulling out of his experience utterances with similar patterns that he then experimented with. He would, for instance, while falling asleep at night, repeat groups of related utterances, such as: "what color, what color blanket, what color mop, what color glass." (Weir, 1962)

This process of generalization about patterns and rules for their formation and for the interchangeability of elements is much more abstract and complex than the process of expansion. A rule, as used here, is not externally imposed by a grammarian but is, in fact, a law by which language behavior is governed. In expansion, children merely become more complete and precise. In generalizing rules, they must reflect on the utterances they use, generalize a pattern, induce a rule, generate an utterance consistent with the rule, and then, on the basis of the effectiveness of the utterances they generate, evaluate the rule and modify it. Just as they had to learn the limits of each utterance, they must now also learn the limits of each rule.

As they learn the limit of generalizations they have made about the similarities and differences between utterances, children slowly become aware not only of words and phrases but also of the complex interrelationships of these words and phrases. They become aware of very common patterns in the structure of utterances such as the subject-verb-object, "I see you," pattern. They also become aware of less common patterns. They discover that some patterns are one-of-a-kind idioms with no parallels, which must be treated as unbreakable units. They learn this through trying out alternatives. "Wait a few whiles," said one 3-year-old.

As children become aware of the deep structure (underlying forms) of language and begin to generate their own utterances according to their half-defined rules, many of their utterances are ungrammatical by adult norms. Thus, their language appears to be less mature than it did earlier. Their early attempts may be clumsy graftings of the type cited before. Later they overgeneralize, regularizing irregular forms or structures. By analogy they create forms that conform to common rules. They may say, "I taked it" (or even, "I takted it"), because they are aware of the most general rule for indicating past tense. This over-generalization shows the use of abductive reasoning by children; they generate new forms by analogy to old forms.

Adults sometimes are disturbed about the errors in children's speech in this stage. They regard it as sloppy and often react in annoyed or sarcastic ways. Actually, children could not acquire control over the rules, patterns, inflectional endings, function words, and intonation systems of language without testing their generalizations as they were formed. Rather than discouraging error making in this stage, adults should respond to the intention when they understand and ask for clarification when they don't. It's through these transactions that the development is furthered. Children may be reluctant to try out their rules if adults constantly correct or ridicule them.

Development of Meaning

Now, as children begin to generate sentences, particular words or phrases begin to take on separable meanings. Previously, only the whole utterance had any meaning. Now children become aware of the element of meaning that is contributed by each word or phrase to complete the meaning of the utterance. This is a complex process, indeed, because the meaning of a word in an utterance is strongly determined by the meaning of the whole utterance. Children must encounter a word or a phrase in many utterances before they begin to know the limits of their meanings.

An indication that children become concerned with the meaning of words and phrases during this phase is that they frequently ask adults, "What does _____ mean?" Sometimes they ask right after they hear the expression, but they are just as likely to ask hours or even days later as they mull over an expression that was not completely understood. A. R. Luria reports that Russian children at about 4½ years begin to respond to the semantic (meaning) qualities of words. Prior to 4½ years they respond impulsively to whole utterances. (Ervin and Miller, 1963, p. 137)

Children's large vocabularies of whole utterances serve as a check on their generalizations about language rules and word or phrase meanings. They develop a feeling for the language, a kind of intuition that is formed of many not wholly analyzed and understood language experiences. The other check comes from the transactions with others as they try out their rules and meanings.

During this discussion frequent mention has been made of words and phrases rather than just words. This phraseology is preferred because children do not break language into words as literate adults might. They become aware, during this stage, of particles of language that are smaller than whole utterances, but these particles are not exactly the same as words. Groups of two or three words, like _all-gone, out-of-doors, pick-up,_ and _fire-engine,_ are heard so frequently together and are so closely bound that children consider them and treat them like single elements. They may even say, "I pick-uped my toys."

The processes of induction (building generalizations from experience) and abduction (building generalizations by analogy) through which each child discovers the fine points of one or more languages is long and slow. Berko reports that American children from 4–7 years of age tend to avoid derivational suffixes like *worker,* preferring compounds like *working man* or syntactic constructions like "the man that works." (Berko, 1958)

On the other hand, preschoolers can identify nonsense words such as *was sibbing, the sib,* or *some sib* as verb, count noun, or mass noun, respectively, by the markers *(was, the, some).* Ervin and Miller conclude that by age 4 most children have learned the fundamental structural features of their language. (Ervin and Miller, 1963, p. 125)

The process of developing less common grammatical generalizations and of learning unusual exceptions continues well past the point where the base structure has been established. An example is an expression such as "he gots it." *Got* is in the process of replacing *has* in some uses. Americans are likely to say "I've got it" or "I got it" rather than "I have it." Similarly, Americans say "he's got it" or "he got it" but seldom "He has it" and hardly ever "He has got it." Because children do not hear the latter, they do not know that the "'s" in "He's got it" is equal to *has,* so they regularize *got* as a third person singular verb, making it *gots* and hence "He gots it."

Language Proficiency and Linguistic Awareness

By the time of beginning school, children have internalized the phonology, the grammar, and a considerable vocabulary of their language so well that language seems to have become virtually effortless or automatic. They generate comprehensible, largely grammatical utterances appropriate to the situations they encounter and can hold their own in conversations with others, particularly more mature others. They can move words and phrases from one structure to another and know with considerable confidence whether they are acceptable in these settings. They appear to do all this with little conscious attention to the language processes themselves. They can tell whether something is wrong or right, but they cannot begin to explain why. They just know. Six-year-olds will often laugh uproariously at an ungrammatical or illogical statement, but they can't tell you what's so funny. It just is.

What has happened is that children's language has become almost totally rule governed. They have enough sense of the contextual and pragmatic constraints of speech acts that they need to give little attention to the form of the language they are using and they can concentrate on the meaning they are trying to express or comprehend.

Effective and Efficient Language

Language proficiency has two aspects: it is effective to the extent that there is successful expression or comprehension, and it is efficient to the extent that it is effective while expanding the least amount of effort. The language is then not so much automatic as highly efficient. People, including children, get very good at the things that they do a lot because they're so basic to their life experiences. With rules for generating language under control, children can use language for most of their needs with very little attention. Of course proficiency is not as high as with adults. There are times when the going gets tough as they deal with new experiences and run out of ways of dealing with them. At times there is considerably more attention paid to language itself. That's true throughout life. Even highly proficient adults find themselves sometimes "at a loss for words." When this happens, generating language requires much more deliberate effort.

Metalinguistic Awareness
Recently there has been interest among those interested in language development in an old issue. How much do language users know about how language works? This has recently been labeled *metalinguistic awareness*. The difference between knowledge of something and knowledge about something is an old issue in philosophy and psychology. Knowing language in the sense of being proficient in its use is not the same as knowing it in the sense of being able to discuss it technically. Confusion between these kinds of knowing has troubled both research and curriculum. There is a strong tendency to judge what people know or how well they've learned by how well they can explicitly and abstractly discuss something. So we have tended to judge language proficiency in children by what they can say about it rather than by what they can do with it. Sometimes we go so far as to think that knowledge about language is a prerequisite to its effective use.

Sometimes schools are encouraged to "put learners in touch" with what they know about language; that is, to help them reach a point where they can analyze what they do when they use language. While children may find this interesting to a point, it's hard to find justification for it as an aid to learning either oral or written language. Encouraging pupils to think about what they're doing when they use language may make them self-conscious and distract them from using the processes to communicate.

Perhaps what we are misled by is that children do ask questions and make comments about language as they are gaining control of it. Furthermore, the more proficient children become in using language, the more they tend to be able to talk about it, since they can draw on their own intuitive knowledge to support their conclusions. Neither of these obvious facts establishes that metalinguistic awareness is a cause for or a prerequisite to language development. Whatever children know *about* language, it is far more likely that they learned it in the course of using and learning language than by being taught or told it. We'll come back to this point when we discuss the development of written language and school language programs in general.

Continued Social and Personal Development
The age at which children become relatively proficient in using language is an age at which they are greatly increasing their conceptualization and the quantity and effectiveness of their language. Their language has moved rapidly from highly individual attempts at communication to an idiolect that falls well within the norms

of their community's dialect. Whatever this dialect is, it is adequate to meet the communicative needs common to persons of their age in their immediate society.

The two opposing forces, centripetal and centrifugal, never cease shaping children's language. All children invent their own language, but the need for effectiveness in communication is so strong that they are constantly moved toward the language of their community, eventually taking on the same structure and dimensions. All this is in the direction of conformity. Most of everyday communication is carried on with common expressions, so common that they seem trite. Discourse seems almost to operate by a series of formulas. To a great extent, this conformity reflects the social constraint on language, pulling it back toward the middle and away from divergence.

Halliday sums it up this way:

> What is the significance of this for the child? The significance is that, because of the functional nature of language, the particular, concrete meanings that are ex pressed in everyday situations become, for him, the primary source for building up the context of culture. . . . So it happens that the child's own early uses of language impose certain requirements on the nature of the linguistic system, de termining the functional basis on which it is organized; with the result that, as these early uses evolve into generalized social contexts of language use, the linguistic system is able to act through them as the means of transmission of the culture to the child. In this way language comes to occupy the central role in the processes of social learning (Halliday, 1975, p. 15)

It must not be forgotten that language is a human invention. However trite and systematic it becomes, it never becomes completely static and unchanging, because people individually and socially never lose their ability to create language. Children never lose their ability to create and creatively manipulate language. This is one of the reasons they enjoy playing with it so much. In childhood there is an increasing ability to conceptualize and think in metaphors and abstractions. So children push language beyond its conventional limits. In teenagers, this creative force surges again.

Creativity In Language
Children, of course, have needs and interests in common that they do not share with adults, so a child subdialect develops. This is passed on from each wave of children to the next. However, there are always some new needs and new ways to meet old needs, and new language is created to express them. Teenagers, particularly, tend to create language. To some extent this is because language is so closely related to perception and life view. To use the language of adults would imply acceptance of adult categories, values, and attitudes. Teenagers must have a language that is uniquely theirs and uniquely able to express life as they see it. The meanings of some terms are even inverted so that generally negative adult terms such as *crazy, mad, tough, bad,* and *wicked* become positive terms in the teen vernacular. Positive terms like *nice, sensible, square, bold,* and *good* become negative.

Other groups in society share with the adolescent the need for a special language to express nonconformist views. In every recent decade there has been a new nonconformist group visible partly by its language. Regardless of the forces that bring new language into being, some of it will find its way deep into the common language of society. New language tends to be colorful and a welcome relief from the cliches that are repeated endlessly. Then again, the perceptions of life and the world that are common to the society are also in evolution. It may be the young who first sense this and supply the language to express it.

All people create language to some small degree, but only the great language artists rival the young in creative use of language. The literary giants and storytellers of all time have in common the ability and the courage to use language in artistic and novel ways and to find unique ways to communicate fine images and emotions with great effectiveness and understanding. They become masters at stretching and varying language to avoid repetition. In their hands, language does not limit the human capacity for self-expression; it becomes the supple tool of thought and communication. The great writers are such masters of language that they transcend language conventions; they make rules work for them.

Creative thoughts require creative language to express them. Emphasis on conformity in language in school or at home stifles not only expression but also thought. Fortunately, the tendency of children to be creative with language is almost universal. Parents and teachers can encourage this tendency. If they do, perhaps eventually there will be more adults with the courage to use language creatively.

The language development children accomplish by the time they enter school, largely without the help of professional educators, is an immense achievement. School programs must be so constructed that they fully accept the language children bring to school in all its magnificent diversity. Teachers must treasure this universal resource of pupils and learn to support the creative process of its development. They must see what happens in school as expanding outward and upward on the existing base. They must create classrooms that are nourishing environments for language to grow in with real learning experiences that will fully support the joint development of language and thinking.

Expanding Language In School

Expansion is the key word in the language program: expansion of communicative need, expansion of experience, expansion of confidence in the use of language, expansion of conceptual ability, expansion of control over the structure of language, expansion of vocabulary, expansion of the range of language that is understood, expansion of the range of language used in expression and the ability to communicate with many different people. A time-honored adage of education is that it must always start where the child is. For the school language program this means that:

The school language program must be flexible to allow for the range of languages, dialects, and language abilities children have when they come to school.

The school and the teacher must be concerned with understanding the language of
   the community or communities the children come from. The teacher must
   accept the language of each child and must build upon it.
Teachers must value and appreciate the language of every child. Children must not
   feel that their language is considered bad. The teacher must not just tolerate
   it; the teacher must cherish it, making children feel pride and confidence in
   their language and their ability to express themselves in their language.
The teacher must concentrate on developing ideation in widening experiences
   with children, thereby stimulating an expansion of language.
Literacy development, reading and writing, must be considered part of this expansion on the existing language base.

   To start where the child is in language, the teacher must listen to the language
of the child carefully and without prejudgment. If the teacher disdains the "terrible
English" of the learners, a barrier is created that not only undermines their
confidence in their ability to use and learn language but also makes it impossible
for them to communicate to the teacher. The teacher, perhaps without realizing it,
may refuse to listen or understand. In some cases, the negativism can be so strong
that children are literally forced to defend themselves. If teachers will not listen to
them, then they will not listen to the teachers. For children to build on their
present language ability, their confidence in themselves must be unshaken; otherwise, there will be a separation between their speech and the language activities of
the school and the larger society that may never be bridged.

Language Opportunities in the School

In order to expand language there must be no artificial exercises in recitation or
copying someone else's language from the board but real speech acts and literacy
events, actual opportunities for children to use their own language to communicate. Children need the opportunity to stretch their language to the limits, to
express their reactions to experiences, and to interact with each other. In this
process they will strengthen and refine the generalizations they have internalized
about language, while at the same time they will feel the need for growm in
language. Children can discover limitations in their language ability only if they
have many opportunities to use it. As communicative needs occur that they cannot
meet, they will reach for more language; they will be self-motivated to expand their
language.

   Every available opportunity for children to use their language in school
should be exploited. Whenever there is a time for natural conversation, it should
be utilized. When children arrive in the morning, they have things to tell each other
and their teacher. It is natural for friends and acquaintances to want to talk over
what has happened since they saw each other last. This informal, spontaneous
conversation is more valuable than any kind of before-school board assignments
could be. This is a particularly good time for the teacher to become aware of any
interesting events or experiences children have had that they would like to share
with the whole class in a more formal sharing time. Recess and lunch periods

are also natural occasions for informal language. How unnatural it is to see hundreds of children sitting and eating their lunches in silence, furtively trying to communicate with each other without getting caught by a teacher or a monitor! Noise may indeed be a problem in many school situations, but if the importance of language opportunities is recognized, solutions other than bans on speech will be found.

When children have something to say, it is at this point that they are most motivated to use language. It is important that children learn to listen as well as to speak, but in too many classrooms the times when speech is "appropriate" are too few. A sharing period may stimulate children to express their experiences and ideas to others, but language must not be confined to a half-hour period a day.

Children also need opportunities to talk about the new concepts and ideas they encounter during their schoolwork. Class discussions meet this need to some extent, but there are also times when it is beneficial for two or three pupils to discuss the mathematics that they are doing, to compare notes on African cultures that they may be researching, or to share their reactions to a science demonstration. In such situations children have the opportunity to seek effective language to express new concepts in a less threatening situation than they have when they must address a whole class. It is not enough that children have heard the teacher use language to describe a new concept or that they have read about it in a book; they must ultimately be able to communicate it to others and to get the immediate feedback from others that indicates whether or not they have been successful.

School must be a place where children know that people will listen. Communicative need stimulates expression, but if no one wants to listen, then there is no point in talking. Eventually, children who are not listened to stop trying to communicate. The curriculum, the weekly lesson plan, and the daily sequence of lessons should be constructed to make it possible for children to use language in many ways.

Throughout these language opportunities, children must be encouraged to find pleasure in their own language. They should be helped to feel pride in a choice idiom, perhaps based in a regional dialect, that expresses an idea or an emotion that cannot be expressed in any other way. They should be assisted in exploring the ways that language can be manipulated to produce a variety of forms and subtle differences in connotation. They should be guided to discover more effective ways of making themselves and their ideas maximally understood. They should be encouraged to be creative, not only in the uses they make of language but also in the language itself. Language must be constantly created and recreated to meet the changing needs of its users.

School Innovations in Organization and Curriculum

Some innovations in school organization and curriculum facilitate language use while others do not. The open-school movement is, by intention, an opening of space, of structure, of limits. If it is well executed it can be an excellent vehicle for stimulating varied, easy use of language in highly informal settings. It can also provide for one-to-one interactions as well as small and large group activities in which language will be used. But the structure itself will not bring about these beneficial effects. They must come from the planning and the commitment of the professional staff. Their minds and the concepts they hold of language, curriculum, teaching, and learning must be open for the classroom to become a truly open learning environment.

Under the heading of "individualized instruction" many schools have all but eliminated any kind of linguistic interaction between learners. This is particularly true in those highly structured "mastery-learning" programs where, in fact, only the pace at which pupils may proceed through a rigid program is individualized. Instruction can be personalized, made relevant to the particular needs and interests of learners, while still making possible thought and language interactions that are essential to human learning.

Expanding Interests, Experiences, and Concepts

School-age children are by nature expanding their horizons, widening their interests, and using language as a tool to do so There is much in their world that is new and wonderful to them that they must express. They must know what things are; they must know where they come from; they must know how things work. They must have language to ask, to name, to share, to explain, and to manipulate mentally. Eventually, children must be able to use language to expand concepts and solve abstract problems, but the foundations for this ability must be built on speech acts and literacy events where language accompanies experience.

Before children can arrive at new mathematical concepts through the use of mathematical symbols such as 2, x, y, $=$, $+$, %, and $, they must first acquire the concepts they represent through the manipulation of representative objects and by hearing language in real situations involving real lengths, quantities, sizes, and intervals. The danger of creating a gap between language and experience is ever present because teachers as adults are accustomed to speaking in abstractions from their backlog of experience.

When language is developed in relation to many real life situations, it acquires limits of definition in relation to the varied experiences that the child has had with it. A dictionary can confirm a definition that the child has arrived arrived at or it can clarify which of several possible connotations is appropriate. Thus, the dictionary is an aid in language development. But a dictionary definition is of no use to children if they have not encountered the words in situational contexts. There is always the possibility of one word being defined in the dictionary by another word, which, in turn, is defined by a third word, until the unfortunate student is led back to the original word—a chain of words all related to each other but none related to anything in the experience of the dictionary user that could give substance to the words.

Perhaps a cardinal precept of a whole-language program must be: No language without experience and no experience without language.

Using Language More Effectively

The first concern in expanding language is aiding children to have more to say and more language to say it with. Of equal concern must be increasing the effectiveness of communication.

During their school years, the language of children becomes fully grammatical within the norms of their own dialects. Not only do they gain control over the structure of the language, but in a sense, the latent structure of language gains control over the language of the child. As children fully internalize the structure of the language, it comes to determine the precise patterns and choice of words of their speech, thus increasing their effectiveness in communication. However, a wide range of language is acceptable by adult standards. Some language is more effective, interesting, precise, or euphonious than other language that is equally correct. In short, beyond the point at which language becomes fully acceptable grammatically, increasing the effectiveness of communication becomes something of an art. The school can assist children in this art of effective communication. It can:

Encourage creativity in language as is done in the arts.

Encourage children to experiment with style, varying the wordings and varying the structural patterns they use.

Encourage children to listen to their own speech and read their own writing while considering: Have I said what I wanted to say as well as I could?

Avoid demanding absolute conformity. If there are many school situations where an answer or an idea must be expressed in only one way and that way is someone else's way, children are not likely to become more effective in communication. They must feel ownership of their language and its uses. If the teacher says, "Put It in your own words" but then rejects those words and demands the words of the text or teacher, children will give back not what they are asked for but what they know is wanted.

Expose children to a wide variety of language. They should hear and read "good" language ("good" here is defined as highly effective), but it is a mistake to limit their experience to "good" language. How can children tell what language is effective unless they encounter language that varies in effectiveness? How can they appreciate the language artistry of the great writer unless they can compare it with the triteness of the hack?

Expand vocabulary. There is, of course, a reciprocal relationship between children's striving for greater language effectiveness and expansion of the fund of language available to them. They are more effective if they have more language available. It is not profitable, however, to short-circuit this cycle by teaching language in isolation. Vocabulary grows as the learner requires it to deal with new experiences and new concepts. The road to greater vocabulary, then, is through a rich, exciting, expanding whole-language curriculum. Directing children to work with word lists and dictionaries can have only a superficial effect on any learner's vocabulary.

Encourage risk taking through language. Children tend to be somewhat hesitant in trying new things; they will tend to do things in safe, tried ways rather than in new ways that may not succeed, particularly if they feel they will be judged by the results. They also tend to use safe, sure language rather than new terms, phrases, or constructions. To overcome this tendency, they must be given the feeling that school is a place for taking risks and for experimentation with language. Their experimental efforts should be praised, not laughed at, ridiculed, or red-penciled. Intrinsic, positive responses for using effective language must be provided. Praise always helps, but the success of com municating one's own ideas lucidly and powerfully to someone else is sweeter.

The pleasure that the teacher takes in language use in its full variety can be as encouraging to linguistic ease and experimentation among students as the narrow, uptight view many teachers take is discouraging to such linguistic risk taking.

Trying something new always involves risks. Traditionally, pupils have been least willing to face risks involving expanding language in school, more so in fact than in any other place. Only teachers can turn this situation around, not just by what they say but by how they act in response to the language of their pupils and how they use language themselves.

Increased effectiveness in language must not be confused with increased formality or floweriness in language. The goal is natural, effective language use. Within this goal, there is a place for the incomplete sentence, the contraction, the newly coined slang phrase, the new use of old words. When a child is asked, "How many kittens are there in this story?", "three" is an effective answer. If the teacher insists that the child must respond in a complete sentence by saying, "There are three kittens in this story," it does nothing to improve the effectiveness of the response. Great writers of dialogue would never use such a response. It is not even grammatical. The rules of discourse require that elements in questions are never repeated in the answers except for special emphasis. Furthermore, it is unnatural. Language can be rich, varied, even elegant, without becoming unnatural. Language lives. It grows, changes, and adapts to the changing needs of its users. It is better to help children understand language change and be part of it than to insist on a static view of language. Such insistence can't prevent language changes, but it can interfere with the language effectiveness of learners.

Teaching Strategy for a Program of Expanding Language: The Double Agenda

The process of language expansion and increased effectiveness is essentially a continuation of the induction and abduction children have been using in all their language learning since birth, during which time communicative need has been the prime motivating force. The school must encourage the process of language growth by providing stimulating interests, by providing opportunities for experiences, by encouraging concept development, and by creating many situations in which language is needed and used.

Language is learned through its use. Development of functions—communicative needs—precedes development of language forms. Furthermore, people learn language best as they learn through language. This means that the bulk of the school language development program is not focused on language development at all but on the uses of language: to describe, to argue, to discuss, to influence, to represent, to learn, to express, and to understand.

In all this there is a double agenda. From the point of view of the learners, they are using language, not learning language. But the teachers monitor both the language growth and the uses so that they may evaluate and plan further experiences to support the language development.

So language development is best served when it is fully integrated in the curriculum. And language is central to the curriculum, not isolated for instruction, or dissected for analysis. From the point of view of the teacher, there is language development in everything pupils do in school, but the pupils' focus is always on comprehension and expression of ideas.

The teacher and the school may select aspects of language development that would not develop as fully or rapidly without assistance and may develop a series of learning activities designed to achieve this language development. The sequence of learning activities directly concerned with language learning is important, but it must not be considered the entire school program for language development. Equal attention must be given to the ways that the school facilitates the children's own induction and abduction of language as they use it.

References

Jean Berko, "The Child's Learning of English Morphology," *Word,* vol. 14 (1958), pp. 159–177.

Roger Brown and Ursula Bellugi, "Three Processes in the Child's Acquisition of Syntax," in J. Emig, J. Fleming, and H. Popp, *Language and Learning* (New York: Harcourt, 1966), pp. 3–23.

P. Eimas, E. Siqueland, P. Jusczak, and J. Vigorito, "Speech Perception in Infants," *Science* (1971), pp. 303–306.

Susan M. Ervin and Wick R. Miller, "Language Development," *Child Psychology,* National Society for the Study of Education Yearbook 62, Part 1 (1963), pp. 108–143.

Michael Halliday, *Learning How to Mean: Explorations in the Development of Language* Y. Goodman, M. Haussler, and D. Strickland (Eds.), (London: Edward Arnold, 1975).

————"Three Aspects of Children's Language Development: Learning Language, Learning Through Language, and Learning About Language," in Y. Goodman, M. Haussler, and D. Strickland (Eds.), *Oral and Written Language Development Development Research: Implications for Instruction* (Urbana, IL: National Council of Teachers of English, 1984).

Roman Jakobson, *Child Language, Aphasia, and Phonological Universals* (The Hague: Mouton, 1968).

Roman Jakobson and Morris Halle, *Fundamentals of Language* (The Hague: Mouton, 1956).

David McNeil, "Developmental Psycholinguistics," in F. Smith and G. A. Miller (Eds.), *The Genesis of Language* (Cambridge, MA.: M.I.T Press, 1966).

Paula Menyuk and N. Bernholz, "Prosodic Features and Children's Language Production," *Quarterly Progress Report,* no. 93, M.I.T. Research Laboratory of Electronics (April 1969), pp. 216, 219.

Hans Tischler, "Schreien, Lallen und Erstes Sprechen in der Entwicklung des Sauglings," *Zeitschrift fur Psychologie,* vol. 160 (1957), pp. 210–263

J. V. Velten, "The Growth of Phonemic and Lexical Patterns in Infant Language,"*Language,* vol. 19 (1943), pp. 281–292.

Ruth L. Weir, *Language in the Crib* (The Hague: Mouton, 1962).

4

Language Development in Social and Historical Contexts

Those who have been persuaded to think well of my design, will require that it should fix our language, and put a stop to those alterations which time and chance have hitherto been suffered to make in it without opposition. With this consequence I will confess that I flattered myself for a while; but now begin to fear that I have indulged expectation which neither reason nor experience can justify. When we see men grow old and die at a certain time one after another, from century to century, we laugh at the elixir that promises to prolong life to a thousand years; and with equal justice may be lexicographer derided, who being able to produce no example of a nation that has preserved their words and phrases from mutability, shall imagine that his dictionary can embalm his language, and secure it from corruption and decay, that it is in his power to change sublunary nature, and clear the world at once from folly, vanity, and affectation.

(Samuel Johnson, A Dictionary of the English Language, 1755)

The English Language in Time, Place, and Culture

The story of the English language is one of differentiation through constant change from its Germanic cousins; it is a story of a peasant language disdained by the nobility as unworthy of noble discourse and official business; it is the story of a language that in many variants has come to preeminence among the world's languages.

High-status dialects of English have displaced the classic Latin and the noble French as the language of the elite, but the process of change continues, always responsive to the shifts in the needs and culture of the language's users.

Yet each modern dialect of English echoes its antecedents. The language and its background form a commonly received frame of reference. As teachers of English, we need to appreciate its complex roots, the changes it has undergone, and the widely varied modern dialects that exist among its speakers. We need to understand what Samuel Johnson learned in 1755: that the greatness of a language like English lies in its ability to change to meet the needs of its users. We need to understand that teachers have the role of facilitating effective use of language, not preserving it from change.

English from Its Origins to the Modern Period

Most of the European languages, as well as Persian and several of the languages of India derived from Sanskrit, have been traced back to a hypothetical parent language called Indo-European. The comparative studies of languages that led to the establishment of these relationships were a great triumph of nineteenth-century scholarship.

English is a Germanic language, belonging to the same general family as Dutch, Flemish, modern German, Yiddish, and Scandinavian tongues. This family is derived from a Germanic tongue that was related to Greek, Latin, and the early Slavic language. All of these were more distantly related to Persian and Sanskrit. It has not been possible so far to establish relationships with such non-Indo-European languages as Chinese, Malay, or Arabic.

In addition to these common origins, English has been built up from cross-fertilizations and borrowings; isolation and differentiation also complicate the picture of language development. When the Angles, Saxons, and Jutes left the continent of Europe for what was to become England (Angle-land), they separated themselves from the other Germanic tribes that remained behind and began to change their language to adapt to a new environment. Also, the natural changes in language varied among those who had emigrated and those who remained behind. Later, with the Viking invasions, the North Germanic language of the Scandinavian peoples came to England, although the languages were still alike enough for the two peoples to communicate. Some of the Scandinavian invaders settled and blended in with the English, leaving recognizable traces of their language differences in the *sk* words: sky, skirt, skin, and skull. The Germanic peoples had eliminated the Celtic people of Britain, enslaved them (in small numbers), or driven them into remote corners of Britain—to Wales, Cornwall, the Scottish Highlands, or across the sea to Ireland. Though the Welsh, Cornish, Scottish, and Irish peoples descended from the Celts, very little Celtic influence was left on English other than in place names, many of which are of Celtic or Latinized Celtic origin. Had the Celts become a subject people in large numbers, they might have influenced English, but the few who remained were in no position to maintain a social group to sustain their language.

Influence of the Norman Conquest
William and his Norman-French followers carried a French-speaking ruling class to England in 1066. Unlike the earlier conquests of the Celts by the Germanic tribes, William's conquest of a stable society maintained that society relatively intact. Although the ruling class spoke French and the populace had, if necessary, to learn a certain amount of French, the language of the majority of the people prevailed. By the thirteenth century the ruling class was speaking English more and more, although English itself had changed radically.

The presence of French-speaking rulers led to a vibrant vocabulary, which has typified English ever since. The point could be made that words having to do with the enjoyment of the fruits of labor were French, while those having to do with producing them were English. Pork is of French origin, while swine is of English; beef of French and cow or ox of English. Words having to do with government come largely from French—govern, reign, realm, sovereign, country—but the claim of legitimate continuance of the English system is shown in certain key English words, such as king, queen, and earl. Words having to do with luxurious living are of French origin, and as education and the church were taken over by the Normans, religious, spiritual, and cultural terms are of French origin. The Norman Conquest, with all its social and cultural side effects, left a permanent mark on the English language. In many cases French and English words existed side by side and both survived. Usually, however, these are not simple duplicates; the French, Latin-based words seem more elegant and formal. We "construct" and "demolish" (French roots), but we also "build up" and "tear down" (Germanic roots).

More important than what French did to English was what English did to itself during the period of French-speaking leadership. Many changes in Old English (Anglo-Saxon) were accelerated. Without educated leadership, which normally acts as a conservative force, speakers of Anglo-Saxon (and the few who wrote) moved swiftly toward reduction of inflected forms (case and tense endings) and toward reliance on sentence position, bringing greater simplicity of language. The basic grammatical form became a much more streamlined Germanic language with a strong admixture of Norman-French vocabulary.

Middle English and Early Modern English

By the end of the period 1100–1500 the language was so changed as to require a new designation, Middle English. The language of the sixteenth century, Early Modern English, is the language of Shakespeare and the other great Elizabethan writers. Previously, only classic languages were considered worthy of use as written languages and little was written in vernacular languages such as English. Shakespeare's continuing popularity in the theater has helped to keep Elizabethan language alive, as has continued reading of the King James version of the Bible. Their language presents no major difficulties for the educated reader of today. It should be pointed out that these writers wrote without the benefit of schooling in correctness of usage or grammar. They used the language freely and unself-consciously, and that was their strength. It is quite possible that academic inhibitions would have cramped their style, particularly if the inappropriate Latin grammar had been applied to it.

This is the form of English that the early settlers brought to North America and which they used to create the early colonial literature, the William Bradford and John Smith histories.

Borrowings from Other Languages

Some attention should be paid to a long history of borrowing from languages other than French and to the impact of this borrowing on English. Cultures have always shown a tendency to borrow from perceived higher cultures when they come in contact with them. Sometimes this is done in a slavish way, sometimes in a very selective way, when only those things needed are chosen and adapted to the language. The Romans borrowed heavily from Greek culture, recognizing its superiority in many areas; they borrowed and adapted words to express concepts and ideas for which they had no words in Latin. The Germanic-speaking people on the continent, some of whom were later to emigrate to England and become the English, came in contact with Roman civilization, mainly through traders.

As the Germanic peoples were not literate at the time, Latin words were borrowed orally, and when they came to be written later, it was not easy to recognize their Latin origin. From this period came such words as *wine* (from Latin *vinum*) and *wall* (from Latin *vallum*), *mint* (from Latin *moneta*), *pound* (from Latin *ponde*), *inch* (from Latin *uncia*), *mile* (from Latin *mille*), *chest* (from Latin *cista*), and *kettle* (from Latin *catillus*). Objects of trade not known to the purchasers would be likely subjects for word borrowing, although not necessarily. In this case, as in all others to follow, it was always possible to use native language elements to achieve a sensorially, psychologically, and semantically sound translation. But a desire to associate an item with the language and people it came from might lead to the adoption of a foreign word. At later stages, second-language snobbery might lead to its use. At a still later stage, when the new, fused culture becomes strong and begins to look with pride on its roots, the borrowed word may be dropped and an older term revived.

After the Germanic-speaking peoples migrated to England and eliminated the Britons—the Celtic and Latin-speaking inhabitants—they were Christianized over a period of years by St. Augustine in the south and by the Irish Christians in the north. Christianity brought Latin terms into use again, and with them came the Latin cultural elements of philosophy and literature that Christianity continued to foster after the fall of Roman political power. Words having to do with Christianity, such as *pope, archbishop, priest, Mass, monk, nun,* and *shrine,* were borrowed from Latin but many terms were translated, such as *gospel* (Anglo-Saxon *god-spell,* meaning literally "good teaching") instead of Latin *evangelium* (borrowed from the Greek). Throughout the Anglo-Saxon period, the tendency was to use native elements of the language rather than to borrow words. Any language is adequate to the culture it embodies and is capable of expanding to meet whatever cultural developments become necessary, within the terms of its own form and vocabulary. There are other successful ways of extending the cultural limits (as English has shown), but it can probably be done more efficiently with native resources.

It seems quite likely that the undermining of Anglo-Saxon national spirit during the Norman period changed the attitude of speakers of English toward borrowing, and this attitude has never been the same since. Even so, a parallel native term has often been available, providing great range and nuance to the language for those who care to avail themselves of the possibilities. Thus, for aesthetic or psychological reasons or for semantic exactness, English-speaking people can use native elements going back to the roots of the language, or they can use borrowings that create quite a different effect. This is not to say that borrowings have no psychological depth or aesthetic texture. After 400–500 years, they are honestly English. *Cry, poor, change, war,* and *peace* are such words. But apart from such short and familiar words, the shadings of difference are always there. In literature, they loom large; in science also, but for other reasons. A doctor, in discussing internal organs with a patient, might not want to emphasize the psychological and sensory impact of *guts.* On the other hand, such a euphemism as *intestines* might strangle a poem.

Influence of the Renaissance and Scientific Age

The Renaissance (mainly sixteenth century in England) brought an influx of Latin terms to accompany the revival of classical civilization. A climate of thought was created that seemed to call for the wholesale borrowing of Latin words, even where French borrowing going back to the same Latin roots was present, as in *adventure* and *debt.* At the same time, there was an effort to create an English vernacular literature of a quality comparable to that of the classical age. Many writers took pride in native vocabulary, scorning the use of "inkhorn" terms, which they regarded as undigested and unnecessary Latin borrowing.

Eventually, usage sifted out many unnecessary Latin borrowings. This was a period of intellectual ferment, and the process was fed from many sources. The result was the heady wine of Elizabethan literature. English developed the range of vocabulary that made refined gradation of feeling and thought possible, while retaining a central native tradition that made for psychological depth and artistic simplicity. The language developed an extensive system of qualifying terms with an underlying grammatical structure that made the language highly analytical at a time when scientific thought could make use of it.

The development of commerce and communication led to a new eclecticism in word borrowing and quickened the process. Speakers of English have borrowed from all lands and languages in the modern period, reflecting mercantile, military, and colonial interests in various areas at different times. Modern science has led to the use of neo-Latin and neo-Greek words for scientific classification and for describing newly discovered processes.

All speakers of the English language call it to life, as they have been doing for over 1000 years. The language has changed and will go on changing, but there is a continuity that ties present-day speakers with the past and the future. They find their way through riches on every hand, some familiar, well-worn, and of proven worth, some waiting to be discovered, mined, and minted. Teachers may lead them to these riches if they know of them.

Language in Sociogeographic Context

In the words of the poet, "The land was ours before we were the land's." (Robert Frost, 1941) He expresses the insight that language must adapt to the experiences of people in the places they live.

The finding of common forms in the various Indo-European languages led to identification of the family and to the establishment of a hypothetical parent language. Those words appearing in a number of the languages were assumed to represent something of the common culture and its original geographic setting. From the beginning it was assumed that the parent language flourished in a limited geographic area before it spread across Europe and Asia. Words appearing only in isolated languages of the group were assumed to reflect a geographic setting of that language after its speakers wandered away from the homeland. The presence of common words for *snow, beech, pine, bear, wolf, ox, sheep,* and *bee,* taken together, suggest a temperate setting; the absence of common words for *elephant, lion, tiger, rhinocerous, monkey, rice, bamboo,* and *palm* adds negative evidence.

In the late eighteenth century, after the identification of the Indo-European family through the discovery of similarities between European languages and the Sanskrit-derived languages of India and assisted by the commonly held idea that Mesopotamia was the site of the garden of Eden, it was held that the Indo-European homeland was in Asia, despite the fact that most of the members of the family were in Europe.

More recently, scholars have postulated the location of the homeland as Europe, somewhere east of the Germanic-speaking area, extending from Lithuania into southeastern Europe and possibly including Anatolia. These interpretations grow out of language detective work, based on trying to match language (or hypothetical language) and geographic context. However, extreme care must be employed in making judgments about a long-dead, unwritten, prehistoric language in an uncertain geographic setting. Tracing associations of language and geography in recorded history or modern times is much easier.

Influence of a New Land on Emerging English

When the Anglo-Saxon people went to England they began to differentiate their Germanic language from that on the continent to reflect their new environment. Their interaction with a new part of the world, together with their isolation from the old, helped to make English a distinct language. There were dialect differences among the Angles, Saxons, and Jutes on the continent (they spoke different forms of German), and when they settled in different parts of England, these differences were continued. Although the common experience of migration and of association in driving out the Celtic Briton might have served to reduce differences, this was a relatively brief experience as language development goes. When political unity of England did come, it helped to unify the language and to keep dialects parallel, but lack of communication, typical of all Europe after the fall of the Roman Empire, left the dialects isolated enough that they continued to develop along their own lines. The general language, Middle English, was realized by each particular social group in the context of each particular geographic area.

Cleaving to the mother tongue was understandable in the early days of North American settlement. The American wilderness may have seemed like chaos to the first settlers, and one way of avoiding slipping into it was to stick to the safely ordered language of society that maintained in England. But the new environment called for new language to express its concepts. The American Revolution was in part the result of the realization that the British Parliament and British ways had little relevance to the American situation; to continue to vest power in a body without the possibility of cognitive and perceptual understanding would indeed be tyranny.

Adjustment of English to the American Scene

Psychologically and aesthetically, the need to adjust English to the American geographical and cultural context was extremely important. Perceptions and conceptions couldn't be slowed by the requirement that every experience be referred to England. The organic and symbolic importance of the colonial pine-tree shilling had its counterpart in language. The need for a thoroughly acclimated and domesticated language was even more important in literature. Noah Webster deliberately introduced spelling changes in his American English dictionary so that American literature could be easily recognized as distinctively American. A very great advance in modern letters took place when writers such as Mark Twain and Walt Whitman finally made the break complete. They evaluated the American experience in its own terms. Once this kind of turning away from the source would have meant a new language, considering the size of North America. But changes in communication and the spread of literacy and electronic media now seem likely to maintain a widespread language community.

Wherever English has gone out into other parts of the world, the pattern of adaptation has recurred, in Australia and New Zealand, in Canada and South Africa. Where speakers of English have faced a new environment without constantly looking back, they have given greater strength to the language and caused a strong literature to emerge.

Meeting the American Experience with Language

From the beginning, English-speaking settlers used Indian place names, recognizing that there is often some special connection between the place and the conventional name it bears. Just so, the Anglo-Saxons, while obliterating the previous inhabitants of England, did not tamper with some Celtic and Roman place names. The feeling for the country has come to be expressed in Indian names— *Oklahoma*, the *Penobscot, Massachusetts*, the *Chickahominy*, and *Alabama*. Words for new flora and fauna and experiences were also borrowed from the Indians: *moose* and *caribou, pow-wow* and *pecan, oposum*, and *skunk, squash* and *succotash, canoe* and *tobacco* (these two from the West Indies), *chili* and *chocolate, tomato* and *tamale* (these four from Mexico). Terms were translated from Indian languages: *warpath, paleface, pipe of peace*, and *bury the hatchet*. Words were contributed by non-English-speaking settlers: from the New Amsterdam Dutch, *cruller* and *coleslaw, sleigh* and *span* (of horses), *dope, spook*, and *Yankee* (derived from Jan-Ki, diminutive for John); from the Spanish settlers (mostly after the westward movement), *corral* and *ranch, lasso* and *pinto, arroyo* and *canyon;* from the French, *bayou* and *levee, cafe* and *portmanteau, portage* and *prairie*. Perhaps most important of all in conjuring up the quality of American experience were the new combinations of old words: *garter snake* and *grizzly bear, slippery elm* and *snap bean, sourwood* and *sugar maple, bullfrog* and *backwoods* (the latter an interesting contrast to the Australian *outback*).

The first English settlers to come to America had grown up in the age of Elizabeth and were Elizabethans in their language. But the life of the frontier did not take the language in the directions it took in stay-at-home England of the eighteenth century, so some Elizabethan characteristics that died in England survived in the "hollers" of Appalachia.

The English Language in America

Dutch settlers in South Africa, isolated from their homeland, evolved a new language, Afrikaans. The new settlers arriving in America from England brought the language of the homeland, but they immediately began to find new words or to use old words in new ways. But continuing political relationship and new immigration served for a time to keep the differences between British and American English to a minimum. The attitude of those in England was that the language was degenerating in the New World because the migration was mostly one way.

Early English travelers, within a few years of the first settlements, commented on the changes wrought in the language by the New World experiences. Although dialect differences came to America and, in some instances, were isolated in pockets, as in some southern Appalachian areas, the fact that the settlers were funneled in through the east coast served to provide a common language denominator. Also, continuing and relatively rapid mobility of people across the continent and new forms of communication made the old isolation less possible, keeping dialect difference within limits. West African pidgin with its English word phrases set in African and Portuguese language structures came to America with black slaves, sometimes via the Caribbean islands. It has enriched the American language as it emerged in southern black dialects.

American Dialects Today

Only a few major dialects with the degree of difference comparable to the much larger number of dialects of England have persisted in the United States. Does a peach have a *pit, seed, stone,* or *bone* in it? Is the same thing found in a cherry or is that known by another name? Your answer will be different depending on where you live and where you grew up. Do you carry the groceries home in a *bag,* a *sack,* a *poke,* or a *tote?* One or more sounds natural to you and the others are either strange-sounding or you may argue that they have quite another meaning. A speaker from southern Illinois amuses his Chicago listeners when he says he will *warsh* his clothes and then *arn* them. A listener in Milwaukee notes inwardly the lack of culture of an educated Kentuckian when he hears him say *dived* instead of *dove.*

All of these are aspects of the differences among the well-established regional dialects of the United States. Such differences have been studied and documented by linguistic atlas field workers who have been engaged for decades in the task of interviewing speakers in all parts of the country to determine the boundaries and overlaps of dialect regions. The task is not yet completed because of the limited number of trained field workers and the lack of the substantial financial support that would be required to complete it.

Three major dialects have emerged: northern, midland, and southern. But each of these can be subdivided. Furthermore, some eastern dialects developed that didn't move west. Eastern New England, New York City, and eastern Virginia are examples. Another such dialect developed in the hollows of the Appalachian Mountains. The influence of the generally westward population movement across the northern, middle, and southern states since colonial days explains the division of the country into the basic dialect groups. A certain degree of insularity explains the more contained dialects of New England, New York City, eastern Virginia and Appalachia. The areas of earliest settlement on the east coast developed the smallest and most easily defined dialect areas.

When the mapping of American dialects is finally completed, it will partly represent an extension of the westward movement and partly reflect major changes in the speed and methods of transportation in recent decades. The population movement into California, Florida, Texas, and the rest of the sun belt, for example, often represents leap-frogging from distant parts of the country.

Class Dialects

The dialect patterns of the major northern cities are influenced by a decided south-to-north movement established as industrialization became a magnet to those leaving more rural areas. This has led to complex socioeconomic dialect patterns within the major cities. The different social classes have been recruited from different parts of the country. Particularly after the migration of Europeans in large numbers ended in the 1920's, industrial workers were recruited from the black and white poor in the south and midlands. World War II accelerated this migration.

Studies of socioeconomic dialect patterns within urban complexes of the United States have only recently begun. In the geographic atlas work there was a strong tendency to concentrate only on the most stable and well-established language in an area. Studies of urban dialect patterns require a look at the speech of all groups in the area across ethnic, racial, and class lines. The patterns of dialect distribution within a metropolitan complex relate to the population shifts in that complex. Immigrants have tended to arrive in the central portions of the complex, to spend a generation there, and then to shift outward toward the outer part of the city and the suburbs. In American cities the pattern has been for successive waves of European immigrants to replace each other, followed by black and white immigrants from the South. In more recent decades a major Hispanic migration from Puerto Rico, Mexico, Cuba, and Central America has been underway. Even more recently there has been an immigration of Asians, particularly from the countries of Indo-China.

Transplanted regional dialects are superimposed on preexisting ones in the cities, and all are in continuous evolution, as is language everywhere. The net result is a picture of great variation, with social-status factors becoming intermixed with linguistic ones in the attitudes themselves. Some language forms—phonological, grammatical, and semantic—become prestigious, while others are accorded the low social status of their users. Some folks' language seems archaic to others. Those who stay home have a "country" quality as distinguished from the "city" dialect of the city folk.

All dialects influence each other to some degree, but upwardly mobile individuals will tend to shift toward prestige forms to gain greater acceptance from high-status groups in the community and to conceal their more humble beginnings. (Shuy, 1967) Each dialect, however, is a bona fide language system. Teachers need to be well aware of this fact in their daily instruction.

English that Stayed at Home in England

Needless to say, English that stayed home did not remain static. The world changes even without travel. Sometimes English changed faster than its emigre cousin. Sometimes the language left behind was more conservative. The Anglo-Saxon settlers in Britain had settled in their different corners, set up their seven kingdoms, and left the stamp of their differing dialects to survive to the present day. An age of slow communication and identification with the land maintained distinctness. There were centers of political power and literary brilliance that pulled at the .

extremes of Lancashire, Yorkshire, Lallans, and Cockney, but through it all the dialects of England and the English-speaking areas of Scotland, Wales, and Ireland maintained their strong identity. The United States has only a handful of dialects compared to some 29 in the Great Britain.

In recent years, both politicians and writers have recognized the myth that there is a pure form of English and the value of dialect differences. Class dialects, as Shaw demonstrated in *Pygmalion,* have been much more clearly delineated in Britain than in other English-speaking countries. This requires a careful educational response, lest difference be confused with deficiency.

The Role of Young People in the History of Language

Young people have played key roles in the evolution of English and will continue to make their influence felt as the language is molded today for the future. They are the protectors of the language that was, conveyors of the language that is, and innovators of the language that will be.

Conservation of the Language by the Young

Young people protect or conserve the language that was and thereby assist in the stabilization of a language. Oral transmission is a stabilizer of language. Transmission of folk tales, folk songs, and rhymes is a good example of how the old language persists for centuries. Children learn some of these rhymes and tales holistically in their early years; at the same time, the children are delighted with the old syntax, the old flow of line, the old rhymes and assonance. Some words persist for generations because of this oral tradition, even though there is no need for the words any longer.

In the United States, *porridge* is such a word. It is firmly seated in "Pease porridge hot, pease porridge cold," even though porridge has been replaced by cold cereals for most American children and has been narrowed to mean only oatmeal for other English-speaking children.

Overly modernized versions of such tales, songs, and rhymes may help children grasp the ideas they express but could also begin to shake the language loose from its roots.

Children also tend to conserve the old language in their own tongue. Children's language in play has changed surprisingly little over the centuries. Although much of the song of children is inventive and gains prominence for the moment, lore passed down in regions and neighborhoods from one generation to the next persists over many generations. Names and places change, but the old jokes and themes of play language are the same.

A remarkable and fascinating book, *The Lore and Language of School Children,* by Iona and Peter Opie (1959), reveals English-speaking children at work in their language The Opies have differentiated the juvenile tongue from the mother tongue of the adult world by making a distinction between the nursery rhyme and what they call the "school rhyme," which is language of the playground, whether it is used in a street, in a barnyard, or upstairs in the attic.

While a nursery rhyme passes from a mother or other adult to the small child on her knee, the school rhyme circulates simply from child to child, usually outside the home, and beyond the influence of the family circle . . . It (the nursery rhyme) is a rhyme which is adult approved. The schoolchild's verses are not intended for adult ears. In fact part of their fun is the thought, usually correct, that adults know nothing about them. (Opie and Opie, 1959)

This child language of rhymes, jokes, parodies, tricks, testing code, nicknames, and epithets is the symbolic content of a universal subculture of youthful society. It is a subculture in which young people learn the language and all its possibilities at the same time that they are learning adult culture and its language. The new language of each generation emerges from an interplay between the juvenile tongue and the mother tongue.

The Opies quote an old ballad of 1725 from which a common playground song developed.

> Now he acts the Grenadier,
> Calling for a Pot of Beer:
> Where's his Money? He's forgot:
> Get him gone, a Drunken Sot.

They then quote the British Museum's record from an 8-year-old child who noted his own version of the ballad almost 50 years later (1774):

> Who's there
> A Grenadier
> What d'ye want
> A Pint of Beer

From that date until now it has been children's coinage and theirs alone.

> Rat a tat tat, who is that?
> Only grandma's pussycat.
> What do you want?
> A pint of milk.
> Where's your money?
> In my pocket.
> Where is your pocket?
> I forgot it.
> O, you silly pussycat (1916)

> Mickey Mouse
> In a public house
> Drinking pints of beer.
> Where's your money?
> In my pocket.
> Where's your pocket?
> I forgot it.
> Please walk out. (1950)
> (Opie and Opie, pp. 10–11)

Though the verse is altered in each generation, perhaps play language remains much the same because it is passed on so quickly. A generation for children's language is only six to eight years.

Many items of the British collection by the Opies sound very close to American play language. Oceans of distance have not held back the carrier children. One of what they call the "tricks inflicting pain" is as common in America as in England.

> Adam and Eve and Pinch-me
> Went down to the river to bathe.
> Adam and Eve were drowned,
> Who do you think was saved? (Opie and Opie, p. 59)

From most categories of child language collected in Britain, there are echoes and even repetitions in the American child culture. Crybabies on both sides of the Atlantic are rebuked with some version of

> Cry baby, cry,
> Put your finger in your eye,
> And tell your mother
> It wasn't I. (Opie and Opie, p. 188)

Children's play talk pervades the child culture and stabilizes the movement of language at an impressionable period in children's language development. Both schoolyard language passed from child to child and the nursery rhymes, tales, and old songs transmitted by adults preserve the oral traditions. Children carry the language they learn in this way into the next generation, when, as adults, they pass some of it along to their children. They put away child language as they put away childish things, but the sense of rhythms and sound-play remains.

Children Expanding Their Language

Children are more than just the conveyors of the language between generations. They actually remold or remake it as they play with it. Even though they tend to be conservative in their passing on of language, they also break away from accepted patterns as they innovate and use shortcuts, particularly as cultures intersect.

Here are a group of circle games collected from some inner-city American black children. These are called circle games because the players stand in a circle. Usually sung, some of these games have motions or movements that go along with the words. The rhythms, like the sounds and grammar, change to suit the singers.

Little Sally Walker

> (Someone is Sally and sits in the middle. A boy would be Tony Walker.)
> Little Sally Walker, sitting in a saucer,
> Crying and weeping for someone to come.
> Rise, Sally, rise, Sally.
> Wipe your weeping eyes, Sally. (Swivel hips
> during next line.)

Put your hands on your hips and let your
backbone slip.
Aw, shake it to the East, Sally. (Shake hip to left.)
Aw, shake it to the West, Sally. (Shake hip to right.)
Aw, shake it to the very one that you love best, Sally.
(On the last line cover eyes with one hand and swing around while pointing with the
    other. The one pointed to at the end is the next Sally or Tony.)

London Bridge, My Baby

London Bridge is oo-atcha-koo, my baby,
Oo-atcha-koo, my baby, oo-atcha-koo, my baby,
London Bridge is oo-atcha-koo my baby,
Work out, Karen. (Child chosen "rocks and rolls.")
With a hip and ho and a rock and roll[1],
(Three times.)
All right, Karen. (Now repeat and Karen calls another name)

Of course there are lots of folk songs that children sing. Here's a version of
one that black inner-city boys sing, showing their response to changing cultural
events.

Mockingbird (The Boys' Way)

Hambone, hambone, have you heard?
Papa's gonna buy me a mockingbird
If that mockingbird won't sing,
Papa's gonna buy me a diamond ring.
If that diamond ring don't shine,
Papa's gonna buy me a bottle of wine.
If that bottle of wine gets broke,
Papa's gonna buy me a billy goat.
If that billy goat runs away,
Papa's gonna buy me a Chevrolet.
If that Chevrolet won't run,
Papa's gonna buy me a BB gun.
If that BB gun won't shoot,
Papa's gonna buy me a baseball suit.
If that baseball suit won't fit,
Papa's gonna say, "Aw shoot, I quit!" (Goodman, 1971)

Language change is available to all its users, young and old, but the young are
more likely to take advantage of change because they have less commitment to the
past. Another group, of course, who exercise their options to change the language
are the great poets and writers.

The language might be radically changed by each generation of children
were it not for their strong need to communicate with adults. When adults are not

---

[1]*Ho* and *roll* rhyme in the dialect of the singers.

present, as in the instance of isolated children (so-called feral children and real victims of extreme adult cruelty), only grunts and groans emerge from the complex speech-sounding apparatus all human beings possess. In a society of only peer relationships—no child-adult confrontations—there could be only minimal language development.

However, as the language is passed on from generation to generation, children, like poets, seem to brighten it and stretch it when they discover new things already commonplace to adults. Even though it would be impossible to find out whether some startling pieces of a child's language ever got into the mainstream of the national language, the freshness and rightness of some of their phrasing suggest that it must have an influence. This freshness can be a mighty resource for imaginative adult speaking and writing if it is not submerged by the formalities of socially acceptable, conforming language taught in school and required for advancing oneself.

Child-Tending Rhymes

Children in large families often are required to tend younger brothers and sisters, and their frustration may come out in rope-skipping rhymes. In Belfast one child commented that her mother didn't like her to skip too much, since it wore out her shoes. Then she began:

> My wee brother is no good.
> Chop him up for firewood.
> When he's dead
> Cut off his head,
> Make it into gingerbread

Another skipper in Belfast added this one:

> Eni eni mino mo
> Set the baby on the po
> When it's done
> Clean its bum
> And give it a lump
> Of sugar plum.

And in the United States, baby care is a problem, too.

> I had a little brother,
> His name was Tiny Tim.
> I put him in the wash tub
> To teach him how to swim.
> He drank up all the water,
> He ate up all the soap.
> He died last night
> With a bubble in his throat. (Butler, 1973)

Street Slang

The slang of the street and the schoolyard has substantial effects on the history of a language, because a certain amount of slang from one generation lodges in the matrix of the language and becomes an acceptable word or phrase for a cycle of years. Teenagers take hold of current slang, using it, stretching it, and adding to it. They do this with all the zest of defiance against parents and their values. To use slang frowned on by parents is one safe way to revolt. Following the early stages of the space program and the emergence of the drug culture, a spate of slang emerged that the young quickly exploited. Being "in orbit" came to apply to more than just satellites and was quickly followed by "spaced out."

The intense popularity of most slang themes seems to last no longer than one youth generation. However, some slang words and phrases hold and are carried into adult life. "O.K." was one of these. A variant, "oaky-doaky," was dropped, but "O.K." has swept across the seas, and it now appears in many languages. "Cool" in its slang meaning is likely to persist, and there is hardly a youth in the "cool" generation who did not use it to describe the car he would like his father to buy or the posture he would like to present to the world. Heaven forbid that he should blow his "cool."

Fostering Children's Language Play

Young people play an important role in the development of language, and this role should be respected by teachers. Traditional language is a valuable inheritance, but fresh and new language should be encouraged. It is improper for adults to intrude upon play language, for once they do, it is thwarted and is no longer an important aspect of children's language. Teachers need to be aware of its existence because it gives them clues to what sort of language interests young people. The rhyme, the chant, the joke, the parody, the shaggy-dog tale, the scary story, the word trick, the pun, the riddle, and the taunt that protects children from other children and allows them to get back at the adult world are all literary forms children enjoy reading and writing.

Children delight in the teasing puzzle of an unfinished story or in a story that starts off sensibly and then takes a foolish turn. These forms can be crudely or artfully executed. Children seem to prefer the artful ones with strong rhythms, delightful shapes, good rhymes, or interesting assonance. Yet many trite, ineffective verses labeled "poetry for children" get into children's readers or into teachers' plan books.

With the world's people having to learn to live together using different speech—and there seems no likelihood of a truly universal language being developed—children need to grow up with a healthy respect for their own dialects, for other languages, and for the history of language. They may not be aware that they share in this history when they go to school, but by the time they leave they should feel their part in the process of language growth.

Dialect Differences and School Programs

When children enter school they bring to it five to six years of language and experience. Because their world, prior to entering school, has been largely confined to their family, their home, and their immediate neighborhood, both their language and experience are heavily rooted in their subculture. The language they speak is their mother's tongue. No matter what other language learning they achieve in their lifetime, this first one is most deeply rooted.

This language has been so well learned that no conscious effort is involved in its use. It is deeply internalized. Children's language is as much a part of them as their own skin. Rejection of children's language may be more deeply disturbing than rejection of their skin color. The latter is only an insult, the former strikes at their ability to communicate and express their needs and feelings—their very selves.

When they hear language, children can judge whether it sounds right or wrong on the basis of the language norms of their dialect. They can detect very fine differences in sounds when these differences are significant in their dialects. They have learned to ignore differences in speech sounds that are not important to their dialects. They have learned to use their dialect's patterns of rhythm and pitch with great subtlety. They enjoy, at an early age, puns in the language that depend for their humor on slight differences in stress, pitch, or phrasing. The puns may be funny only within one dialect of English. Many a teacher has unwittingly created a pun in the dialect of the pupils that is not a pun in the teacher's dialect (sometimes with embarrassing results).

Children, at school age, have virtually mastered the grammar of their dialect to the point where they can create sentences that they have never heard but that are grammatical within their dialect. Their vocabulary falls largely within the vocabulary of their speech community. They have begun to develop concepts based on experiences common to their culture and have learned to express these concepts in their mother tongue. They become ever more effective in communicating with their language.

In all respects, the process of language learning and development is the same whether the child is learning a socially prestigious dialect or learning one with low social status; that is, considered by others to be substandard. When they enter school their language is well learned and is just as systematic as any other and just as important to them, regardless of the social value attached to their dialect in the general culture. It is their means of communication with humanity and with those who are closest to them.

Children with Divergent Speech

Perhaps the greatest handicap to more effective language programs in the schools has been the mistaken assumption that language that deviates from the standard (however defined) is bad, sloppy, or ineffective. Linguists are often surprised that anyone would believe that any dialect of any language could exist without a system of its own. Linguists have learned through studies of countless dialects of countless languages that each dialect is basically systematic and that speakers of each dialect use its system with great consistency. H. A. Gleason says, "All languages are approximately equally adequate for the needs of the culture of which they are a part." (Gleason, 1961)

As long as the schools treat learners as poor users of standard English rather than as speakers of their own systematic dialects, schools will be unable to deal adequately with the language learning of all children.

Children who do not speak high-status English have language that has been adequate for their needs up to the time of school beginning. That same language continues to be an effective means of communication in the child's daily life outside of school. This effectiveness is increased and the dialect is reinforced through contact with adults and peers in the subcultural group. The teacher may say that "I done it" is wrong, but the subculture says over and over again to the child that "I done it" is right.

It is only when children come into increasingly more frequent contact with other subcultures in the general culture that their language may become inadequate for their changing needs. Normally, new communicative needs will stimulate the expansion of children's language. But teachers may frustrate language development rather than facilitate it if they continually attack children's speech as incorrect or substandard. Children may be driven to defend themselves, their families, their friends, and their culture by resisting all attempts to change their language. They may be forced to regard rejection of their language as rejection of themselves. Movements stressing ethnic pride, however, have made speakers of low-status dialects aware that there is power and beauty in their language.

Social and Regional Divergences

In this chapter, standard English is used to mean the dialect form that carries the most social prestige in the larger community. The child who speaks a dialect different from standard English will be referred to as a *divergent speaker*. This term is preferred because it is not value laden. It does not label children's language as worse or less correct, in some qualitative way, than standard English. We use the term divergent also because of the variety of idiolects and dialects found among American and other English-speaking children, particularly in urban areas. Whereas one might find relatively pure forms of geographic dialects in communities with relatively immobile populations, the big cities have populations who have moved more or less recently from other parts of the country. They bring varied social and regional dialects with them. Their children grow up with many language influences—the neighbors, the regional dialects of the city in which they live, and the standardized speech of radio and television.

The language each child brings to school may vary in important ways from all other children's language. A group of children may have speech rooted in the same dialect, but their personal languages—their idiolects—will vary widely, depending on how much they have absorbed other language influences. The idiolects of urban children vary from distinctly divergent dialects toward the standard speech of the community, depending on such variables as origin of the family, the degree of isolation from the general culture of the community, the recency of movement to the new community, and the level of education.

Attitudes are also important; parental aspiration, personal motivation, and self-esteem will undoubtedly influence the degree to which the individual seeks, accepts, or rejects language influences.

Bilingualism

For young people whose divergence goes as far as speaking an entirely different language, influences delineated for speakers of divergent dialects may assume even larger proportions. However, it is easier in many ways for the teacher and the educational system to give recognition to the language of such children in a way that will reassure them and give them pride in their native tongues, just because the gap is so wide and obvious. In the case where some children speak a language or languages other than English, the bilingual situation opens an avenue for the children to achieve greater understanding of language in general, to enhance their awareness of the way their dominant language works as a result of seeing it from the perspective of another language, and to receive cultural enrichment that comes from knowledge of a second language and culture.

Bilingualism, at any level, is beneficial and broadening for all people. It is important that the bilingual program not be conceived by its initiators as simply a back-door induction of speakers of a foreign language into the dominant language. Patronizing and self-congratulatory approaches are another form of rejection of children and their culture and ethnic identity along with their language.

Questions of divergent dialects arise also with people who speak languages other than English. Migrants are rarely the high-class, high-status speakers of the places they move from. So, often children in Texas speaking rural dialects of northern Mexico are told they do not speak proper Spanish. French Canada has language policies that treat Canadian French as improper, and children speaking dialects from southern Italy are informed that the Tuscan dialect is the only true Italian. In Spanish Harlem, Puerto Rican children find the dialects of both English and Spanish that they speak labeled low status.

In most parts of the world, being bilingual or multilingual has been regarded as highly desirable. Parents with the means to do so send their children to special schools that teach in languages other than the national language. In the United States, the "melting pot" view caused schools to ignore home languages or to treat them as interfering with the development of English. For decades, the professional literature on Hispanic pupils in the United States treated their home language as a school problem. Rejection of Spanish was supported by the development of an "interference" theory that treated all first language influences as interferences to be extinguished.

This interference theory comes from a confusion of the linguists' use of the term *interference,* which to them really means simply *influence,* with the behavioral view of interference in learning. When people begin to use second languages, there are influences evident from their first language in phonology, syntax, and vocabulary. Such influences would only be interferences if the influences interfered with comprehension. In fact, there is little evidence to suggest that such influences do interfere, and, if the new language is functional for the learners, any such real interference will quickly disappear as the learners move toward effective use.

A wide range of bilingual programs have emerged in recent years. Some in the United States are responses to federal and state laws requiring schools to offer bilingual programs to pupils not proficient in English. Others, like the French immersion programs popular in many parts of Canada, are designed to teach fluency in a second language to those whose home language is English. Those programs are most effective that put the language(s) in the context of functional use and that encourage pupils to expand on the base of existing language(s).

Divergence, Immaturities, and Deficiencies in Speech Patterns

Teachers must learn to distinguish between speech that is dialect based and speech that is immature. Some fine points of grammar, inflection, and vocabulary may still not fall within adult language norms when children start school. They may even retain a slight problem with the sounds of the language, not being able to differentiate the initial consonants of *free* and *three,* or *red* and *wed,* for example. Also, school-age children are still experimenting with the limits of generalizations about the language they have acquired. Regularizing of irregularities in language (for example, *bringed* for *brought*) is not uncommon among young school-age children. Such immaturities exist in the language of all children regardless of the dialect they speak. The important difference between immature speech and divergent speech lies in the direction of the language growth of the child. Immaturities stem from stages in language growth that are part of the process of development and that will give way to more effective forms that fall within adult language norms. But divergent speech already lies within the norms of the dialect; it is supported by the systematic nature of the dialect—that is, it obeys the dialect's rules. One way for a teacher to differentiate divergent and immature speech is to consider how the pupil's parents would say the same thing. Only by comparison with the speech of the mature members of the language community can any child's language be judged immature. Even then there will be some contrast, since changes within dialects are constant and tend to be more easily noticed in young speakers.

The Myth of Nonlanguage
A myth has grown up among the general public and among many teachers and educators as well, which may be called the myth of nonlanguage. Somehow, the belief has developed that some children, labeled variously as "culturally deprived," "culturally disadvantaged," "low income," "language deprived," or just "slum kids," are virtually without language. This belief is reinforced for many teachers by their observation of youngsters who are inarticulate and unresponsive in the classroom or who appear not to understand what to the teacher is simple, clear language. But the overwhelming evidence of linguistic research should begin to clear up this myth. All groups of people ever studied have language. All normal children learn the language of their subcultures, and they use it on the playground, at home, and in the street. The observed "lack of language" of some children in the classroom,

then, is not a real lack of language but rather a lack of "appropriate" acceptable language and a lack of confidence that their own language and experiences are appropriate for the classroom. Two examples will illustrate this point:

1. A teacher noticed that one of her first-graders was unable to participate in the general discussion after the class returned from a trip to the zoo. She was, in fact, unable to answer the simplest question about the animals. She did not even seem to know the names of such common animals as lions, tigers, elephants, and bears.

   A few days later, the teacher tactfully raised the question with the child's mother during a parent-teacher conference. "You know," she said, "it would be very good for Mai-li if you and her father took her on trips to places like the zoo. She needs experiences like that."

   The mother was puzzled. "As a family we go on many trips," she said. "We get to the zoo several times a year, as a matter of fact. It's one of the children's favorite trips."

   Now it was the teacher's turn to be puzzled. "But Mai-li doesn't even seem to know the names of the animals or anything about them," the teacher said.

   "Oh, she does know about animals," the mother explained, "but, you see, my husband is Old World Chinese. He is very anxious that our children learn to speak Chinese and appreciate their cultural heritage. So when we go on trips we speak only Chinese. Mai-li knows the Chinese names of many of the animals in the zoo. I'm sure she could tell you a lot about them in Chinese."

2. A second-grade teacher had prepared to introduce a story to her reading group. The children all lived in a housing project near the head of Detroit. The story was about a squirrel. Assuming a lack of experience with squirrels, which she associated with suburban residential districts, the teacher had prepared a large cutout of a squirrel to show the children. "I'm thinking," she said, "of a small animal that likes to climb trees and has a bushy tail." Hands shot up, and several children, bursting to answer, almost shouted, "I know, I know!" Triumphantly, the chosen child said, "Squirrel! We got lots of squirrel where we live." "Really?" said the teacher in polite disbelief. "Who can tell me about squirrels?" She called on a black child, literally falling off the front edge of his seat in his eagerness to tell about his experiences with squirrels. "My daddy, he go huntin' for squirrel," he said. "Sometime he take me 'long." "Hunting?" the teacher said in a dull tone. "What do you do with the squirrels?" "First we skin 'em. Then we cook 'em," he said. "They goo-ood!" he added. The teacher responded with a silent look of revulsion. An Appalachian youngster then said, "My papaw can skin a squirrel so the skin come out in one piece!"

   Another boy spoke out without the teacher's permission. "My brother, he 10. He catch squirrel and tie tin can to they tail. Man, they sure fun to watch." "That's enough, Thomas," the teacher said coldly. "Class, open your books to page 37 and begin reading."

The first story involves a bilingual child, rich in experience but unable to express it in language acceptable to the school. The second story illustrates the more complex problem of children who find neither their experience nor their language acceptable in the school. Unable to understand the subtle limits and unstated standards for acceptable language and experience in the classroom, hurt and rejected in their initial attempts at using their language to discuss their world in the classroom, the divergent speakers retreat to the safety of silence. Those who doubt this phenomenon have only to listen to the rapid, flowing speech of young divergent speakers as they speak among themselves on the playgrounds and in the halls as they approach the classroom. The speech is rich in idiom, and its effectiveness in communication is obvious from the response and repartee that ensue. Suddenly the speech ceases at the classroom door at the first sight of the teacher. Only then are divergent speakers transformed into inarticulate, tongue-tied nonusers of language. William Labov reports that inner-city black youngsters observed to be nonverbal in schools and in interview situations become extremely fluent when the situation is made less school-like and peers are present for interaction. (Labov, 1973)

Children have concepts that they can express in their own language, but sometimes they find that this is not the language of the classroom or of the basal reader. In fact, they find that commonplace expressions at home may not be understood by the teacher. Worse, yet, the teacher may be shocked by the expressions, because they have an entirely different significance and connotation to the teacher. Occasionally the opposite may occur. The teacher may find that the language in the book sets the class to embarrassed snickering or to outright laughter. Such was the fate of the music teacher who attempted to introduce to one inner-city 6-year-old group the time-honored children's song "Pussy Willow." Only later in the teachers' lounge did she understand why the class "fell out" laughing at the end of the first line.

Another teacher, in preparing her 7-year-olds for a visit to the fire station, asked how many had seen a house on fire. To her utter amazement she discovered that these slum children had not only seen such fires but a majority had had fires in their own dwellings. She should have realized that fire hazard is a fact of life for slum children.

Teachers tend to prejudge what kids are saying on the basis of their dialects. They reject the low-status speakers' ideas because they reject their language. (Williams and Whitehead, 1971)

Divergent urban speakers are linguistically handicapped in school only by the rejection of their dialects. In fact they have linguistic advantages over speakers of high-status dialects. In general, people learn language in order to communicate with those they interact with. Inner-city kids learn to understand dialects used by others in their communities, such as storekeepers, police officers, and teachers. This receptive language control is well developed by the end of the sixth grade, though the speaker may never move to productive control; that is, speaking fluently in the higher-status dialect. Ironically, teachers tend to expect their pupils to understand them without always seeing the need to reciprocate by learning to tune in to the dialect of the learners.

The Myth of Cognitive Deficit

A related, and even more poorly based, myth is that the language of some children is not suitable for use in learning. In its extreme form this theory relates to a general view that some ethnic or racial groups are genetically different from others in the extent and the way in which they can learn. The language difference is seen as an indication of their general cognitive abilities; limited language comes from limited intelligence.

Arthur Jensen has become a spokesman for this position. (Jensen, 1969) In his view, black Americans perform more poorly on intelligence tests because of genetic differences. They can learn, he asserts, but not as much, not as easily, and not in the same ways.

The argument for verbal deficit is summarized by Labov in six steps. (Labov, 1973, pp. 34–35)

1. Lower-class children's verbal responses to formal and threatening situations are used to demonstrate their verbal deficits.
2. These verbal deficits are declared to be a major cause of the lower-class children's poor performance in school.
3. Since middle-class children do better in school, middle-class speech habits are seen to be necessary for learning.
4. Class and ethnic differences in grammatical form are equated with differences in the capacity for logical analysis.
5. Teaching children to mimic certain formal speech patterns used by middle-class teachers is seen as teaching them to think logically.
6. Children who learn these formal speech patterns are then said to be thinking logically, and it is predicted that they will do much better in reading and arithmetic in the years to follow.

In some programs, such as DISTAR, which is based on this set of premises, students are drilled in patterns until they respond quickly and uniformly. (Engelmann, 1969) The teacher holds up a pencil. "Is this a cup?" she asks. In unison her class responds, "No, this is not a cup. This is a pencil." No other response is acceptable. If a black youngster replies, "That ain't no cup," her response is rejected. Because she uses a double negative, her response is assumed to be illogical and her control over the concept of negation is questioned. Yet clearly she has understood, and clearly her double negative is not illogical but rather a matter of dialect preference. In many languages double negatives are required, "n'est-ce pas?" Are French and Russian illogical languages because they use double negatives? No, they are only different.

The danger in these programs is that they turn linguistic strength into weakness and justify elitist views that treat the language of low-status learners as unworthy.

Labov summarizes his case in this manner (p. 18):

> There is no reason to believe that any nonstandard vernacular is in itself an obstacle to learning. The chief problem is ignorance of language on the part of all concerned. Our job as linguists is to remedy this ignorance. Bereiter and Englemann want to reinforce it and justify it. Teachers are now being told to ignore the language of Black children as unworthy of attention and useless for learning. They are being taught to hear every natural utterance of the child as evidence of his mental inferiority. As linguists we are unanimous in condemning this view as bad observation, bad theory and bad practice.

Influence of Prestigious Forms

Although no one dialect of English has established itself as the world-wide prestige dialect to be imitated by all others (as, for example, Florentine Italian is the preferred Italian dialect: McDavid, 1964), there is a common assumption that a standard American English exists. But there are really a number of regional standards, each approximating the speech of high-status speakers of the region. Perhaps it can be more accurately stated that there are a number of aspects of language that are commonly regarded as nonstandard. These mark the speaker, in the view of the general society, as uncultured, crude, and ignorant. Labov's study of dialect in New York City indicates that there is considerable agreement among people of all social classes, who differ considerably in their actual speech, on what are preferred and rejected forms. In fact, many people think, or say they think, that they use prestige forms when they actually do not.

The Language of Youth and Social Attitudes Toward It

To some extent, this common agreement on prestige forms may be due to the prescriptive efforts of schoolteachers, but this can only explain part of the phenomenon. Labov suggests, in fact, that language differences can be divided into three categories: (1) differentiating factors with no social-discrimination components (the differences, in a sense, are socially neutral). Examples are used of *bucket* rather than *pail* or *soda* rather than *pop;* (2) social markers (these differences are widely considered to indicate nonstandard speech. Examples are "nuttin'," "we was," and "didn't have no"); and (3) stereotypes (these items, such as the use of *ain't,* are so widely regarded as "bad" that they disappear from the speech of almost all Labov's New York subjects in even the least formal contexts). It is in this last category that the effect of prescriptive teaching may be felt, but the second category of the socially important markers is the key one. It's the one that causes the speaker to be socially down-graded by the listener.

Labov has found in his studies that there is a pattern of change among all social classes toward prestige forms, but significantly he has found that this pattern does not begin to form to any significant degree until after the age when most children have learned their literacy skills. He suggests six stages a person goes through in the movement toward socially prestigious language norms.

1. Mastering the basic communicative apparatus of language. Children learn this at home from the family. What they learn is the relaxed, informal, unguarded speech.
2. Mastering the street vernacular.
3. Social perceiving. At about puberty young people begin to be aware of which aspects of language and which kinds of language behavior are more prestigeful. Adolescents, of course, may well deliberately reject the prestigeful forms they have identified in favor of what they regard as distinctively adolescent speech.
4. Learning stylistic variations; that is, not just to hear differences but to produce the preferred form. This, of course, is not an easy task, because the preferred form may involve phonemes, inflections, and syntax outside the deeply learned

patterns of the native dialect. An example of such a difficult acquisition for many New Yorkers is the final *r* in such words as *fear, car,* and *fire.*
5. Maintaining prestige forms.
6. Being completely mobile in language. Few divergent speakers are likely to reach this last stage. (Labov, 1964)

Anxieties Caused by Language Differences

Studies of social attitudes toward language indicate a great deal of language anxiety, particularly in the lower middle classes. Anxiety may lead to supercorrectness. This might take the form of overpronunciation, particularly of final sounds in words, or use of such forms as "she gave it to he and I," or "aren't I." The latter uses a plural verb with a singular subject solely to avoid *ain't. Amn't,* the correct form, has become *ain't.*

Increasing language anxiety may produce more careful speech, but at the cost of expressive ability: speakers devote so much attention to their language that they are then unable to give adequate attention to their thoughts.

There are, of course, economic reasons for teachers, parents, and minority group leaders to want young divergent speakers to achieve socially prestigious speech. They feel that people who do not speak "properly" will be denied many jobs and promotional opportunities as adults. There is some truth to this fear. But educators are well aware that children aged 6 or 7 are not easily motivated to learn on the basis of what someone says their future needs as adults will be. For most young children the need is for language here and now: at home, at play, and at school. Further, although young children can perceive differences in dialects (they may well be able to say, for example, "I say it this way, but you would say it another way"), they are quite likely to be unaware of the social approval or disapproval that applies to one or another way of saying something.

Adolescents are likely to have learned the social lesson too well. "Ya, man, alls I got to do is learn me some pretty ways to talk and they goin' to make me President of the United States" is the way one teenager summed up her awareness that the solution to all her problems does not lie in learning to "walk right and talk right."

Efforts to sell either children or adolescents on the need to change their language because of their future need for socially approved language have been largely unsuccessful. Youngsters who feel a pressing drive to move out of their subculture will be motivated to change their language, just as they will be motivated to change their dress and other habits. But, as Donald Lloyd has said, "Change of speech will follow, not precede, this decision to make his way out of the world he was born to." (Lloyd, 1962) The decision to move out of their subculture forces youngsters to disown their own heritage, to reject the folkways and values of their people. It involves an intense effort, and the possibility of failure is all the more frightening, because if they do fail, they will be left in limbo—no longer what they were nor yet what they aspire to be.

The only approach that may help any large number of divergent children is expansion: not the rejection of their mother tongue but expansion outward from the idiolect and subcultural dialect to the expanded language of the general culture, giving up only what is no longer needed and adding to meet new needs. Teachers can be of enormous help in this process.

Transplanted Regional Speech

Sometimes high-status speech becomes low status when people move from one region to another. It is obvious that a teacher in Atlanta, U.S.A. or York, England ought not to strive to impose the dialect of upper-class Boston or middle-class London on children whose speech falls within the norms of high-status speech in Atlanta or York. But these are times of great geographic mobility. What to do with the transplanted pupils when they arrive in the Boston or London (or Sydney) classroom is not so obvious. What complicates the problem is the ethnocentrism that most people feel for their language: if language is different, it must be bad. Too often, children are shunted into "speech-correction" classes because they have phonemes that differ from those of their new speech communities. Sometimes they are ignored or admonished when they have said a word or gleaned the meaning of a phrase but in their own dialect. Too often, differences in vocabulary, usage, and choice of words are lumped with all other language labeled "incorrect."

Teachers cannot plead ignorance in the case of language phenomena. Educators need to know what regional speech is, what immature speech is, what a lisp is, what an idiosyncrasy of one child's idiolect is. Surely, schools must not attempt to stamp out individuality in speech. A federal judge ruled in the widely publicized Ann Arbor Black English case that school insensitivity to language difference was a handicap to school achievement even when no prejudice exists. (Smitherman, 1981)

The following humorous editorial, from the Pine Bluff, Arkansas, *Commercial,* expresses some of the problems, the futility, and the unfairness involved in any attempt to obliterate regional speech:

Chunkin' in on Fixin' to

Another, Detroit educator, _____, reported that tape recorders have been used successfully in that city to change the dialects of children whose parents bring them to Detroit from other parts of the country, particularly the South.

Samples of these dialects, she said, include the use of such coined words as "onliest," "unlessen," "carry" for "take" "chunk" for "throw," and the frequent use of "fixing-to."

First off, _____ is a punk speller to be trying to teach English to other folk. It's "onlyest," not "onliest"; "onlessen," not "unlessen"; and, by all the verities, "fixin' to," not "fixing-to."

Secondly, those people in Detroit have more vanity and less sense than even we were prepared to believe if they imagine that the abandonment of the verb "chunk" is an improvement in anybody's vocabulary.

We'll take our Southern chunkers against _____'s sanitized throwers in any competition, from beanbag catch to rock fight, and will pound 'em into the ground.

Then there's "fixin' to," which _____ wisely refrained from suggesting a synonym for. She alleges that the word is used frequently but this is, we are sure, a canard based on inadequate listening. Nobody down here, and nobody from down here who has gone up there, is fixin' to do anything very frequently—but when fixin' to time has come, events of great moment will not be far behind.[2]

Dialect in Teaching and Learning

The significance of dialect differences in classroom language arts instruction has been largely ignored. The reasons for this oversight have been touched on earlier, the mistaken assumption that there is one correct standard English, the lumping together of all deviations from the mythical standard as incorrect, the language ethnocentrism of most people, the social and cultural positions of teachers and writers of texts, the myth of nonlanguage, and the cognitive deficit libel.

Dialect-influenced aspects of language learning are not confined to the groups we have called divergent. Because all children speak a dialect, further development in language will be rooted in this dialect. Consider, for example, the following list of words: *frog, log, dog, fog, cog, smog, bog, hog.* Some of those who read this list will pronounce these all as rhymes; the vowel in all the words will be /a/[3] as in *dot; dog* and *dot* will be the same except for the final consonants. For others, the words will all rhyme, but the vowel will be /ɔ/ as in *law.* But for many people the words will divide into two groups: *frog, log, dog, fog, bog,* and *cog, smog, bog;* or perhaps the two groups will be *frog, log, dog,* and *hog, fog, cog, smog, bog.* Perhaps *dog* is the only word in your idiolect that does not rhyme with the others. There is no one correct way to say any of these words.

If these dialect differences are ignored, unconscious errors are made by teachers and texts. In readiness lessons children may be asked to identify words that rhyme for the teacher but not for the learner. The generalization in a spelling lesson may not be a generalization at all for some learners. Because the lessons make an inaccurate assumption about the prior language experiences of the learners, both the teacher and the learners are puzzled by why learning does not occur.

As we have said, a major block to language development and school success is the rejection of the children's language during the teaching-learning process. But dialect differences also enter in many positive ways into the process of acquiring literacy skills. Several aspects of language differences will be explored here.

[2]Reprinted with permission of the editors.
[3]An attempt has been made in this book to avoid being overly technical. But when it comes to comparing the ways words are said in different dialects, no adequate way exists except to use the phonemic symbols devised by linguists to scientifically describe the sounds of English.

Divergent Dialects but Standard Spellings

An important point to remember is that, although there is great diversity in oral language, there is only one accepted spelling for all American English, different in minor respects from Canadian, British, and Australian spellings; for example, *labor/labour, civilize/civilise.* There is a well-known story about a little boy who asks his teacher (as she hears it), "How do you spell rat?" "R-a-t" she responds. "No, Ma'am," says the boy, "I don't mean rat-mouse, I mean right now." R-i-g-h-t is the spelling no matter how it's pronounced in any given dialect.

Most dialects of English have the same inventory of vowel and consonant phonemes, but few words have the same phonemes, particularly vowels, in all dialects. Moreover, each phoneme, since it is not a single sound but a range of sounds, varies its limits from dialect to dialect; some sounds at the extremes will be identified as one phoneme by speakers of one dialect but as another phoneme by speakers of a different dialect.

All phonics programs attempt to get learners to associate sounds and letters. Such programs in reading and spelling instruction either must be adjusted to the phonology of the dialect of the learners, or the learners must first be taught a new dialect if these phonics programs are to be usable for all learners. Teachers sometimes appear to be unaware of contradictions between their own speech patterns and the phonics program: "I can't git those kids to hear the short *e,*" one teacher complained.

A study by Richard Rystrom showed that when rural black Georgian first-graders were taught the sounds of "standard white speech" (based on Labov's New York studies) before reading instruction, they actually did somewhat more poorly than a control group of similar learners with no dialect training. The instruction appeared to interfere with learning. (Rystrom, 1970)

If children say *duh* /də/ instead of *the* /ðə/ and *nuffin* /nəfin/ instead of *nothing* / nəθiŋ /, it may confuse them more than it may help if they learn that the digraph *th* represents the initial consonant in *the* and the medial consonant in *nothing.* The generalization is not appropriate to their speech.

Even if they should learn to say /nəθiŋ/ when they see the printed word *nothing,* it is possible that they do not realize that this is their word /n fin/ and that represents the same concept. Do children know that *four* /for/, which is the name of the 4 they must say in school, is the same as /foh/, which they know to be the number of wheels on a car? Even adults often have the experience of meeting what at first seems to be a new word or a phrase in speech or print and of not recognizing until later that it is one that they know but in another form. For example, Dickens *victuals* are the same as Appalachian "vittles" /vit lz/.

Dialect and Spelling Programs

Misspellings may vary considerably from dialect to dialect; studies of invented spelling are shedding some light on the variations. (Invented spellings are those that young writers invent as they use new words that they don't know how to spell conventionally.) Logically, for example, dialects that soften or only slightly pro-nounce some final consonants will not relate in the same way to standard spellings as dialects with more distinct terminal consonants. So a pupil may spell *desk* d-e-s or *test* t-e-s.

Homophones, words which sound alike, will vary from dialect to dialect. The geographical linguists' favorites *(merry, Mary, marry)* are good examples. Whether two or all sound alike to you or all are different depends on your dialect. *Been* may be a homophone for *bin* or *bean* or *ben* in your dialect. Most spelling programs ignore these differences. Teachers need to be tuned in to children's dialects. A teacher who asked his children to use the word *so* in a sentence was surprised with the response he got. "I got a sore (/sow/) on my leg," said one young pupil. Another teacher, a native Californian, was surprised by her Boston pupils' use of *pack.* "My father found a place to /pak/ *(park)* the car." Still another teacher (a New Yorker by origin) was startled by the definitions her midwestern pupils gave of *borough* (a new word in their fifth-grade social studies text). "I think it's a hole in the ground rabbits dig," said one. "No, it's some kind of donkey," said another.

Phonics programs, if they are effective, may only heighten the spelling problems of some divergent speakers and of speakers of some regional dialects. Some will not only say /aydiðr/ but also spell it *idear.* Others will say /p nkin/ for *pumpkin* and spell it *punkin* (in fact, some American dictionaries list that as an alternate spelling). Every dialect contains many words that are spelled in unpredictable ways. Strong phonics programs produce phonic misspellings.

A major problem with ITA (Initial Teaching Alphabet) and other approaches to achieving one-to-one correspondence between letters and phonemes in teaching reading is that they must either be based on one dialect or they must abandon the principle that there is only one spelling, no matter how diversely a word may be pronounced in different dialects. The word *levers* is spelled, using ITA orthography: lïv3rz. (ITA, 1963) If *lever* rhymes with *beaver* in children's speech, this spelling is fine, but if they say *lever* to rhyme with *never,* they will have a mismatch.

The peculiar belief persists among the public and among many teachers that how a word is spelled determines how it should be pronounced. If this were true it would mean there were no dialect differences in English. It would also mean that written language was invented before oral language, an obvious fallacy.

Inflectional Change

Inflectional changes in words involve the use of suffixes or internal variations in words to achieve changes in case or tense. Although inflectional differences among American English dialects are minor compared with phonemic differences, they are still important. When some children say "he see me" instead of "he sees me," it is not because they have dropped the word ending; it is because in their dialect there is no *s* form of present-tense verbs after third-person singular subjects.

In terms of spelling, the *s* in this use becomes silent. Telling children that it does not sound right to leave off the *s* or that they are wrong if they do not say /siyz/ because the written word has an *s* on the end contradicts their past experience with language. Some children may learn to give the response that school demands, but in so doing the children develop a gulf between their oral language and school language tasks. In any event, problems in reading, spelling, composition, and grammar will result; a continuous effort will be required of divergent speakers to do what to them is unnatural. The problem is not a reading error but a consistent language divergence. Any change sought by the teacher must be treated not as a shift from wrong to right in reading but a shift to a socially preferred dialect.

Morphemic Differences

Most Americans add /iz/ for the plurals of words ending in /s/ *(classes),* in /z/ *(mazes),* and in /š/ *(washes);* but after /sp/, /st/, and /sk/ (consonant blends) they add /s/ *(wasps, posts,* and *tasks).* However, in dialects where final consonant clusters are reduced (was', pos', tas') the form of the plural *s* morpheme will change. When *post* or *desk* become /pos/ or /des/, then the plurals become /pos i z/ and /des i z/ rather than /posts/ and /desks/.

Syntactical Differences

When a child who is a divergent speaker responds during roll call with, "I here, teacher," she is not being "careless" in her speech any more than she is a few minutes later when she volunteers the information that James is absent because "He sick." In her dialect the present tense of the verb *to be* (or the *copula,* as some linguists prefer) is omitted. There is a syntactical difference in her dialect. (A difference in sentence structure.) Use of verb forms and verb markers is one well-known area of dialect divergence: "We was going"; "They done it"; "We come" (rather than "came" or "had come"); and "he clumb" are examples. Hawaiian Pidgin uses only verb markers with no inflections: "I go"; "I stay go"; "I wen' go"; "I been go"; "I goin' go."

Fortunately, such syntactic differences among English dialects are relatively minor. The basic structure of the language, the sentence patterns, and the use of function words *(the, was, in,* and so on) as structural signals are fairly uniform to all dialects.

Children will tend to carry these aspects over to their reading and writing. As children read orally, they will tend to read their own dialect from the printed page. They may "correct" the grammar of what they read to make it fit the norms of the grammar of their own dialect. Such "corrections" are good indications that children are using their knowledge of language to obtain meaning from the printed page. Here is an example of this phenomenon.

A group of second-graders were reading in round-robin fashion. It was Jim's turn. "There was a lot of goats," he read. "There was black goats and white goats."
His teacher smiled encouragingly. "Would you repeat that, please, Jim," she said.
Somewhat puzzled, Jim reread: "There was a lot of goats. There was black goats and white goats."
Still smiling, his teacher stepped to the board. In excellent manuscript she wrote two words. "Do you see a difference in these words?" she said.
"Yes, they have different endings," said Jim.
"Can you read these words?" the teacher asked.
"*Was, were,*" Jim read.
"Good," said his teacher.

"This is *was,* and this is *were.* Now read again what you just read from the book."
"There was a lot of . . ." Jim began.
"No, no!" his teacher said with some annoyance. "It's *were.* 'There were a lot of goats.'
Now, please reread."
"There were a lot of goats. There was black goats and . . . (Goodman,1964)

The teacher, in this example, has assumed that Jim is confusing *was* and *were* on a perceptual level, but, in reality, what he is doing is translating; he is reading his dialect from the printed page. He is using his language system.

Divergent speakers may master some specific tasks in English lessons on correct forms, but they are unlikely to carry the lessons over into their written and oral expressions. They may be able to underline the correct choice: "He (*did/done)* it." But they will still say and write "He done it," or having become uncertain, they may avoid the expression altogether.

Intonational Difference
Dialects differ also in their intonation, the rhythm of stress, pitch, and pause or juncture which characterizes the flow of language. Perhaps the greatest barrier to communication between speakers of different dialects is this difference in intonation. Teachers frequently complain, when they first begin to work with children who speak a different dialect, that they cannot understand the children at all. This is not just a result of the variation in the phonemes of the speakers' language but also a result of the teachers' being out of tune with the intonational pattern of the divergent dialect. After a week or two the children appear to be speaking more clearly. In reality, the teachers have become accustomed to their intonational patterns. Paradoxically, people are often struck with what to them is a poetic quality in dialects that they have not heard before. This sense of a poetic quality stems from the listeners' attention to the intonation of the strange dialect; they have lost their awareness, on a conscious level, of the rhythmic qualities of their own and other very familiar dialects.

Children for whom English is a second language tend to use the intonational patterns of their first language in speaking English. They are thus less likely to be understood by people unfamiliar with their speech. They may also find it difficult to appreciate the subtleties of meaning that depend on slight but significant differences in intonation. For teachers, it is important to remember that no feature of language has any intrinsic meaning; any device in language, intonational or otherwise, has only the significance assigned to it by the users of a particular language or language dialect. Just as identical-sounding words may mean very different unrelated things in different languages, so also may words that vary only in pitch or in variations in relative stress. In comprehending oral language, listeners get cues to the pattern from the speakers' stress, pitch, and pause patterns. In oral reading, intonation follows from the decisions readers make about the syntactic patterns they are dealing with. If pupils read without acceptable intonation it may mean that they are not getting the syntax or meaning of what they are reading. A nonnative speaker will frequently read each word as if it were a word on a list. That's a more likely sign of poor comprehension than shifts toward the intonation of their native language. It indicates that they are naming words rather than processing language.

Vocabulary Divergence

Divergent speakers may experience two types of vocabulary divergence. First is the type that stems from difference in word preference and word meanings. Examples of this were mentioned in the editorial cited earlier. Speakers may prefer to use *chunk* instead of *throw* to convey similar meanings. In some dialects, if you *carry* something, you physically transport it on your self, but, in other dialects, you can *carry* a friend to work with you in your car but you *tote* your books. In some uses, both dialects would agree. Some uses are acceptable in one dialect but not in another. The second type of divergence stems from the relatively limited vocabulary all speakers bring to unfamiliar topics or situations. Basically, this means that the divergent speakers will have more limited vocabulary stocks from which to draw in the situations that schools stress that are foreign to them. They will tend to use their basic stock more widely in their expression, using a single word or phrase in place of several, with subtle differences in connotation. They will use metaphors and similes as well: "the piece that looks like a lady's shoe" rather than "the trapezoidal piece."

It would be well to remember that it is harder for children to learn to spell, read, or write an unfamiliar word than one already part of their vocabulary. An unfamiliar use of a familiar word or phrase may cause learners problems, because in their dialect that usage may be incorrect. Mere manipulation of lists of words is not a solution to these vocabulary problems. *Relevance* becomes a key word here. Relevant instruction and relevant materials capitalize on the language and experience of each learner. Vocabulary differences between cultural groups reflect differences in cultural experiences. One is not a deficient example of the other.

Language and Culture-Bound Tests

Young divergent speakers are at a distinct disadvantage when they are judged on the basis of readiness tests, intelligence tests, and aptitude tests that are based on the assumption that all children have common experience and language. Even so-called nonverbal tests involve pictures of things outside the common experience of many children. Children who have seen and experienced but have not learned are not at all the same as children who have not seen or experienced. However, the tests show them as both the same.

The logic or relationships and analogies built into many test items may not hold in the context of the divergent subculture. Do churches have steeples? The store-front churches that some urban children attend do not. Even if an attempt is made to keep the test itself culture-free, the instructions usually are provided in a dialect other than the learners', and the results are evaluated on the norms of the dominant culture. Teachers can do something about the disadvantage of divergent speakers on standardized tests by remembering that these tests are inappropriate and by tempering the use of the results of the tests in predicting and evaluating learning.

The significance of dialect differences in general has been neglected in teaching language and literacy skills. Children who are divergent speakers are often doubly handicapped. Not only is their language rejected and their form of expression misunderstood and thwarted, but also they tend to be children who are not highly motivated to meet school demands and achieve. They will give up easily and reject education if the school rejects their language.

If teachers and schools are to achieve success with divergent speakers, they must first accept and understand the mother tongue of the learners. Teachers must be very careful to separate immature speech from dialect-based speech. They must avoid complicating the difficulty that divergent speakers have in acquiring literacy by making unrealistic and inappropriate language demands. (Goodman, 1973)

Divergent speakers can build on the base of their own language. They can be encouraged to experiment with language and to meet the increasing need for societal communication by expanding their language. The goal is to move outward from the mother tongue, not to replace it or stamp it out. Dialect differences are inherent in language, and teachers must come to accept those differences and to work with them. Divergence of dialect or a different home language can be a source of personal and linguistic enrichment.

References

Francella Butler, "The Poetry of Rope-Skipping," *New York Times Magazine,* December 16, 1973.

Siegfried Englemann, *DISTAR Reading I,* Teacher's Guide (Chicago: Science Research Associates, 1969).

Robert Frost, from "The Gift Outright," from *The Poetry of Robert Frost,* Edited by Edward Connery Lathem (New York: Holt, Rinehart and Winston, 1970). Copyright 1941 by Robert Frost. Copyright 1969 by Holt, Rinehart and Winston, Inc. Copyright 1970 by Leslie Frost Ballantine. Reprinted by permission of Holt, Rinehart and Winston, Publishers, and Jonathan Cape Limited.

H. A. Gleason, *An Introduction to Descriptive Linguistics* (New York: Holt, Rinehart and Winston, 1961).

Kenneth S. Goodman, "The Linguistics of Reading," *Elementary School Journal,* vol. 64 (April 1964), p 7.

————, "Dialect Barriers to Reading Comprehension Revisited," *The Reading Teacher,* vol. 42:8 (October 1973), pp. 852–860.

Yetta M. Goodman, "The Culture of the Culturally Deprived," *Elementary School Journal,* vol. 71 (April 1971), pp. 376–383.

Arthur Jensen, "How Much Can We Boost IQ and Scholastic Achievement?" *Harvard Educational Review,* vol. 39, no. 1 (1969).

William Labov, Address to the National Council of Teachers of English, Cleveland, November 1964.

————, "The Logic of Non-Standard English," in J. DeStefano, *Language, Society and Education* (Worthington, OH: Jones, 1973).

Donald J. Lloyd, "Sub-Cultural Patterns Which Affect Language and Reading Development," copyright by the author, 1962.

Raven McDavid, "Dialectology and the Teaching of Reading," *The Reading Teacher,* vol. 18, no. 3 (December 1964), p. 208.

I. Opie and P. Opie, *The Lore and Language of School Children* (London: Oxford University Press, 1959).

Richard Rystrom, "Dialect Training and Reading: A Further Look," *Reading Research Quarterly* (Summer 1970), pp. 581–599.

Roger Shuy, *Discovering American Dialects* (Champaign, IL: National Council of Teachers of English, 1967).

Geneva Smitherman, *Black English and the Education of Black Children/Youth* (Detroit: Center for Black Studies, Wayne State University, 1981).

The Story of ITA (New York: ITA Publications, 1963).

Frederick Williams and Jack L. Whitehead, "Language in the Classroom," *English Record,* vol. 21, no. 4 (April 1971).

5

Coming to Know

And this our life, exempt from
  public haunt,
Finds tongues in trees, books in the
  running brooks,
Sermons in stones, and good in
  everything.

(Shakespeare,) As You Like It

Knowledge and Knowing

Children could not achieve by themselves the state of knowing that Shakespeare describes, nor could they reach it with their fellow children only. They would see the trees, the brooks, and the stones, but not being able to engage in discourse about them, they would not come to "know" them in relation to each other and to other events in the "Forest of Order." Trees can speak only when the human beings observing the trees have the power of language at their command to make trees a part of their cognitive maps, of the word-maps that place environmental happenings in meaningful relationships with each other.

Knowing is more than thinking, although thinking is one of the processes by which people come to know. Knowing is a very personal process, involving imagination above all else. Some of our thinking procedures can be isolated and scientifically explained, but perhaps only the poet has the kind of vision that can capture a full concept of knowing. Here Walt Whitman says it well:

> There was a child went forth every day
> And the first object he look'd upon
> That object he became,
> And that object became part of him for the
> day or a certain part of the day,
> Or for many years or stretching cycles of years.
> *Walt Whitman,*
> *"A Child Went Forth"*

Knowing is becoming. As events in the world become part of children's worlds and as they gain their own view of people and things about them, they begin to become persons.

> Once Paumanok,
> When the lilac-scent was in the air and fifth-month grass was growing,
> Up this seashore in some briers,
> Two feather'd guests from Alabama, two together,
> And their nest, and four light-green eggs spotted with brown,
> And every day the he-bird to and fro near at hand,
> And every day the she-bird crouch'd on her nest,
> silent, with bright eyes,
> And every day I, a curious boy, never too close, never disturbing them,
> Cautiously peering, absorbing, translating.
> *Walt Whitman,*
> *"Out of the Cradle Endlessly Rocking"*

Whitman was not the only poet to discover and extol the freshness and intimacy of childhood learning—coming to know—but certainly he showed a profound sensitivity to it in the line "Cautiously peering, absorbing, translating." Poets never seem to outgrow this precious quality of childlike experiencing, of meeting the world head on and coming to terms with it. Somewhere along the educational road to adulthood the wondrous quality of experiencing and coming to know in language can be lost, and personality can stagnate. Teachers can work to keep the intellectual growth going.

Language and Coming to Know

A key educational problem is the place of language in intellectual learning—what we call *coming to know* and what Piaget calls *developmental epistemology*. Language may be seen as a necessary part of the personal process of experiencing and knowing. In this view, the thing is not known until it is discussed and named, and its interrelation with other things is not understood until language embodies the idea. If this function of language is accepted, intellectual education is neither the memorization of words and facts nor the possession of significant experiences but rather the constant interplay of interrelated experiences and language. Since language is pivotal in a person's learning through experience, it is at the very core of the teaching-learning process.

To John Dewey and Arthur Bentley, knowing is a transactional process between the individual and the environment, with language at the center. Coming to know—experience interpreted and intellectualized in language—would then be viewed as the basic goal of education. (Dewey and Bentley, 1949)

Dewey believed that experience would not stand alone as learning but instead must be interpreted through a process of reflective thinking to be made consequential. Knowing is a transaction between the individual and the environment in which both are transformed. There is no such thing as absolute knowledge, only a process of knowing involving actions and word-meanings together. The search of young children for answers to their questions about every new item they see and handle is a natural example of the transaction between the individual and the environment that Dewey describes. This process is always happening, and it never becomes final or fixed. The teacher's role is to keep the way open and the means available for the richest and fullest possible transactions.

One of the most powerful statements of the difference between knowledge and knowing is the one-act play *The Lesson* by Ionesco. (1958) Herr Professor, his student, and his maid are the characters. The play opens innocently enough with the arrival of a new, young female student, but soon the maid interjects a note of foreboding by admonishing the professor not to let "it" happen again. However, the professor, by impressing his knowledge (verbiage) upon the pupil through the means of monotonous recitation, finally overwhelms the pupil and symbolically (although on stage literally) kills her. The Herr Professor could have achieved the same end had he used the more subtle, but equally deadening, modern methods of tightly programmed mastery learning materials or carefully conditioned group processes. The aim would still have been the subjection of the pupil to the disembodied verbalization of the culture. The only possible rejoinder to *The Lesson* is to give the learner ownership over both language and experience and to view language as the matrix in personal knowing. Then the process of education becomes a process of personal discovery under the guidance of teachers who are aware of the validity of this process in their own learning.

Personality Development and Knowing

An individual's cognitive posture in the world—his or her very personal view of the environment—is a manifestation of personality-guiding actions. Psychologists of personality speak of an individual's conceptual schemes or patterns:

> The stored organized effects of past experience . . . we have labeled concepts.
> . . . Concepts in their matrix of inter-relatedness serve the critical cognitive func-
> tion of providing a system of ordering by means of which the environment is
> broken down and organized, is differentiated and integrated into its many psy-
> chologically relevant facets. In this capacity, they provide the medium through
> which the individual establishes and maintains ties with the world. . . . It is on
> this basis, hence, that one's self identity and existence are articulated and main-
> tained. Threat to such ties or severance of them leads to a psychological
> mobilization at maintaining or restoring them, efforts which if unsuccessful may
> result in a major reorientation and organization of ties to the world, or more
> drastically, even to breakdown or destruction of the self. (O. J. Harvey et al.,
> 1961)

Conceptual schemes (Harvey's concepts), using language in great part for constructing webs of meaning, become the basis for self-identity and focus in a world otherwise confused by myriads of disconnected impressions. If the system is thrown out of kilter by too many misconceptions, then the personality can become distorted as self-identity weakens through a state of confusion.

The fact that language is the medium of the psychoanalyst's interview or therapy sessions suggests that it is only by language that the human being can have these conceptual schemes at all. Even the ephemeral emotions are expressed mainly through various language means: gesturing, crying, laughing, and speaking all at the same time. Conceptual schemes can be heard at work when we listen to our internal arguing with ourselves before we make an active choice or when we second-guess ourselves. We reiterate our ideas with the pleasure of being right, or we defend what we did even when we suspect we were wrong, or we try to figure out how we might better approach a similar situation another time. Notice that the words for all these kinds of activities are words describing language activities: "arguing," "second-guessing," and "figuring out."

People are constantly coming to terms with the world by forming their conceptions of it. They are making cognitive adjustments to the world—in a real sense, cognitive conquests of the world. When people are deprived of the stimula-tion of novelty or even of the passing parade, they stop transforming experience into symbol, stop knowing, stop playing with their world, and go mad. Evidently, the process of ideation, of forming ideas, cannot sustain itself for long without the stimulation that comes from playful curiosity about things in the environment. We strive to know more, but when deprived of stimuli, we panic and request relief from monotony.

Motivation for Coming to Know

Robert White's ideas of "competence" and "effectance" help to explain motivation for knowing. Individuals have a need to explore their environment, to gain competence to cope with it, and to find a "feeling of efficiency" (effectance) in it. (White, 1959) This need to explore is evident even in the behavior of the chimpanzee when it continues to search for playful activity even though all its drives are satisfied. The need to explore keeps crawling babies active in the discovery of their world and sustains wandering ornithologists in the discovery of theirs. Both the scientist and the baby gain competence in coping with their environments as they discover meanings in them. Parents or educators can partially thwart this natural curiosity or put it to sleep through denial of the opportunity to explore.

Positive cognitive activity is as essential to well-being as are physical activity and the exercise of the emotions. Education from the earliest time, guided by parents and teachers, is a strong force in developing children's patterns of knowing that are as representative of reality as possible. The use of language with children in the interpretation of experience all through the preschool and school years is critical for sound personality development as well as consistent intellectual development.

Each individual's conceptual system develops uniquely, depending on his or her imagination, thinking power, and language skill for processing data from the environment. When the environment is rich in experiential possibilities, when the culture is nourishing, and when the child's intellectual powers are facilitated, the conceptual system can eventually incorporate the logic of a stellar system or the ethics of a philosophical system. Teachers can maximize the educational development of children through the two things teachers control: environmental enrichment and language-cultural expansion.

Language in Personal Knowing

Two twentieth-century philosophers, Ernst Cassirer and Susanne Langer, have been particularly interested in the place of language in personal knowing. Their formulations about language and other presentational forms in the symbolic transformation of experience are useful for illuminating the educational situation. Their views embrace the whole of knowing through the arts, as well as the sciences, and show concern for values both aesthetic and moral. Language in all its forms becomes a focal concern to them. Langer built upon Cassirer's ideas and extended them:

> The transformation of experience into concepts, not the elaboration of signals and symptoms, is the motive of language.

> For language is much more than a set of symbols. . . . Its forms do not stand

alone, like so many monoliths each marking its one isolated grave; but instead, they tend to integrate, to make complex patterns, and thus to point out equally complex relationships in the world, the realm of their meanings. . . . (Langer, 1956, pp. 105, 109)

The transformation of experience into concepts symbolically represented is a personal, humanizing process of education. In our daily living we respond to most happenings in a habitual way because we come to know them early in life and have developed routine reactions to them. Being served eggs for breakfast requires no cognitive or affective reorientation. However, every so often a slightly novel experience comes our way. We must come to terms with it by comparing and contrasting it with the familiar and, finally, by formulating it into a revised and extended version of what we already know. We may inquire of others, even do some reading, but all the time we are transforming the experience into our own symbols. The process may be slight and only momentary when, for example, we are served an omelet for the first time instead of scrambled eggs. But were we to travel to Japan and experience a traditional Japanese breakfast built around fish, a great deal of symbolic processing of fact and feeling would occur before we fully understood and appreciated this experience and could make it our own.

Teachers have a responsibility for fostering personal knowing in their students by developing strategies for evoking personal response to experiences and making symbolic representations of them. Many teachers sense this when they plan discussions before and after field trips or other experiences. Further, the same place may be visited many times, each time to develop different concepts or to clarify or to extend a concept already begun. In the same sense, rereading a book, seeing a play again, or reenacting an event may extend learning.

Educational Phases in Coming to Know

The following is a free elaboration of Langer's formulations for the purpose of bringing a focus on "knowing" into educational planning.

Learning conceived as coming to know through the symbolic transformation and representation of experience, involves three phases of mental activity:

1. Perceiving new data in the environment
2. Ideating upon the perceptions (ideation includes conceptualizing and generalizing)
3. Presenting ideations to oneself and others

Individuals perceive new objects, events, or ideas in their own way and try to incorporate what is perceived into conceptual schemas through the process of ideation. Then they present them on personal terms to themselves and to others by symbolic representation in media appropriate to each individual's life-style and to the types of ideas. The media of symbolic representation are language, art, music, dance, film, dramatics, or any combination of them. The cycle begins again as those presentations meet new events and ideas that have to be newly perceived and conceptualized.

These symbolizing processes of perceiving, ideating, and presenting one's conceptions go on continually in the waking hours of adults and children. Even during sleep, dream sequences often show that individuals work over their experiences of the previous day. A 2-year-old's persistent questions reveal the spontaneous activity of the transformation process, as do the probings of college students. Parents and teachers either tune into an individual's symbolizing process, or they are tuned out of it by the individual who proceeds on his or her own without the teacher's guidance.

The following sections deal with the phases of the symbolic transformation of experience as they can relate to classroom activity. These theoretical formulations can give new focus and significance to some conventional language-centered classroom activities and can suggest new instructional strategies that teachers can explore. Like all formulations of this kind, they do not account for the full range of cognitive-affective learning. The categories are not perfectly distinct, nor do the process phases that they represent always happen in sequence. Perceiving, ideating, and presenting overlap and interplay almost simultaneously as individuals attempt to come to terms with a new object or event brought into their life-space. Even so, a delineation of the symbolic transformation of experience into phases can be useful to teachers in helping them to see what is happening in situations with potential for symbolic learning and to construct appropriate teaching strategies for fostering such learning.

Perceiving Phase

Meeting a New Object, Happening, or Idea

The perceiving phase can be easily observed when children are meeting new objects and situations.

Aaron, who has just turned 3, is in an airport with his mother. "There's our plane," he says, pointing to the one out the window. "No," says his mother, "that's not our plane. Ours is the one over there. See, it has a big red A and a big blue A with a bird in between." Several days later, Aaron, now on his way home, is grumbling about something. "What's the matter?" asks his mother. Aaron points to the bag of peanuts the flight attendant has given him. "That's not sposta be there!" he says, pointing to the American Airlines logo on the bag. "That's sposta be on the plane. See, it has a red A and a blue A and a bird."

Perceiving is that first contact through the eyes, ears, nose, or skin with an object or an event that people are drawn to or select from the vast complex that surrounds them at any one time and place. These individual contacts are sometimes referred to as *environmental stimuli*. In a sense children stimulate the piece of the environment that attracts them at a certain moment; it comes into focus for them while someone standing by may not even see it. Something from their past experience reaches out and pulls in the object or the event for closer view and consideration.

Students looking out a school window at rain coming down during a storm may perceive many different happenings, depending on their previous experience with storms, their attitudes toward thunder, or what they were planning to do in the recess about to begin. Others in the class may not have noticed the rain at all because they were absorbed in some activity. At times, something in the environment attracts attention because of its bright color, its unusual sound, or its strange feel, and it is perceived in terms of past encounters with similar events. Some persons perceived the first orbital flight of an astronaut as an awesome accomplishment; others, as a foolish exploit; and still others, as a blasphemous intrusion into God's heaven. Others had no sense of its significance at all.

Misperceiving

It is not unusual for individuals to misperceive. They see what they expect to see because of their previous experiences. People living in western urban societies expect that a room they enter will be four-square or oblong, with parallel walls. People with such a concept cannot know rooms without parallel enclosures. For example, they are unable to locate a corner of a model of a room prepared with walls of a trapezoidal shape. They cannot act sensibly and effectively in a distorted space because they perceive it to be conventional, even after they are shown the distortions. Only with repeated successful experience of touching corners with a pointer do they overcome their frustration and perceive correctly the distorted room and others like it.

Children show that they have misperceived when they perceive every family and household as like their own. This kind of misperceiving was evident when young children described the family of the President in terms of their own family life by insisting that the First Lady washed the dishes, cleaned the house, and put her hair up in curlers. Older children perceived the President as a "father-boss" of all the people. One of the widely quoted experiments in perception makes use of a slanted window-frame shape rotating on a pivot. Because observers expect the distorted frame to behave like a regular window shape, they see magic when objects placed on the pivoting frame seem to float in the air. (Cantril, 1950; Kelley, 1947; Kilpatrick, 1961) Such misconception is common in childhood learning. Without historical illustrations a 10-year-old is likely to perceive Roman baths as modern public swimming pools.

Misperceiving may also arise because of differences in cultural setting. American children may interpret "going to the store for fruit" as the fruit section of a supermarket; English children may visualize a green-grocer; rural children may have in mind a farmer's market.

Conventional wisdom says that we can only know what we see, but modern psychology, particularly that of Piaget, says that we only see what we know. All sensory input is organized according to schemas we have formed to organize our transactions with the physical world. When we encounter aspects of this world that cannot be assimilated to our existing schemas, we often reject them, not seeing them at all, or transform them into something we can assimilate. Otherwise, an accommodation occurs in which the schemas themselves must be reconstituted, that is, we must literally change the way we view the world. A good curriculum is constantly confronting learners with experiences that they must assimilate or accommodate. The teacher's role is to monitor the ways in which pupils perceive and to cope with what they encounter, to push the pupils to examine and to consider their perceptions, and to assist in what may be difficult accommodations. Knowing where pupils are coming from, their cultures, values, and life experiences, can help teachers to anticipate their perceptions and to build perceptual bridges for them.

Language-Teaching Strategies during the Perceiving Phase

In a classroom situation, the perceiving moment is a strategic time when teachers can help children to extend their perceptions and to assist them in validating or corroborating their perceptions with those of others, including their teachers. Although the perceiving act probably happens in both linguistic and nonlingual images—visual, auditory, or sensory structures—language cues can help limit the situation to be perceived or can interrupt the perceiving process and cause another "look." After setting the environment to be perceived by the children through a field trip, a demonstration, prepared materials, or a film, the teacher limits the focus by bringing one aspect of the environment to their attention or by asking questions that will cause them to look at a particular aspect. On the other hand, the teacher may want to glean all the different perceptions that the class has about an object or a happening; then the teacher will use an open-ended question, for example: "What do you see there?" or "How do you feel about this situation?" The teacher's tactic of the day depends on whether the purposes require a widening or a narrowing of perceptions. For developing poetic expression a diversity of perceptions in the classroom is admirable; for observing the interaction of two chemicals, a teacher will try to narrow the perceptual field so that all the students' perceptions deal with the same reality. Even then the teacher will monitor the varying perceptions of the pupils and the different schemas they reveal. If children do not perceive what the teacher expects them to perceive, their perceptions may be faulty, they may overlook the factor that the teacher is trying to bring out, or they may be bringing personal schemas to bear on the experience. Unless teachers permit free talk at this moment, they may not find this out until hours or days later when an idea will have been stillborn or a teachable moment missed.

A globe in a kindergarten room may not be perceived for what it is but rather as a spinning ball. This may be the first phase of a growing concept that will eventually permit children to perceive the globe as a model of the earth's surface, but in the early stage the perception desired by the teacher is not made. Pictures of the moon taken by cameras aboard a spacecraft look like aerial views of volcanoes, but to perceive the craters as a lot of volcanoes may be a jump in the wrong direction. Sometimes feelings may dominate or distort perceptions. Children who fear snakes may be incapable of perceiving the interesting features of the harmless garter snake that the teacher is holding.

Confrontation of children with significant objects and happenings to be perceived is the first teaching strategy on the way to children's knowing their world. If teachers are aware of the fact that perceiving may be ruled by past experience and concepts by a cultural set or a conforming view, by emotional disposition toward or against an object, or by the physical placement of what is being seen, they can then plan confrontation and language strategies for both heightening and focusing perception. They can use classroom tactics that will help eliminate confusions in the first step to knowing. They can anticipate mis-perceptions and use relevant examples that will avoid them.

As students encounter the world, they can be helped through conversation and discussion to perceive it richly and accurately.

The importance of setting up a stimulating environment of objects, materials, and authentic experiences cannot be overstressed. Not all of the environment is stimulating—only that which children perceive and with which they have stimulat-ing experiences. In the classroom there is a need for structuring situations in such a way that they will present a "cognitive dissonance" that the child must resolve. The slightly novel situation can be introduced purposefully to create challenge and curiosity. (Festinger, 1957)

In the everyday world children are naturally confronted with novelty to explore; in the classroom teachers can provide an enriched and more focused version of this natural novelty. An interesting, novelty-producing tactic reported by a seventh-grade teacher provoked a half-hour of constructive discussion. In the context of studying France the teacher showed without comment a picture of a cow in the kitchen of a peasant farmhouse. The children, surprised by the seeming incongruity of this situation, started immediately to try to explain it, first in terms of their own experiences and then in terms of alternatives.

Goodlad, in his study of American classrooms, found them dominated by skill exercises with little attempt to promote "intellectual development." Education is seriously retarded in such classrooms in a very real sense. Pupils would fare far better in their intellectual and language growth were they left to wander, provided there were adults and other children about to interact and think with them regarding their experiential adventures. School ought to be a place where children get many invitations to experience, to perceive, and to think and talk about their perceptions. (Goodlad, 1984)

Ideating Phase, Including Conceptualizing and Generalizing

The moment that individuals begin to talk and to think about what they have perceived, the phase of ideating has begun. We must come to terms with what has been perceived. Language, affect (feelings), and cognitive energy come into play as the new "percept" is brought into relation with previous ideational and affectual constructions built through past experience. Intellect and affect are stimulated by novelty and by the need to know just for the sake of knowing.

Coming to Terms with an Object, Happening, or Idea

Langer suggests that this human need to transfer perceptions of experience into one's own symbols is a

> . . . primary activity of man, like eating, looking or moving about. . . . It is the fundamental process of his mind and goes on all the time. Sometimes we are aware of it, sometimes we merely find its results, and realize that certain experiences have passed through our brains and have been digested there. (Langer, 1956, p. 32)

Since ideation is an internal activity, it has been difficult for scientists to find out what actually happens. Only recently have neurologists and biologists found means for beginning to explore the chemical and electrical activity of the brain in response to the perceiving signals sent to it from the senses. In the absence of such data, investigators and, in turn, educators can consider only the expressions and actions of individuals, especially their language expressions when they are ideating. As people are asked questions that call upon their ideas following an experience or are asked to tell what they know about a certain subject, their verbal formulations and gestures probably reveal in part the mental process. There are many ways to picture this activity. The tabula rasa concept in which one impression is thought to be implanted on another is an old way to view ideation. A more fruitful way for educational purposes is to look at how people, including scholars, formulate their ideas in language and assume that some internal process allows the brain to make connections, store the mentally digested matter, and release it at appropriate times through the complex human neurological system. Much of Piaget's research has involved probing, verbally, for the ideating of the learners.

Hermine Sinclair describes this method in commenting on its use in a study of children's development of written language (Sinclair, 1982):

> The Piagetian method of exploring children's thinking through dialogue allows the experimenter to create testable hypotheses about the reasoning behind the child's words and gestures and turns out to be—in this field as in many others—a most fruitful approach. It permits basic ideas held by many children to be distinguished from the passing reactions of a child who is impelled to say or do something, never mind what, just to respond to a question. This method allows researchers . . . to see how a concept that may have taken humanity a great deal of time to establish is recreated by the child.

Forming Personal Conceptions

Transforming experience into symbolic representation can best be called *conceptualizing,* for more than immediate impressions are involved as ideation begins. Concepts must form before generalizing can emerge. "But just as quickly as the concept is symbolized to us, our imagination dresses it up in a private, personal conception that we can distinguish from the communicable public concept only by a process of abstraction." (Langer, p. 58).

Personal conceptions are one person's thematic clusters of related facts, impressions, images, ideas, feelings, and value judgments around an order of phenomena. They are not simply intellectualized and verbalized restatements of public or scientific concepts. If other children or adults are present or an appropriate book is at hand, for example, our conceptions can be influenced by what others say or write about that event or a similar one, but we do the interpreting. A young girl's conception of the moon may be more like an active space station than the barren landscape it is because of her imaginings from television programs. Prior to the lunar landings a 6-year-old boy told his father when they were observing a brilliant full moon together: "I can see the volcanoes where the spaceships land. Maybe I'll go there someday."

A public concept is what is left of a general nature when all specific and personal aspects are taken away. "House," described as a building in which people live, is a public designation for all the individual conceptions that may include a bungalow, a mansion, or a grass-roofed hut. Sometimes a public concept is not scientifically accurate but expresses conventional wisdom or even mythology. "Water divining" and "UFOs" (unidentified flying objects) are as much examples of public concepts as are "rainfall" and "jet flight."

A scientific concept is the aggregate of personal studied conceptions of scientists and scholars, objectivized by processes of verification and abstraction, resulting in agreements among the scholars. Examples in the physical sciences would be "atom" and "gravity"; in the biological sciences, "genes" and "homeostasis"; in the social sciences, "caste" and "enculturation"; and in the humanities, "style" and "justice." Even scientific concepts, however, may be refined or displaced by subsequent knowledge, facts, or reconceptualizations.

Attribute-Classifying in the Conceptualizing Process

A personal concept can be further defined as the cluster of ideas of a thing or phenomenon that will always include key attributes that distinguish it from another concept. These attributes will be a mixture of affectual, judgmental, and factual matter. This cluster of meaningful and significantly related attributes can be labeled by a word-holder or a phrase such as "farm" or "factory" or "polluted water."

Concepts are never completed by any individual but are ever expanding and always being altered. As new, significant experience is incorporated into a person's symbolic structures, attributes are added and old ones are rearranged, some becoming prominent as others recede. Language, as the representation of attributes, is one of the chief elements in the conceptual structure; it is also the mechanism that holds the other attributes together.

There are both inductive and deductive paths to the attribute collecting that makes for personal conceptions. The inductive method is seen easily in the young child's assigning attributes to an emerging conception of "mother." The baby girl starts with a vague conception of a live, warm object that feeds and cares for her. Eventually, she assigns special attributes to this person and distinguishes "mother" from all the other people who do things for her. She hears the word *mother* used by the adults around her in specific contexts, and when she begins to speak, the .

word represents her conception of "mother." This inductive procedure is one way in which a person conceptualizes throughout life.

Because we live in a social framework, we also assign attributes in building conceptions by reacting in a deductive manner to public and scientific concepts already derived by others in the society. This procedure can be seen when parents see an object or happening that they think their little boy should know about. On a visit to a farm they might say to the child, "There is a cow and it gives us milk." The child then has to come to terms with this public concept and to try to relate it in a deductive manner to previous experiences and to the attributes he has connected to "milk" and "animals." He may not gain a conception of "food processing" for a long time, but the public concept of "cow" has started the conceptualizing process on its way.

Throughout life a considerable amount of conceptualizing is abductive. We see parallels in new experiences to more familiar experiences, and we use the schema developed with the old experiences to organize the new ones. A child taking her first plane ride may think of the pilot as the driver, drawing on her car experience. Much of metaphor is based on abduction. If certain music is hot, then it is possible to think of contrasting music as warm or cool; if a bed has a head, then it also can have a foot.

Much of the development of conceptions obviously entails an interplay of inductive, deductive, and abductive processes, as children interact with their environment and speak with the adults around them. They are busy collecting and assigning attributes to things and events. When teachers ask children to talk about an object or a picture brought to class, they are stimulating the process of selecting and rejecting attributes. If teachers are aware of this process, they can lift the quality of ideating and can enhance the substance of such discussion by, for example, injecting negative attributes from other concept clusters into the talk in order to help children confirm their conceptions. This technique can also start them on the forming of subconcepts, such as "dog" to "collie" or of related concepts such as "cat" to "tiger." These categorizing exercises can take on the quality of a game, which stems from the basic fun of trying to put the world together, like completing a puzzle.

The Generalizing Process in Ideating

One's view of conceptualizing can be extended and refined by making distinctions between, on the one hand, concepts and generalizations and, on the other hand, conceptual themes that are developed over long periods of time.

A generalization is a statement of a propositional relationship between concepts. It is a tentative "law" or model of the world, which has been tested or could be tested but which is still open to question. Bringing the concepts of "light" and "plant" into relationship under laboratory conditions suggests a general proposition that light significantly influences the growth of plants. A generalization usually has exceptions, because humanity has yet to encompass the world with its thought.

Also, the world, especially the social world, is irregular and not completely amenable to generalizations. Generalizations are always under the surveillance of doubt, and, therefore, they are subject to reformulation as new evidence is discovered. They last only as long as they are useful as frames of reference or guides in investigating the riddle of the universe. Gravity continues to be a useful generalization about a relationship between objects and force; bloodletting in medicine is no longer a useful generalization from which to study bodily functions.

Sometimes a generalization about some phenomenon seems so assured after repeated testings that scholars call it a law. The generalization that genetic material in the nucleus of the cell regulates the growth and development of that cell and determines its characteristics has been so tested. Freud's imaginative proposition of "ego strength" has not been found to exist as yet. It is a convenient generalization for framing a study of the personality. Generalizations can be either working hypotheses (theories to be proven) or proven hypotheses (tested and accepted theories), or any set of positions between those two.

The scientific generalization, "An object immersed in a fluid loses as much in weight as the weight of an equal volume of the fluid" contains several scientific concepts: "fluid," "weight," and "volume," and implies "force" and "buoyancy." A young child may develop early, vague conceptions that eventually become (after years of experiencing, conceptualizing, and generalizing) a personal version of this scientific generalization.

A 3-year-old girl was observed on a beach, filling a hole in the sand with water that she was fetching in a pail from the pond. She had been lifting the pail out of the water and carrying it to the hole. Then, as if by chance, she dragged the pail one time through the water until she got to the beach's edge instead of lifting it out immediately. Her body posture showed relief from the weight of the water. Her face showed delight in her discovery as she repeated the labor-saving action several times. A glimmering of a conception about water displacement came through in this sensorimotor experience. One could speculate how subsequent similar experiences of the child, such as bailing water from a rowboat or lifting heavy stones under water, might cause extension and refinement of the kernel of such an idea. Perhaps later in kindergarten, water play would include objects that float and sink. An aluminum foil toy boat might be constructed to float and might then be flattened out and sunk. Even later, in general science, a teacher might set up a discovery situation that would involve the weighing of the water that a floating hull displaced from a brimful tank. Quite possibly the girl's generalization that approximates the scientific one might be made at that juncture, but all the earlier ideation would have contributed to the derivation of the generalization finally drawn.

In the process of instruction teachers need to be wary of forcing the act of generalizing before conceptions are made clear through attribute classification and description. On the other hand, teachers need constantly to encourage the emergence of generalization at the appropriate time and at the level appropriate to the children's ability to comprehend.

Many attributes of "sun" have to be clear and fully understood, as do certain critical qualities of "plant," before a relationship between the two can be developed into a generalization. A generalization on a simple descriptive level might be that green plants in sunshine grow faster than those not in sunshine, other factors being equal. This simple idea can then be extended into the sophisticated and logically abstract generalization of photosynthesis when the child is older.

The Growth of Conceptual Schemas

As individual generalizations emerge, when conceptions of a like kind become related, the ideational process continues ad infinitum. However, just as individuals tend to cluster small items around concepts, so do they seem to have the tendency to cluster their conceptions and generalizations around individual schemas. Viewing the world a certain way keeps "making sense" for a person. This kind of ideation may be evident in a person's choice of work or hobby. As he or she puts pieces of the puzzle together, the individual can begin to gain competence in at least one aspect of life. It can be said that he or she knows a lot about such and such. An expert in a field tends to interpret the world through the conceptual schemas of that field. For example, economists tend to claim that the history of humanity at war and peace can be explained in large part by economic theory.

The child-sized glimmer of a concept eventually grows into the adult-sized, full-blown conception that aids the adult in coping with the world. A few children grow up to become discoverers of unique conceptual views, and they are the scientists, artists, scholars, and original thinkers who construct new concepts that eventually become the public knowledge of the times.

When two boys were observed at 3-year intervals playing with the same miniature farm equipment in the same sand pit, a substantial advancement in the sophistication and extension of their concepts of farming into conceptual schemas was evident. When the boys were 6 years of age they used the equipment generally for making a road and for cutting a hay field. At 9 years, the two boys played through the whole cycle of plowing, planting, cultivating, and harvesting. The language, as well as the activity, was more sophisticated. The informal sociodrama at the earlier age was in short repetitive, realistic episodes, and they used appropriately direct, explanatory language. The drama at the later age was highly developed into specific characterized roles, using richer descriptive language that explained reasons for some of their activities.

The development of personal conceptual schemas can be recognized over quite long periods of time when patterns of a child's interests and hobbies are observed. A 12-year-old boy, when asked why he had made an ecological study of forest Indians for a science fair, replied that life in the forest had been his chief interest ever since he could remember. He told about spending many summers in the New Hampshire woods. He recalled knowing an Iroquois Indian who had been a family friend when he was younger. He said that he did not read much but that when he did, he always chose books about the forest and about Indians. When asked what he would like to do when he was grown up, he replied that he would like to be a forest ranger. Particular experiences and personal conceptualizing were developing in this boy a life view around adaptations and relationships to the forest.

Children from urban or rural slums may develop different life views because of the models they admire and because of their own environments. Teachers must be ready to seize upon the clues given them by children.

Teaching for the Development of Conceptual Schemas

Advances over time in ideation and language are to be expected, but the dynamics of concept clustering into schemas may be overlooked because the gains are probably minute from day to day and are difficult for a teacher to see. They are there all the same, and the time for growing is when new aspects of a phenomenon are confronted.

Teachers should preplan their programs so that new complexities of a schema are introduced in an orderly manner. They will also want to return regularly to concepts and generalizations developed earlier. This cyclical planning around conceptual schemas should, of course, be flexible. The sensitive teacher will seize an opportune moment for extending a concept, even though it may arise from an unplanned situation. The abiding conceptual schemas of a student are often revealed when a child shows excitement about an idea in class discussion or freely chooses to write, talk, or draw about a subject. A nonreading fourth-grader of the author's acquaintance did not start reading until the teacher discovered one of his conceptual themes: trains. The local suburban and national train schedules became his primer.

Interest inventories and reading and television selection questionnaires can assist in revealing conceptual schemas. Being aware of students' schemas means that teachers can relate new material to them for concept building and enrichment. In this way the expanding world can continue to make sense to the students.

Faulty Ideating: Misconceiving and Overgeneralizing

Just as children can have misperceptions based on their existing schemas, they can also develop misconceptions. These misconceptions frequently reflect preexisting beliefs and values, but they also simply reflect limited experiences and incomplete schemas. So, typically, there is a natural history of development of reality-oriented conceptions that involves their passing through phases of misconception. Conceptions may be only partially conceived and meanings skewed for various reasons: misinformation, lack of experience, misperception, limited classifying of attributes, verbal confusion, distracting emotion, or overgeneralizing. "Boners" often reveal partial misconceptions within a framework of some sense. Because of the incongruity caused by the misconceived elements, they are funny. These examples are from a fifth grade:

Manhattan Island was bought for twenty-four dollars from the Indians. Now, I don't suppose you could buy it for five hundred dollars. (Inadequate conception of the value of money.)
We don't raise the silkworm in the United States because we get our silk from rayon.

He is a larger animal and gives more silk. (Misinformation and overgeneralizing.)
Heat expands, in summer, days are long.
Cold contracts; in winter, days are short. (Logic of the language is correct but generalizing has come before facts are in.)
The dinosaurs became extinct because they were too big to get into the ark. (Two opposing frames of reference are incorporated into one conception.)

Overgeneralizing is mainly caused by premature generalizing from too few instances of seemingly similar experiences or facts. Prejudiced and short-sighted thinking can result in overgeneralizing if it cuts off further learning.

Precedence: A Cause of Misconceiving

When examples of children's conceptualizing are gathered through individual or group interviews, they reveal in part how conceptions and misconceptions develop. In concept development there appears to be a phenomenon called *precedence:* certain powerful developmental tendencies take precedence over a seemingly logical development of the concept. Schools need to be aware that conceptual development does not follow simply from logical explanations and that these forces can greatly influence how concepts are and are not shaped. Several kinds of precedence can be identified.

Marketplace Precedence The reiteration of commonplace and stereotyped impressions picked up from overheard conversations, comments, and small talk may take precedence over the logical or sensible development of a view of world happenings: "The schools sure are going to pieces these days."

Autistic Precedence An overpersonal identification with events results in every conception's being the way "I" am or the way "I" do things. The individual is at the center of the concept, as in the following pre-detente view of China by a 7-year-old: "If I lived in China, I would kill myself, go crazy, or ask God to help me!"

Operative Precedence Children often tend to view objects in terms of operations, how something works, or how it operates on the individual: "School is a teaching place."

Authority Precedence At early school ages family-approved positions or teachers' pronouncements take precedence over ideas generated by peer discussion: "My mother says" or "My father says" is a common introduction for an idea presented in school. On the other hand, particularly at the time when the teacher becomes an object of secondary identification, children dispute a family idea with a statement from their teachers. There is no argument; the teacher is right. Later, the peer culture becomes the authority. However, in political matters children are likely to reflect the family position completely: "The President spends too much money. He shouldn't spend more than the government makes."

Emotional Precedence   The emotional aspect of a happening can dominate the concept, sometimes distorting it. An emotional word, *brainwash,* caught children's fancy after the Korean War, even though they did not quite understand the word.

The emotional prejudices built up in wartime (hot or cold) seem to carry over in the minds of children many years beyond the period of conflict. Undoubtedly, television shows help these emotional epithets to persist in young people's culture.

Linguistic Precedence   A new adult word, not quite understood, may shape a concept. Eventually, the word or phrase will, as it gains proper reference over time, enable the child to develop a sensible concept around it. A young boy insisted that the Pilgrims "conquered" Massachusetts. Sometimes words are used from the common language of the street before they are understood, except in a purely emotional reference. If language molds the particular thinking or way of viewing the world in each cultural group having its own language, it would seem reasonable that the native dialect will sometimes take precedence over experience in guiding the concepts of the children of that culture.

Precedence of Immediacy   What is most recently experienced dominates the path of a concept in development. Children's concepts of the role of the President are expressed in terms of the immediate public events involving the President. When children in the months following President Reagan's election were asked what they knew about him, they stated separately that he was a movie star, that he rode horses, that he lived in California, and that he made speeches.

Implications of Precedence for Teaching

If teachers are aware of the various phenomena of precedence, they realize that some precedences are too overwhelming to be changed. They simply have to be lived with as part of the process of gaining independence from parents and from subcultural bounds. On the other hand, teachers may, with sensitivity to the growth patterns, strategically intercept a precedence tendency by injecting into classroom dialogue a reality to be confronted or an opposing logic or emotion at the time of the conceptualizing phase. The meaning of the word *conquer* could be clarified and amplified at the time when the child said, "the Pilgrims conquered Massachusetts." In dialogue or discussion with the teacher and other pupils, meanings can, of course, be differentiated as the word is used in conventional contexts, or meanings can be extended. There is a "conquest" element in the Pilgrim mission, particularly from the perspective of the indigenous people, that is often brushed aside.

Teaching to Avoid Unnecessary Misconceptions

Misconceptions are often taught because parents or teachers are not aware of scientific concepts. Sometimes books or pictures used convey the misconceptions or stereotypes of misinformed authors. Children's conception of the life of the Pilgrims has suffered more than most school subjects from this type of misconceiving teaching. Most American children misconceive the Pilgrims as having been tall, idealistic men and women with stuffy, moralistic characters, who lived in log cabins. The misconceiving can be ended when the teacher understands the generalization discovered by cultural anthropologists that socially consistent groups of people moving from one environmental setting into another tend to carry their culture with them into the new land. The Pilgrims, then, are rightly conceived as robust, lower middle-class Elizabethans enjoying the earthly pleasures of beer-quaffing as well as visualizing themselves as new "Israelites." They would not build log cabins, but they would, naturally, construct models of English Tudor country cottages as best they could with the materials at hand.

Another usual cause of misconceiving stems from conceptualizing inadequacies in the adults who surround children. Unless adults have kept open minds and have avoided prejudice or have examined the folk wisdom of their culture, the children will pick up not only the adult misconceptions but also the process of narrow thinking. "A penny saved is a penny earned" is not a sound economic concept. Adults surrounding children are likely to have some commonsense concepts, which are passed on to the children in the manner of conventional wisdom.

A far more serious problem of misconceiving is apparent when adults of a cultural group and even the scholars among them fail to view a whole field of knowledge with objectivity because of their cultural blinders. The white community of the European-American world has failed until recently to recognize that it has written history only from its cultural viewpoint, disregarding the view of Asian-Americans, Afro-Americans or Native Americans. One group of Tohono O'Odham Indian children living in the Arizona desert were asked to write a story imagining they were Pilgrim children landing in Massachusettes. A more sensitive teacher might have realized that the pupils might more readily identify with those who were on the shore already when the Pilgrims appeared.

New research needs to be done and new books written to consider the viewpoint of all peoples involved in history. Teachers can begin, however, to present the views of all cultures or at least to express the need for these views to be considered when new history is written or when past history is rewritten.

Children themselves, because of the immaturity of their thinking processes, make many misconceptions on their own. In the early years they tend to overgeneralize. This is a phase in thinking when they have come upon the possibility of putting two likes together and saying, "These must be always the same."

When children are first making a relationship between phenomena (generalizing), they may fall into logical mistakes. Fifth-graders who had learned that hot air rises misapplied this concept to account for the cooling process. When they were asked to talk about why some tin cans, filled with hot water and covered, would cool if left to stand, their reasoning became confused. One student suggested—and they all agreed—that if the teacher would make holes just in the top of the can, the water would cool much faster. The teacher didn't tell them that they were wrong but asked them to suggest a simple experiment that might test their proposition.

Misconceiving seems to be part of the "growing up" of conceptions and generalizations at various stages of their development. Teachers made more aware of this possibility can be aware that some of the misconceiving is bound to occur. At the same time, they can waylay some of the unnecessary misconceiving and inaccurate generalizing by constructive instructional tactics, such as challenges to experiment.

Language in the Ideating Process

In the perceiving stage there are many cues from the environment that are nonverbal, although individuals do bring their own meaning to a word cue as they perceive it. However, language is crucial to the conceptualizing of both words and images perceived.

> This phenomenon of holding on to the object by means of its symbol is so
> elementary that language has grown up on it. A word fixes something in experi-
> ence and makes it the nucleus of memory, an available conception. (Langer, p.
> 110)

Language frames the thought and imbues it with communicable meaning so that it may be held in memory and used again in interplay with other thoughts. Frances Minor describes the lingual aspects of conceptualizing as an act of "own-ing" words, in which children take possession of the word through a "multiplicity" of their own experiences; the language becomes their personal property: "Children shape the meaning of words from their experiences." (Minor, 1964) Attempts in school to build vocabulary through drills or dictionary exercises circumvent this process of concept building and the sense of ownership that comes with it. Those school words are somebody else's, not the learner's.

Jerome Bruner has described thinking as a mediating process between stimulus input and response, in which an individual is freed from the stimulus by varying the response after mulling the situation over or by keeping the response steady in a varying environment. Language is viewed by Bruner as the "instrument" of thought, not just as a medium of communication. The individual "instructs himself" in the art of "reformulating with language." An idea is shaped by talking it out, alone or with others. Children's thinking, then, is shaped in large degree by the dialogue they carry on with adults, for it is the adult grammar of thinking in language that interacts with the child grammar of thinking. (Bruner, 1966)

In the conceptualizing phases of transforming experience to symbol, social language molds thought as thought constructs the personal language of an in-dividual's private conception of the world. Halliday puts it this way:

> . . . because of the functional basis of language, the particular concrete rneanings
> that are expressed in typical everyday situations become, for him, the primary

source for building up the context of culture. . . . Each instance of 'I want' or 'may I' or 'let me take part' or 'what's going on?' is encoded in words and structures which serve in some measure to categorize the social order and the child's own part in it. . . . as these early uses evolve into generalized social contexts of language use, the linguistic system is able to act through them as the means for the transmission of the culture to the child. In this way language comes to occupy the central role in the processes of social learning. (Halliday, 1975, p. 59)

Language Modes and Style in Conceptualizing

The instrumentality of language in thinking can be seen in the language mode or style used in expressing different kinds of personal conceptions of public or scientific concepts. Youngsters pick up these mocles and styles from the adults with whom they have dialogue, whether that dialogue be with adult writers of books, with directors of films, or with parents or teachers. The language mode is related to the content of the concept, whether it be scientific and factual or value laden, or, as most concepts are, a mixture of both. The mode of an adult's conception of nuclear energy will carry both factual and value content in a mode of "either-or" language. An example of such a combination follows:

I shiver at the thought of the magnitude of force released by the atom. This is a terrible weapon and I fear it greatly, even though I fully realize that it can be applied to uses that will build up our civilization.

Adults are not very different from children in coming to terms with new awareness provoked by environmental stimulation, except that they have a backlog of experience and have advanced thinking capability. The concept of "sublimation" may be as unknown to an adult as Newtion's concept of "falling objects" is to a 4-year-old, yet they both live in a world in which these phenomena occur all about them. When the adult is in dialogue with the common scientific concept, the particular style of the language appropriate to that concept is acquired. In freely reacting to a word like *sublimation,* adults will use the mode of definition and example:

Sublimation is a rational act that satisfies an undesirable and antisocial wish in a socially acceptable way. For example, some people have sadistic desires, and they become surgeons.

A metaphorical mode is evident in this very young child's developing conception of sickness: "I am so sick to my stomach that I feel like I am killing myself." The mode of eliminating negative instances is evident in the statement a 5-year-old made as he was watching a motor boat speeding under the historical Concord Bridge: "That does not belong here; it is too modern for this place."

Teachers have always engaged their pupils in discussion, but when they keep in mind the instrumentality of language in the development of conceptualizing and generalizing, they can set the stage for exploring different stylistic types and can encourage the development of appropriate modes. A scientific conception might emerge from children in imagistic and prejudicial language, but refinement toward a concept should be in the direction of the expository mode. A metaphorical mode

Coming to Know

114

may be more appropriate for conceiving certain aspects of the concepts "farmer" and "farming," such as "love of land" and "the rhythm of the seasons," than explanations in terms of science and agronomy. Literary statements tend to be neglected in a technically oriented society unless educators make the effort to explore the literary modes of thinking with children.

Teaching for Ideation in Contexts

Children constantly traffic in both concepts and generalizations as they come to terms with new events in their environment and as they form conceptual schemas. For teaching purposes, environments can be conveniently conceptualized as various contexts in which conceptions and generalizations are likely to be developed. A context in this sense can be described as a chunk of events from the real world of the present or the past that can be experienced directly or vicariously by children. It could be the geography of a place and the culture of a people living there; it could be the biography of an individual, the history of an institution, or the activities of a community; it could also be the life of the ant, the evolution of a lake, or the phenomena of thunder and lightning. (Grannis, 1964)

Concepts and generalizations about the environment, for example, are most likely to develop in contexts of extreme environmental conditions, such as "desert lands" or "life in Antarctica." The educating process is the interplay between concept and generalization in varying but somewhat similar contexts. The child, teacher, and scholar all strive for an approximation of reality.

Teachers, knowing the general background and characteristics of their pupils, select contexts in which concepts and generalizations can best be nourished. For psychosocial reasons in relation to dependency, "pets" may be a good context in which to develop some concepts and generalizations regarding "domestication" at the early childhood level. On the other hand, in junior high school, contrasting contexts of a "hunting society" and an early "farming society" might be more appropriate for extending the same concept of domestication. Hilda Taba has found the use of opposing contexts of a primitive society and a modern urban society to be very useful in extending concepts and lifting thinking about "shelter," for example. (Taba, 1963)

The old-fashioned "object lesson," in which a teacher focused the lesson upon some natural object that was brought in, might be revived and refurbished as a teaching device for extending concepts and developing generalizations. The "object" to be studied can be a group of objects that imply relationships, such as a set of magnets, a compass, and some nails, or the "object" could be in the social science domain; for example, a film clip of an Eskimo seal-hunting expedition juxtaposed with a clip of the clubbing of baby seals by fishermen and an environmentalist group protesting the slaughter. The discussion of the "object" need not, as in past days, be based on a prepared schedule of questions. It could be a free-ranging colloquy in which the teacher, by astute questioning, can foster the clarifying of concepts and the deriving of generalizations.

The time-honored field trip can be revitalized for the development of ideation. Instead of just a visit to a farm to write or draw about upon return, a tactical plan can be made by the teacher ahead of time to insure that children see concept-provoking objects and happenings. The farmer can be asked to show how to milk a cow by hand and then to demonstrate how modern milking machines work. The intricacies of the farmer's office and computers can be shown along with the barns to highlight the business aspects of modern farming.

The world can be brought to the class or the class can be taken to the world in such a way as to promote or enrich symbolic transformation of experience into knowing. But to make the transformation from experience to knowing requires many teaching strategies as concepts are developed and interrelated into generalizations through the language interchange of guided discussions among students and with teachers.

Developing a Dialogue between Personal Concepts and Public or Scientific Concepts

Students can enhance and extend their worlds of knowing through a mental dialogue between individual conceptions of events and public and scientific concepts found in books, newspapers, magazines, lectures, films, and combinations of them. Scientific concepts are derived from summarizing activities of scientists in various fields of study as they digest the results of recent research and theory and incorporate them into explanations that students and the public can understand. Public concepts are those carried by public means of communication, which vary from accurate accounts of events in newspapers to hearsay passed along in public places of work and commerce. Sometimes they are merely bits of conventional wisdom that seem persuasive at the moment, or they may be as profound as a public policy derived through a legislative process.

In school the teacher serves as both a resource person and a catalyst for getting a mental dialogue underway that fosters interrelationships between students' personal concepts and those in the public and scientific domains. The strategies most available to teachers are the lecture-discussion, the project method developed around topics or issues, the debate, and the research study and report developed by an individual or a small group of students. In open-inquiry education, a small unit of work or a learning activity is the means by which the teacher preplans the interaction of personal conceptualizing with public and scientific concepts.

A useful tactic for engaging children in such a dialogue is a small-scale study contract between the teacher and a student or a small group of students. Such contracts should be jointly developed and based upon the specific capabilities of the learners, including experiential and conceptual background in the area of study, and based upon the specific resources and materials that the teacher can make available to the student or small team of students. A contract should specify the goals and the scope of the study. These might be in the form of a series of mutually derived open-ended questions. The types of resources, their availability, and guides to their use should be designated. Alternative means for expressing the results of the study need to be suggested. A timetable for accomplishment of the tasks is advisable. Criteria for judging the level of conceptualization gained should be set down.

The activity card with an accompanying assemblage of packaged resources and materials is another useful means for encouraging the dialogue between personal and scientific concepts though independent work of individual students or students in pairs or triads. Activity cards need to be keyed to specific materials and need to be small enough in scale to be accomplished within a reasonable time span for the particular age of the students involved. The activity card must not ask more of the learners than they are generally able to comprehend at their age. Above all, it must not be an assignment card of directions; instead, the questions should be stated in such an open-ended and appealing fashion that they will induce self-directed concept learning. (Minor, 1964)

Presenting Phase

After people have conceptualized a perceived event, they then give their conceptions back to the world to be tested against the notions of others. They search for an echo from reality much in the same way that the bat listens to its "radar." They announce to themselves and to the world that these are their ideas of the situation. In a real sense, the presentational symbols that they construct are their world. They can know no other, and the only way that they can make sense of what they know is to present their conceptions for self-reflection or response from others. This is as vital an aspect of knowing as is the need to transform experience into symbols.

The presenting of symbols reaches its peak for artists alone; but even though ordinary people cannot give their presentational symbols the refined qualities of the artist, anyone can present conceptions in all the available modes. Indeed, modern social life would be more interesting if people were encouraged to practice the art, music, and dance modes of expression as folk cultures once did. Often youth, on their own and usually outside of school, have used the musical mode to present their ideas: young jazz and rock musicians improvise; Puerto Rican children in Spanish Harlem create festive street music during summer evenings on oil drums and tin cans; "combos" of suburban youth make up their own music of social commentary with its grim absurdities; break dancing is a social-personal expressive form that began in the urban ghettos. Children of the city have always been sidewalk artists, while their country cousins have been whittlers and sampler makers. The school curriculum should make good use of the many natural modes of presentation by children and youth.

Differing Modes of Presenting

Just as there are different modes for perceiving, dependent upon the senses used, so there are different modes of presenting, dependent on the part or parts of the organism used to convey the meanings. The individual perceives through all the senses. Teachers unknowingly limit the possibilities for perceiving by allowing only two sense organs to be used: the eyes and ears are overworked as the other senses are neglected. Outside, preschool children frequently fondle a new object, licking it, smelling it, and banging it against other objects. Langer points out this need for children to use all the senses by focusing on the kinds of sensations that children receive from objects:

> Childhood is the great period of synaesthesia; sounds and colors and temperatures, forms and feelings may have certain characters in common. . . . (Langer, p. 100)

Synaesthesia, perceiving concomitant sensations through several senses, is not just a phenomenon of early childhood but probably continues to function all through life, opening channels for the play of preconscious intuition. Word-object relationships become vital ideas as they are infused with the effect that develops as the initial stimuli touch the senses. Sensations make ideas vibrant by stirring preconscious memories of feeling and form and by bringing them in relation to the newly developing conceptions. (Kubie, 1961)

Similarly, conceptions come alive as they are expressed through all the presentational modes—art, music, dance, and mime—as well as through language. The organic means by which the various modes are conveyed are the vocal organs, the facial muscles, the movement of the body, and the manipulations of the hands in writing, drawing, playing a musical instrument, or sculpting, or extensions of these through tools or instruments. The presentation, in turn, is prepared to stimulate the various senses.

Language in the Presenting Process

The language mode is used in four ways to present conceptions, one's symbolic world, to oneself and others: soliloquizing, conversing, discussing, and writing.

Soliloquizing

Like Hamlet, we present our own thoughts to ourselves for examination and consideration. We go over these ideas in our minds as we "talk" to ourselves. Conceptions are refined in this way. Often the soliloquy is a precursor to writing or formal speaking. As in Shakespeare's play, it may be simply inner communication. When we stop to listen to ourselves objectively for a few moments, we may be surprised at our own eloquence. It is not surprising, then, that in the hands of an artist, inner thoughts can become great literature as demonstrated by the "stream of consciousness" writers of the early twentieth century; their writing is like one long soliloquy.

Time for reverie is essential to the cognitive process, but rarely are such moments planned for in school. Children will find these moments themselves, but great opportunities are lost when children are so pushed from one activity to another from morning until bedtime that they have no time for contemplation. After the reading of a story, the presenting of a significant idea, or the viewing of an impressive sight, time should be given not only for discussion but also for reverie. A problem with recent "time-on-task" proposals is that they narrow the task and leave no time for reflection.

Conversation and Dialogue

Often conversing is soliloquizing to an audience. It becomes an egocentric activity in which individuals keep presenting their conceptions. They do not hear much that their colleagues are saying, but they use their remarks as cues for further extension of their own ideas. Conversation can be parallel monologue in which each participant has the opportunity to talk out ideas and listen intently to them and look at listeners to see how they are reacting. To hear how ideas sound helps an individual test them and refine them.

Children, during play, often talk past each other in their conversation, yet they seem to sense that playmates and guardians are sounding boards. This phenomenon continues in all conversation. Sometimes a speaker will say to a listener, "You are not listening," and this is probably so, because the listener is too busy thinking about what to present next.

Halliday points out that in conversation there is an alternation of roles necessary for language to achieve its basic social function:

> Dialogue can be viewed as, essentially, the adoption and assignment of roles. The roles in question are social roles, but social roles of a special kind: they exist only in and through language, as roles in the communication process—speaker, addressee, respondent, questioner, persuader, and the like. (Halliday, 1975, pp. 48–49)

In dialogue we alternate between assuming for ourselves the role of presenter and assigning to others the role of listener, or accepting the role of listener while others become presenters. This turn taking is a very important aspect of becoming language users. We learn how to present by listening to other presenters.

As Halliday puts it:

> Dialogue involves purely linguistic forms of personal interaction; at the same time, it exemplifies the general principle whereby people adopt roles, assign them, and accept or reject those that are assigned to them. (Halliday, p. 49)

Conversation at relaxing moments in the day's classroom schedule should be encouraged. A time set aside for conversation rather than for more organized discussion might be useful after an important incident of confrontation. Conversation may serve well as a "warming-up" activity for pointed discussion to follow immediately or the next time the topic is broached.

Discussing

True discussion requires acute listening as well as thoughtful speaking. It is a dialogue of ideas, one thought building on another, a concert of thinking as individuals present their conceptions in relation to those of others. In discussion, the participants agree, tacitly or overtly, on a specific agenda. During the act of discussing, conceptions are actually altered, even abandoned, as new ones take their place. The total process of perceiving, conceptualizing, and presenting occurs almost simultaneously in deliberative discourse.

Plato's records of the dialogues of Socrates are usually too one-sided to be considered literally as discussion. His Symposium does very much fill the requirements, however, as guests explore different positions with regard to all meanings of "love." Socrates, of course, has a firm hand on the outcome of these arguments. In a free dialogue, the several minds of the persons involved influence each other as they seek the truth.

Debate is a formal type of discussion, which in practice is valuable for learning to support a position consistently. It has limited value as an education device, however, because one's believed conceptions sometimes have to be altered to fit the tight pattern of pro or con. No compromised resolution is possible. However, in debate the structuring of the language for meaning is clearly evident. The formal grammar of debate is a reminder of the fact that even in informal discussion there is a special language structure that forces the co-respondents to come to terms with cause, proof, and the conditional. As children become involved in true discussion with adults, the grammatical forms of the dialogue enforce, in a sense, the development of children's thinking about relationships.

A discussion needs to be carefully planned by the teacher as to the kinds of questions to be raised and the "givens" upon which the discussion will be based. At the same time, spontaneity must not be thwarted by overstructuring. The genuine discussion happens in the classroom when even teachers find themselves refining their preconceptions because of challenges raised by the students. An effective strategy for stimulating discussion is to confront the children with an experimental situation in science or social studies, encouraging them to describe what they see and then to speculate on why or how the particular phenomenon happened. Here is an example.

A fifth-grade class in science was studying the problem of body heat and insulation. The effects of fur was the topic of experimentation and discussion. The teacher posed the following question that prompted some interesting dialogue:

Teacher:	If it is 120° where the camel lives, what does his fur do for him? (The students immediately applied previous knowledge in saying that the fur kept out heat. Then a new thought occurred to them.)
Child A:	He must be hot. If I put a fur coat on at 120°, I would be hot.
Child B:	If fur keeps heat out, why don't we wear fur coats in the summer?
Child C:	I think it is because nobody has tried it.
Child D:	How about Arabs in desert lands? Do they go around in swim suits?

(A number of the students knew something about Middle-Eastern Arabs and stated that they do wear quite a large amount of clothing but that it is loosely worn. They pointed out that the cloth was very similar to wool.)

Child E:	If my mother had a fur coat, I'd wear it tomorrow and find out what happens. (Elementary Science Study, 1962)

Discussion is the most common means for presenting one's conceptions to be tested against the ideas of others.

Writing

Written composition is the form of presenting most abused in school. Children are often asked to use it when, in fact, the written form is not the most appropriate means for expression but is merely the best way to keep them quiet and busy. On the other hand, writing in school is rewarding when it is used to hold conceptions for future reference, to pull loose thoughts together, to put thoughts into a form whereby they can be considered reflectively, or to form conceptions into memorable statements.

Writing can be divided into two major kinds: *expository* and *literary*. Expository writing deals with statements of fact and arguments based on them. Usually a minimum of emotive language is present, because the writer is trying to be objective. Descriptions of scientific or social phenomena fall into this category. What was observed is presented. Literary writing is subjective and unabashedly emotional. It is no less meaningful, but metaphor and imagery convey the sense more than lucid simple statement. Poetry is the most literary form of writing, whereas a chemical formula is the most expository. In some writing the forms are ingeniously mixed.

Children should have occasion to express their conceptions in the form that is appropriate. Writing becomes a necessity when seen as a presentation and not as an adjunct skill to the educative process. Children writing their impressions of the first snow is as important to their cognitive lives as writing "Stopping by Woods on a Snowy Evening" was important to Robert Frost.

Louise Rosenblatt uses the terms *efferent* and *aesthetic* to differentiate how these two kinds of writing are read. In efferent reading the reader is intent on "what will remain after the reading—the information to be acquired, the logical solution to a problem, the actions to be carried out." (Rosenblatt, 1978, pp. 24–25) Aesthetic reading is more concerned with "associations, feelings, attitudes and ideas" that the text arouses in the reader during the actual reading.

So two kinds of presentation are necessary to make these two kinds of reading possible.

Nonlingual Presentations

The pictorial, musical, mimetic, and terpsichorean arts offer modes for presenting conceptions that cannot conveniently be expressed in words. Composers in these modes decry every attempt to translate their presentational symbols into words. The music, the sculpture, or the dance each speaks for itself. People when first introduced to modern dance or modern painting inevitably ask what a certain abstract painting or a choreographic episode means, as if the meaning could be put into words. So-called primitive tribes have no difficulty creating or understanding dance, but so-called civilized peoples have been so oriented to literacy that the literacy of the arts often escapes them. Modern society obviously needs education in the modes of the arts as well as in that of letters.

Rather than pursuing the vague concept of appreciation, the arts in the curriculum should fill the need for literacy in these particular modes of presentation. In a real sense, children need to learn how to present their ideas in art forms and how to "read" the symbolic presentations of others. Practice in the arts should be contiguous with practice in language presentation. The study of art, music, dance, and theater is not a frill but is an essential in the curriculum. Dramatic art should hold a special place in the curriculum, because it combines the lingual and nonlingual forms of presentation.

The nonlingual modes of presentation can be used in exposition just as language can. In the pictorial mode, matters of fact can be presented in diagrams or pictograms. Indeed, many of the pictures that teachers ask children to draw after a field trip are not art products but are pictograms showing the facts they observed. Body movement can be used literally to give direction or to describe what someone did. Sculptured objects can literally depict atomic relationships or the anatomy of the body. Drama may be quite literal when role playing is used to present factual happenings. The arts of all these modes, on the other hand, are similar to the literary kind of writing in which the emotive aspects of concepts are expressed directly. There are other sophisticated ways of presenting ideas, such as mathematical and chemical equations.

Presenting is both the culminating phase of knowing and the beginning of it, for every presentation offers something new to be perceived and considered. The phases of knowing are thus cyclical.

Teaching Strategies for Presenting

If presenting is considered an essential phase of knowing, opportunities for its practice must be pervasive in the regular school program. Planned opportunities to soliloquize, converse, and discuss must follow confrontations of significance. When all ideas have been explored, a summarizing activity that will cause reflective and deliberative thinking must be arranged. The modes to be used should suit the subject. Writing is appropriate for either the efferent matters (which can best be described by precise language) or the aesthetic matters (which can best be presented in emotive and metaphorical language). The impact of a great winter storm or of a raging forest fire might best be conveyed by painting. Pictorial diagrams, charts, or tables are better suited than verbal exposition to the presentation of interrelated facts about such topics as rainfall and land productivity. The concept of Thanksgiving may best be expressed in song, and the toil of the fields may best be realized in dance. The teacher needs to introduce children to all the modes as appropriate. Children can experience presenting the same concept in several different modes to see which is most successful for them or to see how emphases are altered in the varied presentations. There are many new media, such as audiotape, videotape, xerography, and microcomputers, that can be used by teachers to extend the modes of presenting.

Valid "Integrating" of the Arts into School Programs

At one time in educational parlance the use of the various modes of presentation was called "integration of art and music with subject matter." A study of the mailman included "making up" a mailman dance, a mailman song, and the creation of a post-office mural. Some of these "integrations" were most incongruous because they were inappropriate. The pictogram mural might serve well to show in one long glance the various procedures in the handling of the mail, but a dance of a mail carrier walking down the street seems to reach too far. A dance depicting the encounter of the mail carrier with the neighborhood dogs might be appropriate, however.

Sometimes teachers mistakenly eliminate one of these modes because they feel it does not suit the age level. For example, not many teachers involve sixth-grade boys in modern dance, yet one brave sixth-grade teacher, with his boys, choreographed and dramatized Custer's last stand, using accounts of the battle as source material. The emotion of that dramatic incident lent itself especially well to the medium of dance. The boys were so impressed with what they could do in dance to present their idea about Indian preparation and white desperation that they forgot for the moment that dancing was "for girls only." The starting point for such an activity could be viewing the film "West Side Story" in which rival gangs dance, or perhaps viewing a music video involving break-dancing.

The various modes are for all ages to explore, but within the children's levels of skill and comprehension. Dramatic presentation with music, dance, and scenery combines several of the modes and is therefore particularly useful in the school setting. Different children can work in different modes as they all center their attention on one comprehensive summary of their various conceptions. These are essentials in the curriculum, not just additions for special occasions.

Using the Presentations of Others for Extending Conceptions

The remarkable presentations of adult writers, painters, sculptors, film directors and actors, composers, and choreographers can be used in the educative process to enrich the content of children's conceptions. Fortunately, modern artists in all fields have applied their talents to presenting their ideas to children. Every year, publishers offer hundreds of books for children of all ages. Many are well written, effectively illustrated, and beautifully printed. Robert McCloskey's *Time of Wonder* with its colorful prose and dramatic illustration can add substantially to children's sense of awe about nature. Byrd Baylor's *Hawk You Are My Brother* with its poignant yet restrained language and its severe but touching illustrations gives children an opportunity to stop in the midst of their daily activities to contemplate the end and the beginning of things. The right book placed in the hands of a child at the right time can accomplish wonders that direct teaching could never do, because with a book there are no thoughts unimaginable or unacceptable.

Modern informational books, like those of Herbert Zim and Enid Blough in science, structure the information with words and pictures in such a clever way that children can build some science concepts vicariously. Modern encyclopedias and the better textbooks combine pictures, diagrams, and text ingeniously to present facts and ideas. Films, filmstrips, and recordings bring into the classroom scientific phenomena that could not otherwise be presented in a structured manner. In film, the science and the fury of a hurricane can be presented all at once by a sequence of pictorial images ranging from views of storm clouds and weather satellites to closeups of family tragedy. Pupils can use photography and videotaping to create similar presentations.

In the social studies, presentations that create a sense of personal immediacy are important. In historical studies the firsthand account, a piece of literature from the time, or some music of the period, will heighten sensitivity and understanding. Smith and Meredith have prepared for children a presentation of eyewitness accounts of the founding of Plymouth, of Columbus's first voyage, and the early white explorations of the Mississippi in *Pilgrim Courage, The Quest of Columbus,* and *Exploring the Great River.* Authentic historical storybooks and biographies are other ways to capture the attitudes as well as the facts of a time. James Daugherty has caught the vigor and excitement of Daniel Boone's story that children will never forget. Esther Forbes's *Johnny Tremain,* a work of fiction, accurately and vividly relates the beginnings of the American Revolution for children.

Studies in geography and the culture of peoples benefit immeasurably by presentations of life in children's books written by residents in the particular culture or by sensitive observers of it. Taro Yashima's *The Village Tree,* through language of simplicity and contemporary drawings of Japanese landscape, gives children a knowledge of life in Japan that an outsider could not produce. Ann Eaton's stories about the Indian cultures in America's Southwest and in South America bring children the feeling of living close to the land and places them in communication with the natural elements. Tom Feelings, author and illustrator, creates in *Black Pilgrimage* a fascinating story of his experiences as an artist in the ghetto and a traveler through Africa. This book offers children a personal sociocultural document in two media.

Using Folk and Regional Presentations for Enriching Conceptions
Literature, music, and plastic art by folk artists from various regions of the world present the symbolism of their cultures. These presentations range from the music of a Watusi tribal dance to a Grant Wood painting of midwestern farm life. They convey through myth, ritual, and language the essence of a people's beliefs and world view. By experiencing folk creations, children can, in a sense, live in the culture they are studying and can learn to respect it. Through folk art from earlier times children can participate in some of their own culture's rich, symbolic background and the backgrounds of other modern children. "Greensleeves" and folk Christmas carols symbolize old England more adequately than hundreds of lines in a textbook. The designs on Grecian vases or the friezes on Egyptian tombs tell stories that no book could convey. The brief, epigrammatic American-Indian folktales and the Japanese haiku tell volumes about those cultures. And no child can hear the bells of Bali or Jamaican drums without gleaning some knowledge of the differences and likenesses of those two island peoples on opposite sides of the globe.

Integration of literature, music, the plastic arts, and dance into the social studies should be for the express purpose of enriching the children's symbolic content about a topic. The criteria for selecting supplementary integrating materials should be appropriateness of media to the subject and artistic quality of the presentational symbol. "America the Beautiful" and "This Land Is Your Land" convey the exuberance and the optimism of the American frontier spirit, whereas "God Bless America" is sentimental and superficial by comparison.

Using the Dramatic Modes

The cinematic form is highly effective in the presentation of ideas to children. Unfortunately, many of the films for children are artless; however, a few great films are produced that are exactly right for children as well as for adults. Robert Flaherty's "Nanook of the North" is one of these timeless masterpieces. The one-to-one relationship of a man to his environment has rarely been more effectively portrayed. A good teacher chooses this old film over the many other more recent selections about Eskimo life because this film catches so much more than the facts. Film loops from "Man: A Course of Study" have these same qualities.

Television has many of the same qualities as theater, cinema, and radio. At its best, it is a collage of sound, pictures, written words, dialogue, images, designed patterns, and color. Television can bring important events, such as the moon walks and flybys of planets, to people at once. It can take its audience back to the days of the Gold Rush or to ancient Rome. Because there is an intimacy about television in the home or in the classroom, the personal and group involvement in watching it is new in the media world. Fortunately, the networks have taped some of the outstanding television specials of recent years, and they have been made available to teachers. Television educational tapes are in abundance, but they are only effective as presentations when they use the full potential of the television medium. If the program is simply a recording of a lecture, it might as well have been audiotaped or printed in a book, but if the producer has used the camera to explore and to take students, for example, from a view of minute sea life to a view of the world from a space capsule, then television can be an exciting means of presentation for instruction.

Microcomputers

Microcomputers offer another form of presentation. At their best they can involve pupils in a highly participatory interaction in which cleverly constructed programs, games, and computer assisted instruction encourage presentation by the learners while presenting them with visual and even auditory information. At their worst, they are simply programmed workbooks that narrowly control response and, too often, present oversimplified misconceptions.

Word-processing programs, some specifically created for children, make possible a new medium for written composition. Special programming languages designed for children can open up new vistas for pupils to explore logical relationships and to develop schemas. Ironically, some of the computer games, particularly the adventure games, provide more opportunities for students to learn than do the computer assisted instruction packages.

There are some promising examples of use of networked microcomputers to permit written conversations between pupils in different locations.

Schools in many countries are making substantial investments in computers. How well they're used depends very much on how administrators and teachers integrate them into the methodology and the curriculum of the school.

Importance of Using All Modes of Presentation

Well-chosen examples of literature, music, art, and dance will not only enhance a study with children but will indeed present the essence of that study. Taba has suggested that a study for children might center about some significant children's books, such as the African story, *Brothers and Sisters.* (Taba, 1963) To this study might be added collections of art, song, and dance. These can become the focus of the study of places, as facts are collected to assist in the interpretation of the books, folkways, and artifacts.

The presenting phase of knowing is double-edged. Children need to present conceptions and to experience the presenting of conceptions in all the modes. Some children will show unusual talent in one mode, and they should be given special encouragement, because in the future these students might become artists, poets, or musicians. However, for most children, literacy in the various modes is sufficient. The experience of knowing, of coming to terms with the world, is not complete without opportunities to present one's conceptions, and teachers must see that these times for presentation are available and fully used.

General Teaching Strategies in Coming to Know

In the perceiving phase of the symbolic transforming of experience, teachers generally help students become aware of significances in their environment. They confront pupils with situations that spark curiosity, raise questions, and activate discovering processes.

During the ideating phase teachers assist pupils in finding problems to be solved and in organizing thinking by raising the appropriate questions. They put the pupils into dialogue with public and scientific knowledge by presenting their own ideas and by offering the conceptualizations of others in books, films, and various instructional materials.

When the presenting phase arrives, teachers devise means for pupils to work through their ideas and present them in oral or written language or in other symbolic forms. They can set up problem-solving situations in differing contexts in which students can test and rehearse their conceptual learnings.

In a sense, each individual in each generation rediscovers, in part, the world's phenomena and their interrelationships. The aid and guidance of scholars past and present are available to all people in their schooling, reading, and listening if they wish to call upon them. The excitement of discovery must be maintained as students traverse the conceptual paths, but the students need to use the guideposts of past and present scholarship to stimulate their thinking and to verify their conceptualizations. Teachers act as guides and questioners as the students transform their experiences into language and symbol.

After preparing the class environment with challenges, teachers engage pupils in a dialogue between their knowings and those established by the discipline. In the words of Whitman, the students "peer," "absorb," and then "translate."

References

Jerome Bruner, *Towards a Theory of Instruction* (Cambridge, MA: Harvard University Press, 1966).

Hadley Cantril, *The "Why" of Man's Experience* (New York: Macmillan, 1950).

Ernst Cassirer, *Essay on Man* (New York: Anchor Doubleday, 1956).

John Dewey and Arthur Bentley, *Knowing and the Known* (Boston: Beacon, 1949).

Elementary Science Study, "First Trial with Animal Temperature at the Fifth Grade Level," mimeographed account of lessons (Watertown, MA: Educational Services, 1962).

L. Festinger, *A Theory of Cognitive Dissonance* (New York: Harper & Row, 1957).

J. I. Goodlad, *A Place Called School* (New York: McGraw-Hill, 1984).

J. Grannis, "Team Teaching and the Curriculum", in J. Shaplin and H. Olds, *Team Teaching* (New York: Harper & Row, 1964).

Michael Halliday, *Learning How to Mean* (London: Edward Arnold, 1975).

O. J. Harvey, David Hunt, and Harold Schroder, *Conceptual Systems and Personality Organization* (New York: Wiley, 1961).

Eugene Ionesco, "The Lesson" in *Four Plays* (New York: Grove, 1958).

Earl Kelley, *Education for What Is Real* (New York: Harper & Row, 1947), chaps. 3, 4.

Franklin Kilpatrick, *Explorations in Transactional Psychology* (New York: New York University Press, 1961), chaps. 8, 13, 14.

Lawrence Kubie, *Neurotic Distortion of the Creative Process* (New York: Farrar, Straus, 1961).

Susanne K. Langer, *Philosophy in a New Key* (New York: Mentor Books, 1956).

Frances Minor, "A Child Goes Forth: Ideas Invite Involvement," in *Individualizing Instruction* (Washington D.C.: Association for Supervision and Curriculum Development, 1964).

Louise M. Rosenblatt, *The Reader, the Text, the Poem* (Carbondale, IL: Southern Illinois University Press, 1978).

Hermine Sinclair, in Foreword to E. Ferreiro and A. Teberosky, *Literacy Before Schooling,* translation from Spanish by Karen Goodman (Exeter, NH: Heineman Educational Books, 1982).

Hilda Taba, lecture given at Merrill-Palmer Institute, Detroit, MI, March 11, 1963.

Robert White, "Motivation Reconsidered: The Concept of Competence," *Psychological Review,* 1959.

6

Development of Thought with Language

In Greek philosophy the very term *logos* always suggested and supported the idea of a fundamental identity between the act of speech and the act of thought.

(Ernst Cassirer, 1956)

Thinking and reasoning have been studied systematically as aspects of the search for meaning in the symbolic transformation of experience. Some of the findings have been selected for discussion here because they contribute to an understanding in the educational process.

The question of how much language there is in thinking is a useless one, because it is impossible to see or to hear the inner thinking process. Investigators can only surmise from observing behaviors and hearing expressions that seem to be manifestations of thinking processes. Obviously, there are aspects of thinking that do not involve language, such as observations in which a child sees adult behavior in one situation and then applies it reasonably to another. Manners and customs are largely formed through this variety of abductive thinking. The little girl who always scrapes the imaginary toast in the sink when playing house because she observes her mother or father doing this one morning is thinking without words.

Apes are able to communicate their thought structures only by doing what they represent or by giving simple signals and gestures; humans, however, can tell about their actions and give their reasons for them, even writing them down for someone's use 100 years later. The human miracle—language—is crucial to the highly sophisticated thinking that distinguishes humanity from the apes and lesser species. Thoughts above the habitual level—and human habit patterns can be quite complex—are so infused with language and so dependent on its load of meaning in word and syntax that language surely is more than a mere carrier of thought. Wordless symbolic structures can be organized from observations, but to be recognized in terms of past experiences and the collective experience of people, these rarefied structures have to draw upon language.

Sign modes of communication other than language, such as music and the arts, behave in the same way as languages when they become infused with the artist's thoughts to the point where artists say, "I can see it on canvas" or "I can hear it in notes."

Language and thinking are so interrelated in most forms of sophisticated thinking that they must be dealt with together. Psychologists need to be interested in the question of where language and thought are separated, but educators need to be concerned with where they fit together, because language is the main vehicle for the teaching of thinking and reasoning. The verbal stages of thought are those that are most manifest and visible. Teachers, of course, must also be aware of the nonverbal aspects of thinking; some problems in geometry and in physics, especially those in which a pictured symbol conveys a thought, are of this variety. However, most of the thinking in classroom situations will involve language structures as well as personal sensorimotor and imagistic structures.

Kinds of Thinking

Several kinds of thinking must be considered. Robert Thompson describes six possibilities. (Thompson, 1959, pp. 13–14)

1. *Autistic thinking:* daydreaming, fantasy making, idle flitting from one half-formed notion to another, expressing underlying wishes and needs
2. *Remembering:* recalling happenings in the past and describing them, trying to think of how one did something
3. *Concentrating:* thinking about what one is doing, sticking with a problem
4. *Imagining:* thinking ahead to possible solutions and their feasibility, projecting present knowns into fanciful new combinations, playing around with ideas
5. *Believing:* valuing one thing or feeling over another, judging one action over another, expressing attitudes of taste or distaste, attacking or defending emotional stances
6. *Reasoning:* reflecting about a happening in the light of past experience, deliberating about an idea in view of knowns or givens, pondering over several possible solutions, hypothesizing possibilities, checking out alternatives, raising questions

All these types of thinking may occur in the classroom and, consequently, may be nurtured there. Although "reasoning" is generally considered to be the highest form of thinking, the other forms are as important. Daydreaming may well be the means to intuitive flashes, particularly when it is combined with remembering. The affective or emotive ways of thinking are most responsible for artistic expression. Who is to say which demonstrates more knowing—a formula by Einstein or a fugue by Bach? Teachers must be sensitive to all types of thinking; they must be able to recognize them and to know how to nourish them. A program in the creative arts is not offered merely to provide activity or to permit a legitimate means for working off aggressions; the arts must be in the school program to generate and refine thinking and to teach children how to respond to these other-than-rational or literal kinds of thought.

Divergent and Convergent Thinking

Getzel and Jackson (1962) report investigations of Guilford's notion that there are two different modes of thinking. Basically, these two modes are:

Convergent thinking, in which the individual converges on patterns in a logical manner, a narrowing of prospects in the field, a closing in of definition as already established. These are tested or seen in new situations.

Divergent thinking, in which the individual moves out from a given situation and imagines many divergent possibilities, breaking away from formula and past or established interpretations, experimenting and exploring with novel combinations. (Getzel and Jackson, 1962, pp. 14, 51, 76, 127)

Both modes are essential to the advancement of learning. However, experiments showed that in school, divergent thinking by children generally was ignored by teachers and in many instances children were penalized for indulging in it. The divergent thinker is likely to be the child who is constantly interrupting an orderly discussion with a "far out" idea that sounds as if it were off the subject; actually, it may be very much to the point, even though it leaps out of conventional and conformist thought. Divergent thinking is the kind of thinking that moves the bounds of knowledge outward. This mode must be cultivated as carefully as the step-by-step processes of logical thought that are so highly rewarded in the school situations of exercises and tests.

Language becomes flat and sterile when it is overrefined in the convergent mode; in the divergent mode it expands and extends as it does in the mind of the poet. Careful syllogism lends itself to convergent thinking; expansive metaphor is useful for divergent thinking. Both of these modes of thinking and their language need to be cultivated in school.

In the following example, the sources of this 6-year-old's syllogism are obvious, and the combination is primerish, but the form of thinking exemplifies a syntax of convergent thinking:

This is Dick.
Dick is eating snow.
Snow is radioactive.
Dick is eating too much snow.
Dick is radioactive.

A teacher's questions and directions of the following types encourage convergent thinking: What is this most like? List all the ones that are the same. Knowing this, how would you account for that? A glance over the kinds of questions asked on standardized tests will reveal other examples of the language that encourages convergent thinking.

When a fifth-grader says that "a globe is a rolled-up map" instead of repeating the dictionary definition, the teacher must stop to listen and take the divergent route with the child. In such instances the child's thought may lead to a splendid discovery. When a girl says, "God's eyes are the eyes of lobsters which can see all around," she is using the metaphorical language of divergent thinking.

Control of Language over Thinking and of Thinking over Language

Language has a certain amount of control over thinking. The collective or public way of describing something or of analyzing the processes of some phenomenon persists if only through the confirmation of long-time repetition. Some linguists have conjectured that language patterns control thought patterns. This position may seem extreme to those who expect originality from the individual mind, but even they must admit that the power of language over thinking—especially in the young—is very strong.

Halliday has put the learning of language in its most general context: learning how to mean. In this he sees language development as being shaped and guided by the need for people to understand and be understood, and in turn the language shapes the way learners think the thoughts they are attempting to express:

A child who is learning his first language is learning how to mean; in this perspective, the linguistic system is to be seen as a semantic potential. It is a range of possible meanings, together with the means whereby these meanings are realized, or expressed. . . . The human brain would have been capable of constructing a hundred and one different types of semiotic system; why is it that language evolved in this particular way . . . with the particular properties it has? . . . We can see that the adult linguistic system is structured in a way which reflects very closely its functional origins. (Halliday, 1975, p. 8)

Two Views of Children's Thinking and Language: Piaget and Vygotsky

Language and thinking cannot be discussed without reference to the somewhat divergent positions of the two most esteemed investigators of children's thinking in this century, Lev Semenovich Vygotsky and Jean Piaget. Working separately, one at the University of Moscow and the other at the University of Geneva, they developed similar concepts about human cognitive development while basing their ideas on somewhat different views of language. A review of their positions regarding language and thinking is pertinent here, because it will summarize the significance of language in thinking and suggest implications for teaching children.

Piaget's Position

The following quotations present the crux of Piaget's argument that a purely sensorimotor type of thought symbolizing precedes and is separate from the translation of those thought symbols into the signs (words) of language.

Words are probably not a short-cut to a better understanding. . . . The level of understanding seems to modify the language that is used, rather than vice versa. . . . Mainly, language serves to translate what is already understood; or else language may even present a danger if it is used to introduce an idea which is not yet accessible. (Piaget, quoted in Duckworth, 1964)

Piaget views language as an outside agent in children's developing thought that comes to serve them by translating their personal symbols or symbolic structure into collective or societal meanings. Children's use of speech and language does not substantially affect the development of personal symbolic structures. They are independently made. As children come to understand language, they have to assimilate and then accommodate the lingual signs to their thought structures, but if they are to find their own meaning, the symbolic structuring must come first and not be confused by adult language structures. Following their own symbolizing, children then translate their thoughts into language and come to terms with adult signs. Of course, the symbolizing and then the verbalizing frequently occur almost simultaneously, but Piaget seems to view them as separate operations. Unless the teacher begins with children's spontaneous structures, adult language as it influences the symbolic structuring is likely to confuse their thinking or allow them to settle for a verbalized statement of an idea without knowing what it means. Piaget based this position on his vast experience in recording and analyzing children's symbolic play and their manipulation of objects. Children can show without words that they understand some ideas by the way they manipulate objects in play and in problematical situations.

Teachers need to take warning from Piaget's notion and to consider his advice. Teachers have, in the past, presented children with an idea to be learned in adult language (that is, in the watered-down adult language of textbooks or in "teacher talk") and then called for examples or set up experiments or demonstrations to show the concept. Typical science or social studies texts or even teacher-made lesson plans often reveal this process.

The trend of educators to structure concepts from the organizational patterns of the disciplines for presentation to children can fall into the same trap. It can force adult language structures upon children's thinking as "subject-matter" teaching did. Piaget's advice is worth consideration: "The question comes up whether to teach the structure or to present the child with situations where he is active and creates the structures himself." (Duckworth, p. 3) He points out that the goal of education is to "create the possibilities for a child to invent and discover" and then warns:

> When we teach too fast, we keep the child from inventing and discovering himself. . . . Teaching means creating situations where structures can be discovered; it does not mean transmitting structures which may be assimilated at nothing other than a verbal level. (Duckworth, p. 3)

Piaget does, however, view language as a key element of social interaction. It is only through an exchange of ideas with adults and other youngsters that the developing child moves from a subjective point of view (egocentricity) to an objective and socialized outlook.

Vygotsky's Position

In contrast to Piaget's emphasis on the structuring of thought symbols by observation and manipulation of the environment prior to the injection of language, Vygotsky's emphasis is on the language of the children and the adult teacher in the creation of thought.

> The language of the environment, with its stable, permanent meanings, points the way that the child's generalizations will take. The adult cannot pass on to the child his mode of thinking. He merely supplies the ready-made meaning of a word, around which the child forms a complex [concept or idea cluster]. . . . The lines along which a complex develops are predetermined by the meaning a given word already has in the language of adults. . . . Verbal intercourse with adults thus becomes a powerful factor in the development of the child's concepts. (Vygotsky, 1954, pp. 67, 69)

Vygotsky's view then is similar to Halliday's. As children learn language they also learn how to mean things the way their elders do. From Piaget the impression is gained that the schemas or cognitive structures are thought connections involving language but not built of language necessarily, whereas from Vygotsky a picture of conceptual structures built through symbolic language is conceived. The early interaction between the child's complexes (similar to Piaget's notion of structures or schemas) and the language of the environment is crucial. The child's egocentric speech becomes the inner speech that is the shorthand of thinking. This speech is not accompanying thought; it "serves mental orientation and conscious understanding." "Inner speech is not the interior aspect of external speech—it is a function in itself." (p. 133) It still remains speech—that is, thought connected with language. Vygotsky views thought as nonlingual, a "subtext" that is conceived all at once, not in a linear grammar like language; he places inner speech, however, just prior to the emergence of a meaning and sees it as the first step toward preparing a thought for communication. He concludes:

> Thought and language, which reflect reality in a way different from that of perception, are the key to the nature of human consciousness. Words play a central part not only in the development of thought but in the historical growth of consciousness as a whole. A word is a microcosm of human consciousness. (p. 153)

From this position Vygotsky, like Halliday, shows great concern for the dialogue between children and adult teachers, in contrast with Piaget's concern for self-discovery before adult language is introduced. The environmental language is as real in Vygotsky's view as the objects in the environment and is pivotal to the development of children's thinking. Words have vague meaning for children even before the children can speak, and therefore language helps shape their first thinking. The development of thinking is enhanced by the presentation of scientific concepts (collective adult statements, knowledge) to children as the child's spontaneous concepts become organized in relation to the adult structure. Vygotsky says, "It is our contention that the rudiments of systematization first enter the child's mind by way of his contact with scientific concepts, changing their psychological structure from the top down." (p. 93)

Vygotsky's experiments showed that children could deal more readily with "because" and "although" thinking in scientific concepts developed in school than in everyday concepts developed spontaneously. (p. 107) However, this does not mean that concepts are only realized from the top down. Scientific concepts, on the other hand, cannot develop unless certain basic generalizations have developed in the spontaneity of living; for example, historical concepts can develop only when the child has a generalized sense of "in the past and now."

When making the investigations reported in *Thought and Language*, Vygotsky was more concerned with the effect of environmental language and adult instruction on thinking than was Piaget in his developmental studies of the growth of children's intelligence. Vygotsky may, perhaps, have overstressed the influence of adult language on thinking. Nevertheless, teachers need to be wary of the influence of their language and their structured concepts upon the learning of children. What the teacher says when developing ideas in the classroom has a profound effect upon children's conceptual development. A faulty concept or a misconception presented to children could seriously delay the child's development of a scientific concept.

A Compromise Position

A position between Piaget's and Vygotsky's could be taken, which would be useful educationally. This position embraces a concept of "dialogue" as defined by Halliday in which the language of children and the language of the adult teachers are brought into interplay at every stage of the development of language and thinking, including an initial "discovery" period. The collective language of the adults in a society is as potent a factor in the development of thinking as the children's own spontaneous formation of structures of relationships drawn from experience. Even though Piaget did not stress language in developing his notion of developmental stages in thinking, certain forms of adult dialogue with children are obviously most appropriate for supporting and encouraging the development of thinking at a particular stage, especially if the adult talk raises questions or alters the situation. This process causes a decentering of older children's point of view, thus fostering objective thinking. The limitations and potential of the children's egocentric and developmentally emerging speech-thoughts need to be recognized. At each stage of children's intellectual development, the adult's teaching language must be appropriately congruent with the children's learning language.

Overall Processes in the Development of Thinking

Both Piaget and Vygotsky postulated and described several stages in the development of thinking. Although the descriptions were built from different data, they correspond roughly and can be combined to aid teachers in considering the thinking capabilities of their students.

Readers must not mistake either Vygotsky's stages of concept development or Piaget's stages in the growth of thought for distinct periods or ages in a child's life when a certain behavior is exhibited, as is done in the usual developmental psychology. Rather, these stages are descriptions of a style, or a mode of thinking, which children use in coming to terms with their environment. When children have exploited and explored a way of thinking sufficiently to have developed the schemas (Piaget) or the complexes (Vygotsky) that will support the next way of thinking, they move on. Thought structures are built that will support new relationships and connections. Children will move from one stage of complexity to the next, depending on richness of experiential background, quality of dialogue with adults and peers, and concomitant neurological development.

Teachers need not only to keep these stages in mind as they plan experiences and "dialogue" activities for their children but also to recognize the limitations and exploit the possibilities of each stage. Children need lots of appropriate practice (perhaps play is a better word) in each stage of thinking to build a base for the ensuing stage. However, these stages are not discarded once children enter the next one, for adults probably use different types of thinking in all stages, depending on the situation and the level of their thinking about a certain matter.

Decentering the Child's View: From Egocentricity to Objectivity

Language and cognitive development are just as important as emotional or social development. They are all closely related. Teachers may either underestimate the stage of development of pupils and never stretch their thinking or may over-estimate their stage of development and never reach them. Baby talk and over-simplification of ideas and language can hold children's thinking back just as effectively as overly formalized language tactics can leave them behind. The value of dialogue between children and their peers and between younger and older children cannot be overstressed. Arrangement for such occasions, which will assist in "decentering" points of view, can be a part of the teacher's strategy in exploiting a stage and leading toward the next. Teachers do not think and speak as children in these stages, but they question and present adult structures at strategic points in the classroom dialogue. They should listen to the children and watch their manipulations, reset situations, introduce new materials, add information, raise appropriate questions, and talk with the children about what they see and think.

A key concept from both Piaget and Vygotsky is that teaching doesn't cause learning; it supports it. Teachers need to see themselves as monitors of learning, carefully observing and offering support when it is needed.

Ferreiro and Teberosky point out this Piagetian view of the roles of teachers and methods in relation to learning:

> The concept of learning (understood as the process of obtaining knowledge) in herent to genetic psychology rests on the basic assumption that there are learning processes that do not depend on methods. . . . A method may help or hinder, facilitate or complicate, but not create learning. Obtaining knowledge is the result of the learner's own activity. . . . An active learner compares, excludes, orders, categorizes, reformulates, confirms, forms hypotheses, and reorganizes through internalized action (thought) or through effective action (according to the level of development). A learner who carries something out according to instructions or a model provided by someone is not, usually, an intellectually active learner. (Ferreiro and Teberosky, 1982, p. 15)

Assimilation and Accommodation

Before a description of stages is made, some discussion of a general process of learning to think is needed in order to show what is happening in each stage and what brings children to the climax of one stage and prepares them for the next. Piaget's formulation has been developed systematically and is congruent in part with Vygotsky's general view of process. (Flavell, 1963)

As the individual meets a new situation, new data is assimilated into old related material; at the same time, these older ideas are accommodated to the new.

This is an adaptive process much like biological adaptation. These clusters of thought (connections of inner speech, meanings, images, and feelings) that form, much as cells grow and multiply, are called structures, schemas, or complexes of concepts:

> A basic principle of this theory is that stimuli do not act directly but are trans-
> formed by the individual's assimilation systems (or assimilation schemes). In this
> act of transformation, the individual gives an interpretation to the stimulus . . .
> and only by virtue of this interpretation does the behavior of the individual be-
> come comprehensible. (Ferreiro and Teberosky, p. 13)

These schemas are not viewed as linear additions or associations or as stimulus-response connections, but more as *gestalten* (configurational totalities whose properties exceed the mere sum of the parts). In concept they are more biological (like cellular growth) than psychological in the connectionist sense. Vygotsky gives the proper impression in a general description of the process.

> The development of the processes which eventually result in concept formation
> begins in earliest childhood, but the intellectual functions that in a specific com-
> bination form the psychological basis of the process of concept formation ripen,
> take shape and develop only at puberty. Before that age, we find certain in-
> tellectual formations that perform functions similar to those of the genuine con-
> cepts to come. With regard to their composition, structure, and operation, these
> functional equivalents of concepts stand in the relation to true concepts as the
> embryo to the fully formed organism. (Vygotsky, p. 58)

Formation of Thought Schemas

Schemas become extended and enriched through both a horizontal *decalage* (coupling) happening within a stage, and a vertical decalage happening through maturity in the next stage. Horizontal decalage is a rehearsal of a cognitive structure gained in one situation by working it out in a slightly different situation.

A young boy in the concrete operational stage has classified "rowboat" and "sailboat" as boats in a seashore situation. When he visits a lake and sees a canoe for the first time, he assimilates it into his class "boats" and then accommodates to it with some differences noted regarding shape and kind of locomotion. Several years later in the stage of formal logic, upon the child's seeing an ocean liner, a vertical decalage would occur. Rather than simply adding to his conglomerate classification by the criterion of one attribute, "goes in water," he would build generalized classes and subclasses based upon a concept of the difference between boats and ships, taking first the viewpoint of a sailor and then that of a traveler. A new type of thought process, logical abstraction, has extended and made more complex the earlier and simpler schema.

The main difference between the early and later schemas is that the earlier "boat" is viewed from only one position (the egocentric) and is held together by one simple attribute, whereas the later schema has developed from taking the view of different people (objective and social) and is intricately bound by a principle.

The older child can hold the concept of boats as objects that go in water while at the same time considering them as carriers. The child can then conserve those two ideas as he or she looks at "boats" according to naval tradition. This is the process of growth of schemas or concept clusters. The developmental goal is decentering, moving away from cognitive egocentricity toward objectivity. The result will be socialized, cooperative thinking in abstractions of principles and guiding themes that encourage hypothesizing and testing of new ideas.

Motivation for Thinking and Language Learning

Vygotsky and Piaget differ somewhat in their explanations of motivation for intellectual development, but they agree that neither the systematized "drives" of the behaviorists nor the primary "instinct" of the Freudians are suitable explanations. Instead, they suggest that there is self-activation to growing in the intellectual dimension, just as there is in the individual's physical growth.

Vygotsky, from his Marxist orientation, emphasizes the social aspects of development. He suggests that the tasks with which society confronts children prompt initiation of the cognitive processes; if this process does not occur naturally, he suggests that it is the role of the adult and the teacher to so set the environment that these tasks will be more evident. (Vygotsky, p. 55)

Piaget, on the other hand, emphasizes more the individual aspects of development. He suggests that an independent exploratory drive and the need to make sense of the physical world are responsible for motivating the thinking process. Children are seen as striving to structure their world with meaning; pupils are active participators in the world, who convert it to their own terms. (Duckworth, p. 3) There need be no devised incentive; the life processes of knowing and adapting are sufficient to explain learning to think.

Lessons for Teachers

These views of learning are complementary. They are optimistic, positive, and transactive. They challenge teachers to support the process of thinking and not to impede its natural progress. In general, the stages of development of thinking as envisioned by Piaget and Vygotsky are supported by mounting evidence through experimentation in many cultures with many individuals. There will undoubtedly be alterations in this concept as research continues. Teachers need to help children stretch their thinking horizontally in the stage in which they are, as well as to support their vertical movement toward the stage that is coming. They should remember that because of individual differences individual children may be at different stages in different areas of cognitive content and that children in the same age group may be generally at different stages.

One of the major mistakes of teaching the so-called basics, reading, writing, and arithmetic, is the reduction of these to a series of abstract skills isolated from the processes in functional use. This is done on the premise that focusing on mastery of such a sequence is the way to simplify learning of complex processes.

Yet children can learn easily when the processes are made concrete in functional use, and they have a much harder time learning isolated abstract skills, such as matching letters to sounds or blending kuh-a-tuh to make *cat*.

Ferreiro and Teberosky (1982) respond to such artificial methodologies from their Piagetian point of view:

> Today we know (again from Piaget's work) that this position is unsustainable regarding elementary math. In the process of acquiring elementary numerical notions children construct logical thought. . . . Piaget's work . . . destroys in its very foundations the conception of first grade math as the acquisition of a non-reasoned mechanistic procedure.

> Our question is: doesn't the same thing occur with reading and writing? . . . What is the justification for beginning with mechanical calculations of phoneme-grapheme correspondences to proceed later, and only later to comprehending written texts?

Ferreiro and Teberosky point up the irony that teachers in both Spanish and English speaking countries often use conflicting teaching practices in dealing with math as compared to reading and writing. "They are Piagetians (or try to be) at math time and associationists (sometimes without meaning to be) at reading time." In their view both math and reading instruction should be based on a view of children as "creative, active, and intelligent" rather than "passive, receptive and ignorant." (pp. 14, 15)

References

Ernst Cassirer, *Essay on Man* (New York: Anchor Doubleday, 1956).

Eleanor Duckworth, "Piaget Rediscovered," *Elementary Science Study Newsletter,* June 1964.

Emilia Ferreiro and Ana Teberosky, *Literacy Before Schooling* (Exeter, NH: Heineman, 1982).

J. Flavell, *The Developmental Psychology of Jean Piaget* (Princeton, NJ: Van Nostrand, 1963).

J. Getzel and P. Jackson, *Creativity and Intelligence* (New York: Wiley, 1962).

Michael Halliday, *Learning How to Mean* (London: Edward Arnold, 1975).

Robert Thompson, *The Psychology of Thinking* (Baltimore: Penguin, 1959).

Lev Vygotsky, *Thought and Language* (Cambridge, MA: M.I.T. Press, 1954).

7

Structuring in Thought: Meaning

... myth, art, language, and science appear as symbols; not in the sense of mere figures which refer to some given reality by means of suggestion and allegorical renderings, but in the sense of forces each of which produces and posits a world of its own. . . . Thus the special symbolic forms are not imitations, but organs of reality, since it is solely by their agency that anything real becomes an object for intellectual apprehension.

(Ernst Cassirer, 1946)

Categorical Thinking

Psychologists Gordon Allport and Jerome Bruner have found the formulation "structuring categories" helpful in describing and analyzing a major aspect of thinking and language. They view the individual as classifying and categorizing events in various ways for the sake of mental economy. The human mind cannot hold, nor does it need to hold, all the specifics of the world. It needs only to collect and combine in categories of relationships those specifics that, when put together, help people make sense of the world and guide them in acting. To put a number of events together into one category is an easy way to remember them and provides a convenient means for deciding on reactions to similar events. Overly simplified categorization brings stereotype and prejudice, whereas reflective and deliberative categorization can bring insight and effectiveness of action. Interrelated clusters of categories become structures of knowing for individuals; when formulated by communities of scholars, categorical and propositional structures become accepted "knowledge."

Studies of Prejudicial Categorizing

Allport, in *The Nature of Prejudice,* developed the concept of *categorization* in relation to the problem of racial and religious prejudices. Categories, in his view, are little generalizations drawn from instances in experience. (Allport, 1958, p. 19)

In their simplest terms they are first-order generalizations tying one simple concept to another according to a theme. After seeing many instances of houses—our house, the house across the street, the house in the city, the hut of a Bantu, the log cabin of a pioneer, the Navajo hogan—the child generalizes "house," and a category is formed. Then Aunt Sara's apartment, Mom's office, and the hospital are eliminated from the category "house" as they are perceived, although they may have been so included when four walls and a roof were the defining attributes that differentiated "house." A category may be extended and revised by finer distinctions; it may become clustered with related categories as the process of making sense out of the world proceeds. Each person's categories and the language that shapes and holds them are personal.

On the other hand, individuals may leap too quickly to categories and settle for a few strongly impressionable instances to make their quick categories. The young white children who wrote the following reactions to "Negro" have, insofar as these expressions reveal their categories, a very limited concept of "Negro."

The first one, by a 6-year-old, has some positive value content. Even so, his category excludes the Negro from the category "Americans." Given a young boy's interest in sports, it is not hard to imagine how this category developed.

> They are good athletes. Most Negro men are good tackles, good in basketball and baseball. They are good jumpers and they are strong. Negroes are stronger than Americans.

A negative instance, reinforced by parental agreement, left this impression with another 6-year-old. Even if the following represents only one aspect of his category of Negro, it is already a prejudiced, closed category that may take years to open.

> Negroes have brown skin. They usually don't work. They are asleep on the job. Negroes don't understand our language and I don't think they can learn it.

Some children, even very young ones, are disposed to keep their categories open-ended and tentative. As one 7-year-old stated:

> I think they're kind of nice and it isn't right to separate them. People are people whatever color they are.

Categories may be rational, irrational, flavored with emotionality of all sorts, or coldly calculating. Some are "autistic," very personally and even selfishly centered; others are freer in their associations and more objective in their outlook. They are built on language, and words become their labels. The speaker who uses racial, religious, or ethnic epithets probably holds a very different category from the one who speaks of Irish-Americans, Afro-Americans, or Italian-Americans. The importance of category labels is well illustrated by the deliberate drive among many "Negro" groups to refuse that label as one imposed by hostile whites and to accept for themselves instead the labels "Afro-American" or "black."

Generally, categories tend to resist change, since they are built by incorporating each new but similar exemplar. However, open-minded people keep their categories tentative. The ability to tolerate tentativeness is in part a personality trait and is difficult to cultivate in someone who does not possess it. On the other hand, open-mindedness can be learned, especially when individuals realize that they will find advantages and satisfaction in being able to look at alternatives. The mind and emotions can be disciplined when personal goals are developed that require self-discipline. In homes and in classrooms in which judgments are not hasty, children can learn by example to be more deliberative about making categories. The inquiry or discovery method of teaching can discourage the making of closed categories and encourage the habit of creating open categories.

Allport's view was not optimistic, because he felt that the individual modes of categorizing are learned so early in the social, emotional, and conceptual set of a family that little can be done through education. Change in categorizing would mean personality change, and that is a slow, complex process. His view that personality is behind categorization points up the close tie between the development of language and that of personality. Parental categorizations impress children, especially when the categories carry high emotional content. Because teachers are viewed by children as parent surrogates, they need to learn how to listen carefully to themselves for the prejudiced categories they may be passing on. They are the models of secondary identification for children. Teachers also need to listen more intelligently to youngsters' emerging categories, for they may reveal the way the youngsters are viewing life about them and show the shape of their attitudes. "All categories," writes Allport, "engender meaning upon the world. Like paths in a forest they give order to our life-space." (Allport, 1958, p. 171)

Despite Allport's pessimism, he stated that educators can lead pupils to open-mindedness and tolerance for ambiguity. Categories can be altered, widened, and extended by strategies of teaching that assault the closed category with opposing proofs and highly emotional attributes of a positive nature.

The study of emotive language, whether it be in journalism, advertising, oratory, or schoolyard fights, can be useful. Demonstrating its power and influence can be helpful in teaching children to objectify categorization. Children need to see that the emotive language that expresses categories is not good or bad in itself but that judgments based on value decisions and expressed in language are crucial. Children will understand, because they understand name calling. Perhaps middle childhood is the strategic teaching period for opening up prejudiced categories.

Gillham reports on an experimental social studies program for extending children's "life-space" in a western community bordering on an Indian reservation. It included class experiences with a third grade designed to attack the category "dirty Indians." After a positive experience with Indian children who had made a visit to their school, constructive dialogues between teacher and children and then between children and parents succeeded, for a while at least, in altering the category of "our neighbors." (Gillham, 1958)

Leaving categorization to pure chance is abdication of education. In guiding children's judgmental thinking toward rational categories, teachers and parents can contribute to the sanity of society.

The Categorization Process

On the subject of categorizing, Allport is the activist, and Bruner is the investigator. Because Bruner is mainly concerned with the "how" of categorization, his experimentation deals mostly with nonlingual matters in order to give objectivity to the experiments. In searching out the strategies individuals use for concept attainment—the locating of "predictive defining attributes that distinguish exemplars from nonexemplars of a class"—the experimenters used abstract pictograms, each slightly different from the others. (Bruner et al., 1956; Brown, 1958; Bruner et al., 1966)

Even though language was not stressed in these studies, it is clear from other writings by Bruner that without the "instrumentality" of language, categorization could not take place in much of everyday life. Words permit the holding of categories in memory and create the possibility of altering them and using them in prediction.

The theory of categorizing is based on the apparent need of the human organism to "reduce the complexity of his environment" by "sorting out" and structuring aspects of it that for one significance or another are useful in understanding the environment and in being instrumental in it. People can put happenings in perspective and can anticipate future events by this means. By "ordering and relating classes of events" and "establishing categories based on defining attributes" they can "reduce the necessity of constant learning." (Bruner et al., 1956, pp. 12–15) A concrete example can serve to explain Bruner's terminology.

Children identify food that they eat as something outside themselves. Eventually, some of that food is identified as vegetable, fruit, meat, and so on. "Food" in this situation is an identity category. At the same time, children might be making further identifications about the same object but in such a different situation that a separate category is set up for the time being. They form categories as they grasp at pretty blossoms in the flower bed or pull a hanging leaf from a lettuce plant in the vegetable garden. As their language develops, words begin to stand for the category as further differentiations are made.

The eventual putting together of these several identities into a hypothesis of relationships is concept formation. Some plants are edible and called food, and/or some plants grow in moist places, while some grow in drier places. A boy buys a plant which he does not know is a cactus at the store. At home he waters it frequently as he does with his other plants, but it dies. His eventual decision, after relating the event to previous concepts of "desert" and "plant," to place it in the category of "desert plant" is part of the process of attaining a concept of environmental relationships.[1]

Bruner and his associates have observed other forms of categorizing based on different types of equivalences that people draw. They also have investigated the ways that people develop categories and the ways that they test their validity.

The exciting lingual-cognitive procedures of categorizing in identifing new instances or playing with the possibilities of new categorical themes are ways for people to discover new relationships in the universe. In this manner they construct their own cognitive maps of the world, a reference for intelligent living. It is the teacher's duty and privilege to assist in the cartography.

Educational Implications Regarding Categorical Thinking

This view of a personal way of cognitively structuring one's world suggests possibilities for curriculum planning and instructional methodology. A number of categorical themes crucial to an understanding of the environment could be set down, and samples of subcategories that support the themes might be delineated. Categories involved in people's relation to water might be one such theme. Teachers could help learners build strategies of categorization that would eventually reveal the themes (important generalizations). However, the teacher's main

[1]Adapted from the text of Bruner's discussion of categorization in *A Study of Thinking* (1956). Examples are the authors'.

strategy, after thinking about some of the subcategories, would be to set the stage—the classroom environment—in such a way that the children would develop their own categories and relationships between categories. The *empty category,* Bruner's term (Bruner et al., 1956 p. 14) for an open-ended category, should be encouraged; in this category the students go beyond the conventional groupings and imagine their own. Teachers encourage the use of cues already identified to anticipate what might follow and what might be possible. With careful questioning attributes can be eliminated or incorporated.

Categorizing Games

Students can take a theme and categorize objects or situations in one way; then they can change the theme and point of view and categorize the same instances in another way, eliminating and adding as required. Different strategies for attaining concepts can be explored while the efficient ones are encouraged. Present categories can be used for predicting future possibilities to encourage children to do some original thinking. The theme "the work we do" in a career education curriculum suggests many opportunities for categorizing occupations and their relation to various social and economic factors. Here is an open questioning strategy for group categorizing games:

1. Make a list of everything we can think of about "work and jobs."
2. Now designate with an appropriate symbol all those that seem to fit together.
3. Choose a label for those with the same symbol.
4. If some fit under two or more labels, think of new labels for them.
5. Which label would you like to be the focus of your study?

Teachers must, however, be aware of "teaching at the child's level" by accepting all responses and letting the learners decide which items are valid under which category.

The injection of a "noisy" attribute into the discussion can disrupt the process. Very often the affective or emotional equivalence will dominate the categorizing of children and obstruct more important equivalences. Rejection of the slimy feeling of a frog may delay the categorizing into the class of amphibian and reptile. Teachers can inadvertently introduce a "noisy" attribute of this kind by an offhand remark or a show of feeling of their own. Exploration of categorical possibilities, on the other hand, is a challenge both to the teacher and the children.

Noncategorical Thinking

Logical, rational thinking can be developed in many ways, but such thinking must not be developed to the exclusion of the nonrational modes of thought. In *Essays for the Left Hand,* Bruner describes the artistic and aesthetic modes of thinking as different from the logical, step-by-step process of concept formation and attainment, which he calls "right-handed thinking."

> The elegant rationality of science and the metaphoric non-rationality of art operate with deeply different grammars; perhaps they even represent a profound com-

plementarity. One is at the center of awareness as desire: it is directed toward achieving an end and is specialized to the tasks of finding means. The other is at the fingers of awareness, a flow of rich and surprising fantasy, a tangled reticle of associations that gives fleeting glimpses of past occasions, of disappointments and triumphs, of pleasures and unpleasures. It is the stuff of which James' stream of consciousness was made. (Bruner, 1962)

Noncategorical thinking has been either neglected in formal education or taught inadequately under the guise of "appreciation" of art, music, and literature. These aesthetic modes of thinking are discussed in other sections of this book as presentational symbols. Their inclusion in the curriculum should be founded upon their value as ways of thinking about the world. Today's students need to practice both "left-handed" and "right-handed" ways of thinking if they are to experience the whole of life and not just the scientific-technological aspect of it.

The Disciplines of Study

The works of Piaget, Vygotsky, Allport, Bruner, and others describe kinds of structures in individual thinking: operational schemas, symbolic structures, and language structures in various combinations. Piaget and Vygotsky find that children structure their experiences into thought in different ways at different stages of their development. Allport and Bruner observe that the adult formulates structures of thought into categories and thematic formations. George Kelly views the personality as an integrated cluster of concepts, or personal constructs or systems of life interpretation, that predispose an individual to act and to talk in a certain way. People, collectively, cluster and structure ideas into aggregate knowing. (Kelly, 1963)

Aggregate Knowing

The launching of satellites, the moon walks, and the ecology and energy crises of the 1970's and the 1980's are examples of those rare moments when whole populations have to come to terms with new discoveries in their environment. The modern speedup of communication caused people around the globe to be confronted almost instantaneously by the arrival of the first space explorations. Another similar event in modern times was the announcement of the exploding of the first nuclear bomb. It is significant that although government scientists had already done their symbolizing much earlier at the firing of the first nuclear device at Alamogordo, the public could not begin to respond until the bombing at Hiroshima and Nagasaki.

In earlier times, the symbolic reaction to new discoveries took generations as the symbolic process filtered down from scholars and scientists to the people. The delayed reactions to the genetic theory and the theory of relativity are impressive examples. The Copernican theories took even longer to disturb the public into rethinking the relationship of the earth to the sun and the universe.

Sometimes the public is slow to incorporate a new phenomenon into its conceptual scheme for reasons other than slowness of communication. In the context of World War II, the use of nuclear bombs did not seem as unthinkable as it did later when a fuller understanding of the horror was realized. Darwin's theory of evolution was widely (and violently) discussed in newspapers and magazines shortly after he published it. However, negative emotion ("He may have descended from an ape, but we didn't") and misconception delayed assimilation of the theory as a public concept.

Today, the theory of relativity in relation to time, space, and speed is becoming a more comprehensible concept to the public as we have more experience with satellites, manned space shuttles, and lunar vehicle launchings. Eventually, most people will have a reasonably accurate conception of this theory as more experience is interpreted and symbolized in light of the theory and through science fiction as well as scientific accounts. They will possess a language for coping with incidents involving relativity.

Evolving Fields of Knowledge

The great minds are the first conceivers; they develop the first new conceptions of the universe and the interrelationships within it. Scholars in a burst of language activity reorganize, restate, and reformulate these theories in terms of the particular and in relation to other bodies of knowledge. As each aspect of knowledge becomes more specialized, a new field is developed. It all began as philosophy. Originally, science was simply another word for knowing, the activity of philosophy. But beginning with Aristotle, perhaps before, the special categories of knowledge began to be developed.

As new discoveries were made by perceptive leaders, disciples followed them by conceptualizing the material into schools of thought; clinical psychology grew out of medicine and philosophy under the leadership of Freud and others as they developed new concepts of human emotions. Anthropology stemmed from biology and philosophy as new concepts under the leadership of Boas and others were developed from evolutionary theory and from the study of primitive cultures. New ways of exploring and studying the world of humanity were devised with each new discovery. A way of thinking, of looking at things, developed with each field. Although there have emerged some agreements and interrelationships, each field is a little different, depending not only on the style and the attitudes of the scholars attracted to the field but also on the differentiated content and methodology.

Today, these special fields are seen in any university catalogue, each with its own conceptual structures, approach to the life-situation, and ways of studying and working. These are called the disciplines, and each has been created in a sublanguage of its own.

The Structure of the Disciplines

The disciplines encompass far more than the personal knowings of any individual scholar. They are the established knowledge of the world at a given time, but inquiry goes on more rapidly now than ever before. New concepts overthrow old ones, and new investigations begin. Only a few years ago, the earth was conceived of as a somewhat flattened sphere. Now it is conceived of as pear shaped. The satellites were able to gather vast amounts of data quickly, and computers were able to process some of the new information within hours. A few closeup color TV pictures with accompanying descriptions by astronauts on the moon have swiftly changed concepts of that celestial body.

Each discipline views the world from a different vantage point, and, therefore, a special set of concepts is derived by a particular type of investigation. There are perhaps three major ways of looking at the world, and these are reflected in the great division of academic studies: (1) the natural sciences, (2) the social sciences, and (3) the arts and humanities. Within each of these three broad fields there are individual disciplines whose scholars investigate particular classes of phenomena.

A discipline is made up of the concepts, generalizations, and procedures of investigation that scholars and creative artists, looking at the world in a certain way, develop as they study a piece of the universe. It is the structure of the knowledge gained from their reflective examination of experience. Disciplines are made in a search for truth. Scholars are curious children grown up. While retaining their childhood zest for inquiry, they develop complex skills for quantifying and qualifying the world about them and for assessing the work of previous scholars. They build language by which phenomena can be studied, explained, and reflected upon. Curious children do the same, but with less sophisticated tools of investigation and more modest language means.

No one adult today, much less a young person, could possibly know all that is presently gathered in any one of the disciplines, although in Renaissance times this was thought possible. Students must come to know how to use disciplines to solve a problem or to understand a phenomenon. They cannot know all the content of the discipline, but they can learn how to work in a discipline and use its findings. They can begin to gain what Schwab calls the "syntax" of a discipline, the "pattern" of its procedure, "its method: how it goes about using its conceptions to attain its goals." (Schwab, 1961)

Language of the Disciplines
There are languages of physics and geology and biology, of psychology and sociology and geography, of economics and government, of history and philosophy, of art and literary criticism, and of such applied disciplines as engineering and education. The expertise of these disciplines involves an effort with language to embrace ideas that attempt to describe the world from different vantage points. The chemist describes and explores a world made up of a myriad of interactions of particles of matter. Each particle and compound is given a chemical name, and relationships between particles and compounds are described in shorthand sentences called *formulas* and *equations*. Knowing something of chemical views helps us appreciate the awesome natural phenomenon of chemical change and aids us in making everyday decisions about cooking, health care, and home repair. Young people learn to know their way around the world much better after seeing the universe of matter and force through the eyes of chemists and physicists. Viewing

the world like biologists can help us explain environmental pollution and the need for personal health. We can also learn to make wiser judgments about practical matters impinging on our lives and that of our fellows.

The language of psychology is interesting in that a most influential branch of it, psychoanalysis, was constructed by one man. The language and idea structures of Freud are fascinating metaphors, which when put together into his great scheme reveal a profound myth of the battle for survival of the self "ego," caught between the devil "id" and the archangel "superego." Freud's life and the lives of his followers were devoted to describing the odyssey of the "ego." This magnificent schema has helped reveal to people the ways of the personality; with continuing investigations of the formation and operation of personality, psychologists continue to alter and expand its concepts and language.

In music, too, there is a language that describes its processes and results. Music cannot be known entirely without knowledge of the musician's terms and of ways of talking about the art. The world of artful sound gains meaning as melody, counterpoint, harmony, color, and rhythm are understood in the context of music making. To teach children to "enjoy" or to "appreciate" music, as educators usually say, can hardly be accomplished with any significance unless children know what music is and how it is created. Understanding of the structure of music must not only be experienced but also talked about. The dialogue with the teacher will not only be concerned with the "pictures" children are sometimes asked to see as they listen to music but should also be concerned about the happenings in the musical structure and the means the composer used to create them.

Art has created a magnificent language of line, color, and form, while dance has created one of bodily movement and gesture in spatial designs.

What Schwab refers to as the "syntax" of the discipline—its pattern, its procedures, its methodology, and the language of its conceptions—are changed from time to time as concept revisions are forced by evaluation of new data. Students need to understand that the syntax of the disciplines is constantly changing and being renewed. The language of tentativeness in propositions and of playfulness in investigations, if used in the classroom, will impress upon children the dynamic quality of structuring thought that makes disciplines.

Structures for Teaching from the Disciplines

The structures of the disciplines are human attempts over time through the process of experimentation, deliberation, contemplation, and generalization to describe, explain, and imagine the universe. Each child makes the same attempt. The scholar's search for meaning in the world differs from the child's quest mainly in quality and in sophistication of tools. Once a child has reached the level of abstract thinking, thought and language structures are developed in essentially the same way as those of the scientist and the artist. The difference is in degree, and indeed some children will become the next generation of scholars and artists. Structures of the disciplines are made by people and are used by teachers to order the world for themselves before they try to help children do it.

The conceptual framework does change as scholars discover new views. Teachers need to keep abreast of major conceptual revisions in the fields they refer to in their teaching. They need to know how to study in those fields and respect the scholar's constant tentativeness about knowledge.

Children must not be led simply to copy and to parrot the aggregate thought and language structures of scholars of the disciplines; Piaget stresses that children will find their own structures and that teachers should refrain from presenting adult structures, particularly those in language, until children have made some formulations of their own. (Duckworth, 1964, p. 4) A danger is the hardening of the categories of each discipline so that alternatives are dismissed as incorrect. The teacher, of course, will know the adult structures and will set the environment, limit it, and rearrange it to facilitate discovery of significant factors. Given the importance of language in thinking postulated by Vygotsky, Langer, and Cassirer, discovery of environmental cues is only the beginning of learning. Children need not only to talk about their discoveries with their peers, as Piaget suggests, but also to tally their thinking with the adult thoughts, as Vygotsky recommends.

Thelen's Dialogues

In his theory of interaction Thelen calls this phenomenon the "dialogue" between "personal knowledge" and "established knowledge."

> Teaching is the facilitative reorganization of thoughts and feelings, and its essence is the control and direction of consciousness in planned and selected experiences. First, there is the stimulation of personal knowledge in a situation selected or sanctioned by the teacher.

> I will call this discovery. It would be possible to raise students to be primarily discoverers. The successful adult result would be the "self made" man—a man who knows a great deal about many things and has opinions about the rest, but does not know which of his ideas are acceptable, valuable and demonstrable. Becoming a discoverer, wonderful as that would look when compared to present outcomes, is not enough.

> Discovered knowledge has to be reflected against established knowledge: this is how the experience of the human race helps the individual. The activities through which this interplay is accomplished will be referred to as dialogue. Teaching method produces an alternation between these two activities of experiencing or interacting. In one, the individual is making discoveries. In the other his discoveries and those of other individuals are confronted by established knowledge in such a way that personal knowledge is assessed, corrected, extended; and in such a way that new tensions generate new questions for investigation.[2] (Thelen, 1962, p. 27)

[2]Reprinted with the permission of the School of Education, University of Wisconsin, Milwaukee.

Sample disciplinary study is one instructional means for accomplishing the interaction of personal and established knowledge in planning curricula. Educators with the aid of scientists prepare a thematic series of investigations for youngsters with simplified materials so that they may live through the same type of investigatory experiences that the scientist originally had. There have been nationally developed programs, for example, in geography, economics, anthropology, and physics. Some educators have referred to this approach as a prescience curriculum, since the young investigators do not have the sophistication of the adult scientist. However, students do experience the ways scientists gain their satisfactions in discovering new relationships between environmental phenomena and the human condition. Cultural anthropology, for example, might be the disciplinary base for multiethnic studies in school.

Interdisciplinary Study

Interdisciplinary study is another way of applying the disciplines in developing school curricula. Several disciplines are drawn upon as teachers focus classroom studies around conceptual themes or life problems, issues, and questions. "Human Dependence on the Sun" is a suitable theme for studying energy and production problems. The disciplines of astronomy, physics, economics, agronomy, and geography might be employed and interrelated in such a study. Educators have also referred to such curricula as integrated studies, stipulating that such studies need to be integrated with the learner's experience and personal thinking style. The focus then becomes the learner's conceptual schema about such matters and how that schema can be enhanced through dialogue with the relevant concepts developed in pertinent disciplines. The concept of the emerging curriculum suits this "integration" need best. Teachers pick up an idea, concern, interest, or question that youngsters express in an open-ended, idea-sharing session like "show and tell" or the "classroom meeting." Teachers then draw upon their own resources and those of the school and community to develop a short-term curriculum plan that will permit further investigation of the thoughts raised. Many teachers collect their own resource materials and cluster them thematically for just such an occasion.

Open Inquiry

The open-inquiry approach to education is structured around perennial child interests and is characterized by preplanned studies on the part of teachers. The interdisciplinary conceptual themes are set down, and appropriate manipulative and reading materials are organized and informally packaged for availability to students. Inquiry type work cards may be attached, allowing youngsters to work through their own selection at their own rate. These compact studies or units can be described as small-scale units for bringing personal conceptions into interaction with scientific concepts.

Sequencing Thought Structures for Teaching

The conventional way to structure the major disciplinary concepts for teaching is to borrow from the pattern of most textbooks. A topic is posed and concepts of equal complexity often drawn from several disciplines will be clustered around the topic, an approach that often results in a mere array of loosely connected facts. Through the work of David Ausubel and others who have studied high-school and adult learners, it has become clear that conventional sequencing is not similar to the way learners actually construct their own thought patterns. A "subsumption process" takes place as learners incorporate or discard new ideas. "As new material enters the cognitive field," Ausubel writes, "it interacts with and is appropriately subsumed under a relevant and more inclusive conceptual system."

> The very fact that it is subsumable (relatable to stable elements in cognitive structure) accounts for its meaningfulness and makes possible the perception of insightful relationships. If it were not subsumable, it would constitute rote material and form discrete and isolated traces. (Ausubel, 1963, p. 219)

Clarity, generalizing ability, cohesiveness, and stability are some of the factors weighed as the new concepts are considered in relation to the existing ideational structure. "Furthermore," he writes, "subsumption of the traces of the learning task by an established ideational system provides anchorage for the new material and thus constitutes the most orderly, efficient and stable way of retaining it for future availability." (p. 219)

This system is not unlike the structuring of the disciplines. Therefore, it seems advisable to structure ideas for teaching in the same manner by identifying the basic organizing concepts for a study from the disciplines and then by developing the "organization of presentation and sequential arrangements of component units." (p. 219)

When completing an instructional plan teachers need to find out about the students' previously developed ideational structures under which the new can be subsumed to further the differentiating process. Ties of an integrative nature need to be planned in an effort to aid the student in perceiving overlapping ideas, similar or related concepts, and ways in which the new can be subsumed under previous organizers or slightly altered ones. The use of advance organizers for this purpose has advantages. They can be in the form of verbal or multimedia presentations, designed to show the principal similarities and differences between the ideas in the new material and the known structure. Such an activity would begin the subsuming process in an oriented fashion.

An Example: Teaching Mathematics as Structure[3]

Nowhere are symbolic thought structures (categories) more apparent than in mathematics. Mathematicians study their subject as to its nature and its uses, its possibilities and its limitations. Users of mathematics are especially concerned with its role in the solution of human problems and its contribution to a better understanding of their own fields. The result of these activities has been a contemporary organization of mathematics unified by basic concepts (sets, relations, mappings), by fundamental structures (groups, rings, fields, vector spaces), and by

[3]This section has been prepared by John Camp, Mathematics Education, Wayne State University, Detroit, Michigan.

the interrelations of its topics. This mathematical achievement, beyond its theoretical value, has valuable applications in all fields of knowledge. Piaget speaks of their tremendous importance:

> A critical account of structuralism must begin with a consideration of mathematical structures, not only for logical but even for historical reasons. True, when structuralism first made its appearance in linguistics and psychology, the formative influences were not directly mathematical. . . . But the structural models of Levi-Strauss, the acknowledged master of present-day social and cultural anthropology, are a direct adaptation of general algebra. (Piaget, 1970, p. 18)

In recent years there have been extensive changes in the goals, methods, and content of school mathematics. Basically, the changes reflect the tremendous recent (since 1960) increase in the amount of mathematical knowledge and the way that mathematics is used in the real world. Educators now recognize that students can no longer be presented with a myriad of unrelated mathematical facts and be expected to absorb them in some mystical way. Instead, at the elementary and the secondary levels, structures are playing an important organizational role in the mathematics education of our youth.

Contemporary Goals

Contemporary goals for the teaching of elementary school mathematics include the following needs: (1) to emphasize the unity of the subject; (2) to embed the important classical skills and concepts in a structural framework; (3) to prepare students for subsequent study of mathematics and fields that rely heavily on mathematics; and (4) to prepare mathematically literate students. Thus, the objectives of instruction in school mathematics relate to knowledge about mathematics, development of skills, and literacy for the future.

Methods

There are also new ways for presenting mathematics within the intellectual stages of development. Due mostly to Piaget's theory, teachers are providing opportunities for students to be actively involved in the learning process by using concrete materials like multibase blocks, cuisenaire rods (simulating mathematical units), geometric models, and operational machines. Students experiment to discover patterns and regularities and to suggest explanations for mathematical ideas. Skill and proficiency thus come from understanding. In fact, by presenting mathematics from a structural point of view, with its unifying concepts and elements, teachers are easily able to develop topics spirally and thus conform to the "learning stages."

Content

The concern for a mathematically literate society also has influenced the content of school mathematics programs. Although the content question is still being debated, most mathematics educators agree that students should graduate from elementary schools with a conceptual understanding of rational numbers and operations on rational numbers (including the four fundamental operations of arithmetic) and, at a concrete level, should be introduced to topics from geometry, probability, statistics, and topology. In large part, computational skills should be developed by doing problems in the areas that require use of the skills.

Implementing the mathematical goals, methods, and content of contemporary school programs requires that there be materials based on the symbolic structure and that the teachers themselves be mathematically literate. Mathematics uses a special language and in many cases uses language in a special way, and teachers need to be able to help students read this language.

Mathematical Literacy: Reasoning in Language and Symbol

When the term *mathematical literacy* is used, it usually refers both to the mathematical competencies that are a "must" for every citizen and to the language and the use of language in mathematics. The two interpretations of the term are related. Mathematics uses not only a special language, but common language and symbols in a special way. All of mathematics can be thought of as arising from basic concepts and structures. Today, most school programs reflect this unified organization of mathematics by developing topics spirally and by emphasizing the concepts and properties of the structures that are central to more complex processes.

A connection exists between language and mathematics in that each may convey ideas or facts. More importantly, both seem to convey certain facts when, in reality, they are expressing ideas that are quite different. For example, the boy who says that he really does not care if he makes the team may or may not mean it. In arithmetic $8 + 8 = 10$ may or may not be true, depending on the underlying system of numeration.

Reasoning in mathematics, in law, or in science involves using accepted ways of proving what seems to be true. A prosecutor proves a defendant guilty by exhibiting motive, opportunity, method, and evidence. A chemist proves that hydrogen is lighter than air by comparing two like balloons, one filled with air, the other with hydrogen. A mathematician proves that the sum of two even numbers is even by using the language and rules that are part of the subject. Some of these mathematical rules and ideas follow.

Statements

There are many kinds of statements that are used in everyday speech; for example:

He was President of the United States.
One-half is a rational number.

These are assertions. Mathematics is primarily concerned with making statements that are assertions and then determining whether the assertions are true or false. The difference between everyday language and mathematics is that the mathematical assertion is either true or false, but it cannot be both in the same context. Table 7.1 illustrates some statements in mathematics.

TABLE 7.1 Statements in Mathematics

statement	True	False
$5 + 3 = 8$	x	
$4 - 2 > 2$		x
Two congruent segments have the same length.	x	
The diagonals of a parallelogram are congruent.		x
$X + 3 = 11$		Not a mathematical statement—as written it is neither true nor false

Compound Statements

As in language, by combining two or more mathematical statements into compound statements, new statements are created. Depending on the truth or falsity of the simple statements, the compound statements are either true or false.

The four most common ways of combining statements in mathematics is by joining them with "and," "or," "if . . . then," or "if and only if." The following are examples of compound mathematical statements using the preceding connectives. Try to determine whether each simple statement of a compound is true or false, and then if the compound is true or false.

13 is a prime number, and $4 \times 0 = 0$.
57 is not a prime number, or 57 is evenly divisible by 7.
If 4 is a prime number, then 4 has only the factors 1 and 4.
$4 < 8$ if and only if $-2 > -4$

At the elementary school level, the connectives "and" and "or" are introduced early in studying sets, in constructing mathematical statements, and in solving open sentences. Implications (if . . . then) and bi-implications (if and only if) are usually not stressed.

The understanding of the meaning and truth values of a compound statement with "and" usually causes trouble. Another problem is that of the linguistic difficulty associated with the connective word "or," because in English it is used in two different ways—inclusively or exclusively. When we say "Paul or Jim will go to the game," we mean that Paul, or Jim, or both will go to the game (inclusive). In contrast, when we say "You may go to the movies or you may stay at home," we mean that you may do one but not the other (exclusive). Students need to understand that in mathematics we must adopt one interpretation for consistency, and so "or" is always used in the inclusive sense.

It is important that teachers understand the use of the vocabulary of mathematics. In addition to the special uses of "and" and "or," some other little words and phrases that have special meanings are: "at least," "at most," "for all," "there is," and "for some." Special language structures also exist for probabilities, time and rate questions, and for the mathematics of the financial system. At each stage of development, the vocabulary and ideas must be mathematically appropriate if the spiral approach to developing mathematics is to work and if youngsters are to accomplish the reasoning language of the structural logic of mathematics.

Learning to Learn: A Disciplined Process

The implications of the theory of thought and language structure for teaching can be summarized in the modern dictum, "education is learning to learn." As children discover structures of knowing that help them give meaning to one instance in the environment and move them toward generalities, they can cope with other similar instances and learn about them on their own. The school cannot possibly teach all there is to know about any subject. Teachers can only show the way to learn, but they should do so effectively.

The school curriculum might include sample investigations made in terms of the structure of the disciplines that explore contexts meaningful to children. Aspects of geography, agronomy, economics, astronomy, and entomology, and of literature and the arts are pertinent examples. The development of thinking processes of various kinds would become the main goal of the curriculum. General strategies might be devised for fostering these processes at the different levels of the child's development of thinking capabilities. Some goals that should be considered and some possible general pedagogical strategies for their realization are listed:

Thinging-Process Goals
Learning to classify objects and events according to various critical attributes
Searching for exemplars and testing the criticality of defining attributes
Validating categories by several means
Hypothesizing about relationships between concepts of objects and events
Developing generalizations by interrelating concepts
Incorporating generalizations and concepts into larger thematic structures

Pedagogical Strategies
Question games with selected arrays of pictures or objects
Field work with observation and collection guides
Dialogue with experts and/or source materials, interviewing
Open-ended experimentation, problem finding and solving
Prepared environment with cues for finding relationships

Experimental "setup" for checking out previously derived generalizations in new contexts

Orchestrating Personal Knowings with Knowns

Bruner calls the function of instruction that will bring together personal and established knowledge "orchestration." He distills the processes of thinking used by adults into three forms of representation—three ways that people represent experience. These forms also probably appear sequentially in the child's development of thinking processes. As formulated by Bruner, they involve some of the same characteristics as Piaget's main stages of intellectual development. (Bruner, 1963, p. 530)

1. Enactive representation by a set of actions appropriate for achieving a certain result (a demonstration of athletic skills or manipulation of objects to show a mathematical concept, a sensorimotor memory).

2. Ikonic representation by a set of summary images or graphics that stand for a concept without defining it fully (for example, a diagram or picture, a climate and product chart, an image in the mind).
3. Symbolic representation by a set of symbolic or logical propositions drawn from a symbolic system that is governed by rules or laws for forming and transforming propositions (language of propositions or expositions of ideas in the mind, spoken or written). (Bruner, 1963, p. 310)

In concrete terms, the stages are quite easy to pinpoint. Young children experiencing the same event (a country fair, for example) probably would not advance in their thinking beyond the enactive or ikonic representations of riding ponies or seeing tractors pull equipment. Older children, on the other hand, are more likely to have built their own symbolic representations regarding the products being displayed, where they come from, and how they are made.

Bruner writes of the importance of language in bridging the gap between the concreteness of reality and the abstraction of thought:

> Once language becomes a medium for the translation of experience, there is a progressive release from immediacy. For language . . . has the new and powerful features of remoteness and arbitrariness: It permits productive combinatorial operations in the absence of what is represented. (Bruner, 1964b)

Teachers "orchestrate" the structured or disciplined representations that they present to children with the probable representational modes of the children. An "economy" in children's learning can be accomplished as concepts are clustered and generalizations are drawn that give them "power" to apply them in new but similar situations. School can then be the beginning of a venture in thinking.

References

Gordon Allport, *The Nature of Prejudice* (New York: Doubleday Anchor, 1958).

David Ausubel, "Cognitive Structure and the Facilitation of Meaningful Verbal Learning," *Journal of Teacher Education* vol. 14, no. 2 (June 1963), p. 16–23.

Roger Brown, *Words and Things* (New York: Free Press, 1958).

Jerome Bruner, "Needed: A Theory of Instruction," *Educational Leadership,* vol. 20, no. 8 (May 1963), p. 530.

——"Some Theories on Instruction Illustrated with Reference to Mathematics," *Theories of Learning and Instruction, NSSE Yearbook* (Chicago: University of Chicago Press, 1964a).

——"Course of Cognitive Growth," *American Psychologist* vol. 19, no. 1 (January 1964b).

——*On Knowing: Essays for the Left Hand* (Cambridge, MA: The Belknap Press of Harvard University Press, 1962).

Jerome Bruner, Jacqueline Goodnow, and George Austin, *A Study of Thinking* (New York: Wiley, 1956).

Jerome Bruner, Rose Oliver, and Patricia Greenfield, *Studies in Cognitive Growth* (New York: Wiley, 1966).

Ernst Cassirer, *Language and Myth* (New York: Dover, 1946).

Eleanor Duckworth, "Piaget Rediscovered," *Elementary Science Study Newsletter,* June 1964.

H. Gillham, *Helping Children Understand Themselves* (New York: Teachers College Press, Columbia University, 1958).

George Kelly, *A Theory of Personality: A Psychology of Personal Constructs* (New York: Norton, 1963).

Jean Piaget, *Structuralism* (New York: Harper & Row, 1970).

Joseph Schwab, *The Concept of Structure in the Subject Fields,* mimeographed material from the author, 1961.

Herbert Thelen, "Insights for Teaching from a Theory of Interaction,' in *The Nature of Teaching* (Milwaukee, WI: The School of Education, University of Wisconsin-Milwaukee, 1962).

8

Language Structuring: Grammar

Language is perhaps the ideal example of one such powerful technology, with its power not only for communication but for coding "reality," for representing matters remote as well as immediate, and for doing all these things according to rules that permit us both to represent "reality" and to transform it by conventional yet appropriate rules. All of this depends on the external resources of a grammar, a lexicon and (likely as not) a supporting cast of speakers constituting the linguistic community.

(Jerome Bruner, 1966)

Which Grammar

The word *grammar* has several meanings. It is, for linguists, the structure of the language and the set of rules by which it is produced, but it is also a theory of the grammar of a language. So we can talk about the grammar of English, but we can also talk about a descriptive grammar, or a transformational grammar, or the grammar of Halliday. Furthermore, for many students and teachers, grammar is a school subject, the study of the structure of language. What complicates this is that if grammar is the structure of language, then anyone, a child included, who speaks a language must be using its grammar, since it cannot be used in any unstructured way. The notion that people learn grammar only in school must be wrong, therefore. People can learn *about* grammar in school or they can learn a different grammar than their own. In this chapter we'll explore different views of the grammar of English and how these relate to school grammars and to teaching about grammar.

Traditional School Grammar: Grammar as Received

Over the centuries a tradition has grown to regard grammar (the structure and system of language) as received. A set of fixed rules was assumed to exist independently of actual linguistic behavior. Taught as prescriptive dogma in school, these rules were to be followed at all costs—language that deviated from such rules was labeled wrong, and teachers worked diligently to stamp it out.

The language ability that children developed before they came to school was largely ignored; it was deemed of little importance compared with the ability they would acquire in school through diligent study of correct, proper, prescriptive grammar.

This traditional school grammar (in a curriculum) should not be confused with traditional grammar (old language scholarship). School grammar was not derived from contemporary language study by grammarians but rather was borrowed from Latin school grammar in England at the time when the English language was introduced into the school curriculum. Previously, all learning had been in Latin and Greek, and English was assumed to be unworthy as a medium of learning and learned discourse; it was a "decayed" language to be fitted into the mold of Latin.

Roots in Latin

The major difficulty with the application of Latin grammar to English has been that Latin is an inflected language (one that depends heavily on word endings), and Modern English is no longer an inflected language, although Old English (Anglo-Saxon) was. The transfer of Latin grammar to English was made under the illusion that English is an inflected language. In fact, inflectional forms in Modern English are vestigial, the remnants of a long-lost central pattern. Most of the grammatical function formerly supplied by case endings has been supplanted by positional indication. In "The man killed the bear," the subject and the object are made known by position in the sentence; put the man in the bear's place, and you have another story. In an inflected language like Anglo-Saxon or Latin, you can put the man or the bear elsewhere in the sentence and the endings of the words make clear what the grammatical relationship is. There are many variations on the basic patterns of English sentences, but there is no doubt that Modern English grammar is different not only from Latin but also from its own inflected ancestor, Old English. The subject, verb, object pattern is central and pervasive in Modern English.

The imposition of Latin grammar on English preserved not only distorted views of English but also the philosophical assumption that rules may exist even though they are not consistent with the realities of language use. These two ideas had the effect of causing generations of teachers to persist in teaching generations of youth rules that were neither verifiable in language use nor productive of more effective language. "Thou shalt not end a sentence with a preposition" is one such rule; this particular dictum results in awkward sentences like: "That's the box in which it came" in place of more natural ones, such as, "That's the box it came in."

Traditional school grammar requires elegant, clever, and intricately tenuous connections to be made between its system and the actual language. Perhaps the cause of reluctance to give it up is the human craving for authority and the need for definition of language in terms of where it came from rather than in terms of what it is or what it does. Strangely enough, the sole source was assumed to be Latin, and Latin grammar was accepted as universal grammar, despite the fact that English is more a Germanic language and is a cousin of Latin rather than a descendant of it.

Language is like an organism in many ways; it changes and grows and is dependent on the human organism in society for its life—a kind of symbiosis. This is true of the spoken language, but it is also true of the written form of language. The latter is anchored securely to the page and is more conservative than the spoken language, but it must maintain the continuous relationship to oral language. When written language becomes fixed and unchanging, as in the case of legal documents, it risks becoming incomprehensible except to very few readers. Literature is geared to the living moment, and when language leaves behind psychological and sensuous embodiment in the human organism, it is not literature, as Dante well knew when he turned away from Latin to the vernacular.

Clearly, for scientists, it is unsatisfactory to continue to accept a grammar that bases itself on traditional authority rather than on linguistic reality. Linguists had to find a more rational alternative.

Descriptive Linguistics: Grammar as Product

Out of a new scientific tradition in language study came a simple, pragmatic view of grammar. In this view language, as it is spoken, is subjected to careful empirical study. No preconceptions are allowed to interfere with this study. Grammar is the structure that scientists find as they describe language, a cultural product of human society. Rules, patterns, and systems do not exist independently of language behavior but in fact are attributes of that behavior. If a grammatical argument is to be decided, it is settled not by citing a rule but by studying language as it is spoken. Descriptive linguistics does not directly produce a school grammar. Instead, it produces a view of language as a human social product from which new school grammars can evolve.

It is important for educators to understand the descriptive linguist's viewpoint, because the structure of language is pertinent not only to the study of grammar but also to reading, writing, and general classroom dialogue. In the following section, some key concepts from descriptive linguistics are discussed. As these are used subsequently, some attempt will be made to redefine them.

Linguistic Assumptions

Descriptive linguists have devoted most of their study to oral language. Putting the emphasis on living, spoken language brings into sharp focus several facts of language:

Language is a code system, using significant sounds as symbols. It has no meaning per se but is a means of transmitting meaning.
Language is systematic and orderly.
Language is dynamic and ever changing.

Viewed thus, language can be studied descriptively. Careful scientific description is the descriptive linguist's basic methodology. Concepts not derived directly from description must be tested against real language.

Phonemes: The Significant Sound Symbols

An important concept of descriptive linguistics is that the unitary symbols of language are not single sounds but are bundles of sounds perceived by the native user of the language as equivalent. The sounds have some key features in common and some differences that are not significant to users of the language. Any characteristic of sound variation can be significant or insignificant.

Out of the full range of available sounds that people can produce, each language develops a limited set of phonemes—bundles of sounds perceived by language users as the same—to use as symbols. Morse code is a very simple analogy to language. It uses variations in the duration of sounds and in the duration of silences between bursts of sound as unitary symbols. Linguists have developed a set of symbols to represent the phonemes of English. A symbol between two slash lines, / /, is always a symbol for a phoneme, not for a letter. Phonemes are perceptual rather than real language units. Thus, language users learn to pay attention to significant, contrasting features of sounds (those that matter in the language) and to ignore others. In studying perception in listening and reading it is important to remember that language users learn what to pay attention to, but equally important they learn what not to pay attention to. Through highly selective attention to only those sound features that are significant the language user functions efficiently.

Morphemes: The Meaning-Bearing Language Molecules

The phonemes of language have no meaning, but when they are combined in certain recurrent sequences, they acquire the power to represent meaning. /b/, /æ/, and /t/ have no meanings, but together they form the morpheme /bæt/ *(bat)*. This morpheme carries meaning that can be indicated in a dictionary, but the precise meaning will depend on its occurrence in the flow of language. Morphemes outside of context represent lexical meaning; full meaning must include contextual meaning. (The boy can *bat* very well. He uses a hickory *bat*. He is *bat* boy for the Tigers. He has *bats* in his belfry.) In these sentences, at least two different homophones are presented by one morpheme. Yet even within one sentence the precise meaning can be obtained only from the whole sentence.

There are two types of morphemes: *free forms* and *combining forms*. /bæt/ *(bat)* is a free form. /s/ is a combining form; with /bæt/ it adds an element of meaning and/or syntax. I *bat*, he *bats* (syntactic difference), or I have one *bat*, he has two *bats* (meaning difference and syntactic difference).

Syntax: The Systems of Language

Only when phonemes are combined into morphemes that are, in turn, formed into recurrent patterns and sequences that form a language text does language become fully capable of transmitting meaning. The study of the system and structure of sentences is syntax. In English there are four important systems that operate.

Pattern and Sentence Order   The most important system in English is that of pattern or word order. The following list of words can only be arranged in a limited number of ways: *horse, man, the, carried.* "The man carried the horse," or "The horse carried the man." The first meaning is less likely but equally permissible. Any other arrangement would sound strange to a native speaker and would not be understood. The only way that the reader (or listener) can know whether "man carried horse" or "horse carried man" is by word order. As indicated earlier, some sentence patterns (subject-verb-object, for example) are very common. There is some disagreement among descriptive linguists about how many basic sentence patterns exist in English, but all the linguists agree the number is small and certainly less than 10. (Loban, 1963)

Word Classes and Functions   Descriptive linguists have not found the many parts of speech of traditional grammar in their description of English. They generally recognize four word classes that are defined by the positions in patterns that they can occupy. Some linguists do not mind using traditional terms: noun, verb, adjective, and adverb for these classes; others prefer new terms. Charles Fries merely numbers them 1, 2, 3, and 4. (Fries, 1952)

Class 1 words fit into the slots represented by the blanks in this pattern: The _____ carried the _____ .

Class 2 words fit into this slot: The horse _____ the man, or into this slot: The horse _____ brown.

Class 3 words fit into this slot: The _____ horse carried the _____ man. Class 3 words pattern with Class 1 words.

Class 4 words are more movable. They fit into this slot: The horse _____ carried the man. But they may also be moved into other positions; that is, the pattern could be: "The horse easily carried the man," or "Easily, the horse carried the man," or "The horse carried the man easily." Class 4 words pattern with Class 2 words.

In most cases, groups of words may replace single words in these four pattern slots. *The white horse I have in mind could very easily carry the heaviest man you could find.* English is quite a flexible language; many words cannot be assigned to a class because their class depends on the slot in which they are found: "I have a *bat;* I *bat* right-handed; He is the *bat* boy."

Descriptive linguists are perhaps more concerned with function than with parts of speech. If the word or phrase performs a particular function (sentence subject, for example) that is what is significant.

Inflectional Changes   Inflection is the system of changes in words to achieve changes in function or meaning. These changes in English are relatively infrequent as compared with other languages. However, some verb endings and auxiliaries that denote changes in tense and mood are still extant, as are the plural and possessive endings in nouns. Most pronouns still retain inflectional forms. A few changes are internal as *mouse* to *mice,* but most are made by addition of suffixes, as *book* to *books, jump* to *jumping.* Nevertheless, formal inflections in English are minimal in contrast with most Indo-European languages.

Function or Structure Words   A fourth system consists *of a* small set *of* words *with* little *or no* lexical meaning *that* serve *as* syntactical signals. Although few *in* number, *these* words recur frequently *and* make *up a* large part *of the* volume *of* language. *The* words *in* italics *in this* paragraph *are* function words. Function words *may be* divided *into* operationally defined groups, just *as the* form classes *were* operationally defined. *Here are some of the* groups *of* function words, named according *to* function (Table 8.1). *The* approximate number *of* words *in each* group (according *to* Fries) *is* also indicated.

The names assigned to these groups are perhaps self-explanatory. Each group of words is a category of structural signals that define and mark off the language structure. "The blobble of garfia was arkpuling and heboling when his wibfrid norped." The sentence doesn't make sense, but it has a ring of sensibility because

TABLE 8.1

Name	Example	Number
Noun markers	*The* man came. (This group also includes possessives and cardinal numbers used in this slot. It is thus the only open-ended group of function words.)	
Verb markers	He *is* coming.	About 15
Negative	He is *not* coming.	1
Intensifier	He may be *very* tired.	25
Conjunctions	The man *and* woman are singing *and* dancing.	9
Phrase markers	They will come *into* the house.	12
Question markers	*When* will they come?	7
Clause markers	They will call *before* they come.	12

the structure is all laid out by the function words. *Blobble* is unmistakably a noun, just as *arkpul* and *hebol* are unmistakably verbs. The markers make this clear.

Intonation: The Melody and Rhythm of Language

Intonation is the system of "signals of pitch, stress, and juncture that clot the utterance into word groups that are meaning groups." (Lloyd and Warfel, 1956) Speakers of English use very subtle variations in relative stress, pitch, and pausing or spacing between sounds to convey important variations in meaning. Is a certain toothpaste "proved (pause) effective'"or "proved defective"? Why do *rebels rebel?* Is a *blackboard* always a *black board?* As an adult highly proficient in both oral and written language, you supply intonation in these written sentences as you determine the grammatical structures and move to the meaning, although you may be hard pressed to pinpoint without considerable effort precisely how you comprehend. Similarly, you know when a woman addressing you wants you to continue listening to her, to respond to a question, or to act on an instruction, although few of you who are not students of intonation could explain the patterns of pitch and stress that you subconsciously interpret and respond to.

Transformational-Generative Linguistics: Grammar as Process

Descriptive linguists begin with a transcription of language as they find it. They seek system within the linguistic product. In recent years another major school of linguists has devoted itself to the theory of the process by which the linguistic product is generated.

All speakers of a language can generate an almost infinite number of sentences in the language, many of which they have neither heard nor uttered before. Yet they and other speakers of the language can easily differentiate sentences that are acceptable in the language from sentences that are not acceptable. These linguists reason that while the number of acceptable sentences in a language is very large, the speaker's generative process must be governed by a much smaller number of rules.

Rules

The rules that speakers master enable them to produce novel utterances that will be understood by other speakers because they are also able to use the rules. Generative grammarians claim that descriptive linguists are concerned only with the surface structure of language, the end-product of the linguistic process, while they consider that each utterance also has a deep or an underlying structure. From this deep structure, the surface structure is derived through a series of transformations that result from the application of obligatory and optional transformational rules. The process is illustrated in this example:

The ball hit Tom.
Tom was hit by the ball.

These sentences, although they differ in the surface structure, have the same deep structure. When the passive transformation rule is applied to the deep structure ("The ball hit Tom"), it results in several changes in the passive surface structure. *Tom* moves to the position of the sentence subject, the verb *hit* takes the auxiliary *was,* and *ball* becomes the agent that *by* introduces. A further transformation could produce the surface structure "Tom was hit." Although an agent is not present in this surface structure (a deletion transformation has removed it), it is present in the deep structure: "(Something) hit Tom." This, by passive transformation, becomes "Tom was hit by something" and then by deletion becomes "Tom was hit." A question transformation could produce another surface structure: "Was Tom hit?" This still has the deep structure: "(Something) hit Tom."

Rules often produce compact, economical surface structures from multiple deep structures. "Mary saw the boy who hit Tom" is a surface structure that combines two deep structure sentences: "Mary saw the boy" and "The boy hit Tom." A relative clause transformation transforms the latter sentence into a relative clause and embeds it in the surface structure noun phrase, "the boy who hit Tom."

Meaning is more significant to the work of the generative-transformational linguist than it is to the descriptive linguist. Transformational linguists add introspection and inference to the tools of linguists. They are not satisfied to work with what they can observe; they seek to go beyond linguistic performance to competence. They are interested not only in what speakers do but also in what they know that makes it possible for them to do what they do. They seek an explanatory theory of language.

Grammar as Social System: Halliday's Semiotic View

Halliday, as we have indicated at other points in this book, sees language as part of the culture. It is as much social as personal. Furthermore, Halliday takes a semiotic approach, one that sees language as a system composed of symbols and in integral relationship to the culture, itself a social system for representing meaning.

For Halliday the system of language is constituted of three levels or strata (Halliday, 1974):

Semantic
Lexicogrammatical
Phonological

> The social system . . . is a set of meaning relations; and these . . . are realized in many ways, of which . . . perhaps the principal one as far as the maintainence and transmission of the system is concerned, is through their encoding in language. The meaning potential of a language, its semantic system, is therefore seen as realizing a higher level system of relations, that of the social semiotic, in just the same way it is itself realized in the lexico-grammatical and phonological systems. (Halliday, 1974)

The middle stratum of human language is what distinguishes human language from animal communication, which has only sound and meaning. And it is this wording/structuring (Halliday sees word choice as functioning at the same level as grammar) stratum that makes it possible to realize the full meaning potential of the semantic stratum. The capability of human societies to achieve almost total communication is thus dependent on there being a grammar to the language.

So grammar both determines and is determined by meaning. Its constraints, its very rules, are at least partly derived from the semantic functions language must fulfill in the social contexts of communication.

Scholars and language users may focus on the grammatical structure, but they cannot lose sight of the fact that this system is in complex interrelationship with the other systems.

What is important in language development in this view is that the systems only exist as dynamic systems in the context of the social use of language. That's why language and any of its aspects or systems are learned best and most easily in context.

Language doesn't happen in one person's head. Grammar itself would not be necessary to the same degree if it were not necessary for language to be understood by more than one person. There must be devices in language for differentiating subject and object, for example, not for the speaker who already knows, but for the listener who does not yet know. Different languages use different grammatical devices to accomplish this, but the alternatives are limited by the phonological system, the semantic system, and the social context.

Unlike the tranformationalists, Halliday's grammar does not just confine itself to the study of sentence structure. To Chomsky a language is the set of sentences the rules of the language generate. But to Halliday a language text, though it is indeed composed of sentences, is not any random set of sentences. The text has very important characteristics that determine how the sentences may relate to each other and how the text itself relates to the context in which it is produced and the meaning it expresses. A text, then, and not a sentence, is really the minimal unit of language, in any functional sense.

Value of Linguistics

It should be clear that looking at language as a product, looking at it as a process, and looking at it as a sociosemiotic system are not intrinsically conflicting views. The information and insight gained can be complementary and not contradictory.

Further, each may be useful for specific purposes and applications. It may be quite useful to look at differences between dialects descriptively, because breakdowns in communication may occur because of differences in phonemes, intonation, and inflectional suffixes (or lack of them), as well as rule differences. A generative view may be very useful in dealing with comprehension problems in reading that result from the grammatical complexity of a noun phrase involving adjectives. And the social view of language is essential to keeping language, its use, and its development in proper perspective. It makes a whole language-thinking perspective possible.

Nevertheless, there has been considerable controversy over these schools of linguistics and over the knowledge they have produced. Coupling any of them with psychological schools of thought tends to increase the controversy. Descriptive linguistics, because it concerns itself with observed behavior, is often combined with behavioral psychology in research and applications to learning. Cognitive psychologists, themselves concerned with the process by which knowledge is acquired, have frequently moved toward a generative-transformational theory. Gestalt psychology can combine with semiotic views of language. Other combinations are also possible. In recent years a group of scholars have called themselves *cognitive scientists,* seeking to unite philosophy, cognitive psychology, artificial intelligence, and some use of linguistics.

Much of what modern linguists produce, as they move toward a more perfect understanding of how language works, will be of limited direct utility to education. The theory, however, will form the basis for the content of instructional sequences that deal with how language works. But the greatest contribution that linguistics will make, particularly as it is linked with psychology and kept in social context, is in the insights it will provide into the developing child as a user of language. In this important area the view of language as social, personal process will be most relevant, and language as the product of this process will be of lesser importance. As teachers seek to help learners become more effective users of language, their success will be contingent to a great degree on the extent to which they understand language processes. Both idiolect and dialect will expand and become more effective language tools as teachers and parents see the communicative power of children's language. In designing curriculums it will be most useful to move beyond attempts to change linguistic behavior to focus on expanding the whole of language competence.

In teaching reading and listening, teachers seek to help learners to use their experiential and schematic base, to be aware of the author, and to construct meaning from a surface representation through an underlying structure. In teaching speaking and writing, teachers strive to help learners formulate their thoughts, to be aware of their audiences, to generate underlying language structures, and then to produce a surface representation that will express the message clearly enough that it will be comprehensible to their readers or listeners. In all this, the teacher must focus on the process while the learners concern themselves primarily with communication.

Why Study Grammar?

By what means can communication skills be taught? I agree . . . that it is extremely improbable that they should be affected at all by instruction in explicit grammar, whether that grammar be traditional or transformational circa 1958, or transformational circa 1965, or on the transformational frontier. Study of the theory of language is probably irrelevant to the development of skill in the use of the language. (Brown, quoted in Moffett, 1968, p. viii)

Grammar and Curricular Goals

Traditionally, language instruction has had three broad goals, all of which have become intertwined in the school curriculum: (1) to help children become more effective language users; (2) to influence children to speak in socially preferred ways; and (3) to provide children with knowledge and terminology so that they may understand and discuss how language works. These relate to the three types of language learning Halliday has described: (1) learning language; (2) learning through language; and (3) learning about language. These three kinds of language learning take place at the same time in natural speech acts or literacy events. (Halliday, 1979)

The relationship of the study of grammar to the last set of instructional purposes and to learning about language is the most obvious and the least open to debate. Language, like any other aspect of human interest and activity, is worthy of and amenable to study. The study of language structure can be a fascinating part of any curriculum, particularly if learners, as linguists do, can draw on their own language experiences and regard themselves as reliable language resources. They have learned to speak the language. They can gain much insight into how language works by carefully observing and examining their own use of language and what they already intuitively know about language structure.

It is also obvious that the schools are obligated to make available to learners the most modern and up-to-date insights, concepts, and information about language. In such a dynamic period of language study as this one, it is not conceivable that schools can be content to present a closed and static system, whether that system is a received one or one that views language as product, as process, or as social semiotic. Even young children cannot be offered misconceptions in the name of simplicity.

The proportionate amount of time and effort that should be devoted to the study of language for its own sake is a good deal more open to question. Here, several considerations are important, including:

The intuitive knowledge about language children already possess

The importance of learning about language as compared to the other language
 goals of the school

The ease of acquisition of the knowledge

The general need for such knowledge among school-age children

The degree to which the knowledge achieved will relate to or bring about the achievement of the other goals

The building of more effective language, helping young people expand their language, is a much greater concern in the competition for time and energy in the school day. Further, a year's intensive study of grammar in junior high school would probably be more productive than several years of time spent in earlier grades. Such terminology as is needed in discussing compositions and other forms of language activity can be introduced in the elementary school as it is needed.

A few basic grammatical concepts should be the goal in the elementary grades. Here are some examples:

Everybody's language is systematic. People couldn't communicate if it weren't.

Language change is continuous and inevitable.

There are many forms of English in current use.

Speakers of a language use its rules as they speak.

It seems so logical to say that learning about grammar will influence the effectiveness of language use and will produce more socially preferred language; but we must clearly separate what is effective language from what carries high social status. Effective language is language that can be used most successfully in expression and communication. It needs to be flexible, rich, and variable so that the user may adjust it easily to the demands of particular situations. Frequently, the language that is called "proper language" tends to be inflexible, narrowly correct, and particularly confining for a language user whose native dialect is divergent from it. Even for the fortunate children whose dialect comes close to the preferred form, it will be necessary for them to achieve a flexible ease in using their language if they are to be fully effective in the varied communicative situations of modern life.

Grammar Study as a Means of Achieving More Effective Language

Early in this chapter, the lack of a substantive base for prescriptive grammar was explored; also considered was the failure of received grammar as presented in standard school texts to explain adequately the language as it really exists. Interestingly, it was not the advent of scientific linguistics or the realization of the inaccuracy of traditional school grammar that caused educators to be dissatisfied with direct instruction in grammar. What bothered teachers was that this instruction did not work. It did not achieve any of its assumed objectives. Children simply did not apply what they had been taught as they used the language in speaking or writing. Teachers became aware that many pupils, confronted in each grade with nouns, verbs, and other elements of grammar, were often unable to learn anything they could retain from grade to grade. Whether grammar was taught directly or by controlled induction, it was necessary to start over again for most pupils in each successive grade in elementary school. Then, in junior high school, and again in senior high school, the curriculum started from the beginning. Unhappily, it could not be assumed, for most children, that any grammar had been learned in prior education. Teachers also noted that some students, after repreated exposure, had indeed mastered the grammar as measured by achievement tests, but this mastery had no noticeable effect on the everyday language of the children. Undaunted, the children persisted in using their "quaint" personal grammar in their routine communications with each other in and out of the classroom. Teachers painfully realized that by emphasizing grammar instruction, they failed to change oral language and written composition and, in fact, they were actually interfering with its effectiveness. Some children became frustrated and intimidated; for them the best solution was to say and write as little as possible. Others learned to substitute stiff, "proper" phrases and constructions for colorful, natural ones.

Research on Teaching Grammar

Dissatisfaction with the results of instruction in school grammar was reinforced by the findings of grammar research over several decades on the cherished beliefs of educators about the reasons for such instruction. The research corroborated what teachers had suspected. Here is a catalogue of beliefs about the value of instruction in standard grammar and usage that were questioned by substantial research findings:

Belief: The study of grammar is good for the mental discipline of the pupil. In 1913, Briggs tested nine typical claims for the value of grammar instruction as a mental discipline and found no improvement. (Searles and Carlsen, 1960, p. 459)

Belief: Grammar study produces a transfer of learning to other subjects. Studies by Rice in 1903, Boreas in 1917, and Bender in 1935 showed no evidence to support this belief. (DeBoer, 1959)

Belief: Knowledge of traditional grammar improves the ability of children to interpret literature. Studies by Hoyt in 1906 and Rapeer in 1913 found no transfer at all. (Searles and Carlsen, p. 460)

Belief: When school grammar is learned well, it remains a useful tool. Macauley tested seniors in Scottish schools who had passed tests on grammar as part of the "11 plus" examinations that they took when they entered the schools. He found that their knowledge of school grammar had virtually evaporated. (Searles and Carlsen, p. 460)

Belief: Knowledge of school grammar aids in reading comprehension. Greene found no important relationship between the amount of grammatical in formation possessed and the ability to read and to comprehend sentences. (Greene, 1947)

Belief: Ability to cite grammatical rules improves grammar in written expression. The research of Bender in 1935 and Catherwood in 1932 says no. (DeBoer, p. 415)

Belief: Grammar instruction is the best approach to teaching sentence structure. In 1934, Ellen Frogner demonstrated that children who were taught sentence structure by thoughtful analysis of their own writing rather than by direct grammar instruction learned better. The time spent on grammar instruction could have been better used in letting children write, she concluded. It was wasted time as far as improving sentence structure was concerned. (Frogner, 1934, p. 578)

Belief: School grammar is the best approach to teaching punctuation. Evans showed in 1939 that it was far more effective to teach punctuation by example as an aid to comprehension than to teach rules of grammar first. (DeBoer, p. 418)

Belief: When school children can cite grammatical rules, they will apply them. Segal and Barr demonstrated in 1923 that there is no more correlation between formal and applied grammar than between any two unrelated topics. (De Boer, p. 414)

Belief: Grammarians agree on what is and what is not standard English. Perhaps the cruelest blow of all was dealt by the 1938 research of Marckwardt and Walcott. They found great disagreement among a group of experts on English grammar and usage about what is correct and incorrect. Furthermore, these researchers found that many usages considered substandard by a majority of these experts were labeled correct by authorities such as the *Oxford Dictionary.* (Marckwardt and Walcott, 1938)

Grammar instruction in school is ineffective. Many children have learned to write effectively while being taught grammar, but probably more have learned in spite of it than because of it.

The Value of Teaching Linguistically Valid Grammar

An important question, not yet fully answered, is whether the content of prescriptive grammar instruction was at fault, or whether the type of grammar and the teaching strategy were also to blame. Was traditional school grammar instruction a failure because it was inaccurate, or did it fail also because children do not learn how to use language through formal instruction in its grammar? Loban states flatly:

> Since formal instruction in grammar, whether linguistic or traditional, seems to be an ineffective method of improving expression at this level of development, one can conclude that elementary pupils need many opportunities to grapple with their own thought in situations where they have someone to whom they wish to communicate successfully. (Loban, p. 88)

Little evidence exists for the value of grammar instruction based on linguistics. Material appropriate to use in school has been available for some time, but there has not been interest in examining its effectiveness as there was in earlier years.

Theoretically, a new prescriptive grammar could be evolved based on descriptive linguistic studies or on generative rules, or on systemic grammar. A new prescriptive grammar would be superior to traditional grammar in that it would be based on English rather than on Greek and Latin. It would, however, still share several faults with traditional grammar:

1. Because language is constantly changing, any prescriptive grammar will lag behind and will be somewhat out of step with linguistic reality.
2. Unless a separate grammar is developed for every major dialect, any standard grammar will be inconsistent to some degree with the language of many people. (This is a problem evident in some linguistically based English/Language Arts text series.)
3. The new grammar would still need to deal with the anomalies of language, instances where the rules do not work or where they become complex. It is possible that no system can completely explain the structure of living language. At any rate, no current system does.

Most proposals for teaching modern linguistic grammar have stressed the use of controlled induction, a system in which rules are discovered in highly controlled situations. Research evidence exists that controlled induction is more effective in teaching grammar than purely deductive approaches, but there is no evidence yet that such knowledge, however accurate it may be, actually improves the effectiveness of the child's language. This objective can be achieved more surely if primary emphasis in the school program is on expanding the language of learners to better serve their communicative needs. If such an approach is followed, learners will build, incidentally, a strong sense of structure of language.

Inquiry in a Whole-Language Approach: Letting the Questions Control the Inductive Process

Inquiry is an approach to learning that organizes around key questions that the learners seek to answer through experimentation and through whatever techniques are available. It has been advocated in science and social studies because it not only offers a highly motivating way of organizing the content but also lets the learners operate like scientists and scholars do in investigating questions in their disciplines. Learners acquire not only concepts but also a sense of the structure of the discipline and an understanding of its methods.

Language study, particularly grammar, is an excellent subject for the use of inquiry methods. Because all learners have already acquired control over at least one dialect of one language, they are their own resources. They can, as linguists do, collect their data from within their own language groups, family, friends, and class—even from within their own heads. They can examine their own language, hitherto the least used resource in school grammar study. They can compare and contrast whole language forms heard in their class, in the community, on trips, in the mass media, in business, and in "old-fashioned" literature. Although language varies, the universal characteristics of language (for example, that it has system) are present in all language, including their own. Furthermore, what they learn provides them with insight into how language works in general, but it also helps them see specifically how their own language works.

Inquiry starts not with rules or sets of preselected sentences but with questions. At the simplest level is a "how come" question, which even a 6-year-old can formulate. "How come we say 'new red car,' but we never say 'red new car'?" In such an inquiry, the pupils may ask themselves what other sequences are possible. They may discover that strings of words in front of words like *car* say something about *car*. They may categorize these describing words (if the term "adjective" is needed it will be introduced after the concept is already shaped by inquiry) as those that show age, color, size, condition, and so on. In the process of deciding what rules are used by class members in ordering adjectives, they begin to get the more general proposition that users of language are following rules that they have learned. They continually discover that language has order to it. They find that words and phrases often are interchangeable in recurrent language patterns. The specific knowledge gained is, of course, never as important as the generalizations it leads to, and, therefore, any real whole-language variety is a useful base for building these generalizations.

Upper elementary or junior high school pupils might well undertake the construction of a descriptive grammar for their own dialects or undertake an inquiry into the comparative use of verb forms in their community. Inquiry need not be confined to grammar, of course; in fact, language inquiry is likely to touch numerous dimensions of language, because it stems from questions that are not always neatly classified. Youngsters might become curious about the use of idioms or slang by themselves, their parents, and their grandparents (for example, what things like *phonographs* have been called over the years). In the course of their investigation, they may find changing forms in phonology, vocabulary, and grammar.

Inquiry has some drawbacks that sometimes discourage teachers. Its direction is often neither predictable nor controllable. Examples in language data are likely to be found that contradict the concepts that the teachers hold or that do not easily fit the rules they know. In many cases the inquiry will lead into unsettled areas where even the most modern, authoritative references disagree or offer no help. So much learning may take place that it may be difficult for the teacher to measure and to evaluate it, and the teacher must trade the role of language judge for that of coresearcher. Teachers who have used inquiry, on the other hand, find that their pupils no longer regard language study as dull and uninteresting, because they are dealing with their own whole, living language.

References

J. J. DeBoer, "Grammar in Language Teaching," *Elementary English,* vol. 36, no. 6 (October 1959), pp. 412–420.

Roger Brown, in J. Moffett, *Teaching the Universe of Discourse* (Boston: Houghton Mifflin, 1968).

Jerome Bruner, *Toward a Theory of Instruction* (Cambridge, MA: Harvard University Press, 1966).

Charles C. Fries, *The Structure of English* (New York: Harcourt, 1952).

Ellen Frogner, "Grammar Approach versus Thought Approach in Teaching Sentence Structure," *English Journal,* vol. 28 (1934), pp. 575–582.

Harry Greene, "Direct versus Formal Methods in Elementary English," *Elementary English Review,* vol. 24 (1947), pp. 273–285.

Michael Halliday, "Text as Semantic Choice in Social Contexts," in T. A. van Dijk and J. S. Petofi (Eds.), *Grammar and Descriptions* (The Hague: Mouton, 1974).

_____, "Three Aspects of Children's Language Development," in Y. Goodman, M. Haussler, and D. Strickland (Eds.), *Oral and Written Language Development Research: Impact on the Schools* (Urbana, IL: National Council of Teachers of English, 1979).

Donald J. Lloyd and Harry Warfel, *American English in its Cultural Setting* (New York: Knopf, 1956).

Walter Loban, *The Language of Elementary School Children* (Champaign, IL: National Council of Teachers of English, 1963).

Albert Marckwardt and Fred Walcott, *Facts About Current English Usage,* Monograph no. 7, National Council of Teachers of English, 1938.

John R. Searles and G. Robert Carlsen, "English," in *Encyclopedia of Educational Research* (New York: Macmillan, 1960), pp. 456–464

9

Composing Letters to the World

This is my letter to the world,
That never wrote to me,
The simple news that nature told,
With tender majesty.

(Emily Dickinson—frontispiece in the first edition of her poems, 1944, p. 2)

Emily Dickinson's "letters to the world" were touchingly conceived, and their artistry finely honed. Few people, even artists, have been able to communicate their reflections and reactions to the life about them so exquisitely, but all people present their thoughts and feelings about the happenings of life in one way or another. Children, like artists, explode with delight in the world and with wonder at its mysteries. Given an opportunity, they will tell it to the world, making their own presentations.

> They are behind you.
> They are holes,
> Holes in the snow,
> Holes in the sand,
> Holes in the mud.
> Your feet make the holes, lots of holes,
> So your mother can find you.[1]

> The beach is peaceful in the winter.
> I often go when I'm disturbed.
> I can sit on the rocks lining the shore.
> I sit and throw bread to the friendly sea gulls.
> I watch the crashing waves tumble in.
> Pretty soon the waves hit my feet.
> The tide is in, so I get on my bike and ride home.
> I feel much better now.
> I sure hate to see the summer come.[2]

> The first thing I noticed when I walked outside in the early morning was a big red-tailed hawk that would send shivers down your back. When I walked farther out into the wet field with the diamond-like sparkle of the dew, I saw a baby red fox go across the field eating the fresh strawberries wet with dew. I followed it past an old barb-wire fence and down an old cow pasture and I stopped at the edge and didn't follow him into the woods because I was looking at a big patch of succulent strawberries and they made me stoop down and I ate them.
> That's what happens in the early morning in the country.[3]

[1]"Footprints," dictated by a 5-year-old child to his teacher.
[2]"Winter Beach," by David Mullis (12 years old).
[3]"At Five Forty-Five in the country," by Jon Smith at age 10.

Like Emily Dickinson's, these letters to the world are addressed as much to the self as to others. Still, children's messages find their way out to others in conversation, in the dialogue of play, in reverie committed to writing, in debates with themselves, and in argument set down, and sometimes in the literary forms of stories and poetry or in descriptions and explanations of events.

Composing: Modes of Presenting

Language is not the only (and not always the most appropriate) medium for presenting one's ideas and feelings about one's world. The expressive relationships of line and mass in painting or drawing, the form of a piece of sculpture, the telling movements of dance, or the harmonious flow of notes in music may be the means that best present a particular letter to the world. That marvelous combination of the arts called "theater" when presented by adults and "creative dramatics" when presented by children is one of the most communicative of the modes of presentation, because it uses several modes simultaneously.

All such means of presenting one's own symbolic formulation should be cultivated. Few children will be artists, but many will find these modes useful and enjoyable, and all will learn, through experimenting with each, to read them in their own forms. What a pity when an adult cannot read, in the artist's terms, the playfulness of a painting by Miro, the passions in a drama by O'Neill, the serenity of a Bach fugue, or the inner conflicts of Martha Graham's choreography.

Communication is a two-way process of output and input, of speaking and listening, of writing and reading, of presenting and receiving. The more artistry there is, the more effective is the communication, and this is where teaching comes in. Teachers create classroom situations that encourage free discourse within the limitations of group operation. These limitations, however, should be only for insuring the kind of orderly working environment that will permit a maximum of individual expression and a minimum of willful self-indulgence. Gaining artistry in presentational modes requires the calm of reflection and the rigor of discipline, as well as the excitement of sharing ideas in discourse with others. Teachers must be sure not to thwart the natural tendency of youngsters to present their symbolic formulations for testing against those of others and the expression of ideas to others in search of reflection and refinement.

Composing in Speech and Writing

Although one needs to keep constantly in mind the possibilities of the nonlingual modes of presenting and communicating, the main concern of the ensuing discussion will be speech and writing. At the outset it is important to state two postulates with regard to writing and its relationship to speech. Although an expression of a notion, an idea, or even a fact in speech is never quite the same in writing, both are expressions of language. They are alike in that the key morphemes (idea units) are essentially the same. The syntax is a little different. Hand-written, typed, or printed matter does not have the benefit of intonation, gesture, or pauses to develop meaningful flow but relies instead on punctuation. Subtle intonation contours make it easy for anyone to follow spoken narrative or discourse, but if it is written down exactly as it is said, it is hard to comprehend. This is why dictated letters have to be rewritten from the rough draft until the author has, through practice, learned to speak in written terms.This is why good dramatic dialogue is so hard to write and so difficult to read. Being oral language, it needs the stage or an imaginative reader to make it live.

Great Shakespearean actors are the ones who really "read" the lines as speech, for helpful punctuation in the old Shakespearean texts is not enough to represent the oral forms of those times; he meter was made for speaking.

Although the differences between speech and writing are important, their interdependence is even more significant. Lyric poetry, for example, is often written to be read aloud.

For teachers the argument just given is a crucial reminder that they can neglect neither speech nor writing; they must develop both modes in relation to each other, because children enter school with a large speech repertoire but only the beginnings of writing. While their speech patterns are continuing to grow in sophistication, children must add written patterns to their speech patterns. The disparity, which is wide at the beginning and slowly narrows over a four-to-six-year period, can cause great frustration.

Differences Between Speaking and Writing

In order to understand the problems inherent in the development of literacy skills, it is necessary to examine some of the special characteristics of written language that are involved in teaching composition, spelling, and handwriting.

Written language first of all makes use of graphic symbols rather than the sound symbols of speech. In English orthography these symbols are alphabetic in nature; that is, they correspond to sounds in speech rather than to syllables or to meanings. Our numerals 1, 2, and so on are examples of the type of symbol corresponding to meaning. They represent the same numerical concept to speakers of English, French, German, Russian, and other languages, although the names the languages give to the concepts may be very different.

The alphabet, as we suggest in the chapters on reading, is more a convenience for writers than for readers. Readers have no more trouble with pictographs or logographs or syllabaries than with alphabetic writing. However, writers are greatly convenienced by a system that uses a small stock of easily formed letters roughly corresponding in number to the number of phonemes the oral language uses.

Oral language, unless it is recorded electronically, is perishable. Once uttered, it is gone. Written language, on the other hand, is more permanent. It can preserve   thought   for   some   later   decoding,   perhaps   long   after   the writer is dead or at a place far distant from the place of writing. Written language is also perfectible. It can be reworked and revised until writers are satisfied that they have used it in the most effective manner to express their thoughts. Perhaps for this reason more precision is expected of written expression.

Written language, as it is being created, has a spacetime sequence, whereas oral language has only a time sequence; that is, the symbols of writing are usually produced sequentially and in a spatial direction (left to right in English orthography), whereas the sounds of oral language need only be produced sequentially. This may explain why writers are more aware of the sequence of letter production than speakers are of the sequence of sounds in speech production. As proficiency in the skills of literacy increases, however, this letter-sequence awareness tends to diminish. Many adults find it necessary to write a word out fully, perhaps in several alternate spellings, so that they can see it as a whole and decide which spelling "looks" right.

Written language is often ambiguous where oral language is not. The intonation of oral language may make clear the underlying structure and meaning of language which is ambiguous in written form. For example: "The store is closed at 8 P.M." This could mean that the time of closing is 8 P.M. or that it's closed at some earlier time and is not open at 8 P.M. Intonation would prevent oral ambiguity. Punctuation does not provide the range of cues to the underlying structure in writing that intonation does in speech. Authors proofreading their own written work are aware only of the structure and meaning that they had in mind at the time of composition; a second person, however, may be able to uncover an unintended ambiguity, a possible alternate meaning or syntax that is equally plausible. In some instances, written language may be less ambiguous than speech. Homophones, words that sound alike, may be spelled differently, for example.

Written language has the advantage of permanence, but this is also one of its disadvantages. It becomes, over time, a fossil that preserves thought encoded in language at the time of writing. It is more resistant to change and, therefore, tends to lose touch with sociocultural reality and become out of phase with the changing oral language. Perhaps the greatest difference between oral and written language is that speech is very likely to occur in a situational context in which there is much to support the language, while writing occurs in a situation that is most often far from the reality it deals with. Speakers can point or motion to things that are visible to their listeners as they speak. The face-to-face character of most oral language communication is even more facilitating. Writers must express their meanings more fully through language because it is removed from any supporting situational context. This difference is, of course, a continuum. Written language in the form of signs, labels, or illustrated texts may be embedded in a situational context, while oral language may deal with abstract ideas or may involve media, such as radio or telephone, which transcend time and space. The use usually made of oral and written language, though, imposes some basic differences on the ways they work, the forms they take, and the factors necessary for their use in successful communication.

Vygotsky, in reporting his investigations of the relationship between school instruction in language and child development of language, states clearly his view of the difference between speaking and writing:

> Written speech is a separate linguistic function, differing from oral speech in both structure and mode of functioning . . . lacking the musical, expressive, in tonational qualities of oral speech. (Vygotsky, 1962, p. 18)

Vygotsky suggests reasons why young children do not find conventional writing and composition easy tasks, even though oral speech is the basis for such composition:

> Our studies show that it is the abstract quality of written language that is the main stumbling block, not the underdevelopment of small muscles or any other mechanical obstacles. . . . Writing is also speech without an interlocutor, ad dressed to an absent or an imaginary person or to no one in particular—a situation new and strange to the child. (Vygotsky, pp. 98–99)

In Piaget's terms, writing is a decentering objectifying process that requires some maturity beyond the egocentricity of the young child. Writing hardly ever becomes as spontaneous as speaking. Writers cannot let their ideas tumble out as they do in speech, although this is where they will begin. If one admits to an "inner speech," as Vygotsky does, the problem becomes one of establishing a relationship between it and oral speech on the one hand and writing on the other.

To Vygotsky, written language demands conscious work, because its relationship to inner speech is different from that of oral speech. The latter precedes inner speech in the course of development, while written speech follows inner speech and presupposes its existence:

> Inner speech is condensed, abbreviated speech. Written speech is deployed to its fullest extent, more complete than oral speech. Inner speech is almost en tirely predicative because the situation, the subject of thought, is always known to the thinker. Written speech, on the contrary, must explain the situation fully in order to be intelligible. (Vygotsky, p. 100)

Even though written language is quite different from speech, language for most people begins with speech development derived from inner speech. The cultivation of speech, the development of speech-thought, is important for its own sake, but students will have little of significance to write about or communicate, nor will they understand sophisticated reading, unless their speech-thought is constantly nurtured in ever widening circles of sophistication.

Often adults take little time for extended conversation with children. Adult-child dialogue about the world could be encouraged in the school, but many teachers say that there is no time for such dialogue because of societal pressure to teach "basic skills." Skill workbooks and programmed skill exercises on computers are no substitute for daily opportunities for talking, reading, and writing about relevant and important ideas. Persistent low reading scores from most schools in slum areas, despite great efforts with drills, may be caused by the overemphasis on sounding and on teaching word-attack skills to the neglect of significant and total language development within the curriculum.

Children from affluent homes often are shunted from one afternoon activity to another with no time to ask questions of their parents or to talk about the multitude of experiences they have had. In school, many children who are failing are subjected to hours of remedial instruction and have no time left for the rich language experience they need.

In the past, the farmhouse and the artisan's house were centers of learning, not only about the day's work but about life as well. Adults and children were in regular dialogue about the events happening to them all. Even though children were supposed to be seen and not heard, they heard the important adult talk and had their questions answered at appropriate times. Even in so-called preliterate cultures the young are in constant communication with adults. In many instances, the fathers and mothers take on the training of the boys and girls by including them in their daily activities. The young hear their elders' discussions and begin to participate in them. The younger children are always in close social contact with the women, and they join in the large social festivities.

In social environments where the young are included in the talk and have opportunities to ask questions and participate in the dialogue of inquiry with adults, children can then develop their speech-thoughts fully. Otherwise, both thinking and speech are held back, and the conceptualizing process never develops sufficiently. The grammar of reasoning is seldom heard. As concepts of the environment become clear through describing, defining, classifying, categorizing, interrelating, and eventually hypothesizing, the thought process develops. If children have never been encouraged in their questions and have never been shown by example how one goes about seeking answers, their minds may not develop fully. A stimulating environment of objects is necessary, but it is not enough. There must also be a stimulating and varied interactive human environment if children are to expand on their uses of language.

Speech-Thought in School

Scientific investigation substantiates the commonsense view that the development of speech-thought requires adults to interact with children, with lots of "good" talk. Yet in our "quiet" classrooms—even in some kindergartens—this activity is discouraged, is considered to be a waste of time, or at best operates at a minimal level of "yes-or-no" questioning. Time is required to nurture speech-thought. Children need to have less content coverage and more time to think out loud about what they are learning.

The school is the only social institution, besides the family, that can reach all children. The school should be the agency that extends the speech-thought activities of the community. However, schools should encourage parents to participate with their children in general cognitive activities growing out of school programs as well as home experiences, rather than discourage them by throwing up fences of educational expertise. Parents should be encouraged to participate in the school program and should be invited to the school when they have particular knowledge or skills to contribute. In some schools, parents have been encouraged to go on trips with the children and to return to the classroom to join in a discussion of the experience. This procedure helps the parents to see how to talk constructively with their children. As talk takes over in home and school, the excitement of learning is conveyed and communication is enhanced.

Relation of Reading to Speaking and Writing

Too often, reading and writing are taught as separate tasks, and reading always receives the greater emphasis—despite the label "language arts." Because both tasks depend on a speech base, speaking, listening, writing, and reading support each other in the school program. They are the main modes for the everyday presentations of symbolic life and our only means of encountering the day-to-day symbolic presentations of others. The way to learn to "read," in the sense of understanding the presentations of others, is to prepare one's own presentations so that they can be more easily "read" by others and to learn to "listen" to what other people are "saying." Obviously, both presenter and receiver should deal with things of concern to both. Relevant reading, listening, talking, and writing need to be a vital part of every child's school day.

Strategies for Developing Speech-Thought

Many classroom strategies for furthering the development of speech-thought were developed during the progressive movement as a means for involving children in "experiences." They were part of a recommended "activities program" that emphasized "doing." Too often, however, the activity was carried out for its own sake, and the next step of language interpretation was not taken with sufficient resolve. In a modern, whole-language view of teaching, these strategies are recommended for their potential in extending language and thinking through relevant language use in functional contexts.

Child Talk in Creative Play

All children aged 3 to 12 years employ speech-thought during periods of concentrated play. These periods are rehearsals, with the play objects simulating the world situation of the child. (Frank, 1960) Past learnings and developing concepts, with associated language, are paraded before the other child or children as each contributes to the emerging drama. Creative play can happen in a housekeeping corner with dress-up clothes, in a pile of building blocks representing an airplane, in a playground sandbox, in a dirt hole under the back porch with little fire engines and police cars, in a pup tent in the woods, or in a cellar space preempted for doll play or car racing. No better empirical proof is needed than the fact of play to show that children are natural learners, busy at making discoveries and testing what they know against simulated reality. If more play were encouraged in school throughout the period of childhood, the teacher would have more opportunities to observe the child's level of operation with ideas and language under somewhat natural circumstances. Children playing with toys create analogues of reality—it could almost be said that play is reality for children. It certainly is their self-imposed work.

Guiding Play Talk

Without forcing play into a contrived educational mold, the teacher can, through the introduction of playthings and simple paraphernalia pertinent to a classroom study, provide a means for concept rehearsal and concept testing. It is not unusual for children to ask adults to enter a play episode in an adult role or as an adviser on the accuracy of their life projections. If an argument develops over a matter of fact, a parent may be invited to discuss it or to provide a needed fact. Teachers can make themselves available for this kind of supportive role, provided they do not dominate the situation. They can judiciously make suggestions or inject a novel object that will cause the children to reconsider or to reorganize their thinking in terms of a slightly different situation.

Substantive Play at Different Levels

Two boys playing in the same sand hole with practically the same miniature tractors and trucks were observed during the same time of year at ages 5, 9, and 11. As expected, the activities, the accompanying language, and the attention span advanced markedly in sophistication over the years. At 5 years of age the two boys talked about playing with their tractors in the sand under the porch, but they were distracted by a number of extraneous things before each began to build a road on which they planned to have their respective farmhouses. Although the following dialogue, along with the appropriate action, reveals some concepts of dirt roads and tractor use, the episode is inconclusive, brief, and ends with the throwing of sand.

Jon:	Here's a road.
Jim:	It won't make a road. This is a dead end.
Jon:	No, this is a farmhouse—right over here is a tall, high farm.
Jim:	Now, here is a dead-end road.
Jon:	No, the house.
Jon:	(Humming rhythmically.) Hey, Jim, help me, I got stuck (meaning his tractor). Help, help, look at the big hole I dug. Anyway, I'm a tractor, err, err, err, err, kach, kach, kach. I'm getting stuck.
Jim:	Why are you getting stuck?
Jon:	Addy, pladdy—hey, it's a sand and dust storm raging across the earth.

At 9 years of age the boys assumed the roles of two farmers, Roy and Joe. They helped each other with the building of their roads and farmhouses as if they were neighbors. They had a much better concept of how a road is built and of the give-and-take that occurs when men are working together with different kinds of equipment on different aspects of a job.

As the observer took his position, the two children were carrying on independent play, one on each side of a clump of birch trees, each developing his own dirt project with trucks and bulldozers.

Jon: Hey, Joe (imaginary character), if you want to work on one side you could make a sand pit with your project. I've made one with all my leftover.

Jim: Can I have the thing that scrapes the roads?

Jon: Why?

Jim: To make a driveway.

Jon: When you're finished with the yellow thing (road scraper), leave it right there. (An array of road equipment has been placed carefully in a row and is ready for use when needed. Jim is developing a similar project with industrious ness, building miniature walks and special areas for the road equipment. It is beginning to look like Jon's. At least 3 minutes of silence pass here.)

Jon: Hey, Joe, anytime you need the dump truck just call.

Jim: O.K. Any rocks in here? I'll dig up the whole row. Wow! See this rock in the way.

Don: Wow!

Jim: No wonder I couldn't plow. (Long silence and much work.)

Jon: Now why don't you come over and see my plan?

Jim: We need clearance here so I can get mine out. These tractors are all ready. Those would be out working.

Jon: They use that on different kinds of farms (constructing a part between them together for mutual improvement). Where are you going to go?

Jim: Up to your farm. We are helpful farmers. Hey, Roy, can we use some of the excess dirt?

Jon: Sure, I'll help you load it up. I'll bring down the bulldozer.

At 11 years of age the two boys worked diligently in parallel play, not because they were in a less mature social stage, but because they each had big ideas for the development of their prospective farms. The farm setting was quickly constructed; the play then became the rehearsal of the highly complex agricultural procedure of preparing the fields for a crop, including sowing, cultivating, and harvesting. There was much less talk; the running commentary was no longer needed. No fictitious role names were used, but they both adopted a "country" accent when they did converse.

It is not unusual to find older children playing in this manner, yet in most schools creative play is the last educational method used in the kindergarten. Play should be continued in more sophisticated forms at least through the primary grades as a means for developing speech-thought. From the play situation It is an easy step to informal dramatics in which children create roles based on stories or incidents that they have experienced or can imagine. Mock telephone conversations and television interviews, which often are suggested in "using English" textbooks can be more than an exercise in courteous usage; they can be rehearsals of ideating language. Telling the class about a story that one group has read is sometimes best done in dramatic form. Role playing social conflict situations taken from classroom life or from big picture sets suggesting social problems between the world of the adult and the world of the child can be expanded into informal dramatics. Modeling adult roles and creating dramatic situations among adults and children are enjoyable activities that are psychologically sound.

Creative Dramatics

Creative dramatics is another natural form of play, popular among older children, which can be used effectively by teachers for speech-thought development. The enthusiasm with which children plan a show to be given in the backyard or basement can be linked to educative purposes if the teacher permits children plenty of time, space, and freedom for exploration in composing. To cut off creativity prematurely, forcing the dramatic play to gel before children have been able to verify their ideas, will leave only the stiff and awkward shell of a drama.

The educational purpose of creative dramatics in relation to social studies units is to rehearse ideas developed in the study. Most of the children should have an opportunity to play and to talk them out; otherwise, the value of the exercise is lost, even though the production might be more presentable at an assembly with only the born actors taking part. A judicious combination of oral and written composition is necessary before the final production.

One fourth-grade play showed possibilities when a composite of the class's ideas is used. It was composed from group discussions and composites of individual writing after the Homeric hymn to Persephone had been read to the class during a study of the early Greeks. The written text was not memorized but became the agreed-upon base for improvisation. It never played quite the same way at any two rehearsals. Music and choreography were composed by the youngsters. A group-painted mural of expressionistic designs suggested by possible happenings in the "underworld" formed the backdrop for Hades' throne.

Other myths, folk tales, or heroic stories from Asia or Africa or from American Indian collections can be the inspiration for creative dramas. In social studies, the struggle for life on the frontier, or the adventures of fleeing slaves in the Underground Railroad, or imagined life in the first moon colony are thematic possibilities for rehearsing conceptual learnings through creative dramatics.

Classroom Conversation

Originally, sharing, or "show and tell," was introduced as a practice to help children bridge the gap between home and school by permitting them to bring an article of attachment from home into the new, strange environment of school. It was felt that if they talked about something of their own, they would become relaxed in speaking before their peers. The practice easily can be abused by overstructuring it into a routine for speech drill and making it into a routine opener for the day, giving the teacher time to attend to milk money and other accounting tasks.

On the other hand, an informal period of class discussion with the teacher about happenings inside and outside the school can be a productive practice that could embellish the old "show and tell." The teacher can be involved in the conversation, raising questions of interpretation, of evaluation, and of relation to matters learned before. When class conversation is well done, it can be one of the most fruitful experiences for developing speech-thought, because concerns are usually ones that the children have brought in and they have immediacy, which heightens curiosity. In this way, the teacher can keep abreast of what is on the children's minds, provided the teacher is truly encouraging in allowing the children to talk about what is on their minds. Very often, clues for later study or for extensions of what the class is already working on are presented.

Glasser's proposed technique of classroom meetings is a relaxed yet organized approach to informal discussion that has proved productive in encouraging children to respond to what is happening to them in and out of school. Frequently, these meetings become the jumping-off point for classroom studies of substance based on the children's concerns and interests. Such "talk-about-anything" periods need not be held every day, but they should be regular enough for children to expect such a time. (Glasser, 1968)

With older students a topic presented by one of them can be discussed in small groups, and opinions can be collected from each group for consideration by the class. The teacher can sit in with different groups and lead a summary discussion. Snack time and lunch time afford opportunities for informal discussion if arrangements are made for conversation on designated topics. Parents can assist as talk hosts. In these situations, teachers have tended to sit back and let the children lead and comment, thinking that the children need the experience, but perhaps it is important for the children to be challenged by a teacher's questions and some adult thinking about a subject of their choice. The dialogue between teacher and pupils will foster improved speech-thought and help the students to consider what they tell each other and what they already know.

A good example of appropriate exploitation of "table talk" is a practice carried on for a number of years by a teacher:

The "Luncheon Club" was held once a week at a special large table set up in the dining room. Anyone from the fifth through ninth grades was invited, provided he was willing to present a brief program about some hobby or interest of his at least once during the year. There was a child chairman who introduced the speaker of the day and organized a question period following each talk. The children rose to this new procedure and participated with enthusiasm partly because it was theirs and partly because it was a role-playing of the adult world. . . . Teachers were invited from time to time as members who participated in the discussion.[4]

Classroom Dialogue: Exposition, Discourse, and Argument

Organized discussion should be used regularly in classroom programs for the social sciences, the humanities, the arts, and the sciences. Teachers consciously will

---

[4]Shady Hill School, Cambridge, Mass. Description by the authors of this regular event led by Helen Hayes, athletic director.

plan a logical outline for the discussion to make sure that various kinds of thinking processes and their accompanying language structures are exercised within the milieu of meaningful content. Sociolinguists have shown that children can gain the rudiments of logic in language, albeit in their own dialects, and can, with practice, develop thinking by analysis, synthesis, and hypothesis.

Dewey's five phases for reflective thinking would be most advantageous as a general tactic for problem solving:

1. Suggestion, in which the mind leaps forward to a possible solution
2. An intellectualization of the difficulty or perplexity that has been felt (directly experienced) into a problem to be solved
3. The use of one suggestion after another as a leading idea, or hypothesis to initiate and guide observation and other operations in collection of factual material
4. The mental elaboration of the idea or supposition as an idea or supposition (reasoning, in the sense in which reasoning is a part, not the whole, of inference)
5. Testing the hypothesis by overt or imaginative action (Dewey, 1933, p. 107)

All these phases involve talking from or talking through an experience. When educators adopt the "doing" aspect of Dewey's recommendations, it is important that they not forget his emphasis on "reflective thinking" during and following an "experience."

Discussions Used as an Invitation to Inquiry

To Joseph Schwab, the older problem-solving methodology advanced by Dewey is too limiting for the kind of investigation modern children should be practicing. He calls the old method a "rhetoric of conclusions," which takes children through experimental steps and brings them to conclusions already attained by predecessors. Instead, Schwab makes an eloquent plea for advancing the "narrative of inquiry" in order to exhibit the "course of inquiry." (Schwab, 1962) The teacher aids the children in finding the "syntax" and the English "style" that will carry the burden of meanings as the course of fluid, open-ended classroom discussion progresses. A problem is described. The data, focused by a scientist, is given or shown, and the scientist's interpretation of the event is described. A further problem is made visible by the outcome of the previous research. "The second enquiry is seen to elicit new data requiring revision of the earlier formulation and so on." (Schwab, p. 88.) Schwab goes on to say, "Care should be taken to emphasize the doubtful aspects of each research, the limitations in scope or adequacy of its conclusions, the questions and problems it leaves unanswered." (p. 93)

Invitations to Inquiry

The teacher, with the children, adopts the attitude of the inquiring, questioning, and always doubting scientist. Schwab suggests a classroom strategy of "invitations to enquiry" that could be adapted for use with children at different levels in school, provided the teacher sets the expectations within the limits of background and thinking capacity of the children. For example, younger children could be asked to make a narrative description for the following question: If we assume that all pets are animals that live with people, are fed by people, given a home by people, and trained by people, then is a cow a pet? This question would require the marshalling of descriptions of different kinds of pets in order to check the hypothetical classifications. Surely, other criteria would be discovered and checked out against the exemplars of pets named in the beginning. The differentiating attributes would be located for cows, horses, goldfish, and so on. The process of inquiry, which describes and classifies the phenomena of our universe in a special language style, would thus be experienced by the children. Young children are capable of descriptive and categorizing inquiries, and older children can cope with propositional and hypothetical forms of inquiry. All children can be "invited to inquire."

Using Novel Objects   The "invitation" strategy is only one of many strategies that could be devised to give children guidance in the development of speech-thought. A statement of observed fact would be useful, followed by a program of provocative questions leading the child into new considerations. A novel object or two can be placed for the children to manipulate freely while raising their own questions and propositions. Teachers, as they observe the playful investigations of the children, can phrase questions growing out of their comments, which will lead them to further description and analysis of previous attempts as the narrative of inquiry unfolds. Scientists are always saying that the questions are at least as important as the answers, so that educating children to frame questions is one way to achieve logical thinking. The "20 questions" technique can be adapted for use with science or social science phenomena, especially in the area of framing questions.

With children in the middle grades and above, such activities can be in self-directed small groups (team learning), as long as the teacher keeps in touch with the ideational movement of the group and guides their questioning. Social science questions and matters of judgment in viewing human situations can be explored in a fashion similar to that of scientific discovery as different kinds of evidence are considered. A parable or a short story that involves problematic situations of questionable morality may provoke as much reflective discourse as a question of space science if it is presented as a matter for inquiry.

Enlightened Opportunism   The Elementary Science Study had as its guiding motto, "enlightened opportunism." All their suggested unit plans encourage the teacher to seize opportunities presented by children to explore phenomena in an enlightening manner. Teachers, being well versed in the science of the phenomenon, intelligently arrange the environment and guide the questioning, while listening to the children's open-ended investigation for clues to be explored. (1962–1964)

The following is an account of several episodes involving first-graders in an exploration of shadows at the Elementary Science Study summer school. (ESS, 1963, pp. 5–9)[5]

---

[5]Reprinted with the permission of the Elementary Science Study of Educational Services, Incorporated.

Upon reaching a sunny, broad expanse of sidewalk, the teacher began to play with her shadow. All joined the game.

T.:   What can you make your shadow do? (Shadows jumped, hopped, skipped, grew short, etc. Shadowmakers talked about their shadows.)

Ch.:   My shadow can do anything I can do.

T.:   I can step on your shadow (shadow-chasing).

T.:   Can you get away from your shadow? How could you make your shadow disappear? (Jumping and stooping.)

T.:   Hold out your hand. Look carefully at your hand and at the shadow of your hand. What do you think is causing the shadow?

Ch.:   My hand. I am.

T.:   What do we have to have in order to have a shadow?

Ch.:   (Tentatively) Well, the sun.

T.:   Could anyone tell how the sun might be causing the shadow?

Ch.:   (Children appeared unable to think further about this question.)

T.:   Can you catch your shadow? Can you pick up your shadow?

Ch.:   (Many children stooped to pick up their shadows; others did not respond to this. Two boys began to talk about the cement and one expressed the idea which both seemed to share: Well, if I could pick up the cement I could pick up my shadow.)

T.:   Well, I know one way you can catch your shadow and pick it up, too! The teacher showed the children how they might trace around each other's sha dows. All the children were eager to do this. . . . Although un-doubtedly tired and restless either from work or waiting, the children were full of talk about these caught shadows and wondering about what might follow. . . . The class wrote a story about shadows. . . .

Another day the teacher planned to probe a remark made by one child which suggested that he had been thinking of his shadow as occupying space.

T.:   Yesterday someone said something very interesting about his shadow. He said it was a funny thing it was there on the ground but it also came up to meet him and touch him (moving her hands up her body as the child had done). Let's go out into the sunshine and look at that person's shadow.

Ch.:   It will look the same as any shadow. The shadow touches all over the front of me. (The teacher put her hand into the shadow in different places. Children began to fish for the shadow)

T.:   Is this body blocking off the sun? Does there seem to be shadow in the air here?

Ch.:   Yes, yes, yes (from those fishing).

T.:   (Walking back under the tree.) Do you think there is a shadow in the air under the leaves? (A few positive yesses as though these were silly questions to be asking.) Could the shadow reach from the leaves to the ground?

Ch.:   (Children looked up and down and seemed to be considering this idea.)

T.:   (Walking out into the sunshine while opening one of two umbrellas she had brought.) Do you suppose there would be shadow in the air under this umbrella? (The teacher raised it high over her head, then lowered it so that her head and shoulders were in the shadow.)

Ch.:   I've seen ladies use umbrellas to keep off the sun.

Ch.:   We used beach umbrellas at our beach.

Each child took a turn with one of the umbrellas in a purposeful way not really anticipated by the teacher. The teacher asked from time to time if they could feel or see the shadow coming down around them. Some children "tested" by raising and lowering the umbrella several times. May mentioned that it was "darker under here." One child said she did not see any shadow in the air anywhere.

Question Cards   Another tactic for encouraging children to think out and report their own hypotheses and solutions is the question card, presented in the following account of work on light and shadow with sixth-graders. (ESS, pp. 10–13)

This lesson started with discussion of x-ray shadows, light shadows, and paint spray shadows. Then each pupil was given a set of cards with different questions encouraging exploration of shadows and the straight-line nature of light:

1. Suppose light moved in the way smoke travels, can you think of some way the world and the things in it might be very different?
2. Is the kind of shadow made by a clear bulb the same kind of shadow as that made by a frosted bulb? Can you predict before you try it out? Then tell us how you tried it out.
3. Can you make the shadow of a straight stick be a curved shadow? Can you make the shadow of a curved stick be straight?
4. Can you invent something to show why one cannot see around corners? How many things can you think of that will let you see around a corner? Tell us about some of these. Or show us one or several.
5. Make a shadow. How many ways can you find to hide the shadow now that you have made it? Can you think of one, two, three, four, five, six?

Each child was asked to read these cards one by one, and then choose one of the questions to explore, alone or in pairs. They were shown boxes and a shelf containing lamps, string, tape, tinker toys, flashlights, mirrors, styrofoam balls, candles, bulbs of various sorts, extension cords, and other materials which they could use to answer the questions themselves.

Picture Sets   In the social sciences, similar tactics can be used for advancing inquiry. Joseph Grannis has experimented successfully with primary-grade children in using pairs and sets of pictures for developing and extending categorical thinking. (Grannis, 1964) The children talk together first in pairs and then as a group about the likenesses and differences in a set of pictures that suggest categories. A class observed by the author conversed about sets of pictures showing the same jobs done by farmers, fishermen, and so on, in different environmental settings. An imaginative teacher who knows the concepts and language of a subject discipline can devise similar discussion games through which children can experience the speech-thought of reasoning.

Sound and Word Play

If a scale has rational scientific discourse at one end, at the other end will be the purely playful and emotive language of the rhyme, the limerick, the joke, the pun, and light verse of all kinds. Poetry, however, is the most intense concentration of both the ideation of prose discourse and the emotive language of verbal play. It is rooted in as intense an observation of the world as is science. It grows from the very core of language energy. The way for children to understand poetry is through a close reflective look at the world and experimentation with the sounds, shapes, colors, and intonations of words and combinations of words in flow that can describe it. Poetry expresses "as ifs" about the cosmos and provides memorable metaphors for recognition. Sometimes, children reach poetry in their speech and writing, as do some adults. Children should come to know poetry and experience its possibilities as a grand vehicle for knowing and as a special form of symbolic presentation—a very special form of communication.

Practice in discursive thinking and speaking has been discussed, but there is left for consideration the practice of sounding the depths of the language through language play with sounds, timbres, and richness of meaning. Youngsters can be observed in the natural state of play exploring their language in all these dimensions.

With this kind of language activity so much a part of the child's own development, it would seem to be only common sense to encourage language play in the school setting. Opportunities for sound play should always be available to younger children. For practical reasons, language play is useful in helping children sensitive to the sounds and rhythms of the language in preparation for more sophisticated use in reading and writing. For aesthetic reasons, such play is the gateway to the feel of language that will contribute to their understanding and love of poetry. This natural tendency can be blocked by strait-jacketed exercises in "making" poetry that rhymes in regular meter, or by force-feeding the "old chestnuts" of grownups' verse to reluctant children.

Extending Play Talk into Verse Talk

Teachers may pick up interesting chants that emerge while young children are playing and may encourage their extension. On the other hand, they may interject into the classroom some words they know from their experience with children and thus prompt extemporaneous sound play. The teachers need not be afraid of permitting presentation of group chants and individual variations at the same time, because this is the way language play develops. A child picks up an idea from another and plays with it in much the same way that jazz musicians improvise on a musical phrase they hear. Children will not become undisciplined in such a session if the teacher gives them a feeling that language play is a constructive enterprise. The following example comes from a home setting, but is not unlike the kind of activity that should be happening from nursery school through the second grade:

A father is sitting in a rocking chair in front of the fire; his son is climbing on his knees, hoping for some roughhousing. The 5-year-old boy begins:

Do it with me on your knees.
Do it with me on your knees.
Clap, clap, clap on your lap.
Lapity lap lap lap.

Do it with Pete on your feet.
Do it with Ted on your head.
Do it with Hans on your hands.

Clap, clap, clap on your lap.
Lapity lap lap lap.

Traditional nursery rhymes will, of course, stimulate extensions. Children will chant them in unison and make up variations.

A related form of language play is making up word pictures or definitions. As children develop their ability to classify and to categorize, they enjoy creating similes or operational definitions. The following examples of similes come from a fifth-grade class:

Jane: Snow is like feathers.
Robert: Yes, like feathers from a flock of geese flying north.
Lucy: Like icy feathers that melt and leave their shape in your hand.
Jimmy: Freezing with a special shape you can remember later in a warm house or even next summer.

Ruth Krauss's book *A Hole Is to Dig* reflects the delight children have in defining things by their use, an expression of the "operational" way they think about the world. Five-year-olds completed "A meadow is. . . ." by saying, "where cows eat grass," "where horses are," and "it's an animal place." A 7-year-old responded to "spring" by saying, "Crocuses are a sign of spring. Why? Because they can put up through the ground and when the ground gets soft that is a sign that spring is here."

Rhyming will come naturally to children because of their delight in word-sound play, but the wise teacher may wish to deemphasize it at first in order to break through to their basic poetic resources. A better pathway for children to the creation of poetry is to start with a joke poem, like and dislike poems, or a comparison—whatever can bring forth honest feelings. (Koch, 1970, 1973)

The teacher can introduce a game in which the teacher begins a story and the children complete it, somewhat in the way folktales have emerged. A trip to the nearby woods or a studied look out the window as a storm gathers can be the subject of delightful verbal interchange. Sometimes these "stories," "reactions," "definitions," or "poems" are worth writing down and saving or preparing to share with another class or with parents. This is one way that narrative writing begins for the young, when the teacher writes down their "stories" to be read; older children, of course, will write down their own. With older children, there will be less talk and more writing at such a time, but talking must not always be replaced by writing. Some subjects are too complex to write about at a certain stage, but they can be thought about out loud.

From Oral to Written Thought

From the nursery school through elementary and secondary school programs, the phenomenon of communication, with its interplay of oral, inner, and written speech, means that there must be much lively practice of speaking as the language of reading and writing is introduced. Children present their stories orally and make comments about happenings and ideas. These are then transposed by the teacher without content change to the written form and are read back to young children or are prepared for the older children to read to themselves. In turn, books are read to the children, who then talk about what has been read. They react to the story, relating it to their own experiences, reflecting upon it and extending it with their ideas. In addition to talking among themselves, they will talk with the teacher. The teacher presents his or her ideas and frames questions that will encourage the children to think more deeply about what they have read. The teacher must confront the children with new experiences and happenings that will warrant talking, reading, and writing about. A cycle of language activities causes one to support the other.

Writing can be scheduled as one of several independent activities to choose from, or at times everybody can work on some kind of writing activity: dictating a first draft into a tape recorder or dictaphone, going over a first draft by reading it aloud with the teacher or another student, peer group critiquing of a first draft, or working on a second draft for display or for publication. Some children, during this activity, can be reading material written by classmates or members of other classes. Reports on social studies or science topics can be prepared. This type of classroom period might well be labeled "The Young Writer's Workshop," and be a valid replacement for repetitious language-usage skill periods.

As children grow older, the same general procedures should be continued, as reading and writing emerge to augment the oral-aural process. And so the school world wags from speaking to listening to writing to reading and back again.

The Teacher as a Guiding Critic

All strategies for teaching the arts of communication must emphasize the movement from speech-thought into written thought and back again. If from the beginning children are helped to be aware of the different language forms and are encouraged to strive for meaning in each form, they should find it natural to punctuate and to phrase properly for communication as the time comes. If children are preparing something significant to them that they wish to be read by others, they will try to put in the punctuation that will make it readable.

Students who write may want help with finding the phrasing that will transpose their speech-thoughts to the written page. In this spirit, teachers can safely raise questions and offer suggestions much as the friendly critic operates in support of a writer. Most authors ask a friend or a colleague to go over their manuscripts for just this purpose. However, the act of criticizing does not mean interference or adult rewriting. Helping children rethink and rephrase a spoken story for reading need not be an infringement of their right to express themselves nor an infraction against the postulates of child development. It is education. Children quickly become able to rewrite their own first drafts for reading. The child must make the decisions to transpose, while the teacher bases critical advice on comprehensibility broadly conceived.

In order to assist in this way, teachers must know what they are doing; they must have a broad view of the language system of English and know of its infinite variety; otherwise, they may not recognize the situation when children in their fresh approach have written more effectively than if they had used more conventional English. One teacher insisted on an alteration of a passage (quoted earlier) about stooping down to eat succulent wild strawberries that deprived it of its power. The original was: " . . . I was looking at a big patch of succulent strawberries and they made me stoop down and I ate them." The teacher's corrected version was: " . . . I was looking at a big patch of succulent strawberries, so I stooped down to eat them." By invoking a rule that inanimate objects should not be given human attributes, the teacher denied the child the use of exception to the rule when the meaning called for it. Teachers must not be purists.

In order to accomplish the role of guiding critic, teachers need to promote an atmosphere in which there is a disposition to use language. They must set up an encouraging and flexible situation in order that children will not feel pressured and become blocked yet at the same time will feel a need to say things or write them down. They must also provide an atmosphere in which intentions can be carried out.

In these ways children will compose their "letters to the world."

References

John Dewey, *How We Think* (Boston: D. C. Heath, 1933), p. 107.

Emily Dickinson, *The Poems of Emily Dickinson* (Boston: Little, Brown, 1944).

Elementary Science Study (Watertown, MA: Educational Service, Inc. 1962–1964).

Lawrence K. Frank, *The School as Agent for Cultural Renewal* (Cambridge, MA: Harvard University Press, 1960).

William Glasser, *Schools Without Failure* (New York: Harper & Row, 1961), Chs. 10–12.

Joseph Grannis, unpublished mimeographed material, Harvard Graduate School of Education, Cambridge, Mass., 1964.

Kenneth Koch, *Rose, Where Did You Get That Red: Teaching Great Poetry to Children* (New York: Vintage Books, 1973).

Kenneth Koch and Students of P.S. 61 in New York City, *Wishes, Lies and Dreams: Teaching Children to Write Poetry* (New York: Vintage Books, 1970).

Joseph Schwab, *The Teaching of Science as Inquiry* (Cambridge, MA: Harvard University Press, 1962).

L.S. Vygotsky, *Thought and Language,* E. Hanfmann and G. Vakar (Trans.) (Cambridge, MA: M.I.T. Press, 1962).

10

Reading and Writing: A Psycholinguistic View

Bright is the ring of words
When the right man rings them,
Fair the fall of songs
When the singer sings them
Still they are carolled and said-
On wings they are carried
Often the singer is dead
And the marker buried.

(Robert Louis Stevenson)

In the next three chapters we'll discuss the reading and writing processes, how they're learned, and how teaching can help development. In this chapter, our primary focus will be the processes: how reading and writing work, and how they're used. The following chapters will deal with teaching reading and writing.

It's useful to focus on one process at a time, but reading and writing can never be completely separated, whether we're talking about process, development, or instruction. So we'll be saying things about writing as we discuss reading, and vice-versa. And we'll be using the term "literacy" to mean control of written language, both reading and writing, at all levels of proficiency.

Theory and Technology in Reading

Early in the twentieth century, Edmund Huey, a pioneer in psychology, recognized the complexity of reading in psychological terms. (Huey, 1908) He presented a view of reading as essentially meaning-seeking and constructive. His work influenced thinking about reading in the first quarter of the twentieth century, but it was lost as attention shifted to the development of a technology of reading centered around the basal reader.

This technology of reading also had its impetus early in the century in the work of the Committee on the Economy of Time, a national committee dedicated to producing more efficient elementary and secondary schools at a time when education in the United States was moving toward becoming truly universal. (NSSE, 1915–1919) For the first time in the history of any nation, virtually every school-age child would be in school. The aim of the committee was to combine a curriculum that used time efficiently with scientifically based methodology. There was great optimism in the 1920's that science would provide solutions to all educational problems, including universal literacy. This "scientism" coincided with an upsurge of behaviorism in psychology and logical empiricism in philosophy. Specificity, sequence, and quantification became the watchwords of American education.

In the field of reading, William S. Gray played a leading role in the work that resulted from the committee's efforts and in the development of the basal reader. (Gray, 1925, 1937) The technology that centered around the basal reader had these main characteristics:

1. Graded materials began with "readiness" in preschool and first grade and carried through to sixth or eighth grade.
2. Focus was on controlled vocabulary. Word lists were used based on word frequency studies such as Thorndike's. The primers, and later preprimers,

introduced only a few words at a time and repeated them frequently. Each subsequent book in the series repeated the use of previously introduced words and added a few more. Publishers competed to see who could produce the most materials with the fewest words. Each book ended with a summary word list. Teachers judged progress by the ability of pupils to recognize words out of context.

3. Workbooks were provided to practice skills and to provide a drill on words. Millions of copies of these workbooks were sold each year.

4. Skill hierarchies were developed, starting with phonics, the relationships between the orthography and phonology. "Word-attack skills" were systematically cultivated through the workbooks. Directed reading of the selections in the pupil books focused the attention of the pupil on the skills and words being taught.

5. The reading program became divided into developmental reading, which was designed to take pupils through a normal progression, and remedial reading, which was designed to teach skills to those unsuccessful in the developmental program.

6. Testing became a major and eventually dominant aspect of the technology. Readiness tests were developed to predict success, achievement tests were developed to measure success, and diagnostic tests were developed to determine deficiencies for remediation. More and more, as the technology developed, the tests became tests of skill mastery, measured outside of the reading of meaningful texts. More and more the reading of meaningful texts in the basal programs became down-graded and the skill-drills achieved central importance. This became more true as public interest and school policy centered around scores on reading achievement tests.

A systematic technology for teaching reading grew based on controlled vocabulary and the development of a hierarchy of skills. The teaching of reading became central to the curriculum through the elementary grades and into the secondary grades. Testing, with a heavy stress on component skills, came to dominate.

If there was a theory of the reading process implicit in this technology, it was that reading is identifying words and putting them together to make meaningful texts. Learning to read was seen as mastering the ability to recognize words and acquiring a vocabulary of sight words (words known at sight). The major controversy, phonics versus whole-word approaches, fits within this view, since the argument is not over the importance of words but over how best to identify them.

Ironically, as reading became dominated by a skill hierarchy technology and the reading curriculum became keyed to gain scores on standardized tests, there was a neglect of teaching writing, particularly in the elementary schools. There was no similar technology for writing instruction, and tests devoted little space to testing writing since evaluation of writing proved to be very time consuming. Standardized tests did measure spelling, handwriting, and mechanics, and those tended therefore to be taught in isolation from their use in written language expression.

A Psycholinguistic Perspective

Starting in the mid-1960's, a new interest in language theory has developed. Linguistic science was gradually shifting its attention from sounds to syntax, and linguistic theory was concerning itself with linguistic competence. Psycholinguistics was emerging as an interdisciplinary bridge between cognitive psychology and linguistics, whose purpose was the study of the interaction of thought and language, and a new psycholinguistic perspective on reading also emerged. This perspective made it possible to understand the reading process and its development so that we could examine our instructional technology. (Smith, 1978; Goodman 1965; Goodman and Goodman, 1978)

Here are some key beliefs underlying this psycholinguistic perspective:

In a literate society there are two language forms, oral and written, which are parallel to each other. Both are fully capable of communication. Both forms have the same underlying grammar and use the same rules for relating this underlying structure to the oral or written surface representation. What differentiates oral and written language most are the circumstances of their use. We use oral language primarily for face-to-face immediate communication, and we use written language to communicate over time and space.

Each form has a productive and a receptive process. Speaking and writing are productive or presentational. Reading and listening are receptive. However, both processes are processes in which the meaning is actively exchanged.

In using language productively or receptively, there are transactions between thought and language. So speaking, writing, listening, and reading are psycholinguistic processes.

Language processes are both personal and social. They are personal because they are used to meet personal needs. They are social because they are used among people to communicate. Because languages are social, though they may differ in basic ways, they all are constrained by the same need to be comprehensible to others. There are only limited ways that languages can vary and still be comprehensible. Therefore, they are alike in their purposes, and they are alike in their limitations.

Furthermore, though the written forms of languages may relate to the oral forms of the same languages in different ways, they all must represent meaning in some comprehensible way that does not depend on converting them into their oral counterpart. Some use alphabetic writing; some do not represent vowels; some use symbols to represent syllables; some represent ideas directly. But written languages are not ways of representing oral language; they are alternate and parallel to oral language as ways of representing meaning. If they could only be understood by converting them to oral language, then they could not serve the special purposes for which written language is needed, mainly communication over time and space. Silent reading is much more rapid than speaking because readers are understanding meaning directly from the printed text.

A Single Reading Process

Written language, like oral language, is a social invention. When a society needs to communicate over time and space and when it needs to preserve its heritage of ideas and understandings, it creates written language. This happens when societies reach a certain level of complexity and size. Oral language texts disappear as they are created. Written texts are more or less permanent, so they may be sent over great distances or stored away over long periods of time.

The oral text is comprehended by listeners as it is heard, and then it is gone, except as it is remembered. The written text may be reread, because it still exists after it is read and comprehended. But both listening and reading involve making sense of texts.

There is only one reading process, regardless of the proficiency with which that process is used. The difference between proficient and nonproficient or beginning readers is not in the process by which they must get meaning from print. There is not a different way for poor readers to make sense of print as compared to good readers. The difference is in how well each reader uses the one process.

There is, likewise, only one reading process for reading all kinds of texts, regardless of their structure or of the purpose the reader has for reading them. This one reading process must be flexible enough to allow for differences in the structures of different languages, in their orthographies, in the characteristics of different types of texts, and in the proficiency and purposes of the readers.

We might compare reading to driving a car or a truck. There are small cars, big cars, old ones, new ones, trucks, buses, light traffic, and heavy traffic. All these differences require flexibility from a driver. But there is still only one way to drive. You can drive well or poorly but you cannot drive without using the accelerator, the brakes, and the steering wheel (or some parts with equivalent functions). Somehow you must make the car move, stop, and go where you want it to go.

Similarly, though there is need for flexibility in reading, the process has essential characteristics that cannot vary. It must start with text in some graphic form; the text must be processed as language; and the process must end with construction of meaning. Without meaning there is no reading, and readers cannot get to meaning without using the process.

The Process of Reading

To understand the reading process, we must understand how the reader, the writer, and the text contribute to it. Since reading involves a transaction between a reader and a text, then the characteristics of the reader are as important to reading as those of the text. (Rosenblatt, 1978)

The relative proficiency of a particular reader is obviously important to the successful use of the process, but so is the reader's purpose, social culture, background knowledge, language control, attitudes, and conceptual schemas. All reading is based on interpretation, and what the reader is able to understand and learn through reading depends strongly on what the reader knows and believes before the reading. Several people reading the same text will vary in what they comprehend, depending on their personal contributions to the meaning. They can interpret only on the basis of what they know.

Everyone speaks at least one dialect of each language he or she uses and usually several registers, or ways of using the language in different contexts. What forms of the language the readers control will strongly affect their reading.

How well the text represents the writer will affect how well the reader and writer can transact meaning through it. The writer's sensitivity to his or her audience and how well the writer has represented meaning for that audience will influence comprehensibility.

Success in reading will also depend on how much the reader and writer agree in the ways they use the language, in their conceptual schemas, and in their life experiences. When you write a letter to a close friend you may take a lot for granted, whereas you must be much more complete and explicit in a business letter.

An important difference between oral and written language is that in written language the two people communicating are rarely in each other's presence, so readers must construct meaning from the text in the absence of the writer. We cannot turn to the writer as we can to the speaker and say, "What did you say?" The transaction is a long-distance transaction between the reader and the writer. The reader must depend on the text for construction of meaning.

Text Characteristics

To understand what readers do we must understand the characteristics of the texts that readers are transacting with. The text is a graphic display, spread out over pages of paper. It has spacial dimensions, such as shape and directionality. English and Spanish are written from left to right and down the page, but Arabic and Hebrew are written from right to left. Chinese and Japanese may be written vertically from top to bottom or horizontally from left to right.

The orthography in an alphabetic system consists of a system of graphemes, usually called letters, which have a variety of forms and styles. The orthography also includes the spelling rules and punctuation by which the letters may be combined to represent the phonemic, morphophonemic, morphemic, syntactic, and pragmatic systems of the language. This orthography, in languages that use the same alphabet, must have ways of relating to the particular sound patterns of the language. So the alphabet must be modified slightly from language to language, but the orthography must also be able to represent the ways that the sounds of the language combine and are modified by the sounds around them. In doing so, choices must be made of which language level to represent. Sometimes we must choose whether words should look alike because they sound alike or because they are related in grammar or meaning.

The orthography must indicate through punctuation the sentence patterns and phrase and clause relationships that represent meaning.

The orthography must be useful by speakers of the language whose dialects differ in their phonology. This means that it must deviate from the consistent representation of sounds in any one dialect. Most languages standardize spellings across dialects so that the writing will be comprehensible to speakers of a wide range of dialects. Thus, the spellings cannot fit all dialects equally well (for example, *Calle, tortilla, caballo* in Spanish, or *Ben, been, bean, bin, being* in English).

The phonological and orthographic systems have different constraints, so they can never have complete one-to-one correspondence between their units. Oral language has time constraints; for written language the constraints are spacial.

The written text has syntactic structure. It must represent the syntax of the language to be understandable. Punctuation, sentence order, and grammatical suffixes all are cues readers use to get at the syntax. Written language sometimes tends toward more formal syntactic structures than oral language, perhaps because it is kept after it is produced. On the other hand, the sentence structure of written language is often less complex than oral language, because punctuation is a different system than intonation and doesn't avoid syntactic ambiguity as well. So writers use less complex structures to avoid ambiguity.

Written texts also have semantic structures. Though stories vary considerably, there are only a limited number of structures that they can have. Partly that's because of the nature of the meaning, partly it is cultural, and partly it is custom. These semantic structures make them predictable to readers. One common story structure has a series of events that build a problem, a climactic event, and then a resolution of the problem. Texts also have cohesive devices that tie the text together and provide a unity for them. For example, repetition of the same word and its synonyms forms a cohesive chain. All these text characteristics are used by the writer to create comprehensible texts and by the reader in making predictions and inferences in building meaning.

Strategies in Reading

The reading process employs a series of strategies. A strategy is a broad schema for gathering, evaluating, and using information. Reading, like all human activity, is intelligent behavior. People do not simply respond to environmental stimuli. They find order and structure in the world so that they can learn from their experiences and anticipate and understand them. Readers develop strategies for dealing with the text so that they can construct meaning or comprehend it. Strategies are used in reading, but they are also developed and modified during reading. *In fact, there is no way to develop reading strategies except through reading.*

Readers develop *sampling strategies.* The text provides redundant cues that are not equally useful. The reader must select from these cues only those that are most useful. If readers used all the cues available, the perceptual apparatus would be overwhelmed by unnecessary, useless, or irrelevant information. However, the reader can choose only the most productive cues because of the strategies based on schemas that the reader develops for the characteristics of the text and the meaning.

Because texts have recurrent patterns and structures and because people build schemas as they are seeking to understand the order in things they experience, readers are able to anticipate the text. They can use *prediction strategies* to predict the ending of a story, the logic of an explanation, the structure of a complex sentence, and the ending of a word. Readers use all their available knowledge and schemas to predict what is coming in the text and what the meaning will be. The speed of ordinary silent reading demonstrates that readers are predicting and sampling as they read. They could not handle so much information so efficiently if they had to process every bit of it. They predict on the basis of the cues from their sampling of the text, and they sample on the basis of their predictions.

Inference is a powerful means by which people supplement the information available to them using the conceptual and linguistic knowledge and schemas they already have. Readers use *inference strategies* to infer what is not explicit in the text, but they also infer things that will become explicit later. Inference is used to decide on the antecedent of a pronoun, the relationships between characters, the author's biases, among many other things. Inference may even be used to decide what the text should have said when there is a misprint in it. Inference strategies are used so much that readers are quite unlikely to recall accurately whether some aspect of a text was explicit or implicit.

Since *sampling, predicting,* and *inferring* are basic reading strategies, the readers are constantly monitoring their own reading to make sure that it makes sense. Readers are actively in control of the process as they read. There are risks involved in sampling, predicting and inferring. We sometimes make promising predictions that turn out to be wrong, or we discover we have made unwarranted inferences. So the reader has strategies for confirming or rejecting prior conclusions. This self-monitoring through the use of *confirmation strategies* is the way that the reader shows concern for comprehension. However, it also is used by the reader to test out and modify strategies. Readers learn to read through self-monitoring their own reading.

The process is a very efficient one. *Effective reading* is making sense of written texts. But *efficient reading* uses as little time, effort, and energy as possible to be effective. It uses only as much information from the text as is needed to get to the meaning and no more.

If readers are successful and self-confident, they take greater risks and increase their efficiency. If they find the text hard to comprehend, they proceed more cautiously but less efficiently. So readers also must have *self-correction strategies* for reconsidering the information they have or for gathering more information when they cannot confirm their expectations. Sometimes this means rethinking and coming up with an alternate hypothesis, but sometimes it requires regression back through the text to look for additional useful cues. Self-correction is also a form of learning, since it is a response to a point of disequilibrium in the reading process.

Reading Is a Cyclical Process

We can think of reading as composed of four cycles, starting with an *optical cycle,* moving through a *perceptual cycle,* to a *grammatical cycle,* and then finally to a ‗

meaning cycle. But then, as reading proceeds, another series of cycles follows, and another, and another. So each cycle follows and precedes every other cycle until the reader stops or the reading is completed.

The reader's focus is always on making sense of the text. Attention is on meaning, and anything else such as letters, words, or grammar only gets full attention when the reader has trouble getting to the meaning. Each cycle is tentative and may not be completed if the reader can move on directly to meaning. In truly efficient reading, few cycles need to be completed before the reader has meaning. But the reader, in retrospect, will know what the sentence structure is and what the words and letters are because the reader will know the meaning. And that will create the impression that the words were known before the meaning. In a real sense the reader is constantly leaping to conclusions.

Since reading is intelligent behavior, the brain is the center of human intellectual activity and information processing. The brain controls the eye and directs it to look for what it expects to find. So even in the *optical cycle* the reader is actively in control of the process. We know what is the most useful information to look for, where to find it, and which information to ignore.

The human eye is an optical instrument. It has a lens with a focal length that can only gather sharp information over a small spot of the text. But around the area of sharp focus the eye also has a fuzzy peripheral field, and the brain can make use of what is dimly seen if it has expectations to guide it.

Our ability to predict language patterns is so strong that what we think we see is mostly what we expect to see. As long as we see enough that is consistent with our predictions and as long as it makes sense, we are satisfied. Once we have made sense of print, we have the illusion that we have seen every graphic detail of the text. This makes the *perceptual cycle* very efficient. We can do very well with very few cues, if we are dealing with meaningful and predictable texts.

Rapid reading is associated with high comprehension, not simply because good readers can process the perceptual input faster but because they are efficient in using the least amount of visual information necessary. They are not distracted by attention to irrelevent text information; they use minimal perceptual cues to activate schemas.

The *syntactic cycle* requires strong use of prediction and inference strategies. Readers must be able to use key elements of sentence patterns, function words, grammatical suffixes, and punctuation to predict syntactic patterns when they begin to process them. Otherwise, they cannot give proper value to each syntactic element and know where to look for the most useful information. Just as you must know where you're going when you start on a trip, you must know the pattern when you start to read a sentence.

The clause is the most important unit of language, because meaning is organized and presented through the clauses and their interrelationships. Readers must be able to predict the patterns of the clauses and their interrelationships, whether they are independent, coordinate, or subordinate, in order to sort out the clauses and get to the meaning.

The search for meaning is the most important characteristic of the reading process, so it is in the *semantic cycle* that everything else takes its value. Meaning is being constructed as we read, but it is also being reconstructed, since we must continuously accommodate new information and adapt our developing sense of meaning. All through the reading of a text and even afterward, the reader is constantly reevaluating the meaning and reconstructing it as new insights are gained. Reading is, then, a very active dynamic process. Readers draw on all their conceptual schemas as they seek to comprehend.

What the Reader Brings to the Transaction

Obviously, the success of any reader in comprehending any text depends to a very great extent on the individual characteristics of the reader. That's as important as the cues in the text itself. Language can carry a meaning potential if the writer constructs a good text, but the meaning must be constructed by the reader. Readers must share with writers common language, common concepts, and common schemas for the transactions to be really successful.

Consider the absurd example of a young monolingual English-speaking girl trying to read an ancient Chinese philosophical tract written in classical Chinese characters. The task is patently ridiculous, but why? First, she doesn't understand Chinese. Even if she did, the modern dialect a contemporary child would know would be very much changed from the ancient dialect of the Chinese philosopher who wrote the text. Communication depends on a common language. If the young reader could somehow overcome this problem, she would still be confronted with a writing system that she did not know. She would not have learned strategies for dealing with the symbols that the writer had presupposed his readers could handle. Even if she could learn that, however, she could not read the philosophical tract because she would not have had the experiences, have developed the philosophical concepts, have shared the culture and life view of the writer, or have the knowledge the writer presupposed of his audience. Her culture would be so different from his that many of the philosophical thoughts would be unthinkable even for the vast majority of adults in her culture.

Young English speakers learning to read English are confronted with problems that differ in degree but not in kind from this absurd example.

Language Facility

People learning to read a language they already speak have a lot of language facility to bring to their reading. All children have mastered for all practical purposes the language of their family, friends, and community. This dialect is deeply internalized in each learner; it has become a part of the learner's personality. Further, each user of language develops his or her own idiolect, different in some respects from those of all other users.

Children draw on this language facility in developing literacy, and the dialects of reader and writer must be mutually understandable if readers are to comprehend what they are reading.

Even though both may speak English, the writer may use a dialect substantially different from any the reader is familiar with. Or the writer may use an unfamiliar register, a variant of the language used by people who share special interests and concepts, used in specific contexts. There is, for example, a school register used by teachers and text authors that may take a while for children to get used to. Every content area has a register of its own, a way of talking about things important in art, mathematics, science, or history.

Beginners, including those who speak standard dialects, have receptive control over a variety of dialects other than their own. Mass communication in this electronic age has widened language communities. Studies by Goodman and Goodman of several different groups of American children ages 7, 9, and 11 with different regional low-status dialects showed that they all have considerable receptive control over the language of texts. (Goodman and Goodman, 1978)

What's important is how children's oral reading is treated by teachers. They will tend to shift to their own dialects in oral reading, particularly in phonology. It's important that teachers keep in mind that meaning and not phonological accuracy in the teacher's dialect is what's important. (Goodman and Buck, 1973)

Even readers who speak English as a second language show considerable ability to make sense of English texts in the Goodman and Goodman study. For many bilingual pupils who are literate in other languages, reading is the first of the language processes to develop. Often they can understand what they read but only express their understanding in the mother tongue.

Physiology

The need for language and the ability to develop it is so strong in human beings that they can overcome tremendous handicaps and still produce and comprehend language.

People who can't see at all can't read print, though tactile reading through braille overcomes this handicap. More recently, devices have been used that translate light into vibrations felt on the fingers as the blind reader scans the pages with a light pen. Furthermore, some people with very limited vision manage to read and make sense of printed texts. People with physical disabilities or lack of coordination may have difficulty producing legible writing. Typewriters and word-processors may help them.

Of course, general physical and mental health interact with economic, social, and emotional factors, and all of these can influence learning and language. But there is no reason to believe that any large proportion of people lack the ability to become literate or are retarded in their literacy development because of physical or mental handicaps.

Some authorities have sought to identify a pattern of factors that produce what they have termed "constitutional dyslexia." They postulate problems of the brain or central nervous system that would interfere with perception and reading and/or writing development. However, if this were a medical condition, it would require some symptoms common to all those who suffer from it and not found in those not affected, and no such set of symptoms have been identified. In fact, usually the diagnosis is made by reasoning backward from the fact that the learner is having trouble learning to read. Research has failed to find any substantial cause for reading failure in children with physical, mental, or perceptual diffculties.

Experiential Background of Learners

Readers depend heavily on their experiential background and conceptual schemas to comprehend what they are reading. Texts are predictable for readers to the extent that the events, places, people, and objects the readers encounter are related to experiences they have had. If they are not, the readers will have difficulty comprehending even though all the language elements may be familiar.

Communication depends on some base of shared experience between the writer and the reader. This base may be the common experience of all those who share the culture or subculture, or it may be the intimate experience shared by a small in-group or even just by two people. The more intimate the base of experience is, the less complete must be the language, so that, between close friends or family members, a nod or a single word may be sufficient to communicate whole thoughts.

The following passage illustrates the kind of language composed of familiar elements that can be understood only by those who share schemas developed through common experiences:

Here comes the new scorcher in BMX: X20R. R as in rugged, race-ready and radical. Look how it's tricked out.
New style Elina UL racing saddle, tack tested by top riders in BMX. Gnarly chrome fork for monster muscle. Oversize down-tube that's totally tough. Dia Compe MX1000 stoppers on front and rear with quick adjust and quick release.

The source of this passage is an ad in a magazine aimed at boys aged 7 to 14. The copywriters know their audience well. What sounds like highly technical terminology is well understood by the large number of young people who are into motor-cross bicycles. They bring their schemas to the reading. Teachers of adolescents sometimes despair that their pupils can handle with ease passages like the one just given, but bog down hopelessly on *Silas Marner* or a sixth-grade world geography text.

Of course, reading itself is experience. This experience can be built layer on layer, so that the armchair traveler, detective, and scientist can come to be almost as much initiates as their real-life counterparts. But this is all vicarious experience. Language is symbolic. It can only evoke images, feelings, thoughts, and visions that have some base in the real experiences of the readers.

A seventh-grade pupil was observed attempting to read a worksheet in a junior high school print shop. The sheet provided directions for printing personal stationery. The boy read with difficulty but paused every time he came to the word *stationery*. Each time his teacher supplied the word, but the next time the pupil would be stumped again. When he had finished reading the sheet, the boy could describe the technical details involved in setting up the lines of print for the job, but he had no idea what the purpose of the project was. The simple truth is that he had no experience with stationery. The writer of the worksheet had presupposed that the pupils had seen stationery in use and would appreciate the value of personalized stationery. This type of unwarranted assumption is frequently reflected in school texts for all subjects at all levels and penalizes children whose experiences are different. Teachers who know their students and preread text material carefully can soften the effect by providing experiences that bridge the gaps to the texts.

Conceptual Background

Just as reading is limited by the experience of the learner, it is also limited by conceptual and schematic development. None of us, no matter how proficiently we read, can read written language that deals with concepts far beyond our existing knowledge, for which we have no schemas. Concepts may be attained or enhanced through reading, but they must be within the grasp of the reader. Indeed, once people learn to read, teachers would be unneeded if this were not true.

When teachers think that language alone conveys concepts and they simply assign textbooks for reading, learners flounder. Concepts are communicated among people through language, the symbolic medium individuals use to manipulate their experiences and ideas in order to develop concepts. But, under pressure, children can manipulate language without understanding the concepts involved. They may state correctly that Michigan is a peninsula and so is Florida without grasping the basic significance of peninsularity. They may just be repeating correct answers in appropriate contexts or in response to particular questions at the ends of textbook chapters, without understanding the underlying concepts.

Vocabulary

Some teachers naively assume that if pupils can translate the written symbols of a written text into oral speech, they are dealing with the concepts being presented. If they cannot read a particular word, teachers consider this a vocabulary problem. But what is labeled a vocabulary problem may involve problems on four very different levels. Here are four cases to illustrate these levels of vocabulary difficulty:

1. Readers understand a word or a phrase and use it in their oral speech but have not seen it in print before.
2. Readers do not know or use the word or phrase in oral language but can grasp the meaning in the context of an otherwise comprehensible text. Their previous experience and conceptual schemas make this easy assimilation possible.
3. Readers do not know or use the word or phrase in oral language and cannot understand the meaning, even in context, because it depends on experiences and concepts they haven't attained.
4. Readers are able to produce an acceptable oral pronunciation for a word or phrase they don't know, use, or understand. By our definitions, if they don't understand, they're not reading.

If there is a relationship, as some have argued, between vocabulary and comprehension, it is that people who read a lot build and extend their vocabularies through reading just as they do so through listening, in relationship to experiences and concepts they are developing. Vocabulary cannot be built in isolation from language and experience.

Getting It All Together

Research on the reading process among readers from low-proficiency second graders to highly proficient adults has demonstrated that the major difference among readers is how well they have the process together. Regardless of level of proficiency, all readers and writers are users of language. (Goodman and Burke, 1973) They use the graphic, syntactic, semantic, and pragmatic language systems to express and comprehend meaning. They all use all systems and all types of cues. Proficient readers and writers are both effective and efficient. Effective writers say well, for their intended audiences, what they mean to say. Effective readers get the most meaning out of the texts. Efficient writers and readers do so with the least effort and energy. Efficient writers produce first drafts that they may or may not edit depending on their purposes and audiences. Efficient writers are highly selective of the cues they use, using only enough to get to meaning.

The more that is understood about written language, the more complex it appears; yet it is no more complex than oral language that children have basically mastered without the school's help. Understanding how written language processes work and how children learn them may turn out to be the key to universal literacy.

The Reading Process in Different Languages

Readers in all languages have the same essential purpose: to make sense of print. To do so they must transact with a text created by a writer to express meaning. Readers in all languages must use the same psycholinguistic cues and the same strategies. They must sample, predict, infer, confirm, and correct. They must pass through the same optical, perceptual, syntactic, and semantic cycles. These are universals across languages.

Of course, the reading process is flexible to allow for differences in the languages and their orthographies. Readers of English expect adjectives to come before nouns; readers of French or Spanish expect adjectives to follow nouns. English syntax depends very strongly on fixed word order and not so much on the grammatical endings of words, so readers of English strongly base their predictions on word order. Readers of Spanish will seek important cues in suffixes and base predictions on them.

Though European languages are written alphabetically, punctuation varies somewhat in European orthographies to adjust for variations in syntax, phonology and convention. Spanish puts the question mark and the exclamation point at both ends of the sentence. English uses them only at the far end. Both systems work because readers in each language learn what to expect and base their predictions on their punctuation schemas. That's a difference in convention. German capitalizes many more nouns than most European languages. This is another difference in convention.

Some differences in orthography reflect language differences, however. Russian has two systems of consonants, hard and soft, so it attaches a "soft sign" to mark some soft consonants. Spanish has some pairs of words that are the same except for the accent, so it includes an accent mark as part of the orthography.

Even within languages there are sometimes variations in orthographies. American spellings are different than those used in England and other English-speaking countries in some respects: *labor/labour, jewelry/jewellery, center/centre,* for example. Part of this difference was deliberately created by Noah Webster in his first major American dictionary. He was part of a movement to make literature created in America look different from British literature.

In the United States many people believe that some languages are harder to read than others and that English, because of the complexity of its spelling, is among the hardest languages to read and to learn to read. It is true that English spelling is complex. That's due mostly to the multiple roots of the language. Some sets of English spelling rules are, Germanic, while others are Latin based. Still others have an influence from the Norman French, and there are some Danish rules in some English words that start with "kn" as in *know, knight,* and *knee.*

There is no evidence that this spelling complexity does make reading English any harder. Readers can tolerate a great deal of complexity. They learn to ignore some cues and use others, since they must sample from the text anyway. What is important to attend to will vary from language to language, but there is a still a universal in reading that in every language some cues are more useful and dependable than others. Readers build schemas for the complexities and variabilities of the orthographies and use them in their reading.

Nonalphabetic orthographies relate to phonology through meaning primarily, although one part of each Chinese character may indicate the possible sound. But the Chinese characters are basically ideographic. They represent meaning directly. That's much like the number system of European languages. 3 + 3 = 6 is written the same way in every language, though an English speaker would read it: "three and three are six" and a Spanish speaker would read it as "tres y tres son seis." It's very useful for science and commerce that we use this ideographic system for our arithmetic, since it is meaningful across so many languages.

Similarly, it is useful in China that they have a writing system that can be read with understanding by people who speak a very large range of Chinese dialects. Readers of Chinese will place much more emphasis on the semantic and syntactic systems in their reading. But the process of making sense of print is essentially the same for them as other readers, once they've adjusted to the differences in the orthography.

The Writing Process

Writers create written texts to present meanings, that is, coherent messages. Readers, intent on comprehending written texts, must transact with the writer's text and create a text of their own, which is parallel to it, in order to make sense of it. So both reading and writing are constructive processes. Writers are intent on creating texts that represent comprehensible meanings to their intended audiences.

However, the two processes are not the reverse of each other; they are not mirror images, that is, not every aspect of reading is present in reverse in writing. Readers keep their focus on their goal: making sense. Because inference and prediction play so large a role in making sense of the texts, they can leap toward meaning without fully constructing their texts. When the going gets tough they process more carefully and completely but they need only to satisfy themselves that they are comprehending.

In writing, the same cue systems are used—the graphophonic, syntactic, and semantic systems—to produce a comprehensible text. But the text must be complete, coherent, and cohesive. Both syntactic and semantic structures must be complete ones. Writers must have the particular audience for each text very much in mind. If comprehension depends on cues within the reader, then writers may not presuppose concepts or experiences that are unknown to the intended readers. They depend on their readers to make inferences and predictions, but only if they have provided sufficent information in the text.

The written text the writer is producing never fully represents the writer's complete meaning. Behind every bit of information made explicit there is a whole body of implied information related to it. The writer's knowledge schemas are always available to him or her. The "inner speech" Vygotsky discusses need only represent these schemas in the briefest manner for the purposes of thinking. But in the written text, there is always a delicate balance between how much must be made explicit and how much the writer can presuppose. Readers will also have relevant schemas to access and provide themselves in constructing their own texts from their transactions with the written text. This balance depends on how much knowledge and experience readers and writers share.

Eco, in discussing how he wrote *The Name of the Rose,* talks about how he spent a year creating, in his own head, the medieval world he was representing in the book.

> I had to know who the monks were, those who do not appear in the book. It was not necessary for the reader to know them, but I had to know them. . . . I conducted long architectural investigations. . . . to establish the arrangement of the abbey, the distances, even the number of steps in a spiral staircase. (Eco, 1984)

Dual Texts in Writing

So, for the writer as well as the reader, there are dual texts. The written text is never the same as the text in the writer's mind with all its referenced schemas, and both of those are changing constantly in the transactions between the writer and the written text. In the process of presenting thoughts, the thoughts themselves are changed. Presentation, as we have said, is one aspect of learning. Ideating leads to presentation, but it is also changed by it.

Readers seldom need to write while they read. (Taking notes while reading textbooks and other informational material is the exception.) Writing, on the other hand, involves a great deal of reading. There are several reasons for this. One is that writing involves producing relatively long texts (as compared, for example, to oral utterances in conversations) at a relatively slow pace. So writers read what they have written to remind themselves of where they are and where they are going in the composing process. Another reason for reading while writing is the absence of the intended audience. The writer assumes the role of the intended reader and reads from that point of view: is my text one the reader will be able to comprehend? Furthermore, since writing usually occurs at a different time and place than reading, the writer has the time to edit and polish the text carefully so it is as good a presentation of the message as possible for the intended audience. Just how much reading, editing, and polishing goes on will depend considerably on the purpose of the writing, the familiarity of the audience, and the disposition of the writer.

A Single Writing Process

We said above that there is only one reading process; so also there is only one writing process. To get from thought to written text, writers must use the same language and cognitive systems. But purpose, audience, proficiency, and orthography will strongly influence what the text looks like and how this single process is used.

From the point of view of generative linguists, any productive language process involves creating a grammatical deep structure to represent the intended meaning. A set of transformational rules produces an internal surface structure from the deep structure. And finally another set of rules produces either the oral or written texts.

The important concept here is that this whole process is rule governed. The linguists' rules are the grammatical counterpart of the psychologists' schemas. Writing and learning to write are much the same as speaking and learning to speak. Learning language is largely a matter of developing the rules by which texts may be generated that will be understandable by other people who are competent in the language.

Together with conceptual schemas, the transformational rules make language production an easy, flowing process. When the writing is going well for a proficient writer, the writer can give full concentration to the meaning. Some writers have commented that in particular works it was as if the characters had taken over the writing, because it flowed so naturally.

As we write, we use the transformational rules to assign syntactic structures. We create and relate deep structure clauses, and the rules then delimit the choice of structures and interact with semantic and pragmatic schemas and with schemas we've developed for certain text types, certain purposes, and certain audiences. Though we are making many choices, the choices are so constrained and so constrain each other that we are rarely aware of choosing one structure over another, one phrase or word over another. In reading and editing what we've written, we may discover ambiguities, see better alternatives, become aware of unneeded redundancies and disruptive writing miscues, but we're rarely aware of any of these during the time that we're composing "at the point of utterance." At that point our focus as writers is where it should be: on the meaning we're trying to express.

Field, Mode, and Tenor in Writing

Halliday provides a compatible perspective to the one we've provided above. All writing utilizes a language register that involves field, mode, and tenor.

> The *field* is the total event, in which the text is functioning, together with the purposive activity of the speaker or writer; it thus includes the subject matter as one element in it. The *mode* is the function of the text in the event, including therefore both the channel taken by the language- spoken or written, extempore or prepared- and its genre, or rhetorical mode, as narrative, didactic, persuasive, . . . and so on. The *tenor* refers to the type of role interaction, the set of relevant social relations, permanent and temporary, among the participants involved. Field, mode, and tenor define the context of situation of a text. (Halliday and Hasan, 1976)

In this view all writing (or speaking) involves a unified context of situation, and the text is created from the constraints it provides. The writer is writing in a context for a reason and chooses the form to use within those constraints. The text produced takes on the characteristics it does because of the characteristics of the context of situation. Writing is then a dynamic process in which field, mode, and tenor operate together.

Writing Miscues

To a certain extent, whether any writer stays with a first draft or edits, polishes, and modifies it is a matter of the writer's personality. Many successful professional writers, like Asimov, are essentially single-draft writers. Others, like Tolstoi, constantly polish and rewrite before they are satisfied that the text is the best they can produce for the purpose. What's important here is that single-draft writing is possible even for literary purposes and that all of us use it for some purposes. Yet, even a single draft will need proofreading for other purposes.

Writers, like readers, produce miscues, points where the written text does not match what they intended. These miscues demonstrate the psycholinguistic nature of the writing process. With the focus on meaning, what is written results from this psycholinguistic process, but the process does not involve composing an entire text or even a single sentence in advance. The process is happening while the writing is proceeding. So a reader may omit, insert, substitute, or reverse letters, words, or phrases. These may involve any of the rules and schemas at work in producing the final form the written text takes. Structures do not always end where the author aimed to end, because the writer may have shifted or modified schemas at the point of writing. Writing miscues are not a matter of poor or ineffective writing. They are intrinsic to the process itself. Furthermore, such miscues are rarely ever totally eliminated from texts even by professional proofreaders, because readers will be able to move to meaning and often will read the text as if the miscues weren't there at all.

Shanklin sees in writing a continuous experimentation that contributes to writing miscues (missed transactions in her terms):

> Viewed as the written expression of meaning, and not entirely worked out beforehand, writing involves experimentation with function and form until writers are satisfied meaning is expressed. . . . It is through such experimentation that development occurs. If writing tasks are in some ways new or difficult, writers will not have an effective means of cue utilization readily at hand. A greater number of decisions will have to be made, the brain's processing capacity may overload, and missed transactions are likely to occur. But such missed transactions at the point of utterance must occur and should be expected if development is to be achieved. (Shanklin, 1981)

Spelling in Writing

Too much concern for standard spelling can divert writers from the need to focus on meaning in their writing. As we say elsewhere in this book, the rules of English spelling are not dependable. Writers develop a set of rules and use them to generate or to invent spellings. But they learn that because English spellings are standardized, frozen, and unchanging, the rules do not always generate standard spellings. So writers learn, over time through reading and writing, the standard spellings of the words. These spellings are then accessed in the process of going from the internal surface structure to the written text.

To some extent, the concern for spelling can be disruptive to the writing process, particularly if the writer is operating on the premise that words must always be correctly spelled, even in first drafts. Most people who are comfortable with their writing have some strategies for checking the spellings of words they may have misspelled during proofreading or editing, and they do not let their attention be distracted from their expressive purpose by letting it focus on how a particular word should be spelled.

Why People Write

Consider a very mundane use of writing, the composition of a shopping list. The function of such a writing activity seems self-evident. It obviously is to create a guide in advance of a forthcoming shopping trip. But why is it needed? Is it possible to shop without a list? Of course, and most people do shop without one, at least sometimes. So why do people write them? Consider the following reasons:

1. To be sure to get what is needed
2. To save time in shopping
3. To avoid impulse buying
4. To economize on expenses through advance planning
5. To guide a shopper who is not the person making up the list
6. To follow a personal, familial, or cultural custom

These reasons are not exhaustive, and of course they may overlap and interact. Furthermore, writing a shopping list may relate to other preceding or concurrent activities. The writer may first plan and write out a week's menus;

perhaps the list is related to preparation of a particular recipe or a special meal and the shopping trip is basically to obtain the needed ingredients; or the shopper may scan the newspaper ads for special offers and bargains.

Custom often plays an important role in such an activity. People may continue a custom that their parents engaged in. So today's shopping list may be a descendant of the shopping order a prior generation handed to the corner grocer, who then stacked the items on a counter for the customer.

Making a shopping list may also relate to a broader personal way of organizing one's life. Some people feel more secure when aspects of their life are planned, organized, and recorded in a visible and consultable form. Writing a list finalizes and formalizes a series of decisions made prior to shopping and assures that they will not be forgotten, so it extends memory. The written record gives the writer a sense of being in control.

Why the shopping list is written also helps to determine its form. Of course, its general form as a list comes from the way it is used. The reader may scan it, but its main reading is done one item at a time to be checked off actually or mentally as it is used. The price per item may be added during the shopping in order to keep a tally of the expenditures. The list may be randomly ordered as items come to the mind of the writer. It may be systematically organized by categories such as meat, fresh fruit, and vegetables, and so on. It may be organized according to a week's menu. It may be organized according to the writer's memory of the layout of the store to facilitate shopping and save time. It may list generic items or specific brand names and sizes such as those on sale.

Even what it's written on and how it's written are partly related to function and use, and partly to personal characteristics of the user. It may be scrawled hurriedly on the back of a used envelope or carefully typed on a fresh sheet of paper. It could even be generated by computer or be checked off on a standard printed form with space left for personal items to be added.

Often the readers of shopping lists are the writers themselves. People write them to use later in their shopping. But sometimes the shopping list is written by one person to be read later by another who actually does the shopping. That makes a big difference. If the list maker does the shopping too, then the entries on the list need only be complete enough to jog the writer's memory. But if the reader is another person, then a lot more information must be included, like size, brand, type, or purpose. Even so, the shopper may surprise or disappoint the list maker because important information was not explicit or because the writer made unwarranted presuppositions about knowledge the reader would bring to the task of comprehending and using the list.

Form, Function, and Audience

We've chosen this rather special kind of reading and writing as a focus of our discussion of the reasons people write, because it is one in which purpose and function are relatively easy to see, form is relatively constrained, and success or failure would be easy to judge. Careful examination of the composition of a shopping list can make clear how writing relates to functions in all kinds of written language. List making as a kind of writing has many things in common with every type of writing.

1. Its purpose and function are usually related to communication over time and/or distance.
2. It occurs in a specific context in which the purpose or function motivates a specific writing event.
3. It has an intended audience of one or more readers.
4. Its content is relevant to the purpose and audience.
5. Its structure and format are suited to the purpose and function that will be familiar to or expected by the reader.
6. It must be so composed that it serves both the writer and the reader.

Writing of shopping lists differs from other kinds of writing in that there is usually only one intended reader, who is often the writer. Writing for one's self represents one end of an audience continuum. At the opposite end is writing for a totally unknown audience. Actually, it would be rare indeed if a writer had no sense of the audience, since he or she would, more or less consciously, have some intentions of reaching particular people or particular kinds of people. Furthermore, the content would itself help to define the potental readers. But it is not uncommon for writers to write for strangers with little personal knowledge of their backgrounds or interests.

As we suggested above, what goes in a shopping list will be read later by the writer while shopping, so it need not be very complete, but writing even a shopping list for someone else requires a sense of audience.

How Form Serves Function

Various kinds of texts develop, in every culture, certain conventional forms. These forms are partly the result of the purposes and contexts in which the text will be used, partly the result of cultural traditions, and partly arbitrary choices for the sake of consistency.

Even the most informal letter, for example, must include a greeting and a closing:

Dear Bob,

....
....
....

Love, Mary

Writers learn partly through reading and partly through writing what these forms are. If they have not said sufficiently completely and well what they wanted to say, they will not be successful in communicating, but if they have used unpredictable forms that violate social conventions or if they have not included certain culturally required features, they will also not be successful. In even the most business-like letter, readers could be offended if the writer simply stated the message without anything else:

Mr. Jones:
You owe us $50. Pay up or we'll sue you.
The Smith Company

It would be much more likely that the letter would include certain expected parts and employ less direct language.

Dear Mr. Jones:
It appears by our records that there is an unpaid balance of $50 in your account.
Please check to see if our record is correct. If so we would appreciate prompt
payment.

If your check is already in the mail, please disregard this notice. We value your
business and hope to serve you again in the future.

Sincerely,

The Smith Company

These subtle social and practical insights that are necessary for successful
writing, like those required for successful speaking, can only be learned in the
process of using language.

References

Umberto Eco. "How I Wrote 'Name of The Rose'," *New York Times Book Review,* October 14,
1984.

Kenneth S. Goodman, "Cues and Miscues in Reading: A Linguistic Study," *Elementary
English,* vol. 42, no. 6 (1965).

Kenneth S. Goodman and Catherine Buck, "Dialect Barriers to Reading Comprehension
Revisited," *Reading Teacher* (October 1973), pp. 409–417.

Kenneth S. Goodman and Carolyn L. Burke, "Theoretically Based Studies of Patterns of
Miscues in Oral Reading Performance," U.S. Office of Education, Final Report, Project
No. 9-0375, April 1973.

Kenneth S. Goodman and Yetta M. Goodman, *Reading of American Children Whose Language Is a Stable Rural Dialect of English or a Language Other Than English.* U.S.
Dept of H.E.W., Final Report, Project NIE-C-00-3-0087, August 1978.

William S. Gray, "The Teaching of Reading," in *NSSE 24th Yearbook,* Part I (Chicago:
University of Chicago Press, 1925).

Michael Halliday and Ruqaiya Hasan, *Cohesion in English* (London: Longman, 1976).

E. B. Huey, *The Psychology and Pedagogy of Reading,* 1908, republished (Cambridge, MA:
M.I.T. Press, 1968).

National Society for the Study of Education, Fourteenth Yearbook, Part I, 1915. *Minimum
Essentials in Elementary School Subjects.*

National Society for the Study of Education, Sixteenth Yearbook, Part I, 1917. *Second Report
of the Committee on Minimum Essentials in Elementary School Subjects.*

National Society for the Study of Education, Seventeenth Yearbook, Part I, 1918. *Third Report
of the Committee on Economy of Time in Education.*

National Society for the Study of Education, Eighteenth Yearbook, Part II, 1919. *Fourth Report of the Committee on Economy of Time in Education.*

National Society for the Study of Education, Twenty-Fourth Yearbook, Part I, 1925. *Report of the National Committee on Reading,* W. S. Gray, Chairman.

National Society for the Study of Education, Thirty-Sixth Yearbook, Part I, 1937. *The Teaching of Reading,* W. S. Gray, Chairman

Rosenblatt, Louise, *The Reader, the Text, the Poem* (Carbondale, IL: Southern Illinois University Press, 1978).

Nancy Shanklin, *Relating Reading and Writing: Developing a Transactional Theory of the Writing Process,* unpublished doctoral dissertation, Indiana University, 1981.

Frank Smith, *Understanding Reading,* 2d ed. (New York: Holt, Rinehart and Winston, 1978).

11

Literacy
Before School

In the literature on learning written language, one finds, basically, two types of treatises: those dedicated to promoting some methodology as being the solution to all problems, and those dedicated to establishing the list of capabilities or aptitudes necessary for this kind of learning. Within the latter group we include the educational literature that attempts to establish the conditions necessary for initiating this learning, conditions commonly referred to as "reading readiness. . . ."

We have searched unsuccessfully in this literature for reference to children themselves, thinking children who seek knowledge, children we have discovered through Piagetian theory. The children we know through this theory are learners who actively try to understand the world around them, to answer questions the world poses. They are not learners who wait for someone to transmit knowledge to them in an act of benevolence. To the contrary, they learn primarily through their own actions on external objects, and they construct their own categories of thought while organizing their world.

We believe that these thinking children play an active role in learning written language. It is absurd to imagine that four- or five-year-old children growing up in an urban environment that displays print everywhere (on toys, billboards and road signs, on their clothes, on TV) do not develop any ideas about this cultural object until they find themselves sitting before a teacher at the age of six.

(Ferreiro and Teberosky, 1982; in Spanish 1979)

Until recently, even teachers and researchers directly involved with very young children have assumed that learning to read and to write are activities that take place in school and are taught by teachers. The discovery of the writing system by human infants, their scribbles and explorations of letter forms and writing functions, their knowledge of books, and their response to print in the environment have been largely ignored and devalued. The reading of 3- and 4-year-olds often has been called "just memorizing," and their initial attempts at scribbling or writing have been thrown away or washed off walls, tables, and floors.

Yet adults will share accounts of literacy events of young children with each other:

How a 3-year-old patiently made rows of circles and lines on a sheet of paper and then said, "Read this to me."

How a 4-year-old pointed to print and asked, "What does this say?"

How another 4-year-old sat for a long time and produced a number of characters, many of which looked like letters of the alphabet, and then said, "This says me and this says Mommy."

We know that in each of these literacy events (events in which the children are actively experiencing reading and writing), children are discovering, exploring, wondering, and playing with the development of the writing system of English or Spanish or Arabic, depending on the spoken and written language or languages in the environment. As scholars began to know more about how the reading and writing processes work and how oral language develops, it was natural that researchers would begin to look within these literacy events for the signs of written language development among very young children.

Researchers like Yetta Goodman (1983) and her colleagues at the University of Arizona and Jerome Harste (1984) and his colleagues at Indiana University began to observe the way in which children interacted with print in their environment. Marie Clay (1975) developed ways of evaluating children's book-handling knowledge and suggested principles of their writing development. Charles Read (1975) provided insights into their development of spelling. William Teale (1984) and David Doake (1982) studied how children's literacy development was influenced by being read to at home. Emilia Ferreiro and Ana Teberosky (1982) worked with an international group of Piagetian researchers to discover children's concepts of reading and writing. Shirley Brice Heath (1981), Gordon Wells (1981), and Alonzo Anderson and Shelley Stokes (1984) studied children's involvement with literacy events in home settings. These studies drew on the theoretical insights of Lev Vygotsky (1978) and Michael Halliday (1975) into how written language development in the young child occurs in a social-cultural context. Social factors were

224

shown to be important as a context for the child's personal contribution to learning.

Researchers began to suggest that an intuitive awareness of the nature of written language develops in 2-, 3-, and 4-year-olds and that children are learning to read and write before they're taught, through their interactions with print in their own homes, on the streets and highways, in supermarkets, and even on television. They suggested that children learn to find order and sense in print as they do in the rest of the world. Researchers came to see that young children realize that print and pictures say things in different ways and that drawing and writing serve different functions. It seemed to these researchers that literacy development may have been confused with schooling and so the learning children achieve before instruction was missed.

Beginnings

The beginnings of literacy development are nonalphabetic. Children know that print says something, but they view the whole as symbolic of meaning. So the front panel of a Rice Krispies box says *cereal,* Crest is *toothpaste,* and Pepsi Cola represents *Pepsi, Coke, pop,* or *soda.* When they write one letter or one letter-like character for their name they say it says their whole name.

Like proficient users of written language, young readers and writers bring their own more limited knowledge of the world to literacy. Seeing the cut-out McDonald's logo from an envelope that had once contained french fries, Maria responded: "That's McDonald's french fries!" She could construct the whole from the logo, drawing on her own experience with the place and the product. When she was asked where it says that, she pointed to the print: "McDonald's," slowly moving her finger from left to right and rapidly saying, "McDonald's french fries," so that she finished both at the same time. She chose the print and not the "golden arches" as the part that said something.

Y. Goodman and Altwerger (1981) report that when preschoolers are shown a picture of an automobile, they usually say "car." If they are asked where it says that they will point to a small printed word, *Chevrolet,* for example, in the upper left-hand corner and move their fingers under the printed word. When print is totally decontextualized, preschoolers no longer tend to treat it like language. One 4-year-old who could read *Ivory* on the label of a soap bar said, "One, five, zero, r, e" when the word was printed on a blank white page of paper.

Preschoolers show that they can recognize print and select cues from it. One 4-year-old was shown a *Chicken of the Sea* tuna label. She said, "That's Chicken. No, tuna! No, it's dog food." It isn't hard to understand where her choices of *chicken* and *tuna* came from. Perhaps she knew the word *chicken* but then disconfirmed it and went to *tuna.* Her final choice, however, was clearly the result of a small red and white checkered symbol on the can label, a manufacturer's logo which she has experienced in relation to dog food.

As young readers know more, they become more tentative. Three-year-olds will quickly say "cereal" when they see *Corn Flakes* or *Rice Krispies*. Five-year-olds respond more cautiously. They'll say, "I don't know," because they know that knowing it's cereal is not enough and that the print says which one it is.

As children develop concepts about print and terminology to express these concepts, they do not always use terms with their adult meanings. *Word, letter,* and *number* are likely to be used interchangeably. Children know they are units of language but haven't yet learned which is which.

A Piagetian Explanation

Ferreiro and Teberosky (1982), Piagetian psychologists, have studied young children's discovery of how print works as a system. They find that children try a series of hypotheses about the nature of print. At one point they may expect large things to be longer than short things: the word *cow* should be longer than the word *fly*, a father's name contains many more letters than a little boy's. At other times they try the hypothesis that words must have a minimum number of letters: three, for example. They also move to the idea that each letter may relate to a syllable of the oral word or phrase. They discard these hypotheses as they gain more insight. A process of disequilibrium occurs, which stimulates new concepts and new hypotheses. A child might write ꟼꟼƆ to represent one cat but when asked to write two cats may write ꟼꟼƆ ꟼꟼƆ for the plural.

The hypotheses youngsters try out overlap, interact, and are cancelled out by others as they sort out which work, which don't, which are used infrequently, and which have no reality in reading and writing at all. This process can't be curtailed by teaching. True concepts can't simply be taught; they develop as children personally and actively interact with a lot of written language in appropriate contexts in which the written language is functional.

This suggests that children, as individuals, are going through the same problems and raising the same questions for themselves that the world's communities went through when they became literate. The needs, the environment, the attitudes, the knowledge, the significant others are all merging to aid each child in becoming a literate human being. It is important that the significance of each literacy event in the life of the child is well understood, so that educators will not ignore the intuitive knowledge children have when they come to school but rather will build on it. This intuitive knowledge is a major asset in becoming literate.

Discovering Principles

Yetta Goodman (1984) divides the principles that children discover into three categories:

1. *Functional principles* develop as children solve the problem of how written language is used by people and how it functions in human communities. They develop their personal written language functions. The specific functions will depend on the child's needs for written language.

2. *Linguistic principles* develop as children solve the problem of the form in which written language is organized in order to have shared meanings in the culture. These forms include the orthographic, graphophonic, syntactic, semantic, and pragmatic rules of written language.

3. *Relational principles* develop as children solve the problem of how written language means what it does. Children come to understand how written language relates to the ideas and concepts people have, the objects in the real world, and the oral language or languages in the culture. The science of semiotics deals with the relationships between systems of symbols. It can help us to understand the complex relational principles children are developing.

Functional Principles

Functional principles grow and develop as children experience literacy events. Children can be involved as spectators as they watch parents, siblings, or teachers reading and writing. The literacy event can involve the child alone using a writing implement on a piece of paper or reading through a favorite book. Or the child can be involved in talking about reading and writing: "What does this say?" "Read this to me." "I see DD - Dunkin' Donuts, let's stop!"

Every such literacy event provides the child not only with information about the function that reading and writing serves in a society but the attitude that community members have toward literacy. Is writing something readily available to the child? Are pens, markers, pencils, papers, books, and magazines accessible, or are reading and writing seen by the child as an activity performed only by adults or by children only in response to schooling? Do children see literacy events as meaningful aspects of living or are they burdens, which result in emotional stress?

Heath (1984) reports how agency workers, in places like social security offices and hospitals, assume that their clients cannot write, and fill out necessary forms for them. Children watching such literacy events build notions about the functions of reading and writing and about who is in charge of the literacy events in such social settings.

From the study of children's writing samples, especially in home settings, it is possible to list various *functions* of writing that children use.

1. To Control the Behavior of Others   Children know that they can produce signs that have an impact on how others behave.

Jill, aged 4, put a sign on her bedroom door that said, "Mnsrs dnjros kepe awt" (Monsters dangerous, keep out). She was able to use that to get back at her older sisters who, she felt, never would let her play with them when they had friends over. Children will put "stop" signs in their drawings appropriately and expect an adult to understand their purpose. One 4½-year-old often reported to her mother: "Daddy didn't stop at the stop sign. He'll get a ticket."

Jon said to his mother as they drove past a school zone, "That says (pointing to the "School" sign) 'Watch out for kids.'"

A 5-year-old drew a picture of a truck. On the side of the truck were the letters "AP." When the teacher asked about them, he responded, "That tells you, don't go near that truck 'cause there's a monster in it. He's going to kill you.'"

    2. Interpersonal   Very early, for some children as young as 2 but for many by age 3, their names are used to identify their pictures and their possessions.

Roberta, age 3, commented to her mother as they were driving, "REVCO has the same face as my name."

Lori was 2½ when her mother asked her to write her name on a picture she had just drawn. Her mother knew that Lori could spell her name out loud but had never seen her write it. Lori immediately picked up the crayon she had been drawing with and made four vertical lines at the top of the page above her picture, saying a letter for each stroke: "L..O..R..I." From then on for a period of 3 or 4 months until she began to make characters that looked more like the letters in her name, she finished each of her pictures by labeling them with her four vertical lines and informing her mother, "See, that says me."

    In homes where children are invited to write letters or notes, they develop a sense that written language can be used to say, "Thank you," "I love you," or something about their daily lives to members of their family or to friends who live some distance away. Children discover that written language is used when face-to-face communication is not possible.

A letter comes from a grandparent, and the child listens to it with excitement as the parent reads it aloud and then carries it away to be "read" later over and over again to anyone who will listen.

Bobby's letter is an example of the interpersonal function. It also provides insight into his development of the form of written language. At age 4, Bobby wrote to his grandmother using his mother's help: she dictated each letter as he wrote so that his letter had conventionalized spelling and punctuation.

4 years old, November:

    DEAR GRANDMOTHER, I LOVE YOU.

    BOBBY.

5 years old, August:

    DER GADMTR i LUV

    YU BOBBY.

By the time he was 5, Bobby was able to generate his own spelling, had the confidence to do so, and was in an environment in which his explorations were admired and accepted.

    3. Pretend-Representation of Real/Imagined Experience   By age 4, children have a repertoire of stories, which they recite appropriately as they read. They incorporate their stories into their play. Two-year-old Reuben puts on his dad's cap and calls out, "Caps for sale. Fifty cents a cap." Many young children begin to present their own imagination in written language. Early in the development of this function, the written language of the story may be not even visible but buried under pictures. The child may have started writing, moved to drawing and forgotten the earlier writing, becoming more concerned with the process of creation than with any product. Or the written language may have been a form of scribbling or letter-string writing, which is not yet communicative to adults. However, when children are observed or questioned during their process of drawing and writing, _ their intentions become obvious. Children draw, write, and talk, weaving back and forth among a variety of symbol systems. Harste et al. (1984) discuss these works by children and suggests that children are negotiating from one symbol system to another, depending on the pool of written and oral language and art information that children have available and what they need at the particular moment of creation.

4. Explanation and Information   As children begin prior to school to read signs in their environment, they also start to label their own drawings in order to explain them or in some way to represent in written language what they have represented in drawing.

Holly's work, at age 5, showed such a representation. As we follow her discussion with Andrea, who was sitting next to her in their kindergarten class, we can also gain insight into some of the children's ability to talk about language at the same time that they are participating in the act of writing and drawing.

Holly had written the word *zoo* on her paper, and on the next line she wrote the letter *l*. She then said out loud to no one in particular, "How do you write /ay/?" (she made the sound of the letter *i* as in *lion*). Andrea replied, "Apple . . . *a*" (naming the letter). Holly then responded, "Andrea . . . *a*" (also naming the letter) and wrote an *n* next to the *l* to represent *lion*, which had been drawn in a cage at the zoo.

Children expand on their use of written language to explain what they've learned about plants, babies, fire trucks, or anything else when they are writing reports of events in their diaries or are writing letters sent off to tell others what has happened and why.

At 4 years of age children will recognize that supermarket ads in newspapers say "Buy ketchup" or "Coffee costs less." Aaron asks to see the TV guide and then looks for his favorite program with his father's help. Children become aware that different parts of the newspaper provide different kinds of information and that each is organized in a particular way.

5. Memory Extension   Children learn that written language can be used so that something won't be forgotten. They can find phone numbers and use them to call their grandparents. They may list their possessions or things they need to buy. Or they discover that they can leave their parents a note when they go outside or write themselves a note to remember important things.

Jennifer, a 4-year-old, was sitting in the back seat of her car and asked her mom, "How do you spell 4th?" Her mother responded, "You can write it by putting down a 4 with the letters *t* and *h* after it." When they got to the end of the ride, the little girl showed her mother a note on which was written:

4TH O   IN MY ⬭

The child then said to her mother, "You know how sometimes I buckle my shoe too tight and sometimes I make it too loose. Well, today it's just right so I wrote myself a note so that I would remember to put the silvery thing in the fourth hole in my sandal."

A parent is making a shopping list and says to the child, "What else should I put down on the list?" The child says, "Cocoa, don't forget cocoa," and the parent writes something on paper.

Each function is developed separately with little transfer from one to another. Children learn how writing is used in a particular context and develop their understanding of different functions by being part of the literacy events in these contexts.

Linguistic Principles

A second group of principles is linguistic in nature. Children come to know that written language takes certain forms, goes in a particular direction, and, if alphabetic, has spelling and punctuation conventions. There is no orthographic system in oral language, so this aspect of written language is a totally new system that children come to understand. They also come to know that written language has syntactic, semantic, and pragmatic rules that in some cases may be similar to oral language but in other cases are different.

1. Orthographic Principles   Orthography generally refers to spelling, but other aspects of written language are also part of what are considered here to be orthographic principles. These include the alternate forms of the writing system, such as cursive and manuscript handwriting, and different print fonts, as well as the various forms that individual characters can take, such as capital and lowercase. In addition, orthography includes the direction of the writing (in English, left to right), punctuation, and spelling.

The written form of English is usually thought of as a particular type of published text: line after line of print, each sentence starting with a capital followed by lowercase letters in a highly conventional fashion. However, if you look around any commercial urban area, it is easy to see that written language also occurs using all capitals or all lowercase letters. It can be vertical as well as horizontal or even in zig-zags or in circles.

Most writing in markets, on streets, on television, on toys, and on foods is written in capital letters. Most of the writing that children see adults producing in front of them is horizontal and cursive. It is no wonder then that children's early attempts at writing resemble adult cursive forms, that their early use of letters or letter-like forms closely resemble capitals, and that their control over the horizontal direction comes very early. At least this appears to be true of children's writing development in the United States.

There is also evidence that children who grow up with other writing systems scribble differently, producing characters or letter-like forms that resemble the orthographic system in their own culture, and they tend to write in the direction most conventional for their culture. What is important to understand is that scribbling and letter-string writing are important aspects of the development of orthography. Katie's, age 4, scribbling includes several English letters, including *k* and *a,* and some things that look like English letters but aren't. Fatima, also 4, scribbles too, but her Arabic scribbling has a cursive sweep with lots of dots above the curlicues. Rudy, age 6, separates the words and letters of his writing with periods rather than blank spaces.

These children are discovering the form that written language takes in representing meaning. Very young children know that there is horizontal directionality in English print, that it takes up space, that it uses letters, that the letters are patterned, that punctuation marks off the patterns, that books are opened in one direction, and that some of the beginning pages are skipped over to begin reading. They learn these linguistic principles by interacting with and using written language functionally.

Alois Legrun (1932) and Gertrude Hildreth (1936) suggested stages of scribbling development. Clay (1975) discussed stages of early use of alphabetic characters and words. Evelyn Lieberman (1985) characterized the developmental moments of the name-writing of 3-, 4-, and 5-year-olds. Myna Haussler (1985) showed how children move from reading texts holistically to growing more aware of the alphabetic principle in their reading development. Although additional longitudinal studies are needed to gain even greater understanding of the development of these early forms of literacy, it is important for teachers and researchers to appreciate these as part of writing development. Adults recognize babbling and holophrastic speaking as the beginnings of the oral language of the child; it is time to recognize scribbling, letter-string formation, and invented spellings as the beginnings of reading and writing.

Directionality is another orthographic principle that children explore and develop. By 4 or 5 years of age children in English-speaking homes produce writing that is horizontal, although for a while they may write from right to left or they may make their first line from left to right and then snake back in the opposite direction. Children's reversals in writing may be explained as explorations of aesthetic and linguistic principles and are not likely to be due to any problem with brain dysfunctions, as some have assumed.

Bryan, who is 3½, is drawing a dinosaur on a big sheet of paper. He finishes at the bottom of the paper, but he wants to write the name of the dinosaur on the sheet. He writes *TY* on the lowest right corner and *ran, usor, us,* and *rex* on successive lines, one above the other, using the available space and snaking up toward the top right of the page. He's writing alternately from right to left and left to right, but he's guided by the aesthetics and space availability on his picture, not simply by language conventions.

The development of spelling in young children is well documented by Read (1975), Chomsky (1975), Bissex (1980), Henderson and Beers (1980), and others. Their major conclusion is that children develop rules about spelling before they are given instruction.

One key insight that emerges from research on natural spelling development is that, like the other forms of language, writing is invented and not imitated. Children invent ways of spelling the words they want to use. They do so by trying a series of hypotheses based on their accumulated knowledge of how the spelling system works. Read (1975) concludes from his research that children's spelling development reflects their search for relationships between oral and written language. He and others hypothesize a developmental sequence moving from a letter-naming strategy, to control over consonants and then certain vowels, and on toward conventional spelling. There is evidence that this development is quite independent of instruction. Henderson extends these conclusions to other writing systems. (Henderson and Beers, 1980, p. 11)

> From our exploratory work across languages (Finnish, German, French, Spanish, Chinese) I am inclined to believe that these progressions have a marked commonality even though they are expressed in different writing systems.

Spelling development is more than inventing a set of phonics, rules for how sound patterns relate to letter patterns. Children discover the visible features of the orthography. Although many young writers spell *telephone* and *elephant* with an *f,* some children are already using the *ph,* perhaps from seeing the word *telephone* on so many signs. Children could not move toward conventional spelling unless they were relating the visual forms of what they read to the forms of their invented spellings. Invented spelling rules can get them close, but they can't produce reliable standard spellings.

Where words end in both oral and written language is by no means obvious. The features that mark speech into units do not systematically correspond to the white spaces between written words, so we find the principles children invent for marking off words in writing going through stages of development. Bissex (1980) provides examples from her son's writing at age 5:

> *Efu wauth kloz I wel gevua wauthen mathen.*

(If you wash clothes I will give you a washing machine.)

A Native American six year old wrote:

> *It livdina kav.*

(It lived in a cave.)

This concern for segmentation in written language is mirrored in children's development of punctuation. Bissex reports that her son used the exclamation mark before any other form of punctuation. Other children discover the use of the period, sometimes overgeneralizing its use as a word boundary marker before they control the use of space to separate words. The more that children use written language that makes use of punctuation for purposes that make sense to them, the greater their control over punctuation grows.

Jennifer used dialogue in her writing in the first grade when she was 6, but it was not until she was 7 that punctuation related to dialogue appeared in her story writing.

January, Grade 1:

> *. . . the mastr yald at hem you onle have*
> *two galns of hone he tot to the flor*
> *he sed tri to gev me som mor natr. . . .*

(The master yelled at him, "You only have two gallons of honey." He talked to the flower. He said try to give me some more nectar . . .)

March, Grade 2:

> . . . *"so he said I will go to the camping*
> *stor, and I will ask what I need to go on my trip"*
> . . . *so he "said Im going camping"* . . .

Most orthographic features have no direct counterpart in oral language, yet they fit in the visible system of written language. Children develop orthographic principles as much through reading as through writing. Exclamation marks in cartoons, which show POW!, SMASH!, and so on, may explain the early use of the exclamation mark. Periods are the most frequent punctuation mark in English and are controlled and overgeneralized earliest by young readers in a variety of settings. Frank Smith (1981) believes that writers who learn to control spelling and aspects of the syntactic system do so primarily through their reading. Bissex (1980) also offers a similar conclusion as she discusses her son's punctuation development:

> Most of Paul's knowledge of punctuation came from reading, such as his use of the colon and ellipsis . . . His formal instruction . . . had not included such uses. (p. 181)

2. Syntactic Principles   The syntactic principles children learn will again depend on the functions of writing that they see used and in which they participate. There are many syntactic features of written English that do not occur in oral language. For example, in oral English it is unlikely that a speaker would report a dialogue between people using "he says" or "she said." Usually dialogue is reported in oral language through the use of the indirect quotation form, such as "Mother said that you may go outside." Even if a "mother said" might occur in someone's oral speech, rarely would one find the form "said Mother" or "said Pinocchio." Yet, in Jennifer's story (other excerpts appear above) she did use the dialogue carrier form of "said the bee" without the quotation marks:

> *I am soo cold sad the bee* . . .

Early in their writing, children show developing control over the principle that some morphemic endings are kept the same, regardless of their phonological composition. For example, at ages 5 and 6 children may spell words such as *walked, jumped,* and *kissed* ending with the letter *t*. It is later that they realize that *ed* tends to be the most common graphic representation of past tense in English.

Two first graders showed overgeneralization of this morphemic principle in their spontaneous writing. Carolyn, in writing a letter to her grandparents, spelled the ordinal numbers *first, fourst, sixst* as she reported what grade she and her siblings were in (Milz, 1983). When she read the letter to her teacher she orally produced the appropriate English forms. Michael, a Native American first grader, wrote to a friend about his "sidiren" and "bidren" (sisters and brothers). Could these morphemic endings have been overgeneralizations from the word *children?* Again, when he read this out loud, he read the words appropriately as *sisters* and *brothers.*

3. Semantic and Pragmatic Principles   In the same way that children learn the ways written language is similar to or different from oral language syntactically, they also learn whether meaning is represented in written language in the same ways or in different ways than it is represented in oral language. Children who write "Once upon a time" at the beginning of a story indicate an awareness of story structure. Of hundreds of children's letters examined, there was not one letter that a child had written to anyone that started with "Once upon a time." Most letters start with something like "Dear _____," or "How are you?"

The syntax and semantics of oral and written language are similar in many respects, but written language uses space linearly, the way oral language uses sequence in time. There are other features of syntax and semantics unique to written language. Children learn the similarities and differences through their explorations of reading and writing.

Relational Principles

Language is a symbol system. That's true of both oral and written language. In oral language the speaker must relate the oral symbol, whether it's a word, a phrase, a metaphor, or a sentence, to its meaning or idea as well as to the reality that each represents. This is also true of written language, and as children read and write they develop these relational principles. Children must relate their writing to the ideas, concepts, or meanings they are writing about.

If they grow up in an alphabetic writing system, children also learn that there are aspects of speaking and writing that relate to each other. Such relationships are not simply letter-sound correspondences; they are much more complicated than that.

The developing writer must come to know that writing can relate to the object and to the meaning of the object being represented, to oral language, to visual perception of the orthography, to different text formats, and to the interrelation of all these relationships.

1. Relating Writing to the Object and to Its Meaning   When young children are asked why a dog is called a dog, they may reply, "because it has four legs." It is the property of the object itself that provides its label. Children use this same concept when they begin to discover that written language can be directly related to the object or to the meaning of the thing being written about. Ferreiro and Teberosky (1982) describe children who believe that the older or bigger someone or something is the longer that person's name or the label for the thing should be.

Ali, a 2-year-old child, when asked to write his name, produced the first initial of his name only. He then proceeded to use that letter to represent himself in pictures he drew. He put the *a* in the center of the page and drew around it, showed his mother the pictures, and said, "That's Ali on his bicycle."

Early pictographic writing and the logographic writing that appeared later were similar attempts of iconic representation of the object or the meaning or conceptualization of the object in written language. In much of children's early writing development, there can be parallels made to the development of writing systems by the human race.

2. The Visual Perception of Orthography   As discussed earlier, children show evidence that they are aware, quite early, that orthographic features represent meaning in organized fashions, although certain features become more salient than others. Initial and final consonants in English seem to be controlled early by many young children. Kindergarten and first-grade children who are asked to write "McDonald's" often make some letters in the word *bigger* than others even when they are all produced as capitals. There is evidence that suggests that children often know how many letters a particular word should have even if they forget the particular letters. (Lieberman, 1985)

A 5½-year-old wrote *opn* for open as he was writing in his diary. He looked up at his teacher and said, "That needs one more, it needs *e* at the end." He didn't bother correcting the writing, however.

3. Different Kinds of Texts   Children also relate certain kinds of language to certain kinds of texts; for example, they know that letters start "Dear Grandma, . . ." and that signs that turn on in airplanes contain warnings.

Sara, aged 4, turned to her 2-year-old brother when the "No Smoking" sign came on in the jet as they were taking off to visit their grandmother. He was happily sitting next to her, sucking his thumb. She jerked the finger out of his mouth, saying sharply, "See that sign? it says no bad habits!"

When children write to Santa Claus they use list form for their requests.

Listening to and participating in story reading builds functions of connected discourse in books. Children begin to pick up wordless picture books and say "Once upon a time . . ." They know that books can tell stories and that the stories have a certain form and use a particular kind of language.

Conclusions

Each of the principles has its own developmental pattern, constrained in relation to the development of the other principles. Each varies with the learner's use and the significance of a particular literacy event. However, what is most significant is that for each function of written language the beginning writer comes to know not only the function of the event and how it relates to meaning but also the orthographic, syntactic, semantic, and pragmatic systems necessary to produce that piece of writing.

This section has presented the principles about written language that children begin to develop prior to coming to school. The major purposes of this discussion of written language development in young children have been, first, to point up just how much written language development has already taken place before children begin school, and second, to suggest the complexity involved as children develop their reading and writing systems. These complexities children face are sorted out at the beginnings of reading and writing development and they become less formidable as the learner becomes more proficient.

Children must deal with the many principles and systems as they learn to read and write. None of these announce themselves separately to the child. They occur in a complex social cultural environment and in a complex array of forms for complex purposes. It is from this complexity that the beginner at reading and writing evolves the functional purposes for literacy, the organization or form of the writing system, and the ways these all come together and relate to meaning and oral language.

As children make these discoveries, they must test out many hypotheses and discard some conclusions as they decide that others are more appropriate. They must learn which principles are more significant, which are insignificant, and how and when significance changes.

Finally, much of the research reported suggests that children are participating in many literacy activities before they come to school. These continue outside of school. The evidence is unfortunately abundant of children who are actually using literacy for a variety of functions before they come to school but who stop their reading and writing because the instructional process makes them believe that their explorations are inappropriate. There is an instructional function of written language that children often develop as part of their schooling experience. Unfortunately, some children begin to believe that the only function for reading and writing is for instructional purposes in school with only the teacher as audience.

If teachers understand and respect the developmental aspects of literacy in young children—what they have learned and how they have learned it—then they can develop instructional programs that will build on the principles that the child is already developing. Expansion is the key word in a school program in developing literacy.

If the job of schools is to start "where the learners are," then teachers must be aware of what children know when they come to school. They must be able to accept and build on the literacy children achieve on their own and understand the miscues and misconceptions children produce as also being indicators of development.

Literacy development begins for children growing up into a literate society long before school starts. Development of literacy continues outside of school. The school's job is to build on the base, support the development, draw on the outside school literacy events, and work with the children as they grow.

References

Alonzo B. Anderson and Shelley J. Stokes, "Social and Institutional Influences on the Development and Practice of Literacy," in H. Goelman, A. Oberg, and F. Smith, *Awakening to Literacy* (Portsmouth, NH: Heinemann, 1984).

Glenda Bissex, *GNYS AT WRK: A Child Learns to Write and Read* (Cambridge, MA: Harvard University Press, 1980).

Marie Clay, *What Did I Write?* (Auckland, NZ: Heinemann, 1975).

Carol Chomsky, "How Sister Got into the Grog," *Early Years* (November 1975).

Emilia Ferreiro and Ana Teberosky, *Literacy Before Schooling* (Exeter, NH and London: Heinemann, 1982; oringinally published as *Los sistemas de escritura en el desarrollo del niño,* Mexico D. F.: Siglo XXI Editores, S.A., 1979).

Hillel Goelman, Antoinette Oberg, and Frank Smith, *Awakening to Literacy* (Portsmouth, NH: Heinemann, 1984).

Kenneth S. Goodman and Yetta M. Goodman, "A Whole-Language Comprehension-Centered Reading Program," Tucson: Program in Language and Literacy Occ. Paper No. 2, University of Arizona, 1981).

Yetta M. Goodman, "Beginning Reading Development, Strategies and Principles" in Robert P. Parker and Florence Davis (Eds.), *Developing Literacy* (Newark, DE: International Reading Association, 1983).

———, "The Development of Initial Literacy," in H. Goelman, A. Oberg, and F. Smith, *Awakening to Literacy* (Portsmouth, NH: Heinemann, 1984).

———and Bess Altwerger, "A Study of Literacy in Pre-School Children," Occ. Paper No. 4 (Tucson: Program in Language and Literacy, University of Arizona, 1981).

Michael Halliday, *Learning How to Mean* (London: Edward Arnold, 1975).

Jerome Harste, "Children's Language and the World: Initial Encounters With Print," in J. Langer and M. Smith-Burke, *Reader Meets Author: Bridging the Gap* (Newark, DE: International Reading Association, 1984).

———, Virginia Woodward, and Carolyn Burke, *Language Stories and Literacy Lessons* (Exeter NH: Heinemann, 1984).

Myna M. Haussler, "Transitions into Literacy: A Psycholinguistic Analysis of Beginning Reading in Kindergarten and First Grade Children," Occ. Paper No. 11 (Tucson: Program in Language and Literacy, University of Arizona, 1985).

Shirley Brice Heath, "Toward an Ethnohistory of Writing in American Education," in M. Whiteman, *Variation in Writing: Functional and Linguistic-Cultural Differences* (Hillsdale, NJ: Lawrence Erlbaum Associates, 1981).

———, *Ways with Words* (Cambridge, MA: Cambridge University Press, 1984).

Edmund Henderson and James Beers, *Developmental and Cognitive Aspects of Learning to Spell: A Reflection of Word Knowledge* (Newark, DE: International Reading Association, 1980).

Gertrude Hildreth, "Developmental Sequences in Name Writing," *Child Development,* vol. 7 (1936), pp. 292–303.

Alois Legrun, "How and What Do Preschoolers Write?" *Zeitschrift fur Padagogische Psychologie,* vol. 33 (1932), pp. 322–331.

Evelyn Lieberman, "Initial Name-Writing Development," unpublished doctoral dissertation, University of Arizona, 1985.

Vera Milz, "A Psycholinguistic Description of the Development of Writing in Selected First Grade Students," doctoral dissertation, University of Arizona, 1983. *Dissertation Abstracts International,* Vol. 44, 3279A.

Charles Read, "Children's Categorization of Speech Sounds in English," Research Report No. 17, Urbana IL: NCTE, 1975.

Jesse Reid, "Learning to Think About Reading," *Educational Research,* vol. 9, no. 1 (1966), pp. 56–62.

Frank Smith, *Writing and the Writer* (New York; Holt, Rinehart and Winston, 1981).

Raghnild Soderbergh, *Reading in Early Childhood: A Linguistic Study of a Preschool Child's Gradual Acquisition of Reading Ability* (Washington DC: Georgetown University Press, 1977).

William H. Teale, "Reading to Young Children: Its Significance for Literacy Development," in H. Goelman, A. Oberg, and F. Smith, *Awakening to Literacy* (Exeter, NH: Heinemann, 1984).

Lev Vygotsky, *Mind in Society.* M. Cole, V. John-Steiner, S. Scribner, and E. Souberman (Eds.) (Cambridge, MA: Harvard University Press, 1978).

Gordon Wells, *Learning Through Language: The Study of Language Development,* Vol. 1 (Cambridge, MA: Cambridge University Press, 1981).

12

Learning and Teaching Reading:
Strategies for Comprehension

Methods for learning to read come and go across the educational arena like the march of super-numeraries upon the stage. Each is heralded as the final solution of the problem of learning to read; but each in turn gives way to some later discovery. The simple fact is that they all lack the essential of any well grounded method, namely relevance to the child's mental needs. No scheme for learning can supply this want. Only a new motive—putting the child in a vital relation to the things to be read—can be of service here.

(John Dewey, Quoted in Betts, 1957)

In this chapter we'll consider current instructional practice and then present a whole-language view of reading development and the teaching that serves that development consistent with the view of language and thinking that has been developed throughout the book. Dewey's view of education places the learner at the center of problem-solving experiences. A whole-language view of reading instruction is rooted in the humanistic approach of Dewey. It sees learning to read as the problem solving of Dewey: learning how to comprehend the written language encountered as the child grows up in a literate environment. It sees learning to read as the discovery of the order in the physical world of Piaget. Becoming literate is growing into literacy. Teaching is supporting that growth.

Views of Reading Implicit in Instructional Programs

Because the technology of instruction in reading developed without a firm base in theories of the process, much common practice incorporates narrow views of the processes and creates conflicts for the learners as they attempt to make sense through language while also trying to do what they're taught. The technology tends to reduce reading to small aspects of the whole process. The focus tends to be on form outside of whole-language context and outside of the context of functional use.

Limitations of Phonics Approaches

We define phonics as the set of relationships between the sound system (phonology) of oral language and the visual system(orthography) of written language in an alphabetically written language. Some kind of direct instruction in phonics is included in most reading and spelling programs, but some programs limit instruction to teaching these associations. These are called "phonics programs" by their developers. Other terms are "phonics first" and "intensive phonics."

Phonics reading programs teach children to associate sounds with letters, reasoning that if children learn letter-sound associations they can sound out words;

240

that is, recode print to speech, and thus read. In one kind of synthetic phonics children are taught to read *dog* by saying sounds for each letter: *dub, aw, gub.* In analytic phonics, words that fit certain spelling patterns are presented and children are encouraged to analyze them into the sounds they start with, end with, or otherwise have in common.

Phonics, as a method of instruction, has a certain attraction to uninformed people. There are only 26 letters and only 40 or so sounds, so it seems that once children can associate the letters with the sounds they will be reading and writing; but as we have seen, reading is making sense of print, not sounds, and language is much more than a sequence of letters or sounds. Phonics methods keep being reinvented and then fall into disrepute for several important reasons:

1. Each sound in written English is not regularly represented by a specific letter. For example, consider these rhyming words: *go, know, though, hoe, sew.* And some letters may represent several different sounds as the *o* does in *do, so, won, women,* and *not.*
2. Sounds and letters, taken out of context, are abstractions. And, as Piaget and Vygotsky have shown, abstractions are hard for young learners to deal with. So it's not surprising that many children who can read have trouble with phonics lessons. There are also children who learn the phonics but can't make sense of print.
3. Many phonics programs teach unscientific phonics generalizations based on erroneous views of language. Division of English vowels into long and short vowels is an example. So-called long vowels are actually vowels plus glides. There are several vowels that do not fit either the long or the short category; for example, the vowel in *caught, bought, dog* in most dialects of American English is the "open *o*"/ɔ/.
4. Dialect differences mean that the phonic relationships vary from dialect to dialect, since sounds vary but spelling remains constant. What is the vowel sound in these words: *frog, fog, log, bog, dog, smog, cog, hog, jog?* How they split varies from dialect to dialect. In only a few dialects of English are the vowels in these words all the same.

A more scientific phonics would not solve the problem. Phonics programs concentrate on letters and treat every one as equally important. Readers are selective and use only as much of the print as necessary to predict the meaning and confirm predictions.

Word-Focused Programs

For many decades most American reading programs have put their main emphasis on words. The central task at the start of these programs is getting children to develop a sight vocabulary (words recognized at sight) and to develop "word-attack" skills to "unlock" or "decode" other words. In these programs it becomes important to control the words used. That means using word lists derived from studies to determine which words are most frequent in the language. Then controlled vocabulary, the careful, systematic introduction of words in each successive primer or basal reader, dominates the construction of the reading series.

Each successive book uses the words introduced in the prior books and adds a few new ones. The teacher's editions list the words in the back, and the teachers have to judge whether their pupils are ready to go on by testing them on the word list.

Language is More than Words

Many teachers highly committed to phonics or word-recognition methods have been successful—to a point—in teaching children to read. Enthusiastic learners with dedicated teachers can probably learn to read regardless of method—and most children do learn to read. What these methods miss is an understanding of how readers construct meaning from language. To apply these insights and to come to understand why some children do not respond to traditional instruction, teachers must let go of their preoccupation with letters and words and take a broad look at reading as making sense of written language. Children learning to read have learned to make sense of oral language. They use the language systems to construct meaning. Only a small fraction of this power over language is put to work through phonics or word-recognition programs.

What phonics and word approaches have in common is their focus on words. Both focus the learners' attention on getting each word right. Both treat all words as equally important, and both limit the learners to cues within words rather than to cues in their transactions with connected discourse—the whole flow of language.

But language is learned from whole to part. Readers have the meaning of sentences long before they can dependably recognize each word in isolation. Overreliance on phonic and word-attack skills in the early stages of learning how to read leads young learners away from meaning and away from the extensive knowledge of language that they bring with them to school. Such instruction focuses them on minute detail, and then they must find their own way back to meaningful language. Students and teachers may become so concerned with word-attack skills that the pupils may not even be aware that there is any meaning or that they are supposed to be making sense of what they read. Few children who have problems later are unable to attack words; they just can't get meaning.

Reading is More than Naming Words

As we've said before, there has been a tendency to treat language as a string of words and reading as attacking these words. Instead, we should see words as bits of discourse, like cells of the body deriving their nature from the whole, of which they are parts, and the function of that whole.

Suppose young readers find an unfamiliar word, *monkey,* in a short passage:

Tom heard some music coming from a big box. A man was turning a handle and making the music. He had a little monkey. The monkey clapped his hands. He took a cup and held it out to Tom. Tom gave the monkey a penny. The monkey bowed to Tom.

If they are limited to the cues within the word, the readers can sound it out or attack it using its shape, little words in the big word, or compare it to other similarly spelled words. If they know *donkey,* that may or may not help, depending on their dialects. But if they find it in a real text such as this one, they can make use of all the cues that connected discourse provides and deal with the new word in the context of the meaning of the whole passage.

They can use the sentence patterns to realize that *monkey* is a word that can be the subject of a sentence: "The *monkey* clapped his hands." Or, it can be an object: "He had a little *monkey.*" The readers will get semantic information from the the whole passage and from each occurrence of *monkey* in it: it's little; it has hands; it can hold things; it acts something like a person.

Function words help to set up the sentence patterns. In the story, *monkey* is literally marked as a noun: first it's a *monkey,* then *the monkey.* Here's a verse from Lewis Carroll's "Jabberwocky" with only the function words shown to illustrate how function words serve as cues to the syntax and the meaning:

'Twas_____ and the _____y ____s
Did _____ and _____ in the _____.
All _____y were the _____s,
And the _____ ____s _____.

These function words are very repetitious in connected discourse because their functions occur often and there are not very many words to fill the functions. Even in the simplest passages they must be present, but their lack of meaning makes them difficult for children to learn in isolation. Many teachers have noticed that children can remember *birthday* but not *the, on, or,* or *was.* Many of the function words are also irregularly spelled; they are likely to contradict phonics rules commonly taught. Some examples are: *of, for, to, do, from, was, what,* and *can* (pronounced like *kin* as a function word.) Yet these same words have been part of the speech of young learners since a very early age.

Pronouns provide cohesive ties in the passage with *monkey* in it. *He* held . . ., *his* hands. That provides more sense of what *monkey* must mean.

Word callers are so busy attacking words by using cues within words that they make little use of cues in connected discourse. They may get some of the words, but they can't get the meaning of the story a word at a time. They see the trees, but they don't see the forest.

Using All the Language Cues

To illustrate the difference between reading whole language and reading words, let's consider a passage in which all the words other than function words, the content words, have been replaced by nonsense.

Here are these nonsense words in a list form:

Gloopy   klums   poved   jonfy   klorpy
borp   Blit   Ril   rom   lofs
lof   floms   lo   bofd

Except for the three capitalized words, which are probably proper nouns, we have no sense of meaning of the words in this list. But now consider this primer story, in which the words have been substituted for all the content words, with everything else left intact.

Gloopy and Blit

Gloopy is a borp
Blit is a lof.
Gloopy klums like Blit.
Gloopy and Blit are floms.

Ril had poved Blit to a jonfy.
But he had not poved Gloopy.
"The jonfy is for lofs,"
Blit bofd to Gloopy.
"You are a borp."

Gloopy was not klorpy.
Then Blit was not klorpy.

This story presents the problem of readers seeing, in context, words they have never seen before. Yet there seems to be some sense to it. In fact, there are many cues to the meanings of the unknown words, and if we apply our knowledge of English, we can come close to understanding the whole story.

The title presents two nonsense words joined by *and*, so the words must be of the same class, nouns or verbs, for example. *Town* and *country* can be joined by *and* as can *red* and *green*, *run* and *play*, *quickly* and *quietly* but not *town* and *green*, or *red* and *play*.

The first sentence provides more cues. By its position in a familiar pattern, we know that *Gloopy* is a noun, probably a singular name, because it is not preceded by a noun marker like *a* or *the*. *Gloopy* must be singular because *is* goes with singular nouns. *Borp* is a noun, we can see, because it follows *a*, a noun marker, and because it occupies a particular position in the equation-like sentence. Similarly, we know that *Blit* is most likely a name and *lof* is a noun, perhaps a category contrasting with *borp*.

Three cues tell us that *klums* is a verb: (1) its position in the sentence, (2) the inflectional ending *s* marks it as a singular verb confirming that *Gloopy* is a singular noun, and (3) it patterns with *like*.

Floms is a plural noun, we know from the plural left side of the equation-like sentence, the copula *are*, and the *s* ending. We also learn that *borps* and *lofs* can be *floms*. The cohesion tells us that. Notice that this little story is lavish in the cues it provides. Seldom are we given only one cue for a specific bit of information. Note also that our guessing, our tentative information processing, is not random. We are malting inferences on the basis of text cues.

Ril is another name. We know *poved* is a verb from the verb marker *had*, the inflectional ending *ed* that sets the whole sentence in the past, and its position between subject and object nouns. By their positions before and after the verb in this sentence pattern we know that *Ril* is the subject and *Blit* is the object. It was *Ril* that poved *Blit*; *Blit* didn't pove *Ril*.

The pronoun *he* here must refer back to *Ril,* even though *Blit* is closer. This is because of the parallel patterns of this sentence and the preceding one. So, whatever *Ril* did to *Blit, Ril* did not do to *Gloopy.*

In case we were confused about which noun the pronoun coreferenced, the next sentences clear it up. We get a sense of cause and effect. Blit is addressing Gloopy here, we know from the quotation marks that enable us to supply proper phrasing and syntax. The reason Gloopy was not poved, Blit bofs, is that the jonfy is for lofs and Gloopy is a borp. *You* is a singular pronoun that takes the plural copula, *are,* and refers to Gloopy.

Because this is a coherent and cohesive story, the sequence gives us further cause and effect. As a result of not being poved, Gloopy was not klorpy, and this led to Blit also being unklorpy. If Gloopy had been a lof instead of a borp then Gloopy would have been poved to the jonfy too.

We can come very close to understanding the whole little story (a possible case of sex discrimination), even though all the important words are nonsense. Yet when these were presented out of context they meant nothing to us at all. Proficient readers can use phonic generalizations to pronounce the words in the list, but that isn't reading, because no meaning is involved. *Reading is not reading unless some level of comprehension is involved.* Readers, even beginners, engage in the same process that we've just gone through when they read texts, although not on so conscious a level. They can't help using their cognitive and linguistic strategies for trying to make sense of texts.

Redundancy

In the story, "Gloopy and Blit," we noted the generous number of cues for the same bits of information. Redundancy is a term used by information theorists to describe the tendency of languages to restrict the sequences in which language patterns can occur, to provide several cues for one bit of information, and thus to be less than 100 percent efficient in the amount of information transmitted per unit of language.

To be completely efficient in this sense, our language would have to allow for every sound or letter to occur after every other with equal probability. Likewise, every word would need to follow every other with equal frequency. However, words like *ngopr* can't occur in English, though *prong* can. Nor can a sentence like: "Penny a monkey the gave Tom."

The language is made predictable for readers because some sequences are very common, some are rare, and some are not permitted to occur at all. The process by which a reader deals with unfamiliar terms or phrases such as *monkey* or *floms* is a kind of zeroing in or what Smith calls reduction of uncertainty. (Smith, 1972)

Successive sets of redundant cues keep narrowing the possibilities and making inferences more certain. Reading is a guessing game in which readers use their knowledge of language, their past experience, and their developing conceptual schemas. If they make mistakes there are almost always abundant cues to tell them that they are wrong and to help them correct themselves.

It's clear that reading is much more than attacking words. It's also clear that readers do not have to know all the words in order to make sense of texts. In a study by Goodman (1965), children in first, second, and third grades were able to read in stories two-thirds to four-fifths of words that they had not been able to identify on lists.

Whole-Language Reading

A whole-language approach builds on the language and cognitive strength of the learners; it rejects the view of young learners and nonlearners as deficient or defective. This approach is rooted in science as well as humanism. It is based on modern theory and research on language development, language processes, and language learning, including research on both oral and written language learning. This research has shown the universal language strength of all learners, including handicapped pupils, those who speak two or more languages, and those whose home language is a low-status dialect.

The whole-language view incorporates a psycholinguistic view of the reading process, but it also draws on the psychology of Vygotsky, Piaget, and Bruner in their views of language, thinking, and learning. Perception is viewed as schema governed and as contextually controlled by the learners' knowledge. So a whole-language view is a psycho-socio-linguistic view that sees personal language functions and learning based in sociocultural development and function. The major features of a whole-language reading program (as well as the writing program we discuss in Chapter 13) are:

1. It is positive, respecting the strength and health of the learner.
2. It seeks to be relevant and personalized to particular learners, expanding on their experiences and schemas.
3. It treats written language as transactional with the learners actively in control of their own texts and their own development as readers and writers.
4. It's dynamic and process oriented. Reading and learning to read cannot be stopped, frozen, or dissected. They must be examined as they happen.

Old and New

Much instructional material, reading curriculum theory, and reading teaching has suffered from a lack of accurate knowledge of how language works. Generalizations about teaching of reading from psychology, sociology, physiology, and pedagogical sources are less inaccurate than incomplete. A new whole-language framework can unite old knowledge and new to produce more effective school programs. Any strategy of reading instruction based on a single principle or tactic is incomplete, no matter how valid the principle or how sound the tactic. Reading instruction must be based on complete understanding of the complex reading process.

Children do not learn in the same way that linguists or psychologists study language. Nor do they learn one piece at a time as do laboratory rats and pigeons. They learn like people. Reading instruction must reflect an understanding of language, of learning, and of people learning language.

Just as important as the proper concepts and tools are enlightened teachers who make the difference between whether some learn or all learn. The purpose of this section is to show what teachers need to know and do.

Principles of a Whole-Language Program

The whole-language approach is based on a number of key principles dealing with the reading process, teaching, and instruction. (Goodman and Goodman, 1981)

Reading Process
1. Reading is constructive. Meaning is constructed in listening and reading. Readers use their background of experience and concepts while transacting with the text.
2. Reading is efficient and effective. Effective readers construct coherent meaning. Efficient readers use prediction, inference, selection, confirmation, and correction strategies. They use as little input and effort as possible.
3. Language systems are inseparable. The *text* is the minimum unit of meaningful discourse. Grapho-phonic, syntactic, semantic, and pragmatic systems cannot be broken apart and decontextualized during instruction without creating abstractions and nonsense.
4. Comprehension is the one objective. It is always the goal in listening and reading.
5. In writing, as it is in speaking, expression is the one goal.
6. Comprehension depends on prior knowledge. Meaning is both input and output in reading and listening, and what is comprehended is always partly what was known before reading.

Learning Principles
7. Language learning is the same in and out of school. Literacy begins outside of school and is an extension of natural language learning. In school or out, it happens most easily when it is functional and internally motivated by a need to comprehend.
8. Form follows function. Development of function usually comes before and motivates the development of form in reading and writing.
9. Literacy is developed during functional use. Expression and comprehension strategies are built during the functional use of relevant, meaningful, self-motivated language, so skills can't be learned prior to their meaningful use. There is no sequence in which skills develop and no hierarchy of language skills. They are learned together in the context of their use.
10. Literacy develops in response to personal-social needs. Since the need for literacy begins before school, literacy also begins before school.
11. Teaching cannot control learning. The teacher motivates, arranges the environ-

ment, monitors development, provides appropriate materials, and provides timely experiences. But there is no one-to-one correspondence between teaching and learning, and, ultimately, learners themselves decide what to extract from the learning environment.

12. There's a double agenda in the whole-language classroom. The learners learn language while keeping their focus on the meaning and the function. Teachers monitor both the use and the development.

13. Risk taking is necessary to language development. Readers and writers must try to use language before they control it. They must take chances, make mistakes, make miscues, predict, infer, and guess as they move toward meaning. Teachers must see this all as a natural part of development and create an atmosphere that encourages risk taking.

Instructional Principles

14. The language must be whole. Everything that children are asked to write must have a purpose and an audience. Everything they're asked to read from the beginning must have all the characteristics of whole, real, functional language. They must want to know what the texts mean.

15. There's no place for bits and pieces. Exercises that fragment language and turn it into bits and pieces have no place in the program. A letter is harder to read than a word; a word is harder to read than a sentence; a sentence is harder to read than a paragraph; and a paragraph is harder to read than a story.

16. Materials must be predictable. Predictability is the most important factor in determining whether a given reader will find it easy or hard to comprehend.

17. Focus in instruction is always on how to make sense of the whole rather than on words, letters, or patterns.

In a holistic approach we expect learning to go from whole to part, from general to specific, from gross to fine, from highly contextualized to more abstract. That means that we expect children to read familiar, meaningful wholes first. We expect that they will read easily predictable materials that draw on concepts and experiences they already have. As they acquire a repertoire of such known wholes, they begin to read familiar words and phrases in new wholes and eventually to handle unfamiliar parts in familiar uses anywhere. In this method, we see no sequence of skills or language units and certainly no hierarchy for the ordering of instruction in skills or language units. Beginners must use the same information as proficient readers to make sense of print. Development is a matter of getting the process together: learning to use, in the context of reading real language, just enough print, language structure, and meaning, and keeping it all in proper balance and perspective.

We build comprehension strategies, ways of using information to construct meaning, that will help students become both efficient and effective in using this process. Readers, as they develop their strategies, must become more flexible as they move through broader ranges of materials with content further removed from their own direct experiences. We try, as teachers, to help pupils to use reading to learn—to extend and acquire concepts, as we try to avoid misusing reading in instruction by expecting textbooks to carry the burden of teaching.

Most crucial in the holistic method is the new role of an enlightened teacher who serves as guide, facilitator, and kid-watcher. Such a teacher can capitalize on the language competence and language-learning ability of children and help make literacy an extension of their natural language learning.

The Whole-Language Base

The reading beginner is not a language beginner, so the base of the whole-language curriculum is the language development—oral and written—that children bring to school. Because all children do not start at the same point, the reading program must be flexible from the beginning. All hearing children bring oral language with them to school, and all who are growing up in a literate society have developed some of the roots of literacy: they've begun to respond to print in the environment, to know that it makes sense, and to experiment with writing, but they vary considerably in the dialect(s) and language(s) they speak, their experiences, conceptual development, motivations, interests, and the exposure they've had to books.

Haussler found that preschool children all had a considerable amount of print awareness but they differed considerably in their ability to deal with print in books. (Haussler, 1983)

Holistic instruction begins where it ends, with whole language—mundane, useful, relevant, and functional language—and moves toward the full range of written language, including literature in all its variety.

In a whole-language program, the language of the bilingual pupil or the pupil whose dialect is different than the teacher's is accepted and expanded upon to develop literacy and flexibility in language use. In the case of the bilingual learner, the objective becomes biliteracy, the ability to read and write both languages.

It's important, at all grade levels, for teachers to find out where their pupils are in their development and expand on that base.

Objectives

Understanding what is read is the one central goal of the reading curriculum: to construct meaning that substantially agrees with that of the author. All other goals are secondary to this one. Here are some of the subsidiary goals. In a holistic program they are all developed at the same time and there is no hierarchy and sequence. Learning to read is part of a broader goal of the curriculum, expanding the ability of learners to communicate effectively.

1. To develop strategies for sampling and selecting grapho-phonic, syntactic, and semantic cues
2. To develop prediction strategies and schemas for anticipating meaning, syntactic patterns, and orthographic patterns
3. To develop inferential strategies using text and nontext information to infer what is not in the text or has not yet been encountered in the text
4. To develop confirmation strategies to check predictions and inferences against subsequent cues

5. To develop self-correction strategies to detect and correct miscues that disrupt comprehension
6. To develop flexible strategies for dealing with a wide variety of materials: environmental print, expository materials, literature (both fiction and nonfiction), instructions, forms and directions, content area materials, including school texts and materials particular to content areas such as charts, tables, and recipes
7. To develop critical strategies for judging the validity of information gained from reading
8. To develop flexibility in the use of the reading process for different purposes:
   a. Coping with a literate environment
   b. Information seeking
   c. Occupational uses
   d. Recreational and aesthetic uses

Objectives in so-called mastery-learning programs treat reading as a sequenced set of minute steps, each a separate skill to be learned one at a time. Each phonic relationship or each word is presented to learners as a separate unit to be mastered. These sequenced lists, sometimes hundreds of objectives long, have the appearance of logic, order, and tangibility, but language isn't learned piece by piece. Fractured, it becomes abstractions that are hard for children to learn. Language, whole and in proper relationship to relevant meaning, is easy to learn.

In a whole-language reading curriculum the focus is always on meaning. For the teacher, the most important question is, "How is this contributing to comprehension?" The most important question for both the learner and the teacher is, "What's the sense of this?" Readers can judge their own success by whether or not what they read makes sense. They learn also to reject nonsense.

Motivation

Children learn language because they need to communicate. Their oral language is continually polished and improved to make it more efficient and effective. In the process it becomes more like the language of the family and the community. It is the need to be successful in communication that is the internal motivating force behind this expansion and polishing. Children don't learn language for its own sake or to please adults; they learn it because they need it to communicate.

Communicative need is the most important motivation in reading and writing, as it is in oral language. In literate societies, illiterates are at a great disadvantage because there is so much written language communication everywhere: streets and stores are labeled, warnings and instructions posted, letters written, boxes and wrappings printed upon. Children become aware that all around them there is language that is being used and understood by readers. Some are so aware and so highly motivated to understand that they learn without professional help before they come to school. But all become print-aware. And the internal motivation, the communicative need, is always a force to be tapped and supported in school.

No M & M's or pretty stickers are needed or permitted to reward effort or success in a holistic approach. Nor is any negative, "assertive discipline" response justifiable or useful. Such rewards and punishments distort the purpose for reading. Relevant meaning is reading's own reward and the only appropriate one. When language is functional for the learner, motivation to learn is high and children know when they are successful, since they have met their own needs. Extrinsic rewards and punishments can force-feed dysfunctional learning. At best the learner comes to rely on someone else's judgment that what has been learned is good.

Intrinsic motivation is at its highest when the learner makes the choice of when and what to read. The reader must have a sense of ownership—of owning the process and deciding when to use it and for what purpose—so teachers must plan to create situations in which children will choose to read, and they must have available appropriate materials that they will select themselves.

Children from highly literate homes have the additional stimulation of large numbers of books of all kinds and the frequent example of adults and siblings reading these books, as well as magazines, letters, work related materials, and so on. Children who are read to frequently develop a sense of the function and form of literary language. The function of reading for leisure—for the pleasure of it—becomes established and in turn becomes an intrinsic motivation for personal reading.

Children from highly literate homes with a high expectation of school success may be able to carry their general enthusiasm and confidence through extended learning periods in which little self-motivated meaningful reading is involved. The school programs may provide instructional materials in which there is no coherent message or literary quality. The hours spent drilling on isolated "skills" may be unrelated to any communicative need or goal the pupils can discern. But such learners may be sustained through all this by the knowledge that at the end of the process they will be members of a prestigious society; they will be readers.

For many children, however, the relationships between reading and its functional uses may be permanently or temporarily forgotten unless reading is kept whole, meaningful, relevant, and functional. If children have had little experience with books, then their teachers need to read to them, provide many books for them to handle, and establish the base of experience and function that other children may already have. These are the children who will suffer from the fragmentation of isolated skill drills. They will require more and more rewards and punishments to keep them on meaningless and dysfunctional tasks, and they will profit less and less from the tasks. They will feel no sense of ownership; rather, they will feel like field hands laboring in someone else's field.

Advocates of many approaches to teaching reading have claimed the learners' success at each stage is motivation for the next stage. Reading teachers know from experience, however, that this kind of motivation involves only a minority of children whose motivation is not so much to learn to read as to be successful: to get grades, smiles, or gold stars. Reading then can become a contest or a school chore, a daily ritual unrelated to language, communication, or life.

A whole-language program starts with the premise that all learners are intrinsically motivated; they want to understand written language; they want to be able to read. To sustain the natural motivation of all children, then, reading materials at all ages must be worth reading; they must be self-selected as much as possible by the learners; they must be real language with real stories or real messages that are interesting to the children and that are broadly within their realm of conceptual schemas and experience.

Perhaps teachers need to consider that if children need to be bribed or forced to learn, there must be something wrong with the program, a mismatch between the learners and the materials.

Implementation of a Three-Part School Reading Program

A whole-language school reading program expands on preschool and out-of-school development and experience. It is also integrated with the other language arts, writing, speaking, and listening, and with the content and substance of the curriculum. There is no isolation of skills for instruction, no drill on processes apart from their functional use. The key guiding concept in building the school reading program is that language is learned easiest and best when the learner's focus is on its communicative use.

For the purposes of focus we'll divide our discussion of the school program into three topics: beginning reading, developmental reading, and revaluing. It will be obvious that this is a continuum with common principles, objectives, and criteria for selection of materials and development of experiences.

Beginning Reading

Clearly, a whole-language reading program accepts and extends the beginnings children have already made. This means that some old concerns and debates in reading instruction need to be reconsidered. In the past the argument over when reading instruction should begin was based on the view that most children are total novices as far as literacy when they enter school. One group advocated early direct instruction to produce earlier readers. Another group, citing research from the 1930's by Washburne and others, argued that children are not "ready" for literacy until they achieve an optimal mental age, about 6 years and 6 months. They advocated starting with prereading readiness activities and beginning introduction of formal instruction in first grade, or in some cases later (Morphett and Washburne, 1936)

If children have already begun to develop literacy at early ages, then these arguments are irrelevant. Teachers of young children in preschools, kindergartens, and primary grades will want to monitor and to support literacy development. They will want their classrooms to be literate environments, enriched versions of the environments outside of school that have been nurturing literacy. They will not impose reading and writing on any children, but they will make available books, writing equipment, and everything else related to literacy that the children might need. They will be as concerned and aware of the literacy development of their pupils as they are of their oral language and cognitive development.

Particularly, they will want to support the development of the functions of reading and writing in their pupils so that the natural internal motivation to learn will be fostered.

Key Premises
Beginning reading in a holistic program:
1. Encourages what's already happening by helping children to value and to use the literacy events of their lives.
2. Creates an enriched literate environment in the classroom. Attractive print is everywhere in this classroom where it is functional and the pupils' transactions with this print are supported and encouraged by the teacher.
3. Expands on the experiences of the learners with books, building a sense of what they're for, how to handle and use them, and how they work.
4. Builds a sense of the style, form, and function of written language. Teachers will read to and with children and write to and with them.

Communication and cooperation with parents are vital in a whole-language program, since it depends so heavily on children's out-of-school experience. Children are encouraged to carry books from school to home, and vice-versa, and meetings with parents inform them of what to look for and encourage in their children.

Literacy Experiences For Preschoolers
As print is introduced in the classroom in charts, labels, and bulletin boards, teachers call their pupils' attention to it and solicit their support in its creation. They tell children what things say or ask them to guess. They build for print awareness.

When the children walk around the school and the neighborhood they react to print they encounter. The teacher encourages them to think about what it might say and to bring the print into their pictures and drawings.

Books are abundantly available. Teachers, aides, parents, and older kids read to and with the pupils in small groups and one-to-one on laps. The preschool classroom has a center for listening to tapes or records as pupils follow books. Another center has all kinds of paper and all kinds of pencils, felt pens, and crayons for writing notes, lists, and picture captions, or just scribbling. The pupils are encouraged to play at reading and writing, and the values and functions of literacy are stressed in role playing as children cook, shop, build, and dress up.

Kindergarten and First Grade
Kindergarten extends the same type of activities in a whole-language program except that the teachers are aware that many children will already be reading and writing productively and so they support and encourage their growth. The teachers help pupils to be aware of what they are able to do and foster pride and confidence in their language and their growing literacy.

Because of the wide range of development, it's important in a whole-language program that teachers concentrate on the strengths of pupils and not compare them or draw constant attention to what they cannot yet do. They should neither hold pupils back nor force their pace. The genius of a whole-language teacher is in knowing where pupils are and in helping them to grow. School beginners are encouraged to be confident risk-takers—to take chances and to try when they're not sure.

Control of the form of print is built in the context of functional use. The program builds for strategies, not specifics. The teachers are concerned that children develop the alphabetic principle, not the *bl* blend. Children are encouraged to seek meaning, to predict, to draw inferences, to sample, to confirm or disconfirm, and to self-correct. The teachers are monitors, facilitators, and cheerleaders.

Kindergarten and first-grade classrooms must be rich print environments. Teachers and pupils label centers and create charts for rules, attendance, and jobs. Bulletin boards may feature autobiographies of pupils and messages of interest to them. They're designed to encourage pupils' transactions with them. There are store corners with cartons, boxes, signs, and price tags. Each pupil has a personal mailbox in the class post office for receiving mail and messages. Rugs, tubs, and cubbies invite readers.

Whole-Language Beginnings

In a whole-language program pupils are encountering whole meaningful texts from the very beginning. There are a variety of whole-language techniques to ease them into the process.

1. *The "lap" method.* Many parents and children invent a natural game as they share books. The child sits in the parent's lap, and both attend to the book as the parent reads. Pretty soon the parent is pausing slightly before certain key words or repeated phrases. The child then anticipates what comes next and supplies it. Many children can "read" books completely after just a few such readings.

In the past this has been dismissed as "just memorizing." If it were memorizing it would be remarkable because 3- to 5-year-old children would have difficulty memorizing anything like a list of comparable length. Actually, this ability to learn whole stories is even more remarkable. It's holistic remembering. It's easy for children because they have learned the structure of story books. They have a sense of the whole, and within that it's easy to remember what follows what and what happens next. They can do this because the text is a sensible, structured whole. In fact, children will often substitute more familiar words and phrases in their readings, which shows that they have not memorized per se.

Variations on the lap method are often used in whole-language classrooms. The key is in having a patient, more experienced reader, even an older child, read with the beginner. Some techniques that work similarly are popular.

2. *Assisted reading.* This formalizes the lap method. A teacher or a tutor reads with the child. Gradually the child takes over the reading.

3. *Read-alongs.* In this variation the young reader follows a book while

listening through a headphone to a recorded reading of the book. There are several commercial programs available, including Bill Martin's Instant Readers. Many teachers make their own cassette tapes using their own readings or those of a friend. Several children can be quietly involved in this type of read-along at a listening center. (Martin, 1972)

4. *Shared-book experience.* This is a technique developed in New Zealand, where whole-language approaches are very common. (New Zealand Department of Education, 1985) A very much enlarged copy of a children's book is obtained or made using projections from an opaque projector on tag board. The first time the story is used the teacher uses the big book and pupils follow in their own small books. They read chorally with the teacher. In subsequent readings one pupil may read the big book while the other pupils follow and read chorally in their own books. As with the similar techniques just mentioned, the pupils are encouraged to reread the book many times. Children are quite willing to do so if the story is one that they enjoy.

Several publishers now have published "big books."

5. *Predictable books.* The books that work best in all these techniques are those that have strong, simple story lines, repetitious refrains, and appealing language. Many such books for young people could be termed predictable books. They are predictable because of the way the books are written and because they are within the language and cognitive schemas of young learners.

One reason that children like to hear some stories over and over is that they enjoy being able to anticipate and predict what's coming. This means that the kids are learning to read while they are enjoying and building a sense of story for children's literature. It also means that they are getting practice with whole, real, meaningful language rather than with letters and words. Every whole-language classroom should have a good collection of predictable books available for the pupils' use.

The Department of Education in New Zealand has for many years published their own series of culturally relevant, predictable, self-contained little books. These are the main reading materials used in the beginning reading program.

Here's an excerpt from one of these books with a universal theme—washing the dog:

Hana and Te Popo chased Paru under the house,

around the tree,
through the gate,
up the hill,
down the hill,
and into the shed.

"Now we've got him,"
whispered Te Popo.
They waited until Paru
ran out, but . . .

Paru ran up the hill,
   down the hill,
   through the gate,
   under the house,
   and . . .
back to the big yellow tub. (Hunia, 1983)

6. *Language experience activities.* Language experience has become a popular technique in whole-language and other classrooms. It involves a child or a group of children creating their own story with the teacher, which is transcribed and then read as a group and individually.

Here's an example of a story created by a first-grade group when a class member brought her spring ducklings to school:

Wendy's Ducklings

Wendy's got two cute ducklings.
She brought them to school.
One duckling is yellow and the other is black.
The yellow one is Salt. The black one is Pepper.
They like each other. They peeped and peeped
until Salt found Pepper.

Experience stories have several virtues: (1) the children see that oral language can be written down, so they see oral and written language as parallel; (2) the content of the story is a real event that happened to them; and (3) the language of the text is their own language as they use it.

Many teachers start using experience stories by having children draw pictures and then dictate something the teacher writes on the picture.

It is particularly important in transcribing children's stories not to change the grammar or the vocabulary. If the child says "Me and James was chunking the ball around," the teacher who changes this to "James and I were throwing the ball to each other" will confuse the learner and the issue. The goal is literacy, not changed speech.

In the next chapter we will discuss a beginning writing program in fuller detail. But we need to note here that reading and writing develop best when learners are actively engaged in both. Language experience involves the children in dictating a story to a teacher or an aide, but children should also be encouraged to do their own early writing as well. This self-generated writing does not diminish the value of language experience activities but rather adds to the opportunities available to pupils.

Though language experience does not require published materials, R. Van Allen has published a kit, *Language Experiences in Reading,* which helps a teacher to organize and develop a language experience approach. (Allen, 1979)

7. *Breakthrough.* A program developed by the British Schools Council, *Breakthrough to Literacy,* includes a number of whole-language activities. To facilitate composing, kits of letters and common words are provided that the young

pupils can use in composing their own stories. The program also includes small, self-contained paperbound books. (McKay, 1973)

8. *Microcomputers.* Though most software for school use is little more than computerized workbook pages, there are some promising "interactive" programs that involve pupils in reading predictable texts, responding to what they read, and otherwise engaging in authentic reading and writing.

A Full Range of Reading

It's important in beginning reading that children encounter a wide range of print. They need to continue learning to make sense of print in their environment. That can be built by using polaroid cameras and taking walking tours of the school and its neighborhood. The classroom itself is a literate environment in which the teacher and pupils provide important messages to be read. One example is a door chart. Every day when the pupils arrive at the door of the room there is a chart with an important message, for example:

Today is Maria's birthday.
Happy birthday, Maria!

The children discuss what the chart says as they enter the room. It doesn't occur to them that this is a reading lesson. They learn to read while trying to find out what the print says because they want to know.

They need to develop informational reading. The charts and bulletin boards in the room can lead to exploration of newspapers, television directories, phone books, advertisements, menus, and other common information sources. Children can begin also to use books and magazines to find information for social studies and science projects.

They need to explore occupational reading and writing through their play. They can role play a police officer and write tickets, or a grocer and read labels and lists at the store, or a mail carrier who delivers the mail and reads the names and addresses. In all these activities there is a double agenda. The pupils are aware of what they are using reading and writing for. The teacher is aware of that and also of their development as readers and writers. Beginning reading is a matter of growing into literacy.

Developmental Reading

In reality, of course, all growth in reading is developmental. We use the term here to focus on the part of the reading program that helps children who have begun to read to become more proficient, more flexible readers who are able to deal with a widening range of types of texts, functions, and purposes.

Objectives

The objectives of the developmental reading program are expansionist in all respects. The goals are to expand the children's ability to deal with print in the environment, to expand their ability to get information from print and to know how and where to look for it, to expand their ability to deal with occupational reading, including coping with school texts and other tasks requiring reading, and to expand their ability and desire to read for personal, aesthetic, and recreational purposes. It is not enough to build the ability to read; schools also must be concerned with whether pupils will *want* to read. Too many adults can read but don't choose to because they learned in school to think of reading as tedious and difficult—something only to do when they had to.

Three Focal Points

In the whole-language reading program, the developmental phase has three major focal points:

1. It creates a classroom climate that encourages risk taking. People develop most when they are trying to do things somewhat beyond their current ability. In reading they need to feel that it's alright to try something that looks interesting but hard. They need to know that it's alright to guess, using their best information, at what a word or a phrase means. They need to know that everybody must make inferences and predictions but also check themselves to make sure that these work out and that the reading produces sense.
2. It keeps the readers' focus on meaning. Readers can judge their own success if they keep reminding themselves that things are supposed to make sense and that if they don't something is wrong. Teachers need to help pupils achieve the attitude that they ought not to tolerate nonsense when they read.
3. There must be a lot of authentic reading going on. Essentially, as we have said in a variety of ways in this book, people learn language through using it. They learn to read by reading. Plenty of time must be provided for reading real texts. Time spent on decontextualized skill exercises isn't reading. The teacher's focus should be on finding as many ways as possible to stimulate the pupils to choose to read. Language is learned best when it is self-motivated. Self-selection also helps in developing taste and flexibility.

The belief in the dichotomy between learning to read and reading to learn is unfortunate and not acceptable in a whole-language program. People don't learn to read for the sake of learning to read. They improve their control of reading as they try to understand what is being said and as they seek to comprehend. Self-motivation, choice, is vital because *wanting* to comprehend is a necessary condition of comprehending.

Personalizing Instruction

The heart of a developmental whole-language reading program is the personalization that provides freedom for the learners to choose from a wide variety of interesting books, stories, and articles under the supervision of a competent teacher. This approach is often called an *individualized reading program.*

A natural transition from the whole-language beginnings we've cited into an individualized reading program avoids artificial language and synthetic methods and materials. There is no need for basal readers and the homogenizing of children into groups or levels for instruction. In an individualized program pupils can develop at their own pace while self-selecting from available materials. They don't have to wait for others to catch up, and the teacher doesn't have to force the pace of those who move more slowly.

The Teacher in an Individualized Program   The teacher is very important in all reading programs, but in an individualized whole-language reading program the teacher is of critical importance. The teacher provides stimulating and appropriate materials for the children to select from. The teacher is a kid watcher, monitoring the development of all children and offering support and help for those who need it and encouragement for those who don't.

The whole-language teacher is an informed professional who knows language and how it develops, who knows how children learn, and who knows how to help that learning take place. The whole-language teacher knows how to tell where the pupils are and help them to grow, and how to become more proficient and more flexible with broadening interests and sharpening tastes. The whole-language teacher is guide, monitor, and facilitator.

Other approaches to reading instruction are frequently highly structured and provide teachers with tight sequences or even scripts to follow. Whole-language programs require a great deal of careful but flexible planning by the teacher with extensive systematic record keeping. The learners need to be involved with the teacher in this planning and to do a considerable amount of the record keeping.

Even young pupils can keep a log of their readings and their responses to what they have read. Pupils can note sections in things that they read that they want to discuss in conferences with their teachers. They can rate what they have read and comment on their own ease or difficulty in reading particular things. They can assist the teacher in maintaining the class library, ordering books from the book clubs and the libraries, and surveying needs for materials. They can maintain book and magazine exchanges.

Conferencing   In a personalized developmental reading program the teacher will need to have conferences with individual students at regular intervals, depending on their age, grade, ability, independence, and other characteristics. During and after these conferences the teachers will need to make anecdotal records of events that typify the strengths, weaknesses, and progress of the pupils. At their convenience, the teachers can also make informal observations of their pupils' reading and use of what they read and they can record significant insights.

With such ongoing evaluations, whole-language teachers have little use for standardized tests, particularly since they focus on isolated skills.

Miscue Analysis   If the teacher needs in-depth information on a new pupil or a child who seems not to be progressing, miscue analysis can be useful. Miscues are unexpected responses in oral reading. They show the readers' strengths as well as their problems. Each unexpected response is the result of the same transactions between the reader and the print as are expected responses.

Miscue analysis can be used more or less formally. A formal way would be to use a device like the Reading Miscue Inventory (RMI). (Goodman and Burke, 1972; Goodman, Watson, and Burke, 1987)

The teacher has the child orally read a whole story selected to be somewhat difficult for the learner. The teacher then notes the miscues on a typescript of the story and analyzes the miscues, asking questions like these:

Does the reader change meaning?
Does the reader change syntax?
Do substitutions look and/or sound like the expected response?
Is dialect involved?
To what extent is meaning lost or maintained?
To what extent do pupils self-correct miscues that reflect loss of meaning?

If the RMI is used, then profiles of the miscue patterns are developed and the teacher can then see the patterns of strengths and weaknesses. Many teachers who are familiar with miscue analysis incorporate it informally into their day-to-day interactions with pupils and make general notes in the pupils' records of their miscue patterns.

Some teachers encourage each pupil to read a story periodically into a cassette tape recorder. The pupil chooses the selections, puts his or her own cassette into a tape recorder, and tapes the reading in a corner of the room or in a corridor. Then the teacher evaluates the miscues at a later point. The tape is also a useful record for use in conferences with pupils and parents to show progress and strengths.

Stimulating Reading   In an individualized program the teacher plans for stimulating the interest of pupils in reading. Book displays are regularly created with the help of pupils to highlight particular authors, topics, or genres. The teacher gives regular book talks to showcase particular titles or authors and encourages pupils to present books and stories they've enjoyed to small groups of other pupils. Even at advanced grade levels the teacher reads to the class every day, choosing books and stories that will expand the reading horizons of the class. The teacher encourages pupils to correspond with favorite authors and to try their hand at writing on similar topics or in a similar style.

Since an individualized whole-language program depends on having a wide range of materials easily available, the teacher will take advantage of every resource possible for bringing materials into the classroom. Both the public and the school libraries can be tapped for a rotating collection of books. They should cover a wide range of topics, ability levels, and genres. Books—both fiction and nonfiction—that relate to thematic units should be available.

There are a number of paperback book clubs that make children's books available inexpensively. Children can be encouraged to join and to exchange their books with each other. Many local school authorities have begun to use some of their budgeted funds to provide paperback collections for every classroom instead of or in addition to basal readers.

Magazines, both general and children's, should be available, as well as newspapers and free or inexpensive informational material. Distributors often will provide unsold past months' magazines free to schools. Many local newspapers have special liaison staff to facilitate getting and using newspapers in the classroom.

Resourceful teachers also take old, discontinued basals and cut them up to make sets of the better stories for the use of their classes. The important thing is for teachers to have as much available as possible for their pupils to read.

Integrating Reading and Writing in the Curriculum

Whole-language teachers are concerned about reading and writing and plan time for both. But they are also concerned with integrating reading and writing into the total day's curriculum and they utilize every opportunity to facilitate literacy development. That's part of the double agenda we've often mentioned. Teachers need to be aware that literacy develops as it's used, and they need to be opportunistic in facilitating that growth.

Thematic Inquiry Units   Planned integration is very much facilitated by use of thematic units. These may be built around science topics. For example, a first-grade class could plan a unit around mice, stimulated by a cage with pet mice. It could include science activities that are also literacy events, like keeping records of what they eat, when they sleep, and how much they exercise. Pupils could make charts and record the information. They could use single concept books about mice. They could read or hear literature read about mice, like *Stuart Little*.[1]

Thematic units could involve social studies topics; for instance, fifth-grade pupils might plan a unit around the American Civil War. They would decide what main questions they wanted to answer and plan themselves what information they would need and where they might look for it. The teacher would help them to find and to learn how to use the informational resources they need. Scenes from books, like *Across Five Aprils,* could be dramatized. (Hunt, 1964)

Or thematic units could also focus on literature. A seventh-grade class in the Southwest built a unit around books about Indians of the Southwest. They drew up their own bibliography and made one of their main concerns checking the historical and geographic accuracy of the fiction they read. From the teacher's perspective it was an excellent opportunity for critical reading and for dealing with stereotypes in literature. It also provided opportunities for pupils to compare the quality of a wide range of books and stories.

Skills and Strategies

Developmental reading programs are traditionally built around sequences of skills that are part of or assumed to be part of "skilled" reading. In such programs the term *skill* is not very well defined and often turns out to be anything that can be specified and tested, such as letter or word naming, "blending" letters to make sounds, or finding the "main idea" in a paragraph. Such isolating of bits and pieces

---

[1]This idea originated with Debra Goodman.

of reading is one of the major things whole language teaching seeks to avoid. Most of the real constituent skills of reading will develop gradually for most pupils as they learn to read, provided the material they are reading meets the criteria we have discussed.

Strategy Lessons　　A whole-language program is concerned with building general comprehension strategies, ways readers use cues from the printed text and from themselves to make sense of print. Comprehension strategies develop as pupils learn to select and sample from the available cues, to draw inferences and make predictions, to monitor their reading in terms of whether it makes sense, and to self-correct when necessary. Goodman and Burke provide useful exemplars of strategy lessons. (Goodman and Burke, 1978) Sometimes the strategy lesson is a general one that the teacher establishes over time, drawing on the pupils' own developing insights and experiences. One such general strategy, as we mentioned earlier, is not tolerating nonsense. The pupils are helped to see that they should not proceed with reading if what they are reading is not making sense. They can then try rereading or reading ahead for possible clarifying cues; these are other general strategies. Both the teacher and the pupils must be prepared, however, to decide that it is not possible without building more background for the particular pupil to comprehend the particular text. That's a much more sensible solution than staying with something that is incomprehensible. it also helps the reader to realize that the problem is not always with the reader—some texts are meant for different audiences, and some texts are poorly written and hard to comprehend for even highly proficient readers.

The teacher can be of great help at such a point, helping the readers to find alternative materials that they can handle or to build the concepts necessary to come back to the original texts.

Some pupils create their own general strategies for dealing with recurrent problems in their reading. One such strategy is how to handle unfamiliar names in reading. Names, even relatively common English names such as Thomas, John, Marcia, George, Margaret, and Katherine, come from many language sources and often have relatively unpredictable spellings. Family names are even more diverse. So even proficient readers aren't always sure how to pronounce a name they encounter in their reading. And how the name is pronounced has little or no bearing on the comprehension of the story or passage. Confident readers have learned not to worry over names. They assign something close or even use initials, calling Aloysius "Mr. A." Less confident readers need to have this naming strategy legitimatized. They need to have a teacher's help in recognizing that all words are not equally important and that with names, once the reader realizes that they are names, a naming strategy will work fine.

Sometimes whole-language teachers will design specific strategy lessons for small groups of pupils who seem to have a common need. Here's one such strategy lesson:

A teacher notices that a few pupils are substituting *what* for *that,* and vice versa. As the teacher pays closer attention, she finds that they also tend to do so with *when/then* and *where/there* but that they do not have any general *wh/th* confusion. *Whistle* and *thistle* are never confused with each other.

In planning a strategy lesson, it is important to carefully delimit the phenomenon being dealt with. In this case the teacher notes that these interchanges are happening only where both words could make some sense and fit grammatically, so she finds or writes a meaningful passage in which each time one of the words is used it is the only one that can fit. The passage must be whole, real, sensible language. The teacher's purpose is to have the pupils experience disconfirmation each time they make a miscue that involves the related terms. That will help them to develop their confirming and correction strategies, not only for these pairs of words but for reading in general. The lesson will also help them to make better predictions. It's unnecessary to call the attention of the pupils to the specific word pairs, although the teacher may want to pick up comments the pupils themselves make to help them realize the strategies they are developing.

Content Area Strategies   Reading in particular content fields often requires pupils to develop special strategies for dealing with the style and content of the field. In reading road maps, for example, pupils can be helped to realize that orienting the map to their own position is a necessary first step.

Here's an example of a general strategy for dealing with "story" problems in arithmetic. Pupils are encouraged to read three times:

1. To decide what information is being sought
2. To decide how to solve the problem; that is, to choose algorithms and lay out equations
3. To get specific information and check it against the text

This is a very different general strategy than people use in reading fiction or a newspaper article. Furthermore, each successive reading has a specific purpose that requires different strategies and different use of cues.

In planning for development in content area reading whole-language teachers employ a general plan. First, they review the general and special uses of reading in the field. Science, for example, will require reading expository material with a fairly heavy load of new concepts and terminology. But it will also require reading instructions for how to conduct an experiment. It will involve writing and reading observational notes.

Second, they consider what new kinds of texts pupils will encounter. In science much information is often presented in graphs, charts, and tables. Special abbreviations and conventions are employed. In other fields there are recipes, instructions, scripts and many other text forms.

Third, the teachers decide what strategies, background, and personal resources are needed. In science, the teacher frequently performs demonstrations or provides other experiences for the pupils before they are asked to read.

Fourth, the teacher determines where the pupils are in relation to the special needs for reading in the field.

With such careful consideration and planning, the teacher can facilitate the pupils' building the background and special strategies they need to comprehend content area materials.

Teachers can also avoid, through careful planning, one of the most serious abuses of reading—misuse of textbooks. Just because students are generally proficient readers does not mean they can read and comprehend anything. Most problems with reading content area textbooks, even at college levels, are in no sense reading problems per se. They involve having insufficient presupposed knowledge about the topics being dealt with or insufficient experience in reading in particular subjects and text types. The textbooks are virtually useless until background knowledge is built.

Adapting the Basal

As we've said, a whole-language program requires no basal readers. The program, rather, involves pupils in a wealth of written language available in children's books, newspapers, magazines, resource materials, and in the environment itself. Yet the reading material most likely to be found in contemporary classrooms is one or more basal readers. Teachers and schools wanting to adopt a whole-language approach to reading may find it most feasible to use the basal as a point of departure and adapt its use so that it ceases to be the focal point of the program and becomes one resource among many in the classroom.

In most cases, except where the basal is too tightly structured and skill based, this is possible. The modern basals generally make heavy use, beyond primer levels, of the growing wealth of children's literature. Women and minority groups have sensitized editors and publishers to provide a wide range of content and characters and to move away from the purified and sanitized white suburban family in which little girls play in dresses, mothers wear aprons, fathers wear suits and carry briefcases, and no problems ever happen. There is now a lot more ethnic diversity and a much wider range of settings and plots than in earlier basals.

In a whole-language program all pupils shouldn't have to read the same stories in the same order. No publisher ever claimed that the stories are perfectly sequenced by difficulty. Some pupils may find little interest for some stories, some selections may be irrelevant for some populations, and some may fit better into thematic units than others. Pupils may read some stories and discuss them with others, or they may read them as they become interested in them. Both the pupils and the teacher should exercise selectivity.

Whole-language criteria for choosing among basal stories and other selections include:

1. Language must be natural, authentic, and cohesive, not fragmented and artificially controlled.
2. Language forms and content should be predictable for the pupils.
3. Content should be relevant and interesting.
4. Illustrations should support but not replace the text. They should create a context of situation for the text.
5. Ethnic, racial, or sex stereotypes should not be present.

The teacher should read the basal manual to get a sense of what principles have been used to organize the program and determine inclusions. Then whole-language criteria should be used to choose which advice and activities in the manual to use. The key is to retain only those aspects of the basal that suit the whole-language program.

Not much of the workbooks of most basals will meet these criteria. If the selection uses a complete, comprehensible passage of appropriate length that involves content relevant to the pupils, it may be useful for a strategy lesson. Most of the skill materials will not meet these criteria.

The adapted basal beomes one of several resources to serve the curriculum but not to dominate or become the reading curriculum.

Some commercial programs have been designed with a focus on whole language and meaning. Bill Martin's *Sounds of Language, Reading Unlimited, and Breakthrough to Literacy,* and R. Van Allen's *Language Experience in Reading* are a few. Scholastic provides kits of paperback books keyed to extend themes in specific basals.

Having plenty in the room to read will help teachers to ease away from keeping pupils occupied with skill drills and workbooks. And time spent reading will be far more productive.

Readers in Trouble: Revaluing

The third part of a whole-language reading program has its focus on readers in trouble. The term "readers in trouble" is a nonjudgmental term for those in and out of school who can't read as well as they or someone else thinks they should.

What these people have in common is that they are their own worst enemies. They have come to think of the world as divided between the people who can read and the people who can't. They believe people who can't read can't learn to read, and so they put themselves in that category.

In societies in which large numbers of people have little or no access to education, many people who are illiterate are not stigmatized and they do not think it is their fault that they can't read. Readers in trouble in developed countries have had many unsuccessful school experiences. They believe that it is their fault that they can't read. They assume that failures in instruction were failures in learning. They think that if only they could master the phonics rules, memorize the vowel charts, or get enough word-attack skills, then they would be good readers.

Readers in trouble have succumbed to the medical-pathological view of themselves that has been built into remedial reading programs. They believe something is constitutionally wrong with them, that they lack a magic button that makes the letters and words make sense, that they've got some wires crossed in their heads, and that they just can't learn like normal people learn.

Some older readers in trouble even have adopted some of the jargon of remedial reading: they describe themselves as learning disabled, dyslexic, mixed dominant, myopic. In a Peanuts cartoon sequence, Charlie Brown ran this whole gamut, and Lucy finally said, "Maybe you're just stupid."

There is no reason to believe that reading and writing require any more intelligence, perceptual ability, or physical coordination than oral language does. In fact oral language is developed without professional assistance and without the established language base that hearing learners have before they develop literacy, so oral language development is a more impressive achievement than learning to read and write.

Readers in trouble cannot become proficient readers until they revalue themselves as learners and users of language and revalue the reading process as a transactive, constructive one rather than a technology of phonics rules and word attack. They must be helped to rid themselves of the self-blame and derogatory labels and trust their own ability to make sense of print using the language strengths they've built in making sense of oral language (or sign, in the case of hearing impaired learners). To accomplish this revaluing they need the patient support and help of teachers.

Revaluing the Process   If readers are in trouble, there is a breakdown in the transactions between the readers and the text. They aren't able to use adequately what they bring to the text—experience, attitudes, concepts, and schemas. They tend to treat the text as a string of equally important words to be perceived or recognized in linear order. They tend not to treat the text as syntactically structured, semantically cohesive, and coherent. They lose the overall unity of the text as a representation capable of varied interpretation and variable comprehension.

To become readers they must revalue the process as a psycholinguistic process in which thought and language interact as the reader builds meaning. They must realize that they are not the prisoners of their eyes, that their brains are seeking sense as they read. They must become confident that they have schemas that they can use to predict and to infer where the meaning is going, what sentence patterns are coming, and what words and phrases are expected.

Readers in trouble need to revalue reading as a process of making sense of print in which perceptual, syntactic, and semantic information is processed. Readers can tell whether they've been successful if the print makes sense. Risk taking, self-monitoring, and self-confidence are the essence of a revaluing program.

Teachers' Revaluing the Learners   Teachers cannot be the patient, sustaining support that readers in trouble need unless they believe strongly that the learners can learn and that they are capable. They need to understand where things have gone wrong and why otherwise capable language learners have not succeeded.

Children growing up in a literate society are already responding to print. As they see print used, they come to know what it is used for and what it means. The search for order and comprehensibility that is characteristic of all humans is the key to this learning. Teachers must understand that all learners bring this tremendous strength to learning to read and write. This insight can help teachers to understand that the failure of nonachieving pupils is a school failure. Somehow schools have not built on their strengths. Their lack of success in school is because language has been made too abstract and too difficult for them in the name of making it simpler and easier.

Readers in trouble are, like everyone else, trying to make sense of their world, including the language in it, but at the same time they are trying to read by the numbers: sounding out, attacking words, using phonics skills. Getting words right becomes an end in itself, and they lose the value of getting to meaning, so every unfamiliar word is a potential defeat, a major obstacle. Readers in trouble are afflicted with the "next word syndrome." They think that successful readers never meet a word they don't know or can't get by pressing some internal magic button. They think that it is impermissible to go on unless each word is read accurately.

Readers in trouble are more likely to suffer from too much skill instruction rather than not enough. In conventional remedial reading programs they have had repeated intensive instruction in phonics and word-attack skills. They know the instruction hasn't helped them, but they persist in diligently using skills that don't work for them, assuming that the reason they don't work is their own deficiencies as learners. They persevere on single words, producing many nonword attempts and phonic near misses. Their miscues are frequently misinterpreted by diagnosticians as proof that more phonics is needed.

Besides this overreliance on word-attack skills, these learners have a second strategy. They become dependent on the teacher to supply the word that they can't attack successfully. Each time they meet a problem word or phrase they wait a few seconds; the teacher then will supply the next word. The learners come to feel that they are inadequate without the teacher's interference. The teacher hasn't really helped but only sustains the basic feeling of defeat and inadequacy.

Teachers need to understand that this sense of inadequacy is greatly exaggerated among readers in trouble. They don't believe that they know anything or that they have any useful reading strategies. They often believe that the successful things they do in coping with print are cheating, particularly if they get to meaning without getting all the words.

One common problem shared by readers in trouble is a strong distaste for school. They've spent the time that more successful pupils spend on reading and learning getting extra doses of worksheets, flash cards, and remedial skill drills. When these don't help they're kept in from recess and lunch periods, kept out of physical education, art, music, social studies, and science, and kept after school to do more of what isn't helping.

Once they've been referred for remediation, they've been given a heavy battery of tests that confirm that they don't do well on tests and that they don't respond well to skill drills. The net result is continuing cycles of dull, tedious, repetitious, decontextualized remediation and less and less of anything new, interesting, or useful.

Sometimes when a new cycle of remediation is begun the learners perk up. They enjoy the special attention, particularly if the teacher is warm and enthusiastic, and this shows in somewhat improved scores on tests, but soon enough the decontextualized skill instruction leads to frustration and despair. Pep talks to get the pupils to try harder build personal guilt or hostility, or both. Meanwhile, the time spent on remediation is the time other pupils are spending building concepts, reading, writing, and doing things. Ironically, the pupil who rebels may be showing a healthier reaction than the pupil who meekly submits and withdraws.

So teachers trying to help readers in trouble to revalue themselves and the reading process must understand that they are dealing with pupils who have the ability to learn to read, who are better readers than they think they are, who have little belief in themselves as language learners, and who have aversive reactions to schools.

Pupils Revaluing Themselves   The answer to all this has to be revaluing. The pupils must revalue themselves as learners, and the reading process as the construction of meaning in response to print. They must come to appreciate their own strengths, to recognize and use more confidently the productive strategies they have and to build positively on those. They must come to view reading as transactions between themselves and authors through texts.

When they put proper values on themselves, they can come to see that no reader, no matter how proficient, can comprehend everything, that what readers know before reading strongly determines what they can learn from it. They need to realize that some things are hard to read because they're poorly written, while other things are hard for them because they present a lot of new complex ideas. They need to know that everybody doesn't have to like everything in print but that everyone can find things that are useful, entertaining, interesting, and comprehensible in print. They need to be aware that the things they know the most about and give them the most satisfaction are the very things that will be easiest for them to read.

Helping readers in trouble to revalue themselves is both very easy and very hard. What's easy is that the essential method involves getting readers to read real, meaningful texts and thereby to strengthen and gain appreciation of their productive strategies while dropping nonproductive strategies. What's hard is the long, slow rebuilding of the sense of self and sense of reading. It's hard because it requires great patience and gentle support from teachers. The egos of the learners are very fragile, they're easily discouraged, and they've had years to become convinced of the futility of trying to learn.

However, the very conflict that readers in trouble experience every time they read can be a positive force for teachers to help achieve revalued reading. They are experiencing what Piaget calls disequilibrium, a point in learning where learners have unresolved conflicts. This unbalanced state has become reading for many readers in trouble. But the seeds of resolution are contained in this very uncomfortable condition. The reader is engaged in trying to make sense of a text no matter what else he or she is doing. Patiently, in the context of supporting and emphasizing the reader's search for meaning, the teacher helps the reader shift away from preoccupation with getting each word, from sounding out, and from teacher dependency. Very patiently the teacher helps the learner to trust his or her own linguistic judgment, to believe in the inferences and predictions the reader is making, to take risks, and to self-monitor. The teacher keeps the focus on meaning by urging the reader to apply the key test: Does it make sense?

Gradually the learner becomes aware that the reading is making sense; an accommodation occurs and graphophonic, syntactic, and semantic cues are used selectively as they are needed. Any exaggerated value attached to letters or words or to any one cue system gives way and all are put in proper perspective with proper values accorded.

Teacher as Catalyst   The teacher is the crucial catalyst in this process, shifting the balance in the conflict away from nonproductive strategies towards more productive ones and shifting the reader away from getting the next word to making sense. The teacher does this by supporting the reader's intuition, by showing approval when the reader takes a risk, or by asking a timely question when the reader falters, such as:

What's going to happen next in the story?
What do you already know?
Did that make sense? Why or why not?

The teacher, as with all learners, must find out where the learner is. That's not easy for readers in trouble because there is so much scar tissue to penetrate, so much shame, confusion, and despair covering over the ability. Diagnostic tests won't help either. All they reveal is the pupils' great fear of failure and the ease with which they surrender themselves. Rather, the teacher invites the learners to read a variety of things that vary in content, function, and complexity. The teacher finds out what the learners are already reading and uses that to get a sense of what they do when they read. It's only as pupils relax that they reveal themselves and trustworthy insights can be gained. Often it turns out that they are much farther along than either they or the teacher had realized.

The teacher is quite likely to find that the pupils are not at all ready to accept this new approach to helping them. They have often so strongly internalized an expectation about how reading ought to be taught, even if it has not worked well for them, that they reject any alternative. It is important for the teacher to help the learners see the progress being made and to help them find new ways of judging their own progress. A trust needs to develop, and that takes time. The goal is for the readers to see that progress comes through a focus on making sense out of meaningful texts, and that, of course, is the very central premise of revaluing.

The instructional situation must be made completely nonthreatening from the beginning. For some readers who are in serious trouble, it will be sufficient, as a beginning, to encourage them to follow as the teacher or aide reads. As the reader becomes more at ease and builds confidence, a variety of environmental and informational kinds of reading can become instructional materials: signs, catalogues, advertisements, manuals, menus, television guides, and so on. It's vitally important that what is used for reading, both narrative and expository, be based on the personal interests and experiences of the learners and intrinsically motivating.

In this way, the teacher can expand on the base of pupil interest and ability and broaden the scope of reading while building their self-confidence.

The older people are, the wider their interests range. So what is highly motivating reading material for one learner may not be interesting at all to another. Teachers need to take their lead from the pupils and to continue to be there to offer support, encouragement, and appropriate materials. The learner sets the pace as well, with the teacher tracking behind but offering the right help at the right time.

Content Reading for Readers in Trouble   Even as readers in trouble begin to improve in their ability and self-confidence, they are likely to still have trouble coping with content area texts. It is very important that teachers be as honest as possible with the learners. School texts are hard for many pupils at all grade levels and they will be doubly hard for pupils who've missed out on content area concepts in earlier grades because they were busy being remediated. In revaluing themselves as readers students need to understand that there are several reasons why texts may be difficult:

1. The pupils may lack background that the text authors have presupposed. All teachers, whatever they teach, need to be sensitive to this issue. Too often what is dismissed as a reading problem is a mismatch between the text pre-suppositions and the background of the learners.
2. The texts may be poorly written. Authors of subject matter texts often are authorities in the field who do not necessarily know much about their intended audience or how to make things meaningful for them. Vocabulary may be unnecessarily technical and insufficiently supported by context.
3. The texts may present too much information too superficially and too rapidly. This is a particular fault with upper elementary and junior high school texts, which tend to cover large areas introducing but not developing many concepts. Teachers can help pupils by providing experiences and by being selective about which topics they ask pupils to explore. Trade books that deal in depth with single topics may be more useful for readers in trouble.

Readers who are in trouble have a lot of catching up to do. Teachers can help them deal with content area learning by finding a range of resource materials to supplement or replace grade level texts.

Once readers in trouble begin to gain confidence, teachers often find they become enthusiastic writers. They often have had little experience writing since they may not have been asked to write much. They usually go through the stages of development of younger learners but much more rapidly. Their first efforts are clumsy and contain a lot of misspelling and shaky mechanics. The teacher needs to encourage all their efforts and not be prematurely concerned with errors and form. More will be said about this in the next chapter.

Teachers of readers in trouble need to work not only to help them learn how to read but to make them enthusiastic confident readers who will begin to think of reading as a source of pleasure and knowledge, something they can do while travelling, when waiting, when a quiet, personal activity is needed, when there's nothing good on television and nobody to hangout with. The goal is that they reach a point where they will choose to read for their own purposes.

Teachers can help readers in trouble to find their way to becoming productive and confident readers. The means is to help them revalue themselves and the reading process.

Conclusions

The whole language reading approach this chapter presents treats learning to read as a natural process. People develop strategies for comprehending written language in a literate society where reading becomes meaningful and functional in school and out. Teachers who appreciate and understand language and how it is learned build on that knowledge to support the literacy development of their students. They provide a classroom environment in which reading is used to learn about significant aspects of the total human experience.

Reading, in a whole language program, is always a means to an end, always comprehension centered.

References

R. Van Allen, *Language Experiences in Reading,* a kit (Chicago: Encyclopedia Britannica, 1979).

Emmett Betts, *Foundations of Reading Instruction* (New York: American Book Company, 1957).

Department of Education, *Reading in Junior Classes* (Wellington, NZ: Government Printer, 1985).

Emilia Ferreiro and Ana Teberosky, *Literacy Before Schooling,* (Exeter, NH and London: Heinemann, 1982).

Kenneth S. Goodman, "A Linguistic Study of Cues and Miscues in Reading," *Elementary English,* vol. 42 (October, 1965).

Kenneth S. Goodman and Yetta M. Goodman, "A Whole-Language Comprehension-Centered Reading Program," Occ. Paper No. 1, (Tucson: Program in Language and Literacy, University of Arizona, 1981).

Yetta M. Goodman and Carolyn Burke, *Reading Miscue Inventory* (New York: Richard C. Owen, 1972).

Yetta M. Goodman and Carolyn Burke, *Strategies in Reading: Focus on Comprehension* (New York: Richard C. Owen, 1978).

Yetta M. Goodman, Dorothy Watson, and Carolyn Burke, *Reading Miscue Inventory,* 2nd Edition (New York: Richard C. Owen, 1987).

Myna Haussler, "Transitions into Literacy," Occ. Paper No. 10 (Tucson: Program in Language and Literacy, University of Arizona, 1983).

Fran Hunia, *Paru Has a Bath, Ready to Read Series,* Schools Publication Branch, Department of Education, Wellington, New Zealand, 1983.

Irene Hunt, *Across Five Aprils* (New York: Grosset & Dunlap, 1964).

Bill Martin, Jr., *Sounds of Language* (New York: Holt, Rinehart and Winston, 1966, 1974).

David McKay, *Breakthrough to Literacy* (Glendale, CA: Bowmar, 1973).

M. V. Morphett and C. Washburne, "Whom Should Children Begin to Read?" *Elementary English,* March, 1931, pp. 496–503.

New Zealand Department of Education, Shared Book Experience Procedures, Unit 6, Early Reading In-Service Course, Wellington, New Zealand, Department of Education, undated.

Helen Robinson et al., *Reading Unlimited* (Glenview, IL: Scott, Foresman & Co., 1976).

Frank Smith, *Writing and the Writer* (New York: Holt, Rinehart and Winston, 1982).

13

Learning and Teaching Writing:
Strategies for Presentation

Of course, experience is not innocent. The very act of turning language upon it robs it of innocence, conceptually, affectively and ideologically in one fell swoop. It is nevertheless where the interaction of language, thought and society is passionately lived out. It is much more than a passive mirror image of dominant ideology realized as messy and impotent 'common sense.' It is not motionless and inert: it incites ideas, speculations and questions, often in the form of stories and poems. The experience of pupils in the inner-city and elsewhere leads them to doubt and question in language saturated with thought and feeling. In any case once real dialogue starts there is no way of keeping experience out.

That is why for so many English teachers the word 'experience' has so much resonance. . . . at its best it has unleashed in classroom stories, poems, autobiographies and drama of a kind never seen before in schools, a huge demonstration of the ability of children and young people to speak with authenticity, quite unlike the bogus, half-strangled essays which have filled mountains of grimy exercise books.

(Harold Rosen, 1981)

Writing, perhaps even more then reading, needs a whole-language program to support its full development. That's because there are fewer natural literacy events in which learners experience the role of a writer before school, so it is less common for pupils to develop a full sense of participation in the functions of writing than the other language processes. Children do begin to write before school begins, as we illustrated earlier. And writing is learned for the same reasons and in the same way as the other three language processes. But, surrounded by print, children experience the role of reader much more often. So school writing programs must provide many authentic, meaningful literacy events in which the learners will take on the roles of writers—people who need to say something to someone through written language.

Ironically, there has been very little authentic writing in school. The form of writing has been taught in a particularly fragmented nonholistic manner. From early elementary school the focus is on learning to spell words and form and join letters. And little allowance is made for growth and development. Even when children are asked to write, the focus has been more on error-free spelling, form, and mechanics and less on writing as a form of presentation. Many people leave school without having established a clear set of personal functions for writing, without any confidence in themselves as writers, and with a strong distaste for the process.

A Whole-Language Writing Program

The key criterion of a whole-language writing program is that school writing activities must be authentic literacy events in which the student writes because there is something to be said by the writer, to a particular intended audience, using written language because it best serves the function and purpose. The writer must feel a sense of control, of ownership of the process and its use. Keeping this key whole-language criterion in mind will help teachers and curriculum makers decide whether current and proposed instructional activities are useful and desirable. If they don't meet the criterion, they should not be used no matter how much tradition lies behind them.

A holistic writing program builds on the writing experience learners have had and keeps the development of the forms of writing in the context of their use. It starts with the literacy events in which the writer is closest to the audience to build a sense of function, a sense of audience, and a sense of story or text. It is concerned with providing a full range of writing experiences, including everything from writing lists and keeping journals to writing fiction and persuasive, logically organized essays.

A whole-language writing program is developmental. It is built on the expectation that like everything else people do, writing will be imperfect and immature in its early stages. Because of the fragmentation of writing into component skills, there has been a tendency to think that one must know how to spell a word before it can be used in writing, that one must be able to write a sentence before one can write a paragraph, and that only after one can write a perfect paragraph can one write a story or even a letter to a friend.

Whole-language writing teachers expect parts to be learned in the context of the whole. They understand that the form of written language develops in the context of trying to say something in writing; they assume that there will be a lot of misspelling on the way to reasonably good spelling and a lot of clumsy and disjointed attempts at presentation on the way to proficient writing.

A whole-language writing program sees perceiving and ideating as necessary aspects of a whole-language program. Every true written text, no matter how mundane, has a purpose and content for the writer which involves becoming aware of a situation through perceiving, and developing ideas through ideating. So teachers must plan for time to perceive and to ideate before and during the writing.

Furthermore, a whole-language program accepts the concept that presenting is also part of learning. Writers have a sense of what they want to say, which incorporates what they think they know, but in the process of presenting—that is, of writing—they continue to learn, to assimilate and accommodate, and to form their conceptual schemas. So a writer can never be sure of what the final text will be before it is written.

Relationships Between Reading and Writing

Reading and writing are part of the world of children, we said above, but not in equal proportions. Children growing into literacy find people around them reading more often than they write and for more obvious purposes. There is a world of already existing written language, including but not confined to books. Adults call the attention of children to print and invite their participation in reading. Such reading does not require the reader to assume the role of writer.

There is an important influence of reading on writing. People use in writing what they observe in reading. But they also must be reading like writers. They may notice characteristics of print in their environment, but it is only when they try to create written language that this observation focuses on how form serves function.

Here are some key points about the interrelationships of reading and writing from the point of view of development:

1. While both oral and written language are transactional processes in which communication between a language producer and a language receiver takes place, the interpersonal aspects of oral language are more pervasively evident than those of written language. Productive and receptive roles are much more interchangeable in a speech act of oral language than in a literacy event of written language. The contribution of listening development to speaking development is easier to identify than the similar contribution of reading to writing. One reason is that oral interaction is more easily observable than written interaction.
2. Both reading and writing develop in relation to their specific functions and use. Again, there is more parity for functions and needs of listening and speaking than for reading and writing.
3. Most people need to read a lot more often in their daily lives than they need to write. To put it simply, that means they get a lot less practice in writing than in reading.
4. Readers certainly must build a sense of the forms, conventions, styles, and cultural constraints of written texts as they become more proficient and flexible readers, but there is no assurance that this will carry over into writing unless they are motivated to produce themselves, as writers, similar types of texts.
5. Readers have some way of judging their effectiveness immediately. They know whether they are making sense of what they are reading. Writers must depend on feedback and response from potential readers, which is often quite delayed. They may, of course, be their own readers; in fact, it's impossible to write without reading.
6. Readers need not write during reading, but writers must read and reread during writing, particularly as texts get longer and their purposes get more complex. Smith puts it this way:

   > There appears to be an asymmetrical if not parasitic relationship between reading and writing, Writing needs reading, but reading can do without writing, even though writing may provide short cuts in understanding aspects of reading. (Smith, 1982)

   The process of writing must result in a text that is comprehensible for the intended audience. That requires that it be relatively complete, that ideas be well presented, that appropriate forms, styles, and conventions be used. As writing proficiency improves through functional communicative use, there will certainly be a pay-off for reading, since all of the schemas for predicting texts in reading are essentially the same as those used in constructing texts during writing.
7. Reading and writing do have impact on each other, but the relationships are not simple and isomorphic. The impact on development must be seen as involving the function of reading or writing and the specific process in which reading and writing are used to perform those functions.

Basically, written language came about as a means of communicating beyond face-to-face situations over time or space, or both. In most types of literacy events, the writer and reader are not involved at the same time. Young readers may be only dimly aware, if at all, of an author's involvement. Most traditional school language arts programs do not help students to develop a personal functional need for being authors themselves of poems, stories, news reports, books, essays, or biographical sketches. As they progress in school, they will encounter school tasks that require writing. But, too often, the purpose of such tasks from the writer's point of view is to satisfy an external demand and not an internal need to present or to communicate.

Furthermore, teachers have tended to be evaluators rather than audience or respondents. Often, school writing assignments involve either imaginary audiences or no explicit audience at all.

In summary then, people not only learn to read by reading and write by writing, but they also learn to read by writing and write by reading. For the teacher trying to support written language development, the key objective is to keep the pupils actively involved in both processes. A successful writing curriculum will be one that is holistic, that builds on personal writing, that builds the functions of interpersonal writing, and that helps pupils to find frequent authentic purposes for such writing with real audiences. A successful reading curriculum involves pupils in reading with awareness of the role of the author.

Implementing a Three-Part School Writing Program

An effective school writing program needs to begin where the learners are and to carefully expand on the characteristics of literacy events in which people participate as readers and writers. Such a program needs to be built on the full range of personal uses of written language so that literacy may develop in the context of natural, functional use.

Furthermore, as much as possible, when students write in school they must have something to say, they must choose to write, and they must have an intended audience in mind.

Three Key Concerns

The three key concerns of the reading program are equally important in the writing program:

1. There must be a strong focus on meaning. Writers, at all levels of development, must be writing because they have something to say. The focus of both the teacher and the pupil in considering what is written is whether meaning has been presented comprehensibly for the intended audience and whether the writers have said what they meant.
2. Students must feel comfortable to take risks in their writing. Risk taking in writing means using words they're not sure they can spell, trying forms they haven't tried before, and letting others know through writing what they're thinking and feeling.

Presentation of any kind involves risks. Even professional writers feel this sense of risk. Most educated adults have high levels of writing anxiety; they feel highly vulnerable about their writing. Young people who feel that they won't be embarrassed or punished for the risks they take in writing are less likely to be uptight about their writing as adults.

There's no place in the classroom for sarcastic, caustic, or punitive responses to pupils' writing, no matter how tentative or ineffective their efforts are. This is not a matter of not having standards. The teachers and students have a constant standard for judging writing: does it make sense; can it be comprehended? Teachers have to encourage their pupils to take the risks writing involves and then support their efforts to say well in writing what they need to say.

3. There must be lots of writing. Development as a writer depends on doing a lot of writing. And developing writers will be writing what is most useful to them if they're doing it because they have purposes, because they have something to present, and because they care whether they've been understood. The key to an effective school writing program is a teacher who knows how to use, find, and create situations in which pupils will want to write.

Reading, as we have said, contributes in important ways to writing, so there must be a lot of reading going on too, but as Smith says,

> Writing provides the incentive, the purpose for learning about writing from reading. Unless one wants to write, and sees oneself as a writer, there is no reason to be responsive to the facets of writing demonstrated in text. The key to learning about writing from reading is to read like a writer. (Smith, 1982, p. 179)

The Beginning Writing Program

Writing development has begun before kids come to school. A key objective of preschool and primary teachers is to keep the process going, to involve their young pupils in purposeful, voluntary writing, and beyond that, in the context of their use of writing, to support their increasing control over the form of written language.

Every preschool, kindergarten, and primary classroom should have a corner or center where a variety of paper and writing utensils are always available. Young children should be encouraged to play with these and to play at writing as many have already been doing at home. Teachers need to observe what they produce in their play, to respond to their questions, to ask them to read what they have written, to treat their writing seriously even if it bears no discernible resemblance to comprehensible writing, and to respond to the intentions and the message appreciatively.

Studies by Milz (1983) and others reveal a natural development of the writing of school beginners if they're supported and encouraged:

1. Their first efforts are not interpretable by others and, in fact, they themselves will be unable to read them half an hour after they are written. Primary teachers can make a habit of asking pupils to read what they've written and then writing

this on the back of the page or lightly over the lines, not for the pupils to compare, but so that they may remind the pupils of what they had intended to say.

2. Fairly soon the writing progresses to the point where the pupil and a concerned adult, teacher, or aide who is familiar with other writing of the child can read the writing. At this stage the invented spellings become relatively consistent for words each time they are used, and rules are evident as the child generates new spellings.

3. Some time after that the writing reaches the point where anyone can, with a little effort and imagination, understand it. There are still many misspellings, and punctuation is only rudimentary, but the child is able to present comprehensible meaning through writing.

These stages are very much like the sequence of oral language development, and just as oral language development is very much facilitated by adults and older siblings wanting to understand and going more than half way to assure that the child is understood, so it will help children's writing development to have teachers and parents who show similar delight in the kids' early writing efforts and who go more than half way in trying to understand them.

There will be a steady and quite rapid development in letter formation, spelling, and punctuation through these stages, and the writing will show continuous movement toward adult norms without an undue focus on or teaching of these norms.

When children are involved in role playing situations, whether it is playing house or gas station in kindergarten or interviewing famous people as part of a social studies unit in upper grades, the implements and materials necessary for reading and writing should be readily available so they can easily make shopping lists, label the costs of items, write out receipts, or take notes as appropriate to the activity. These might include typewriters and word-processors as well as paper, pencils, and markers.

Whole-Language Beginning Writing Activities

Here are some whole-language writing activities primary teachers can use to encourage and support writing.

Names and Labels Children are provided with name cards and encouraged to personalize their belongings, their areas of control, and their work. Mailboxes and cubbies can be labeled. If they have their own work areas, such as a desk or table, these may also be labeled by the children. Children can be designated as mail carriers or box stuffers so that the labeling becomes functional in the classroom as everyone has to learn to read all the labels in the room for some real purpose.

A unit on language or on different countries might involve learning how the children's names might be written in other languages or in other language forms such as calligraphy. Children could change their labels during the year, depending on what is being studied, to maintain interest in the activity.

With real function in mind, the pupils can help the teacher label appropriate centers or special areas of the room where specific work takes place. The restrictions related to the use of these areas may also be developed and written by the students so they know what is expected of them. Warnings about how to care for plants and animals or about unsafe areas in or near the school may be made by the pupils. These might emerge from a unit on animal or plant care or safety. Danger and warning signs on drug containers, household cleaners, and so on, can be used to focus on the significance and utility of such warnings and the problems in understanding their meanings.

Letter and Note Writing   Some teachers write a short note to each child before school starts, welcoming them to school and inviting them to write back a letter that they can mail or bring on the first day. That first day each child is presented with a personal mail box in which another note from the teacher is waiting for them.

Teacher Response Journals   Each pupil keeps a journal in a spiral notebook or composition book. They are encouraged to write anything they want to write in the journal. The only requirement is that they must write in it at least once a day even if all they write is, "I have nothing to say today." The teacher reads each journal every few days and responds. The responses are not evaluatory nor does the teacher mark or correct the child's handwriting, spelling, or grammar. But the teacher's responses will give the pupil a "demonstration," as Smith calls it, in a context of high interest to the pupil, of how a proficient writer deals with the topic. Teachers often notice their pupils picking up spellings, phrases, forms, and ideas from their comments in subsequent journal entries.

Bookmaking   Even school beginners can create their own books. The class should have a bookmaking center where books can be typed, cut, and bound in cardboard covered with contact paper, wallpaper, or fabric. Pupils may either write themselves or dictate a story or personal experience to a teacher, aide, parent volunteer, or older child. The teacher and the class may establish procedures for how stories are selected and what process of editing they will go through for publication. In many classes there is agreement that invented spelling is acceptable in other writing but that standard spelling will be used in published books as it is in the printed ones in the classroom library. An editing process is introduced for this purpose. When the book is published it is added to the classroom library for everyone to read. Bookmaking is a good way to encourage imaginative creative narrative writing. It helps pupils to realize the relationship of authors to texts and to audiences. Teachers should not be offended or surprised if pupils pick up themes and story lines from favorite books, television shows, and successful classmates. What might be called plagiarism in adults is, in young writers, using their experience to explore narrative forms, purposes, and styles.

Writing from Experience   In Japan a movement has existed for many years called "Writing from Experience" (Sei Katsu Tsuzari Kata). Kitagawa describes the origins of this movement:

> In the 1920's in Japan some teachers of very poor children began to encourage their students to write descriptive narratives of events in their lives. The goal was neither excellence of compositions nor elucidation for the world beyond these poverty pockets, but rather to help the children come to a level of self-actualization within the reality of everyday situations. They stressed reaction and multisensory perception. By building upon these dimensions teachers became aware of the children's writing process rather than the product. (Kitagawa, 1982)

Here's an example Kitagawa cites together with the teacher's comments:[1]

> Teacher, last night at midnight I woke up wanting to go to the bathroom, but I was thinking that, if I go to the bathroom and a ghost comes, I might faint, so I did it through the window. At the same time, a thief cat was coming down the mountainside with a fish in its mouth. The cat looked up at me, I got embarrassed. The cats eyes were really shining brightly. I thought of splashing the cat and aimed toward it. But I ended up really splashing it. I felt bad and said, "Sor-r-r-y." The cat shivered, shook its head and ran off to the tangerine tree. I almost began to laugh but, because Mom and Dad were sleeping, I covered my mouth, closed the window and very qui-et-ly went back to bed.

Some of the teacher's comments (interspersed in the text) are: (1) It began thus because you wanted to tell this to the teacher; (2) this is where you told clearly why you used the window; (3) you are recalling the cat's behavior very well, aren't you?

The teacher's comments pick up the ways the young writer has followed the basic premises of writing from experience without being strongly directive. This concept starts from the premise that young writers will find it easiest to narrate their own personal experiences and that this will generally promote writing development and also create a sense of narrative, which will then facilitate creative writing. In some senses pupils do this anyway even if they are given assigned topics to write on. Emphasizing writing from experience helps the learners realize that they have experiences they can present and that other people will be interested in reading about them.

Developmental Writing

In past decades, writing programs in elementary schools in North America have been all but nonexistent. Handwriting, spelling, and mechanics have been taught and pupils have been required to write on worksheets, do some individual and group reports, and write answers to questions. Little of the writing has been initiated by the learners because they had expressive purposes to meet through

---

[1]"What Happened at Midnight" by Toshikazu Mizusaki, quoted in Nakamura and Kuniseki, "Sono Toori ni Kakoo" (Let's Write as It Happened) *Sakubu to Kyooibu* (Composition and Education) 350 (1979) 123–124. Cited in M Kitagawa, 1982, translation by Chisato Kitagawa.

writing. Now and then pupils have been encouraged to write stories or poems. But none of this really adds up to a developmental writing curriculum.

Secondary schools have tended to teach some formal characteristics of writing sentences, paragraphs, or essays, but there has been little creative writing in secondary schools and, again, one could not really say that there has been a writing curriculum in most schools. A study by James Britton in England showed that writing for most secondary students there is confined almost completely to what they are assigned to do by teachers.

Ironically, this neglect of the full range of writing development may be at least partly due to the difficulty of putting a writing program into a text series. It also makes it somewhat easier to initiate a whole-language writing program in schools than it is to initiate whole-language reading programs where the long tradition of basal readers has to be overcome.

A whole-language developmental writing program draws on the out-of-school writing experiences young people have. It expands on these mundane uses of writing in school and helps learners expand the functions and uses of writing in and out of school. The writing program includes, but is not confined to, creative writing of stories and poetry. It includes, but is not confined to, writing of notes and letters, journals, news reports, scientific observations, research reports, essays, and statements of belief. And it is holistic in all senses:

1. Writing is integrated with reading and other language processes.
2. Writing is always in the context of its use: the skills and strategies of writing are not separated from the process of using it.
3. Writing to learn isn't separated from learning to write. In a whole-language developmental writing program there is attention to writing across the curriculum. Teachers are as concerned for the opportunities to develop writing through science, social studies, art, music, mathematics, as they are for the development of cognition and learning through writing.

If all involved in the literacy development of children can understand the strengths children have when they come to school, if they believe children have already started to read and write as they have actively participated in their literate environment, a curriculum will be developed which expands on children's knowledge. This kind of understanding is a much more supporting notion for learning than ignoring the degree to which children come to school understanding the nature of written language.

Building on Daily Experience

One way to build on daily experiences is to examine the wide variety of functional writing experiences that can be turned into daily curricular experiences. Teachers can write down everything they write or read for a 48-hour period. The children can be asked to add to this list by observing and interviewing family members. A Friday and Saturday or Sunday and Monday are good days to choose, since these include a school day and a weekend day, which will expose different kinds of language functions in at least two different settings. Everything that is even scanned or glanced at quickly, such as toothpaste containers or recipes, should be included. Then the teacher can sit down with the list and ask: "How can I turn each activity into a written language experience for the children in my classroom?" or "How can I relate these things to the studies I am already planning for my class?" The writing experiences can be planned so that they are done by the children alone, or they can be a collaborative effort by the teacher with the children.

Many of the activities will involve both reading and writing, which can take place almost simultaneously. Many of the activities that begin as personal writing will become interpersonal as children expand their focus on self to a focus on communication with others.

All of these activities take time. They should not be started in a school or classroom unless teachers understand their significance, are enthusiastic about what they accomplish, and believe in the priority of such activities. If these are simply added to an already overcrowded curriculum, then both teachers and children become frustrated and the activities lose their significance.

Since these activities involve the functional use of reading and writing, they include spelling, handwriting, dictionary use, and language analysis. The teacher should therefore spend less time focusing on the latter in workbooks and ditto sheets, which isolate their development from use. Instead, the teacher can begin to gather evidence, through their daily use of reading and writing for many purposes and in all kinds of settings, that children's spelling, handwriting, and grammar develop significantly through varied language use.

Goods and Services Functions

Using mundane functions of writing, like shopping lists in the classroom, can be helpful, because all members of a literate community participate widely in the pragmatic functions of reading and writing that Michael Halliday has called the "goods and services" function of language. These are the functions of written language that help us go about the business of our daily lives—reading bus schedules, writing notes to tell family members where we are, jotting down doctor's appointments and birthdays.

Children often are involved in these literacy events. In such literacy events the relationships between reader and writer are very explicit. Reader and author are more likely to be in close contact. Reading what is written is more immediate and feedback is faster.

Too often, parents, teachers, and children themselves do not recognize these activities as legitimate reading and writing. Therefore, children are not helped to realize that they are significant to the development of reading and writing and building knowledge about written language, including its various functions and forms. If children understand the significance of these forms of reading and writing, then school instruction is seen by them as an extension of what they are already doing and it does not become such a foreboding task.

The shopping list, explored as an example of the writing process in Chapter

9, is one of a small number of relatively frequent writing activities that writers engage in with themselves as intended audience. Other activities in which writers are their own intended audience are:

1. Other list making, such as things to do, invitation lists, holiday lists
2. Information jotting, such as names, phone numbers, addresses, odd bits of information, personal histories
3. Note taking during lectures, while reading or observing, during interviews

All of these writing activities have purposes that are personal, involving use of writing as a means of extending memory. Because this type of writing happens very frequently, students see its use and develop awareness of its function quite early.

Children can be involved in making or reading lists in the classroom. List making might include: attendance taking; keeping track of which children go where during the day; grouping for centers and activities; keeping track of addresses, phones, school personnel, and birthdays; cataloging the class library; preparing lists of educational places to go after school and on weekends to send home monthly to parents; listing completed assignments and accomplishments. All of these eventually lead to a need for organizing, categorizing, and alphabetizing to involve students within a functional and personal use of written language.

Diaries and Journals

Another type of personal writing is the diary, log, or journal. It differs from the other personal writing in that it's intended to be kept longer and is usually much more complete than less formal personal writing. Often, a diary takes the form of a written conversation with an imagined alter ego, sometimes addressed as "Dear Diary." It has the very personal function of recording not only events but feelings, longings, and imagined events. As it is used by teens and preteens, it comes after other writing functions and forms have developed and shows a sense of the historical function writing can have, which makes possible later recall and reconsideration of the past. Like less formal personal writing, it represents an extension of memory.

Teachers might capitalize on this kind of memory extension by keeping a group classroom diary to remember important classroom events. Middle-grade teachers might want to model this on the log of Starship Enterprise with entries made daily as a means of summarizing the day's activities. Pupils can take turns being the captain making the entries, reading them to the class for additions and editing.

On a personal level pupils can be involved in jotting down information in short partial sentences for further reference or elaboration. These could later be used to write a classroom letter to parents about "What I learned this week!" They could also become part of a classroom newspaper.

This type of diary writing is different from the journal writing we discussed for beginners if the teachers read and respond to the pupils' entries. Such journals become extended written interactions. They continue to be appropriate for older pupils who want to participate. The teacher's goal may be to create a meaningful purpose for the pupils to write frequently so that they may have practice in using writing to communicate. The pupils use their writing to tell the teacher about their feelings, the events of their lives, and to complain or make requests. The writing does not have the immediate purpose of extending memory, nor is it personal in that the audience is intended to be the writer. The students may enjoy reading what they have written, but they are not their primary intended audience.

Teachers have begun to make extended use of school journals because they've become aware that while the personal writing young people do builds a strong sense of function, it does not involve the pupil in the role switching characteristic of most uses of oral language, so the writer does not have the opportunity to get feedback from a reader and to build a sense of audience. The teacher-response journal is a kind of written language transaction in which some kind of attention to the interests, characteristics, and background of an expected audience is involved.

Teacher-response journals have most recently been discussed by Milz (1983) and Staton (1980). Teachers must understand the importance of the response. Time must be set aside to read and respond to the journals on a regular basis. The importance of this is seen in a second-grader's disappointed note to his teacher in his journal:

I

won't write

no mor

til yuo write

me back

In personal writing the writer may find out later, as a reader, how successful the writing has been and what changes are necessary to make the writing better serve its purpose, but there is not the same awareness of audience that emerges when language is interpersonal, for then the writer can build a sense of how completely a message must be represented and how form must support function. Language is both personal and social, but it is its social interpersonal use that makes the user aware of how well or completely and in what form it must be expressed to be successful.

One activity, described by Carolyn Burke as "written conversations," is especially helpful for middle-grade children who may need help to focus on interpersonal writing. It is literally a conversation on paper, usually between two people, initially including the teacher. But as the activity becomes familiar to the children, either the teacher's role can be taken by another child or a third member may be added to the team. For very young beginners or insecure writers, the teacher may read aloud as the message is being penned. An exarnple of written conversation follows:

Teacher:	Pedro, how are you today?
Student:	Fine. How are you today?
Teacher:	I feel great today. Pedro, do you have any hobbies?
Student:	No, do you?
Teacher:	Yes, Pedro. I like to cook and swim. Mrs. W. told me you play kickball. Is that right?
Student:	Yes.
Teacher:	Do you like it?
Student:	Yes. Do you like it too?
Teacher:	Yes, I like it a lot. Are you on a team?
Student:	Yes, I am on Bobcats. Do you like the team?
Teacher:	I have never seen the Bobcats play.
Student:	Why don't you come and see.
Teacher:	Thanks! I would like to!

But this form of written dialogue, while very useful, does not yet represent a common need in our culture. Ironically, there are not many common writing situations in which there is some kind of parity between the number of readers and writers involved.

Microcomputers have recently made possible a new form of written conversation. To some extent computer users can holcl conversations with computers as they use "user friendly" programs. Many owners of home computers "talk" to other computer owners through their keyboards and modems. Some experimental use of such electronic writing has been conducted in several school settings. (Scollon and Scollon, 1984) Especially in remote communities, microcomputers make writing a more immediate experience by minimizing the time of getting responses to messages. Such written conversations involve readers and writers in the role-switching characteristic of oral conversation and provide immediate response to each utterance. Deaf and hearing impaired people have been using teletype telephones for some time in place of the usual phones, which are not functional for them.

Notes and Letters

Note and letter writing is one type of writing that most often involves a single writer with one or more readers. Furthermore, this is another type of writing that children observe adults using. They also have early experiences with receiving cards, notes, and letters, so children build an early sense of the function of letter and note writing. Their early efforts are often successful and very well received, because the recipients of children's notes and letters are often close relatives and friends who are willing and able to extend themselves to comprehend and respond. The more readers and writers have in common, the less writers need to consider audience needs, the more readers may infer, and the less complete the expression need be. That creates an optimal situation for language learning.

Note and letter writers learn the form and purpose from receiving and reading or hearing them read and quickly adapt form to function as they write. (Green, 1983; Cholewinski, 1982)

Writing letters to people less familiar than classmates, teachers, and family members provides new audiences for children. Writing to a favorite author to express approval or to ask a question about a book, to a company for free and inexpensive materials, to find answers to questions raised in a science or math unit, to the President, or to the editor of the local newspaper to echo agreement or disagreement with some significant policy all provide challenges for writing, which often demand shifts in style and conventions.

> Dear Mr. President,
> Please help Detroit.
> Do not let people carry guns.
> We see you on T.V.
>
> Our neighborhood is dirty. There is junk everywhere. The windows are busted out. Please don't let people bust out the windows.
>
> Please make a lot of houses pretty. Not with holes, filth, and bugs, and rats. Please let butterflies be flying on your hand.
>
> Paulie

Although the children often get the opportunity to read responses, they may also discover that important people do not always answer their mail.

Narrative Presentation

Commonly, schools have called writing of stories creative writing and have differentiated such writing from other writing pupils do. The term is not a very good one, however, because it implies that the other forms of writing, some of which we've previously discussed, are not creative. That should not be true. If readers are using writing to present, then all forms of writing should be creative. They should feel the same sense of personal purpose and ownership of a letter or a journal entry as they do of a story or poem.

What distinguishes the writing of narratives, then, is not how creative the process is but the narrative purpose and the use of imagination. Rosen believes that narrative is so fundamental it exists "in those forms which are as universal as language itself." He sees narrative as a "predisposition of the human mind to narratize experience and to transform it into findings which as social beings we may share and compare with those of others." (Rosen, 1982) He quotes Barbara Hardy:

> My argument is that narrative, like lyric . . . is not to be regarded as an aesthetic invention used by artists to control, manipulate and order experience, but as a primary act of mind transferred to art from life. . . . (Hardy cited in Rosen, 1982)

Children begin to produce narratives at early ages. They become aware, through listening, that people share their experiences through language. As early as 3 years old they will begin to store up experiences to tell Daddy, Mommy, or Grandma, planning quite deliberately what will be told and how and what the listener's response will be.

Children who are told or read stories begin also to develop a sense of the aesthetic. They enjoy hearing and later reading stories, and so it is natural that they would begin expressing their own imagination through storytelling. Some children will begin to include stories in their journals that are either real personal experiences or imaginative experiences that may incorporate personal experiences. Other children will begin to create their own narratives when they hear those created by their classmates.

One of the most important ways teachers can stimulate narrative in students is to create a classroom atmosphere in which the students' written narratives are valued. That will grow out of beginning writing activities such as bookmaking and writing from experience. It will be helped by the teacher reading pupils' narratives aloud and encouraging pupils to share their writing in small groups, with the whole class, on bulletin boards, or in class magazines. One must have audience reactions if one is to develop a sense of audience.

There should always be time for writing planned into the school day. One form this can take is a time called "uninterrupted sustained silent writing." During this time, which may vary in length depending on the age and motivation of the pupils, every pupil is expected to do some writing. Perhaps it would be better to call it a quiet time rather than a silent time because, though writing is usually an individual activity, collaboration should be encouraged, and a certain amount of social interaction, sharing, giving, and seeking advice is healthy in writing. But it should also be possible for pupils to write at other times of the day as one of several quiet activities they can choose from.

Teachers have used a variety of devices to get pupils to write. Since getting started is one hard part of writing, teachers will often let pupils choose from among several story starters, such as, "It was a dark and stormy night. . . ." or "I'll never forget the time. . . . "

Other teachers feel that giving pupils topics is necessary to get them to write. If topics are used, there should always be choices (including choosing topics of their own), and the choices should build on the interests and experience of the pupils. In a classroom where narrative writing is well established and the pupils think of it as an important aspect of what they do in school, such devices aren't needed. The best writing will come when pupils choose to write and choose what they want to write about.

On the other hand, there are times when teachers may suggest, particularly in the context of a thematic unit or a social studies or science assignment, some appropriate assignments that will encourage pupils to use their imaginations and to incorporate new ideas and insights into their personal schemas. If a class is studying the American Revolution, the teacher may want to read the class a novel, such as *Johnny Tremain,* and then suggest to the students that they imagine themselves in the role of a participant in the events of the time.

In developmental reading instruction one of the main goals is to expand the range of texts pupils comprehend and their flexibility in dealing with them. So also in developmental writing the teacher seeks to support the expansion of the range of narratives pupils can produce and their flexibility in producing texts that suit their purposes.

Teachers need to keep collections of what pupils write. They need to make responsive comments on their papers and discuss them with the pupils in personal conferences, and they need to find ways of stimulating pupils to broaden the scope of their presentations and to take risks if they aren't already doing so.

Expository Writing
At the same time that teachers are encouraging pupils to develop their ability to produce personal and imaginative narratives, they need also to provide situations in which they will need to produce nonnarrative texts. Like all language, expository writing must have a real purpose for the pupils and a real audience, and the form used must be appropriate to both.

One kind of expository writing can occur naturally in response to common occurrences. There are a number of naturally occurring situations in the course of school activities that could stimulate expository writing:

Reacting to a group experience
A class trip
A film, videotape, or play
A dispute, argument, or fight involving other students

Reacting to an event

A natural event, such as a flood, earthquake, blizzard, wind storm, or heat wave

A news event, such as an election, demonstration, assassination, strike, or space exploration

A sports event, movie, television special, concert, festival, or family celebration

Responding to a personal experience

A trip or vacation

A new sibling or cousin

New possessions, such as books, games, sports equipment, clothes, furniture

An exciting happening involving the student, friend, or family member

Any of these may serve as the basis for expository writing. Teachers can help students take advantage of them by providing opportunities and encouragement for writing, helping to identify audiences, and creating an atmosphere in which the writing is highly valued.

Of course, teachers can overdo demanding that every experience lead to writing. That could turn writing into an academic chore. Rather, what teachers want to do is to lead pupils to see the value of putting their experiences, reactions, thoughts, feelings, and views into writing.

One teacher was able to get four 11-year-old boys to do some pretty zealous expository writing. They were brought to her for fighting on the playground. Two had been in the original fight, and each had a friend who came to his aid. Each told the teacher very loudly what had happened and who was to blame. The teacher told them she couldn't hear them because they were all talking at once. She asked them to sit down and write down everything that had happened. When they had finished she asked them to read over what they had written. She observed them carefully editing their original drafts. Then she asked them if they wanted to read what they had written to each other. She asked them to each listen so that they could compare the different versions of the events. Though there was no unanimity, the boys were intrigued by the process, and their tempers cooled considerably. Two of the four wrote more in this context than they had ever written before.

Much of the expository writing students are asked to do in school is related to their other studies: reports for social studies and science, book reviews, or short answer questions on tests and in workbooks. Sensitive teachers can make this incidental expository writing, or writing across the curriculum, very productive in terms of writing development. Again, however, if it is mishandled or overdone, the effect can be to turn writing into "schoolwork," work done in school with no personal purpose and no sense of ownership. Some key factors can make the difference:

1. Pupils should be involved in planning units and studies. They should help to decide what they want and need to know, where they will find it, and how they will share what they find.

2. There should always be choices for them about how they will present their material. Presentations may be expository writing, but they can also take the

form of plays, poetry, stories, oral reports, demonstrations, pictures, graphs, dioramas, songs, or dances. There are many forms of presentation. Students can't learn the importance and utility of written presentation unless they can also explore alternatives. All students should have experience with and become comfortable with expression through expository writing. Some will find it their preferred form for many functions, but others will find they express themselves better, for some purposes, in alternative presentational forms.

3. The time to help pupils learn to control form is in the context of using it. When they've elected to write an essay, a descriptive report, or an advertisement and have prepared a first draft, then they are ready for help in making their efforts as comprehensible and effective as possible.

4. Teachers need to keep in mind that pupils are taking risks when they write for new purposes and audiences. They need to be supported and encouraged. Teachers also need to bear in mind that writing is developmental and that they cannot expect perfection at all points of development.

Editing in Developmental Writing

A key difference between oral and written language is that written language may be perfected and polished before it is presented to the intended audience, whereas oral presentations usually are not. That's because speech is usually heard at the same time it is produced. Whatever editing is done of oral language is usually in the form of restatement if the listener indicates a lack of understanding. There is usually time for the writer to edit before the writing is to be read by the intended audience. Since there is no usual counterpart in oral language to this editing, it is something that pupils must develop in the course of becoming writers.

Not everything written needs to be edited in the same way or polished to the same extent. All writing involves some reading as it is being produced, and that may lead to a certain amount of editing to correct miscues and to change directions as the writers reconsider how they wish to proceed and how well they've considered their audiences. But personal diaries need considerably less editing than narrative or expository writing intended for reading by unknown readers. This is a reality teachers can help pupils cope with.

One dimension of editing is being sure that what is said is what was intended. The other dimension is being sure the intended audience will understand. So effective editing depends on a strong sense of audience, and editing proficiency can't be developed as mastery of a set of absolutes. It depends strongly on the purpose and intended audience of the writing.

Many teachers find it useful to have pupils work in pairs and small groups so that they may serve as an audience for the developing work and provide the feedback that will help the pupils know whether they have written comprehensibly and suggest ways to each other that they can improve their expression. These small group editing conferences also can help developing writers to establish a set of criteria for judging their own work.

Comprehensibility is the major basis for self-evaluation and editing. But writers become aware that the same message can be conveyed and the same story can be told in a variety of different ways and that some ways are more pleasing and more interesting to their readers than others. They become aware also that some ways of saying things may be offensive to readers and have unplanned results. Through writing, getting response, and editing, writing should become not only more comprehensible but also more interesting and more acceptable to the intended audience. Again there are no shortcuts to this. One can't teach style or sensitivity to pragmatics before the writing. Only in the context of writing and reader response can insights be developed that will pay off in more effective writing.

Time is a major requirement for good editing. Teachers need to be flexible in how much time pupils have to complete their writing.

Priorities also need to be developed. In many traditional classrooms there is so much preoccupation with spelling, handwriting, and the mechanics of writing that pupils feel they must continually edit for these surface aspects of their presentation and so they become frustrated and distracted from what they are trying to say. During writing and after completion of a first draft, editing should focus on how well the text says what the writer intended to say. When that's taken care of, then the writer can proofread for spelling, handwriting, and other surface aspects before preparing a final draft. Again, it helps to have pupils work in pairs and serve as proofreaders for each other, since it's very difficult to detect one's own writing miscues.

Revaluing Writing

Many people feel they are inadequate writers even if they can and do write; in fact, even most educated people are not comfortable with their writing. Partly this is due to the broadly negative and decontextualized way that writing has been taught, particularly in secondary schools and colleges. Partly also it results from the perennial complaint of academics and business leaders that schools don't teach people to write.

Ironically, the assumption that ineffective writing shows a lack of schooling is really the opposite of the truth. Nonwriting may reflect a lack of opportunity to learn in school. But most weak, ineffective, or clumsy writing comes from people having learned in school to write that way. It reflects their attempt to produce writing by following a set of arbitrary rules like:

A preposition is something you should never end a sentence *with*.
And never start a sentence with *and* or *but*.

Such writers are unable to use confidently their own sense of language, of text, or of audience and are continually tripping over the mechanistic rules they've been taught. Writers in trouble, like readers in trouble, need to revalue themselves and the process. They need to move back to a view that one writes when one has a purpose, a message, and an audience. They need to think of themselves as competent language users and learners who can make writing work for them when they need to use it.

Writers in trouble will be most successful when they have a strongly defined purpose and audience and when they're dealing with ideas and information that they strongly control. That means starting with what they want and need most to write: that could be letters to family; it could be messages and orders that are related to jobs; it could be lists and records. The audience may be themselves or someone they know very well.

All this makes self-evaluation both easy and realistic. It will take a while for pupils to move away from using external criteria to evaluate their writing to realizing that they can judge their own writing in terms of whether it works, whether the intended readers can understand. Most writers in trouble, like readers in trouble, have a considerable amount of literacy. The problem is that they get in their own way and are easily discouraged. Helping them takes patience, gentle support, and continued encouragement, because they're used to being told in red ink all over their timid efforts how bad, sloppy, and unacceptable their writing is.

The initial purpose of any teacher must first be to get pupils writing and feeling relatively at ease in doing so. Then, within the purposes they've set, the teacher can help them identify what they're doing that works and what is getting in the way. Criticism should always be in the context of the purpose of the writing. Solutions for problems should be elicited from the students, and suggestions should relate specifically to what they're trying to say and to whom.

Older children and young adults often experience a great burst of enthusiasm when they discover they can write. They write extensive entries in journals, ten-page letters, essays, stories, autobiographies, and even novels. Teachers need to support this outpouring of energy and understand that it is the single best way for them to improve their writing effectiveness. Bogging them down in mechanics, stylistics, and heavy criticism will only burst their balloons. That is not to say that they should be told that they are suddenly producing great literature. What they need to know is that they are on their way and they *can* write.

Writers in trouble need to work with others in pairs and in small groups. They can serve as audience for each other. But it also helps to realize that each is not the only student who is uncomfortable about writing. The teacher will need to set the pace and tone of these interactions by showing the students that they need to keep their focus on how well their classmates have said what they intended to say and by showing them how to be critical in a positive way. The pupils working together need not be at the same level of ability and confidence, but the teacher should make sure they have some common interests.

Teachers should also have firm expectations that writers in trouble will write. It's easy to slip into not expecting or asking for any writing of some pupils. Students may try to avoid what has become an unpleasant activity for them, but they will write if they get patient support and if they know that their willingness to take risks will be appreciated and that their efforts will not be ridiculed or punished.

Teachers must search for and create natural literacy events in which writers in trouble will want and need to write.

The Form: Spelling, Handwriting, and Mechanics

Traditionally, much of the language teaching in schools, particularly elementary schools, has been focused on aspects of the form of written language: spelling, handwriting or penmanship, and the mechanics of written language (often mistakenly lumped with "grammar," which, as we said elsewhere in this book, is the system of the language itself, the rules by which it works). These have been treated as skills that are taught in exercises isolated from the written thought presentation that the skills are intended to facilitate.

Presentation through written language is a process of encoding meaning and using a system of graphic symbols for the purpose of communication. Writing is productive, or generative, like speech. Isolating skills from the communicative and expressive uses of language makes them abstract exercises unrelated to the encoding process.

Isolated Skills versus Skills in Context

Children can learn specific skills in isolation: how to spell *dog,* how to form a cursive *B,* how to indent to start a paragraph. But for many children the gap between isolated skills and written thought may never be fully bridged. The assumption in drill on skills is that a transfer of training will occur, with the skills being transferred to the writing of compositions, letters, essays, notes, and other real language uses. Research has failed to demonstrate this transfer. Yet many teachers still operate on the seemingly logical view that children can't present in writing until they have mastered basic literacy skills. "I can't let them write yet," said one second-grade teacher. "They don't know how to spell."

Such a view, if applied to speech thought, would mean that children couldn't express themselves orally until they had fully mastered all the phonology of adult speech as well as all the intricacies of its structure. This view, of course, is absurd. The need of children to express their thoughts, needs, and feelings will furnish their motivation for developing oral language, and their control over the sound system comes as they attempt to use it to communicate.

In the same way, children move toward adult norms in handwriting, spelling, and mechanics if they are involved in real literacy events. They want their written thought to be understood just as they want their speech thought to be understood. This force would make many learners quite adequate in spelling and handwriting even if they had no exercises explicitly devoted to their development.

There are vital part-whole and ends-means relationships that must be in teachers' minds in planning all language activities. Written language is not a matter of stringing together a series of attractive, efficiently formed letters into a series of correctly spelled words that are properly spaced on the page with correct headings, margins, punctuation, and paragraphing. The whole is much more than the sum of its parts, and it is only in relationship to the communicative purpose that the value of legible handwriting, correct spelling, suitable punctuation, and form becomes clear. These are not unimportant; rather, their importance is relative. Skills will develop if teachers stimulate pupils to write frequently and purposefully, but neither skills nor effective writing will develop if the focus is on isolated skills.

English Spelling

Some time ago, a child in a familiar comic strip announced proudly, "I got an A in spelling. When I grow up I'm going to be a speller." This illustrates how spelling has been lifted out of its proper place as a means to effective written presentation and has been made an end in itself. There are some historic reasons for this exaggeration of the significance of spelling. A hundred years ago, spelling instruction preceded reading instruction because it was thought that before children could read they had to learn the spellings of a stock of words. The first book encountered in school was a speller, not a primer or a reader.

Another reason spelling is overstressed in schools is that poor spelling is equated in folk humor and popular belief with ignorance and lack of education. The spelling bee, as a competitive activity, developed because spelling English is something of an art. There is enough variability and complexity in English spelling that people who are highly accurate spellers are rare enough to be considered phenomenal when they become champions.

One dichotomy makes spelling in English and in most languages different from other language systems. Spelling is rule governed. But because writing is used to communicate over time and space, with an alphabetic writing system the spelling rules would need to change as the phonological system changed in order to maintain consistent relationships between the two systems. Furthermore, the spelling rules for one dialect community would not be the same for other dialect communities. The resulting dialect differences in spelling would partially defeat the purposes of written language.

So alphabetic writing systems are faced with a choice: they can have consistent rules that change as phonology changes, or they can have consistent standardized spellings that are the same for all users of the language regardless of dialect differences and changes over time in the oral language. Almost all languages have chosen to standardize spelling even if it means that rules have become inconsistent for some or all speakers.

This lack of dependability in rules does not cause problems for readers, who are sampling and predicting in order to construct meaning. Readers seem to be able to tolerate considerable diversity. But it does account for the variability of spelling accuracy among even educated writers, and it makes learning the spelling system different from other language learning.

Rules for Learning to Spell

Language learning is largely a matter of learning a finite set of rules by which the language is produced. And as people learn to write, they are learning the rules of the spelling system. But in all other language systems, once learned these rules may be used with total confidence. In spelling, they may not. The writer must become aware that many words are conventionally spelled in ways that are not consistent with the rules. These frequent exceptions must be learned separately.

As we indicated, there is abundant evidence in the current research literature that young children are finding order in the orthography and creating rules to use to invent spellings in their early attempts at writing. At some point, young writers also discover that there are conventional spellings. Often they go through a period of being inhibited in using their rules to invent spellings and insistent on being told the correct spelling. This makes for a developmental spiral in the spelling pupils use in their early writing efforts.

The Spiral of Spelling Development

In the beginning children use invented spellings with a few holistically remembered words conventionally spelled; sometimes only their own names are spelled conventionally. When they begin to write in school they use the resources of the classroom. So the teacher's name and the date will always be conventionally spelled since they copy those onto their papers. As they formulate rules for inventing spellings and gain confidence in their rules, they begin to generate spellings even for words they previously copied. So, as so often happens in language development, they appear to become less effective and poorer spellers as they use their rules to generate spellings for words they had previously copied. They're taking risks.

At the point where they discover, or someone points out, that there are "correct" spellings, they may misspell fewer words, but they are also likely to be more reluctant to write and to write less when they do. It is important that teachers be sensitive to these developmental indicators. They need to help pupils realize that, though there are standard spellings, it's good for pupils to take risks and to try to invent spellings as they need them. They need to help pupils be realistic about understanding that the time to be concerned about correct spellings is when final drafts of certain kinds of texts are being prepared.

Teachers themselves need to understand that pupils need to find the limits of their own rules and strike a balance between using the rules and being aware that the spellings they produce are not consistently reliable. Ironically, teaching pupils a set of spelling rules is likely to compound the problem. If the rules they are using are their own creation, pupils will treat them as tentative. But if the rules they are using were taught, they have the weight of authority behind them and the pupils are likely to become phonic misspellers.

Predicting English Spelling

Can a literate user of English predict the spelling of English words from the way the words are pronounced? This is a crucial question because its presumed answer is the basis for spelling programs provided in schools. If spellings are highly predictable, then it would make sense to help pupils develop the rules for making these predictions.

A study by Cronnell (1971) suggests that one can use one of the 166 rules he has identified to decide how a word is spelled. So large a set of rules itself poses a problem, but their use in deciding how to spell words is more complicated than that.

Here are two common English patterns, for example:

ea/ee			a-e/ai
eat		ale	ail
beat	beet	bale	bail
		dale	
feat	feet		fail
(great)	greet	gale	Gail
heat		hale	hail
			jail
meat	meet	male	mail
neat			nail
peat		pale	pail
			rail
seat		sale	sail
teat		tale	tail
		vale	avail
wheat		whale	
			wail
		Yale	

Nothing in the sound of the words can tell a listener that a word is spelled *meet* or *meat*. Developing rules for the correspondence of English spelling patterns and sound patterns will help the listener to know which alternatives exist but not which alternative is the right one. The listener must know which *mail* gets stamped, which *tale* is told, which *sail* is unfurled.

Vowel patterns, particularly those using two or more letters to spell the vowel phonemes, are very hard to predict. Vowels are highly variable from dialect to dialect. Add to this the fact that any word with an unaccented syllable will have a schwa /ə/ in that syllable, which may be spelled by any vowel or combination of vowels, and the situation is indeed complex.

So the answer to our prediction question is "maybe." Listeners can develop rules for generating possible spellings of English words. Rules can only be depended on to produce a useful invented spelling, not a standard spelling. Writers will need to hear words in meaningful contexts and they will need to appreciate their morphemic structure (base, affixes, and their relationship to syntax and meaning). In many cases they will simply need to know which of several possible patterns a word fits. In final proofreading this will help the writer know where to begin a dictionary search. The dictionary does not establish meanings and spellings; it records and reports them. But spelling is standardized, so the dictionary is an authoritative source on spelling and remains so. Meaning is always in motion, but spelling stands relatively still.

Accuracy in Spelling

Two groups of spellers have been informally studied with some interesting results. Bird and Altwerger studied two adults who considered themselves very poor spellers. (Altwerger and Bird, 1982) Both had been classified in school as learning disabled. They found that less than 36 percent of the running words they wrote were not spelled conventionally. The spelling errors, while noticeable, were not likely to interfere strongly with reader comprehension. It would appear that English-speaking societies have an intolerance for spelling errors that may be disproportionate. There is some evidence that misspellings are not considered as important among writers of Spanish and some other languages.

Hodges informally studied the strategies of champion spellers. (Richard Hodges, personal communication) He found that they would first ask for the word to be used in another sentence. That would establish another context for the word. Then they would ask for the origin of the word, that is, whether it had Greek, Latin, Germanic, or other roots. Knowing a word's origins might help the speller to know whether it begins with *n, pn, gn,* or *kn*. Only after exhausting these strategies would they resort to using rules for generating the spelling. Their overall strategy would seem to be first to try to remember how a word is spelled using specific and general contextual information. Then, if that fails, they would use rules to generate a spelling.

This seems to be the general strategy of average spellers as well. Goodman and Wilde (1985) report that over time children tend to shift toward standard spellings and that misspelled words are more likely among words not used previously in the students' writing.

A seemingly heretical question that must be answered in setting up spelling instruction is, "Just how accurate must spelling be?" Setting aside the issue of standardized spelling, the key issue becomes how much misspelling will interfere with readability. How much is tolerable depends on how closely reader and writer know each other, how familiar the reader is with the topic, and how far from expected spellings the invented spellings are. So it appears that the answer to this question is that misspellings are less a problem for the writer's readability than for the writer's acceptability.

The attitudes of intended readers towards misspelling seem to be the problem. Readers will judge character, education—even intelligence—on the basis of a few misspellings. Such judgments are clearly unwarranted, but they indicate a reality that must be dealt with. Intolerance of error has the worst effect on writing if it comes from teachers. The ability to use standard spelling, particularly in final drafts of particular writing, is the ultimate goal of education. But demanding only standard spelling at all stages, in all written work, no matter what the purpose, is both unreasonable and self-defeating. It's unreasonable because there are many occasions involving less formal uses of written language in which total accuracy is quite unnecessary for effective writing. It is also unreasonable because no aspect of any language process is learned perfectly at all stages of development. Language learners move toward adult norms in phonology, grammar, meaning, and pragmatics. They also move toward adult norms in spelling, but misspelling is to be expected on the way to this goal, and here is where intolerance of error is self-defeating. The greatest progress in spelling comes through writing. As youngsters use a wider and wider range of vocabulary in their writing, their spelling continually improves, but if teachers insist pupils must spell every word correctly they discourage risk taking. The pupils use only those words they are sure they can spell correctly. Consequently, both their writing and their spelling suffer.

Reading and Spelling

Earlier we argued that if students write, they will read like writers and their reading will have a strong impact on their writing. There is no doubt that reading has such an impact on spelling development.

Goodman and Goodman (1963) studied the spelling ability of a 6-year-old who had learned to read on her own before coming to school. They found that, on a dictation test in which each word was said by the tester in a sentence, she was able to spell correctly 60 percent of the words from a third-grade story she had read. Many of the words she wrote without hesitation. Usually these were spelled correctly. On some words, however, she would tell the examiner she didn't know how to spell them. Subsequently, she would spell some correctly and some incorrectly. But in both cases she seemed to be making use of generalizations to invent or generate spellings. She only resorted overtly to these rules when she doubted her ability to spell the words.

As a second phase of the study, she was given a test on the words she had misspelled. This time, however, she was asked to pick out the correct spelling of the word from a list of four possible spellings, including her own misspelling. Together with the results of the first test, this raised her score to over 90 percent. Clearly, she could recognize the correct spellings of words when she saw them in print although she could not yet confidently spell them herself. This appears to demonstrate the role that reading played in her spelling development.

It's not uncommon in a primary classroom to see a pupil pause in writing, go over to the bookshelf to get a book, quickly locate a particular word in a particular line on a particular page, and then use the spelling there to continue writing. Spelling development, then, depends on involving students in reading as well as in writing.

Spelling Instruction: A Whole-Language Alternative

Two main approaches have dominated spelling instruction. In one the curriculum is designed to teach a set of rules on the assumption that these rules will produce accurate spelling. Words are selected in patterns that demonstrate the particular rules. The alternate focus is on learning words as individual units. This trend in spelling is parallel to the word focus in reading. Words are selected because they are frequent and are grouped for instruction around common topics: a group of common words relating to farm animals might make up a lesson. Combinations of these two alternatives have also been used in spelling programs, with both words and rules taught.

In teaching spelling, study routines have employed sight, sound, and feel. Pupils look at words, shut their eyes and try to recall the image, say the word, and trace the word in the air or write it to get its kinesthetic feel. A variation on rule-centered instruction involves using contrasting spelling patterns to lead the pupils to form their own generalizations.

There is a limit on how many words can be explicitly included in a spelling program. Usually a program presents 15–20 words a week. Over a 6- or 7-year span the total number of words that can be presented is something under 4000. This number is considerably less than the conservative estimates of children's vocabularies at age 6. Furthermore, many children seem to be unable to learn the spellings of up to 20 words a week.

We've already discussed the problems and limits of teaching rules to students. Both major approaches, thus, seem to have considerable limits. No word-centered program could possibly enable even 6-year-olds to express their written thought in the vocabulary they choose with all words spelled correctly. Neither could a simple set of rules taught deductively or by controlled induction produce the "spelling power" to generate standard spellings for the variety of words pupils use. And there is the risk that putting the authority of the teacher behind such rules will cause pupils to overrely on them to produce phonic misspellings.

A Whole-Language Alternative

Teachers and schools need to take a new, whole-language view of spelling development. Some key aspects of this view are:

1. Spelling should facilitate communication of written thought, not limit it. Rather than being limited to writing with words they are sure they can spell, children should be encouraged to use their language as richly as possible. Then they will tend to learn to spell the words they use.
2. Spelling is developmental. That means that as children expand their writing in terms of its scope of function and purpose, the breadth of its content, and its types of texts, they will be using an expanding vocabulary. They will be spelling more words correctly, their invented spellings will be rule-governed and comprehensible in context, and they will develop strategies for finding standard spellings as they need them.
3. The need for standard spelling should be kept in proper perspective. Pupils should understand:
   a. That there are standard spellings.
   b. That nonstandard spelling is stigmatized by society, particularly in published materials, formal letters, and other writing intended for an unfamiliar audience.
   c. That the concern for use of standard spelling should not be permitted to interfere with the creative process of composing. Checking and correcting spelling can be considered a part of proofreading and editing.
   d. That few people become such good spellers that they rarely ever misspell and that even the best spellers never become such good spellers that they never have to check the spelling of a word.

4. There should be no special spelling curriculum or regular lesson sequences. The time to teach spelling is in the context of writing, The focus should be on strategies, on taking risks, and on ways of checking spelling when editing or proofreading.
5. Strategies for spelling include:
   a. Discovering and using rules for generating invented spelling. Teachers can support this process by encouraging pupils to notice and to think about some of the less common and more subtle relationships. Picking up, for example, on a student's comment that *tissue* is spelled with two *s's,* the teacher might ask pupils to think of similarly spelled words and to decide on what the rule might be. The purpose of such a lesson is not to support each and every rule. Rather it is to call attention to the nature of spelling rules and the pupils' ability to discover and use them.
   b. Learning to cope with the limited utility of rules. As important as inducing the rules is learning their limitations and what to do about them. Teachers can help pupils to be alert to words they encounter in their reading that aren't spelled in the most predictable ways. Pupils can be encouraged to keep a collection of such words in a personal dictionary or card file. They can also be encouraged to go back to materials they've read to find the spellings of words. Another strategy teachers can support is writing a word in several spellings to see which looks most familiar.
   c. Learning to know whether words are spelled correctly or not. Any proofreading or checking procedure depends on being able to detect, at least in a general sense, which words need to be checked for spelling. It's clearly impractical to check every word. Some lessons could be devoted to having pupils look at texts containing some misspelled words to see if they can detect which words are probably misspelled.
   d. Learning how to find the spelling of a word in the dictionary when you're not sure how to spell it. This is a matter of using their rules to invent possible spellings. It's also a practical time to develop the students' use of alphabetic order and how to use the key words in dictionaries to zero in quickly on which pages to go to for a particular spelling.

It's crucial in a whole-language spelling program that any direct focus on spelling strategies as such should be based on the pupil's own writing. So, for example, in working on the use of the dictionary the words the pupils are looking for should not be a general list produced by the teacher or taken out of a spelling book; they should be words the pupils have collected from those they have wanted to use in their writing and which they don't already know how to spell.

Part of each writing conference with pupils can be devoted to spelling, not for the purpose of admonishing pupils about misspellings, but for finding out if they can detect their own likely misspellings and if they have developing strategies for determining the standard spellings.

The key to spelling development in a whole-language program is to keep it in its place, that is, as a necessary part of writing. Ultimately, students who read and write a lot will spell reasonably well and will know how to check their spellings and standardize them when it's necessary to do so.

Handwriting

There was a time when the most significant objective of instruction in handwriting (or as it was commonly called, penmanship) was beauty, conceived as something quite apart from function. Perfection in form, embellished by ornate flourishes was the desired end. It was actually considered to be more important to have a beautiful handwriting than a legible one. Children not only practiced forming de-contextualized letters but spent endless hours in the "push-pulls" and spirals of the penmanship books. For well-coordinated children these exercises were tolerable and a source of some satisfaction, because they won praise and penmanship awards. But for others they were at best dull and meaningless and at worst pure torture. Many children were endlessly rehearsed in tasks at which they didn't get any better because they were not physically ready and because the tusks had no intrinsic purpose. As adults, these losers in the handwriting game may find consolation in the fact that there is no correlation between handwriting and intelligence or achievement in other fields.

Fortunately educators have become aware that handwriting is not an end in itself, but a means to effective communication. In this holistic view, the objectives of a modern handwriting program are legibility, efficiency, and attractiveness, in that order.

As speech develops it becomes intelligible as it moves within the range of adult speech norms. It may vary considerably, however, as long as it avoids ambiguity which could make doubtful what the speaker is saying in a particular sequence. Similarly, handwriting is intelligible to the extent that it falls in the range of variation that avoids ambiguity.

Legibility

If language is considered a code, it can be seen that illegibility is, in a sense, a kind of noise on the communication channel. When an *o* begins to look like an *a* in a particular context in cursive writing, then a perceptual problem that might interfere with communication is created. The forms of letters, particularly in combination with other letters, must be perceived by the reader as the writer intended. There are limits, therefore, on the variability of letter form. These determine the parameters of acceptability if legibility is to be achieved. To some extent, the task of staying within these acceptable limits is influenced by the complexity of the letter forms. There has been a tendency to eliminate unnecessary letter parts to achieve maximum simplicity.

Ease of Production

There is also a tendency for writing systems to evolve over time to make it easier to produce writing rapidly. Development of cursive forms of writing is an example. But what makes writing easier in this sense may make it harder and less legible for the readers. An optimal writing system is one that is relatively easy to produce and also maximally legible.

Handwriting requires a great deal of coordination and small muscle control, perhaps more than many 6 and 7-year-olds possess. Two measures have been used with great success to minimize this problem. First of all, manuscript writing, a system of unjoined letters composed of circles, part circles, and straight lines, is now widely used as the initial medium for writing in school. Secondly, schools have recognized that young children are not ready to write with pens on finely ruled paper, so the inkwells have disappeared from the desks and a wide variety of paper and writing implements of all kinds and sizes are available to pupils. Beginners are encouraged to use pencils, magic markers, and crayons, and to write on lined or unlined paper.

These reforms in handwriting instruction came about in the 1930's and were so effective that schools found it possible to deemphasize the teaching of handwriting. School handwriting coordinators were largely eliminated, and the proportion of time spent on direct handwriting instruction reached a sensible minimum. As often happens, however, school administrators and teachers can forget the history of this shift in handwriting programs. Ignorance has sometimes brought back earlier, less holistic practice as well as the problems that go with it.

Teachers' Attitudes Toward Writing

Perhaps more important than these reforms is the attitude of teachers toward children and the writing task. It is vital that teachers remember the great variability among learners and keep ends and means in proper perspective. Children vary greatly in their coordination, and their handwriting will reflect these differences. In working toward the goal of legibility the teacher must accept progress and not demand perfection. The teacher must also keep legibility clearly separated from other demands made on children. Neatness is, no doubt, a virtue, but messy papers can be legible. In fact, some of the messiness may reflect a child's progress toward legibility: awkward erasures may result from trying to make the initial attempt at a letter-form come closer to the child's view of the norm.

When a teacher offers help to children it should be specific and easily related by them to improved legibility. In the context of real literacy events with real intended audiences, the teacher can help the learner to evaluate his or her own handwriting by considering if it can be read and understood.

Efficiency

Like any physical skill, the skill of forming letters rapidly and legibly in the context of writing can be performed with varying degrees of efficiency. Generally, people who use a skill continuously and purposefully over a long period of time will tend to become more efficient on their own. However, they may take a long time to arrive at a high degree of efficiency and may still preserve some inefficient movements and procedures. Furthermore, it is possible that writers may achieve efficiency at the expense of legibility; their writing begins to incorporate shortcuts and deletions that create ambiguity and illegibility for their readers.

Teachers can eliminate a good deal of trial and error and, in many cases, head off the formation of inefficient writing habits by presenting a set of letter formation procedures that have proven to be efficient for most people. Demonstrating efficient ways of placing the paper, holding the pencil, and sitting will be helpful.

Some teachers may be concerned over the differing guidelines provided by different commercially published handwriting programs. The differences exist to a considerable degree for their own sakes. To copyright a handwriting system it must have a number of points of difference from all other systems. Therefore, every system contains many arbitrary elements; each chooses ways of doing things that are just as ekiciently done another way.

Teachers must keep in mind that the goal is efficiency and not slavish imitation. Studies of different handwriting systems show that while some techniques are more efficient than others for most people, there are always some people who find alternate techniques more efficient.

The teacher can start with a particular system of writing and concentrate, within real literacy events, on efficient handwriting. From the beginning, however, the teacher must be willing to accept deviance. Forcing youngsters who have learned one system to learn another just for the sake of conformity should be particularly avoided.

Attractiveness

Although beauty in handwriting is not necessary to its effectiveness as a meduim of written thought, it does affect the receptivity of the reader. College students know very well that unattractive handwriting on an examination question will probably result in a lower grade than a similar response in a more attractive handwriting. On the other hand, beautiful but illegible handwriting won't get very high grades either. To some extent, then, students should be encouraged to produce writing that is attractive as well as legible and efficient. Beautiful writing does have an aesthetic quality. Calligraphy is an art form that is still cultivated for special purposes in writing English.

It will be easiest to work with children on the appearance of their writing when they have produced something that they want to be well received, such as a letter home or a story to be posted on the class bulletin board. All of us vary in our handwriting depending on the occasion and purpose. A scribble is adequate to remind oneself of something or in composing the first draft of a story. A clean style is necessary in a letter of application or a note of condolence. However, in most of the more formal uses of written language the typewriter or word processor have virtually replaced handwriting, and when these are not available, as in filling out forms and applications, writers are often admonished to print.

Is Handwriting Obsolescent?

The occasions in which an attractive personal handwriting is necessary are certainly declining and largely confined to school for most people. And with the development of cheaper, smaller, easier to use computers for word processing, school uses of handwriting could change rapidly too. It's not hard to visualize a classroom in the near future in which every pupil has a small battery-operated composer, a bit bigger than a pocket calculator, with an LCD display large enough to show 8–10 lines of print and sufficient memory to store a text of 1000–1500 words. The composer would have a typewriter-like keyboard and have wired into its memory a "user-friendly" word-processing program simple enough for a young child to use easily. It would only be necessary to have one printer in each classroom because the children would edit the text on the composer's display and only print it out when they were ready to turn it in.

The technology for all this already exists. Book-sized computers with most of these characteristics, selling now for a few hundred dollars, are in wide use by newspaper reporters and others who travel a lot. All that's necessary is for some manufacturer to recognize the potential and bring the costs even further down. The costs have been steadily dropping. Some variation of this is surely on the way. It would do for writing what the calculator has done for mathematics—take the tedium out of the process. For beginners it would make a tremendous difference because they could compose much more rapidly. For developmental writing it would create a different response to editing and perfecting writing because it's so easy to make changes in a text stored in a word processor and then produce a revised copy.

Some people may not be happy about writing that doesn't include the same kind of physical act as handwriting. But most of the world's writing now is done on machines, and it would be hard to argue that the quality or quantity has suffered. This is not to say that such technology in itself will produce more or better writing. Like all technology, it can only be as good, useful, or productive as the use made of it. In a whole-language writing program any technology that makes writing physically easier can be a boon.

Handwriting is certainly not yet obsolete, and whole-language teachers will need to cultivate and support it, but it is certainly changing in its relationship to alternative means of producing written texts.

Handedness

Left-handed pupils have been at a great disadvantage in many schools. Right-handed readers of this book may assume that the horror stories of mistreatment of left-handed learners are all from the dim past. But virtually every left-handed person reading this book will have personal experiences to recall that show such rejection and misunderstanding of human differences still exist.

Although few teachers try to force children to become right-handed as in days past, many teachers teach them styles and techniques designed to result in writing that looks right-handed even if they are awkward, uncomfortable, and inefficient for left-handed people. Left-handed people need to produce legible writing; they do not need to produce writing that looks right-handed.

People who are left-handed are in the minority. Like all minorities, how they are treated will affect not only their writing but also their self-image, their treatment by other pupils, and their general attitude toward school. Their only real handicap is the one schools may impose.

Variety

It is a remarkable fact that studies of people taught a common writing system show that a great deal of variety has entered their handwriting by the time they are adults. This may happen because they have discovered alternate techniques that are personally more effective. Or it may be because they are consciously or unconsciously seeking to personalize their handwriting. Preteen and teenage girls frequently experiment with highly stylized writing. People communicate effectively in an infinite variety of voices. They can also communicate with an infinite variety of forms of handwriting. Legibility, not conformity, is the goal of instruction.

It may be apparent in this discussion of the teaching of handwriting that though an attempt has been made to present a positive position, a good deal of attention has been devoted to what *not* to do. This is because so many problems are created for students and teachers by ill-considered, inappropriate, and insensitive instruction.

At the risk of some oversimplification, we present a list of do's and don'ts that may help avoid some unnecessary anguish.

Do

Keep the focus on legibility in teaching handwriting. Efficiency and beauty are subsidiary goals.

Keep handwriting in its place—a *means* to written expression.

Teach handwriting as part of a whole composition process with components in a normal relationship to each other.

Accept differences and allow for them in teaching and evaluating handwriting.

Make left-handed pupils feel normal and accepted. Be sensitive to their difference and provide for it.

Be open to variation within the system you teach. Accept another system already learned.

Keep in mind that maturation and differences in coordination are factors in developing handwriting skill.

Don't

Judge all handwriting by an adult model and insist on conformity to that model.

Use drills on isolated letters or letter parts. Don't make children write line after line of strokes, single letters, word parts, or individual words.

Teach handwriting apart from its use.

Make students feel inadequate, abnormal, or defeated because their efforts at handwriting are not very effective. Don't make major issues out of minor deviations.

Let handwriting interfere with the need for learners to express themselves.

Require pupils to copy papers over and over in the quest for perfection.

Require pupils to write dictated exercises.

Make a big thing of what kind of pen, pencil, or paper young pupils use.

Surround handwriting with a set of absolutes and fetishes. Handwriting must be kept in realistic perspective.

Forms: Pragmatics, Rules, and Arbitrary Conventions

Because writing has been taught as if it were a matter of learning a set of arbitrary, conventional constraints, some very different things get confused in curricula and methods for writing development.

Pragmatics

Some things that constrain writing are linguistic and cultural pragmatics. There are pragmatic expectations that when people meet they will exchange conventional greetings: "Hello," "Hi," "How are you?" if the person is known; "How do you do?" and "Pleased to meet you," if the person is just introduced. When people part they are expected to say "Goodbye" or some equivalent parting words. So too, written language has pragmatic constraints on different forms. Letters almost always begin with a formulaic greeting: "Dear," and end with a formulaic ending: "Sincerely yours." Minutes are usually signed, "Respectfully submitted."

Folk stories carry oral formulas into written language: "Once upon a time" is such a formulaic beginning. Young writers often use these formulas in their first narratives.

Punctuation

Punctuation is another matter. It serves a purpose in written language of marking off the grammatical structure. That makes it have functions and rules for its use in meeting those functions similar to those served by intonation in oral language. But punctuation does not represent intonation. Oral language exists over time, and the intonation is a contour for the whole utterance. It has variable stresses, pitches, and pause patterns so the information conveyed to the listener is not confined to one particular point in the utterance. Linguists say it is "suprasegmental."

On the other hand, writing takes up two-dimensional space; it's linear and directional. Punctuation uses marks at the ends of structures. A period, question mark, or exclamation point will confirm for a reader that a sentence has ended, but that's very different from the information conveyed to a listener by the intonation contour over the full length of the sentence.

Punctuation is part of the writing system that writers learn from reading and writing, but it performs its function quite differently than intonation. Studies by Goodman and Milz showed that full, consistent use of the punctuation system takes longer to develop than other aspects of writing. In Milz's study of six first-graders' writing, they ranged from only 3 percent to 39 percent conventional punctuation. (Milz, 1983)

Goodman found that third-graders used about 43 percent conventional punctuation and that the same subjects as fourth-graders used about 57 percent. (Goodman and Wilde, 1986) Milz found subjects using space and distribution on the page as alternative ways of marking off phrases and sentences without punctuation.

It's very hard to teach the rules of punctuation as such. Telling pupils that a sentence always starts with a capital letter and ends with a period, question mark, or exclamation point doesn't help the pupil who doesn't know dependably where new sentences begin and end. One subject in Goodman's study learned that a period always preceded a capital letter, so she very consistently used them together for a period of time in her writing with rather unconventional results. Gradually, she abandoned this strategy and moved toward a more conventional rule.

If punctuation rules develop slowly, the only way to support their development is to stay in the context of the pupils' writing. In a conference with one pupil or in a discussion with several pupils, the teacher can ask pupils to think through how use of periods, commas, and question marks could make the meaning of the text clearer. If pupils have begun to use direct speech in their narratives, then it may be fruitful to look together at how this is handled in the books they read so that they may evolve a rule for when quotation marks are to be used and how.

Conventions

Some conventions of written language are quite arbitrary, but they usually relate to some particular circumstances of writing. Margins must be provided for binding, marginal notes, comments, and also for the sake of appearance, for example. If there is a need for agreement on a set of conventions within the classroom concerning the form of written work, the teacher should discuss the reasons and the limits in which decisions must be made and allow the pupils to participate in making the decisions. Is there a need for the writer to be identified on written work? Why? What other information is necessary: date, subject, time, assignment, teacher's name? Is this all necessary, all the time? Should it always appear in the same place on every pupil's work? Why? Where could that place be?

It's important for teachers to get straight in their own minds when form is a matter of pragmatics, of rules, or of conventions: these are arbitrary but necessary decisions. Traditions are particularly hard for many teachers to consider objectively. Having the writer's name on the paper is usually necessary. Having the writer's name on some uniform place on the paper may be convenient for teachers and monitors who are returning them to the writers. But whether that uniform place is at the top left, top right, after the title, or at the end of the paper is an arbitrary decision, and in many circumstances one decision is as good as another.

Form in footnotes is an example of an arbitrary convention. Certain information is needed. Consistency is useful and desirable. But the several popular footnote forms are all equally useful.

Again, it must be emphasized that the focus of a whole-language writing curriculum is expression of written thought. If students have something important to say to an intended audience, then they will want to say it in the most effective form and they will be responsive to help in doing so.

References

Bess Altwerger and Lois Bird, "Disabled: The Learner or the Curriculum," *Topics in Learning and Learning Disabilities,* vol. 1, no. 4 (January 1982), pp. 69–78.

Mitzi Cholewinski, "Comar Postal System," *California School Boards,* 41 (December 1982).

Bruce Cronnell, "Annotated Spelling-to-Sound Correspondence Rules," Tech. Report #32, Los Angeles: Southwest Regional Laboratory, 1971.

Kenneth S. Goodman and Yetta M. Goodman, "Spelling Ability of a Self-Taught Reader," *Elementary School Journal,* vol. 64, no. 3 (1963), pp. 149–154.

Yetta Goodman and Sandra Wilde, "Writing Development in Third and Fourth Grade Native American Students," Occ. Paper #14 (Tucson: Program in Language and Literacy, University of Arizona, 1985).

Jennifer Green, "The Nature and Development of Letter Writing by Hispanic and Anglo Children Using a School Based Postal System," NIE Final Report, Washington, DC, 1983.

Barbara Hardy, "Toward a Poetic of Fiction: An Approach Through Narrative," in *Novel: A Forum on Fiction,* Brown University. Cited in Rosen, 1982.

Mary M. Kitagawa, "Expressive Writing in Japanese Elementary Schools," *Language Arts,* vol. 59, no. 1 (January 1982), pp. 17–25.

Vera Milz, "A Psycholinguistic Description of the Development of Writing in Selected First Grade Students," doctoral dissertation, University of Arizona, 1983 (*Dissertation Abstracts International,* Vol. 44, 3279A).

Harold Rosen, *Neither Bleak House nor Liberty Hall,* University of London, Institute of Education, 4 (March 1981).

Harold Rosen, "The Nurture of Narrative," Presentation, IRA Convention, Chicago, 1982.

Suzanne B.K. Scollon and Ron Scollon, "]RUN TRILOGY: Can Tommy Read?" in Goelman, Oberg, and Smith, *Awakening to Literacy* (Portsmouth, NH: Heineman, 1984).

Frank Smith, *Writing and the Writer* (New York: Holt, Rinehart and Winston, 1982).

Jana Staton, "Writing and Counseling: Using a Dialogue Journal," *Language Arts* 57 (1980), pp. 511–518.

Jana Staton, Roger Shuy, and J. Krefft, "Analysis of Dialogue Journal Writing as a Communicative Event," National Institute of Education, Final Report No. NIE-G-80-0122, 1982.

14

Children, Literature, and the Arts

In literature, language is deliberately exploited for its expressive effect rather than to indicate, denote, or describe things for practical purposes. . . . A work of literature is not meant as a series of literal propositions, but as a construction to stimulate the imagination of the reader.

(Phenix, 1964)

Author's note: This chapter has been written with Frederick Burton.

Literature as Presentation

Literature is one of the chief modes by which men and women present their knowledge about the world. There are the logical, analytical modes of scientific description, formulas, and diagrams and there are the aesthetic modes of written composition, art, dance, and music. Because language can describe both scientific events on the one hand and personal, emotional events on the other hand, the word *literature* is used for the description of both kinds of events, as in *scientific literature* or *English literature*. Children's literature involves both kinds: discursive, factual books and literary storybooks. Children need to learn how to read both. Discursive, factual writing can be carefully done and can have literary merit; however, most often "children's literature" refers to storybooks, poetry, and informational books.

The Case for Children's Literature

As previously discussed, the process of "coming to know" about things in the world is transactional in nature. This is also true of our experiences with literature. Drawing heavily on Dewey's and Bentley's philosophy in *Knowing and the Known,* literary critic and scholar Louise Rosenblatt describes the reader's literary response or experience as an active force in which the reader and text mutually affect one another.

> The literary work exists in the live circuit set up between reader and text: the reader infuses intellectual and emotional meanings into the pattern of verbal symbols, and those symbols channel his thoughts and feelings. Out of this complex process emerges a more or less organized imaginative experience. (Rosenblatt, 1976)

Such experiences do not involve endlessly dissecting poetry or stories, line for line, or relentlessly searching for the one true meaning or message they are thought to hold. Instead of this more traditional, static view, our literary experiences are better characterized as a transaction of reader and author intentions through the medium of text and the flow of time. Furthermore, because of the dynamic nature of this transaction among readers, texts, authors, and points in time (that is, the total environmental context), many different meanings, perspectives, and "messages" can emerge.

The values of engaging in these literary transactions, and thus of children's literature itself, are many. An obvious, yet often overlooked, value is the simple *pleasure* that comes from books. The fact that Judy Blume's humorous novel,

Superfudge, went into its second printing before it was released and soon after sold over 1 million copies is evidence that children are finding satisfaction in reading real books. (Would they buy basal readers like this?) For years, children have enjoyed the deep friendship between a pig and a spider in E.B. White's *Charlotte's Web* or have journeyed with Max to the land Sendak has created in his book *Where the Wild Things Are.* The sounds and rhythms of language itself are often savored by children. They delight in and are challenged by the language play found in books like Schwartz's *A Twister of Twists, a Tangler of Tongues.*

Literature also helps to develop children's imaginations by encouraging them to ask and to seek answers to "what if" questions. What if I could "tesseract" like Charles Wallace in L'Engle's *A Wrinkle in Time* or fly like Georgie and the Goose Prince in Langton's *The Fledgling?* What if I could visit and explore other possible worlds like Narnia, Prydian, Never-Never Land, or a place in Arnold Adoffs poem, "Dinner Tonight," where a "parmesan cheese breeze" blows and "broccoli logs" are real?

Children's literature presents readers with the universality of human experience. We become a little more human as we gain an awareness of our emotions and begin to develop compassion for others. Children also get insights into human motivation and behavior as they read about the timeless struggle between good and evil in books of fantasy like Susan Cooper's eerie tale *The Dark is Rising* or realistic fiction like Katherine Paterson's *The Great Gilly Hopkins.*

Children's literature also can be instrumental in a child's learning to read. Margaret Meek, in her book for parents, *Learning to Read,* discusses the adverse effects of basal readers (or "reading schemes") and proposes that good stories themselves "teach" reading.

> If you have already experienced the effects of a reading scheme on your child's view of what reading is, you are bound to take steps to counter its influence, not by suggesting to your child that his teacher is incompetent, but by making the most of every chance you have to read real books and to enjoy stories. . . . Literature makes readers in a way that reading schemes never can. (Meek, 1982)

Selecting and Evaluating Literature

The line that separates children's literature from adult literature is nebulous at best. One may find Saint-Exupery's *The Little Prince* being read and enjoyed by a 10-year-old child in an elementary school or a 20-year-old student in college. *The Hobbit,* one of the most widely read books of fantasy among adults, was originally written for children. Another popular book of fantasy, Richard Adams' *Watership Down,* was published for children in England and for adults in the United States. When asked who he writes for, Maurice Sendak replied:

> Well, I suppose primarily children but not really. Because I don't write for children specifically. I certainly am not conscious of sitting down and writing a book for children. I think it would be fatal if one did. So I write books, and I hope that they are books anybody can read. (Haviland, 1978, pp, 243–244)

Although there are no clear-cut recipes or formulas for distinguishing a child's book from an adult's book (other than the experience and understanding of individual readers), there are certain literary elements that one should be aware of when selecting and evaluating any work of fiction. These elements are plot, characterization, setting, theme, and style.

Plot

If a book does not first and foremost tell a good story, it will likely have a low readership, regardless of its other literary merits. The structural treatment of the subject of a child's book should not be overly complex. Simple and straightforward plotting, short but potent description, and life-like, swift-moving conversation will not tax the child's conceptual limits or deter the child from comprehending the scope of a story. Children like action-packed plots where interesting characters face and resolve opposition and conflict. Max's adventure in Sendak's *Where the Wild Things Are* is a classic example of such plotting for younger children. Books like Mollie Hunter's *A Stranger Came Ashore,* which is based on a legend from the Shetland Islands and is about the mysterious Selkies or seafolk, have logically developed plots that are exciting and complex enough to hold older children's interest.

Characterization

Characters in stories for children should be revealed in ways that make them convincing and believable. Authors successfully develop their characters through narration, dialogue, and by disclosure of the thoughts and actions of those involved in the story. Because a good book often allows the reader the luxury of becoming intimately acquainted with the strengths and weaknesses of the characters, they sometimes linger in our memories long after we have forgotten the story itself. It is because of well drawn characterizations that children never quite forget the delightful unpredictability of Ramona Quimby, or the courage of Bilbo Baggins. It is also through fully developed characters that children come to know themselves and gain knowledge about their own and others' behavior.

Setting

Setting is where and when the action takes place. At times, it may be intentionally general. Because very young children lack a mature sense of time and distance, vague settings like "once upon a time in a faraway land" are usually enough to transport them back in time. But settings may be much more specific and complex, yet still have universal applicability. For example, this is true of Mildred Taylor's *Roll of Thunder, Hear My Cry,* which is about a particular black family's struggle with racism in a small, rural town in Mississippi during the 1930's.

With stories of high fantasy like Alexander's "Prydain Chronicles" or LeGuin's "Earthsea" trilogy, authors create a totally imaginary sense of time and place. Believability is often rendered through the consistent portrayal of details in these imaginary settings. Writers of historical fiction and biography must not only be concerned with believability but also with the authenticity and accuracy of their settings. Authors like Jean Fritz and Erik Haugaard often spend a great deal of time researching in libraries, examining documents and artifacts in museums, and actually visiting the places where an historical event occurred.

Theme

The theme of a book is its underlying meaning. A good book may have several themes, all of which should be worth imparting to children. Themes such as "the importance of being one's self" are simply, yet effectively, portrayed in picture books such as Oxenbury's *Pig Tale,* as well as explored in more detail in young adult novels like Cormier's *The Chocolate War.* Many picture books have themes that may be interpreted on several levels. For example, the Swiss picture book *Rabbit Island,* by Jorg Steiner, can be interpreted as a simple story of the importance of friendship or as the complex, dehumanizing consequences of industrialism. Likewise, Leo Lionni's *Frederick* has a simple "be yourself" theme on one level, but it is also a statement on the role of the arts and the artist in society. Themes should grow naturally out of the story and never overpower the plot or resort to heavy didacticism.

Style

Style consists of how the author uses language in the telling of a story. Language style needs to be straightforward but intensified by imaginative selection of words available to children in their oral communication. Use of obscure and unfamiliar terms without contextual support will disrupt comprehension. On the other hand, flat, repetitious language will also bore youngsters. A successful writer of children's books needs to have the same lingual imagination as the poet. The flow of the structures must have music as it develops contours of meaning. This does not mean that the prose will be flowery, but in its economy it should carry weight and color and have the rhythm and cohesion of pleasant conversation. Economy of style and repetition are effectively used in Rebecca Caudill's story of a 6-year-old Appalachian boy in *A Pocketful of Cricket.*

> This boy, Jay, lived with his father and his mother in an old farmhouse in a hollow. He was six years old. All around his house Jay could see hills. He could see hills when he stood whittling in the kitchen doorway. He could see hills when he swung on the gate in front of his house. When he climbed into the apple tree beside his house, he could see hills. (Caudill, 1964, p.1)

The opening page of Mollie Hunter's *A Stranger Came Ashore* reflects the cadence and language of the folktale. One can almost feel the presence of this master storyteller when reading her books.

> It was a while ago, in the days when they used to tell stories about creatures called the Selkie Folk. A stranger came ashore to an island at that time—a man who gave his name as Finn Learson—and there was a mystery about him which had to do with these selkie creatures. Or so some people say, anyway; but to be exact about all this, you must first of all know that the Selkie Folk are the seals that live in the waters around the Shetland Islands. Also, the Shetlands themselves lie in the stormy seas to the north of Britain, and it was on a night of very fierce storm that it all began. (Hunter, 1975, p.1)

The unique style of Mollie Hunter, as of all successful authors, speaks directly to children and is never condescending or presumptuous.

Avoiding Sentimentality

Many areas of life explored in literature can have meaning for both children and adults, but there are some areas that belong exclusively to children, and adults can only respond to them through fond memory. Unfortunately, adult memories of childhood often are rose-colored and misrepresent the realities of childhood. Authors who write from such distorted memories do not make successful books for children. Sentimental and "cute" stories may attract the book-buying adult and boost sales, but such books lie idle upon library shelves. To get inside children and view the world as they do is a feat accomplished by only the great authors of children's books. Usually Robert McCloskey captures the child's world and writes penetratingly about it, as in *Homer Price* and *One Morning in Maine*. Joan Anglund's *A Friend Is Someone Who Likes You* is another example of an adult point of view transferred in part to the child.

To discover the child's world is the first task of an author of a child's book. Teachers need to apply the same discipline as do the authors in putting aside sentimental memories when they select books from which children will choose. They need to listen to children and watch them to have a sense of what is appropriate content.

Genres of Children's Literature

From the sixteenth to the nineteenth century, many of the books that found their way into children's hands had only one purpose: to teach and to instruct in matters of religion, morals, and the right way to live. One such book was John Cotton's (1646) lengthy titled *Milk for Babes, Drawn Out of the Breasts of Both Testaments, Chiefly for the Spiritual Nourishment of Boston Babes in Either England, but May Be of Like Use for any Children*. Another was Maria Edgeworth's (1796) *The Parents' Assistant: or Stories for Children*.

In the late nineteenth and early twentieth centuries, some adult authors began to write books for children, stories that could be read to them and at the same time enjoyed by people at a different level of comprehension. Lewis Carroll's *Alice in Wonderland* was the forerunner, but later *Winnie-the-Pooh* by A. A. Milne won the hearts of almost all.

Today we are living in a golden age of children's literature. Newspapers and periodicals like the *London Times, The New York Times* and *Time* magazine have special sections and issues devoted to the reviewing of children's literature. There are currently over 40,000 children's books in print. These can be divided into seven major genres: picture books, traditional literature, modern fantasy, contemporary realistic fiction, historical fiction, poetry, and informational books.

Picture Books

Just as young children learning to speak do so by attending to and interacting with the purposeful language that surrounds them, young writers and readers grow and develop as a result of being exposed to well-written stories. The first books that children usually encounter are picture books. Very young children enjoy "lap books"—those books that are intimately shared in the company of a warm, friendly adult. Books such as Kunhardt's *Pat the Bunny,* Spier's *Crash! Bang! Boom!,* and the Mother Goose rhymes encourage children to participate in interactive dialogues as they point to details in the illustrations and discover language patterns in the text. There are several interesting variants of the traditional Mother Goose rhymes. N.M. Bodecker's translation and illustration of Danish nursery rhymes in *It's Raining Said John Twaining* and the Canadian rhymes compiled by Edith Fowke in *Sally Go Round the Sun* are examples.

Picture books also include the subgenres of ABC books, counting books, and wordless picture books. While reciting the alphabet is not a prerequisite to being able to read, ABC books can serve to stimulate talk, writing, and children's metalinguistic awareness. Many of these books are beautifully illustrated. Well-known illustrators of children's books (many of whom have works exhibited in museums) who have their own version of an ABC book include Mitsumasa Anno, Leonard Baskin, John Burningham, and Brian Wildsmith. Furthermore, many artists (for example, Anno and Sendak) have published their own counting books as well.

Wordless picture books represent one of the most rapidly growing subgenres of picture books. These books, with their fast-paced stories portrayed through connected sequences of illustration, not only link into the child's preference for action and pictures, but may also serve as a springboard to language activities. Teachers can use wordless books to encourage oral narration simply by asking a child to "tell about the story." Author/illustrators who have done several wordless picture books are John S. Goodall, Fernando Krahan, and Mercer Mayer.

Of course, by far the largest and most popular subgenre of picture books are the picture story books. Many of these stories, like novels, contain the literary elements mentioned earlier—plot, characterization, setting, style, and theme. Young children sometimes enjoy following major characters through several books. Russel Hoban's stories about a lovable badger named Frances and Arnold Lobel's "Frog and Toad" books are both fine examples of series books. Author/ illustrators who are perennial favorites of children include Carle, DePaola, Hutchins, Keats, Lionni, McCloskey, Sendak, Steig, and Zolotow.

Traditional Literarure

Traditional folk literature makes for an especially suitable introduction to literature for children because in the main it was created and recreated in family and community settings that included children. Not only are they stories that contain plenty of action, but they also lay the groundwork for more complex literature. As children begin to pick up the patterned story structures in folktales, such as clear-cut characterizations, straightforward plots that require the protagonist to accomplish a task, and events that usually occur in "threes" (for example, three wishes, pigs, billy goats gruff, and so on), they gradually acquire a literary framework or a "sense of story." This acquisition of literary form enables them to make informed predictions when encountering other similar stories. Children learn what to expect from stories.

There are hundreds of beautifully illustrated single versions of folktales. _

Teachers can share several versions of the same tale with children in order to compare their story structure and illustrations. For example, it is interesting to compare Walt Disney's cartoon illustrations of Snow White to Nancy Burkert's carefully researched illustrations of the same tale. Burkert actually visited the Museum of Decorative Arts in Paris so that she could sketch tapestries, crockery, and other objects in order to create illustrations that authentically reflected the story's medieval setting.

Comparing cross-cultural variants of folktales can be done with older children. A variant of a tale has the same plot but usually contains a different setting and characters. For example, *Tattercoats* (English), *Vasilisa the Beautiful* (Russian), and *Cenerentola* (Italian) have the same basic plot and are variants of the "Cinderella" story. There is even a Norwegian "Cinderlad," which can be found in Haviland's *Favorite Fairy Stories Told in Norway.* In fact, over 500 variants of this story have been collected in Europe alone! Cross-cultural comparisons can also be done by country, character archetypes, and motifs (for example, use of magical objects). Such comparisons convey and help children to understand the universal dimensions of human desires and feelings that exist across the centuries and over the borders of nations.

The folk rhymes that parents say with their children are another introduction to the folk language and wisdom of the past. "Nimble" might well have left the language long ago had it not been for the nursery rhyme "Jack be nimble, Jack be quick, Jack jump over the candlestick." Even though Jack probably was originally a politician who was either too hasty or too sluggish in his decision making, the rhyme conveys the meaning of an old word and a suggestion to the young about keeping alert.

> Oral rhymes are the true waifs of our literature in that their original wordings, as
> well as their authors, are usually unknown . . . having to fend for themselves. . . .
> If Arden and Garret's definition of poetry, that is "memorable speech," contains
> no more than a tincture of truth, it is yet enough to dye the rhymes with the
> tints of poetry. They owe their existence to this one quality of memorability.
> (Opie and Opie, 1963)

The memorability of the language of folk rhymes is derived from their strong rhythmic patterns and tongue-tickling sound play of rhyme and assonance.

> Goosey, goosey gander,
>   Whither shall I wander?
> Upstairs and downstairs
>   And in my lady's chamber.

> Oranges and lemons
> Say the bells of St. Clements.
> You owe me five farthings
> Say the bells of St. Martins.

Folksongs are natural means for building bridges to the pupils' own ethnic heritage. In them the delight and the sadness of simple living are conveyed through strong rhythm and colorful language. The melodies of the songs come also from the wellspring of folk living.

> The folk art lives upon the lips of the multitude and is transmitted by the grapevine, surviving sometimes for centuries because it reflects . . . the deepest emotional convictions of the common man. This is truly democratic art, painting a portrait of the people, unmatched for honesty and validity in any other record. (Lomax and Lomax, 1947)

The battle between people and machines is etched forever in memory by the ballad of "John Henry."

> John Henry told his old captain,
> Said, "A man ain't nothin' but a man;
> Before I let your steam drill beat me down
> I will die with the hammer in my hand,
>   Oh Lordy,
> Die with the hammer in my hand."

During the depression of the 1930's the longing for comfort and three square meals was expressed in the hobo song "The Big Rock Candy Mountain."

> In the Big Rock Candy Mountain
> All the cops have wooden legs,
> And the bulldogs all have rubber teeth
> And the hens lay soft boiled eggs.
> The farmer's trees are full of fruit
> And the barns are full of hay.
> O' I'm bound to go, where there ain't no snow,
> Where the sleet don't fall and the wind don't blow
> In the Big Rock Candy Mountain.

Many of these songs have been illustrated and appear in a song and picturebook format. Peter Spier's detailed illustrations for *The Erie Canal* give the reader a feel for life on a canal boat during the 1850's. Children enjoy singing and using Australian terms like "jumbuck," "billabong," and "tuckerbag" in the song and picturebook *Waltzing Matilda* by Paterson.

Myths are a special form of folk literature that convey cosmic themes of the human struggle with the elements, the battle with the forces of our own passions, and our relationship to powers beyond us. The Homeric "Hymn to Demeter" not only attempts to explain the mystery of the seasons through the saga of Persephone's capture by Hades but also deals both with Demeter's passion of anger at the loss of her daughter and with the question of the judgment of Zeus. The very elements of human existence are at stake in the epic, mythical narratives of Greece and Scandinavia. The same qualities abound in the untapped storehouse of myths from Eastern Europe, Africa, Asia, and the Americas. Older children respond to their challenges as they themselves begin to ask "why" questions about the order of the universe.

From the roots of folksongs and folktales has sprung the world of literature. The writing down of the great epics constituted the first stable literature, and epics were steeped in myth and folklore. From the folk ballad and the lyric song came poetry. This folk tradition of oral transmission has continued, even as written literature has burgeoned, because of human delight in telling a story or a joke.

Contemporary Realistic Fiction

In recent years there has been a trend for writers of literature for children and youth to deal with subjects that were avoided by publishers of an earlier period because of the controversy surrounding the subject matter in the story. Called the "New Realism" by some authorities in the field, this movement is characterized by such authors as Maia Wojciechowska, Judy Blume, S. E. Hinton, John Steptoe, and Louise Fitzhugh, who write books that deal sensitively with pregnancy, sexuality, drugs, urban life, the life of the migratory workers, and various counterculture lifestyles. *My Darling, My Hamburger* by Paul Zindel reveals the novel's plot through the opening dialogue: " 'It was Marie Dazinski who asked how to stop a boy if he wants to go all the way!' Maggie whispered" (Zindel, 1971, p.3)

Many of these authors are writing for the adolescent market. Even books for the very young, however, have become concerned with controversial themes—Maurice Sendak, for example, explores the realistic dreams of children through his fantasies *Where the Wild Things Are* and *In the Night Kitchen* (the latter has received reactions from librarians and parents because Max, a preschooler, floats through his dreams sans clothes). Louise Fitzhugh deals with the problem of the onset of menses through the eyes of preadolescents in *The Long Secret*. Fitzhugh's main character in *Harriet the Spy* has great influence on her readers. A teacher reported that a 13-year-old girl reacted to Harriet by writing, "I always wrote in a diary but after reading about Harriet, I used her writing as a model and the way I wrote my diary changed."

Not only do the plots, characters, concerns, and values take on a contemporary, realistic outlook with which young people can identify, but also the language of the story itself reflects the speech used by real people in real places. In *Stevie* by John Steptoe, the narrator is Robert, whose dialect is represented in the narration as well as the dialogue sequences in the story:

> And that time we was playin in the park under the bushes and we found these two dead rats and one was brown and one was black. And him and me and my friends used to cook mickies or marshmallows in the park. (Steptoe, 1970, p.19)

These books may pose a problem for some teachers in some communities, but they are popular with young people for good reasons. The students relate to books that deal with people much like themselves. "How does Judy Blume know how I think?" is a question commonly asked by her young readers. Teachers need to become aware of the existence of these books, the impact they are having on readers, and the reasons students react with genuine interest to them.

Fantasy

Nothing is quite as real as a well-written novel of fantasy or science fiction. Books of fantasy like Alexander's *Westmark* and *The Kestrel*, or Engdahl's *Enchantress from the Stars,* often make important political and sociological statements about today's world. Good fantasy also encourages the development of our "inner" worlds as well.

And what do we, and they, find, when we read fantasy? The escape and encouragement are there, for sure—but in a different form. This time, when we depart from our own reality into the reality of the book, it's not a matter of stepping across the street, or into the next county, or even the next planet. This time, we're escaping out, we're escaping in, without any idea of what we may encounter. Fantasy is the metaphor through which we discover ourselves. (Cooper, 1981, p. 16)

While exposure to folktales provides children with a literary base and starting point into fantasy, there are also some novels that can act as a "bridge" into this challenging genre. Works like Alexander's *The Cat Who Wished to Be a Man* contain many folktale elements yet are still best described as fantasy. There are books that help children move from the shorter folktale format to the longer, more complex novel of fantasy. Murphy's *Silver Woven in My Hair* is an expanded Cinderella story for elementary school children. Middle school children enjoy Skurzynski's *What Happened in Hamelin,* the story of how the Pied-Piper lured a group of children from Hamelin, Germany. The author has based this serious novel on actual documents that showed that 130 children really did mysteriously disappear in Hamelin on June 26, 1284. For adolescents, Skurzynski has written a similar story, this time based on a medical fact about the werewolf legend.

Series books allow children the luxury of revisiting and accompanying familiar characters as they encounter new adventures. Children that become "hooked" by one book in a series often are not satisfied until they have read them all. There are several superb series books of fantasy written by Lloyd Alexander, Michael Bond, Lucy Boston, Eleanor Cameron, John Christopher, Susan Cooper, Sylvia Engdahl, Ursula LeGuin, Madeline L'Engle, C. S. Lewis, and George Selden.

Historical Fiction, Informational Books, and Biography

Historical fiction breathes life and humanity into what is traditionally viewed as history—that is, the memorization of facts, dates, and events. Yet through literary presentation, children can begin to experience vicariously the dreams, joys, and agonies of those who lived before us. Moreover, they may begin to sense the "connectedness" of past events to their own lives and gain insight into human motivation and behavior across time.

Erik Haugaard is especially known for his two Viking adventure stories, *Hakon of Rogen's Saga* and its sequel, *A Slave's Tale.* The nightmare of Nazi Germany is vividly portrayed in books like *The Upstairs Room* by Johanna Reiss and Hans Peter Richter's *Friedrich.* Many critics would agree that one of the finest writers of historical fiction for children is Rosemary Sutcliff. Teachers will want to be aware of works like *Scarlet Warrior,* set in the Bronze Age, or her story of Norman England called *The Witch's Brat.* Kathryn Paterson brings medieval Japan alive in *The Master Puppeteer.*

Outstanding informational books are also literature. Some straightforward, factual books are designed simply to supplement textbooks, but some so describe the world and human relationships with it that they cause children to contemplate with awe the phenomena of nature and to relate personally to them. Such books are fiction in the sense that, although the details are factual, the author's skill intensifies the experience. Adult readers have this experience when they read books like Rachel Carson's *The Sea Around Us*. C. Holling in *Paddle-to-the-Sea* and Alvin Tresselt and Leonard Weisgard in *Rain Drop Splash* have accomplished artistic presentations of the factual for children.

Accuracy and authenticity are of utmost importance in the writing of informational books. Yet this must be done in a way that does not bore the child. In *Pilgrim Courage,* Smith and Meredith have prepared for older children a text based on the first outstanding piece of American literature, Bradford's *Of Plimoth Plantation*. For younger children there is a picture book based on the same text, called *The Coming of the Pilgrims*.

Jean Fritz has written several biographies that present children with dimensions of historical figures that would rarely be found in history textbooks. She uses a lively, colloquial writing style to reveal details about her subjects. In *Where Do You Think You're Going, Christopher Columbus?*, Fritz depicts Columbus as a very religious, optimistic master seaman but also as a somewhat stubborn man who poorly managed his crew. She skillfully weaves humor into her historical portrayals.

> Columbus named the island San Salvador. Certainly it wasn't Japan. There were no palaces and the only sign of gold was the gold rings that the natives wore in their noses. Indeed, that was all they wore. The people were as naked, Columbus said, "as their mothers bore them" which, of course, was pretty naked. . . . But if the Spaniards were surprised to see naked natives, the natives were even more surprised to see dressed Spaniards. All that cloth over their bodies! What were they trying to hide? Tails, perhaps? (Fritz, pp. 31–32)

Other biographies by this author are *And Then What Happened, Paul Revere?*, *Can't You Make Them Behave, King George?*, and *What's the Big Idea, Ben Franklin?*

Poetry

Ann Terry in her study of poetry preferences (Terry, 1974) found that children responded favorably to (1) contemporary poems; (2) poems dealing with familiar, everyday experiences; (3) humorous poetry; (4) narratives or poems that "told a story"; and (5) poetry that had strong elements of rhythm and rhyme. Although until recently most poems for children were actually more appropriate for adults, there are now several excellent poets who write for children rather than about them.

Every year the National Council for Teachers of English presents its "Annual Award for Poetry for Children," honoring excellence in a poet's overall work. In the past, outstanding poets like Aileen Fisher, Eve Merriam, Myra Cohn Livingston, David McCord, and Karla Kuskin have received this award. A recent winner was John Ciardi, a writer of adult poetry. His poem "Mummy Slept Late and Daddy Fixed Breakfast" was voted the favorite poem by the children in the Terry study.

One favorite writer of children's humorous verse is unquestionably Shel Silverstein, author of the extremely popular *Where the Sidewalk Ends*. A more recently completed volume of verse is called *A Light in the Attic*. This book has poems titled "Messy Room," "Homework Machine," and "How Not to Have to Dry the Dishes." Michael Rosen's humorous poetry is similarly popular among children in England.

Although children in the Terry study preferred contemporary poems, there are collections of traditional poetry that many children enjoy. Robert Louis Stevenson's *A Child's Garden of Verses,* Walter de la Mare's *Come Hither,* Carl Sandburg's *Wind Song,* and an illustrated collection of poems by Emily Dickinson called *I'm Nobody! Who Are You?* are some examples.

Periodicals for Children

Magazines for children can be found in bookstores and on supermarket shelves. Like many adult periodicals, some magazines for children are long on sensationalism and short on content. However, many of them deal with subjects, ranging from animals to teenage idols, that are of genuine interest to children.

There are a few children's periodicals in which the quality of writing and illustrations is especially outstanding. *Cricket,* a monthly magazine edited by authors, illustrators, and other experts in the field of children's literature, contains puzzles, poems, articles, stories, and book reviews, all of high literary quality. Another monthly, *National Geographic World,* primarily features informative articles about animals, sports, and children around the world. The photography is everything one would expect from a National Geographic Society publication. *Ranger Rick's Nature Magazine,* a monthly with interesting articles on the plant and animal kingdoms, also has high-quality photographs. The same publisher has *In Your Backyard* for preschoolers. Lastly, *Stone Soup* has well-written stories, poems, and book reviews as well as outstanding artwork. This magazine is especially unique in that all of the writing and artwork is done by children themselves.

Strategies for Using Children's Literature in the Classroom

Children need to learn the value of the public library and how to use it. One way to get used to sharing books with others is for the teacher to set up a lending library in the classroom, using books borrowed or donated by children or others. Some teachers set up a permanent library corner either in their rooms or in a hall space, or, where classrooms are clustered, in conjunction with other teachers. These collections can be supplemented monthly from local and school libraries. The reasonable cost of paperback books permits teachers to buy them for their classroom libraries, a few each year. In many British schools the child's feeling for possessing a book for awhile is very highly regarded—so much so, in fact, that new paperbacks, written at several reading levels and abundantly available in most classrooms, may be taken home if the child so wishes. They are considered in some schools to be expendable materials like paper. The paperback books now available in the United States are often used in the same expendable way through book clubs and exchanges to build classroom and home libraries. Parents can be encouraged to buy children books from time to time instead of other items. Paperback book fairs are popular in many schools. Also, public libraries periodically have sales in which children's books can be bought at greatly reduced prices.

With the classroom library there needs to be a regular time set aside for individual and paired reading and for sharing books. Adults enjoy telling their friends about a new book they have read; children do also.

Rather than relying on the formal book report, reporting and sharing of feelings about books can be accomplished in a variety of ways. For example, after hearing and discussing Sendak's *Where the Wild Things Are,* children could express their interpretation of the story in several ways. One group of children might choose to dramatize the story or act out an improvised conversation between Max and his mother. Another group could choose (or compose) music and create a dance of the "Wild Rumpus" in the story. Some might want to make a mural of Max's journey or construct sack puppets of the "Wild Things." Still others could make a "Wild Thing" gameboard, which would require players to move markers on a course leading to the land of "Wild Things" and back home again. Drawing cards could be made for the game that contained messages like "Wild Rumpus begins, go forward 3 spaces." When collaboratively planned with children, such activities are valuable because they often require that children go back to the book and reexamine the story and their responses to it.

In addition to providing opportunities for children to respond to books in a variety of ways, teachers will want to use literature "across the curriculum." Stories (for example, wordless picture books) can be used to encourage oral composing and act as a springboard to imaginative writing. Poetry like Sandburg's "Arithmetic" or Morrison's collection of science poems, *Overheard in a Bubble Chamber,* should be a part of math and science studies. DePaola's *The Popcorn Book* or Hautzig's *Cool Cooking: 16 Recipes Without a Stove* can be displayed in classroom cooking areas in order to help children to see the connection between disciplines. It is through integrated curricular experiences that children begin to see learning as a related whole rather than a meaningless fragmentation of subjects and skills.

The Arts as Presentation

Language by itself as an idiom for knowing has limitations. Even when used to the fullest by the great poets it cannot present immediate gestalten. It cannot catch in an instant the whole horrible absurdity of modern war in the way Picasso's "Guernica" does. Nor can it convey the sublime repose of Michelangelo's "Pieta" nor the simple grandeur of Mozart's "Jupiter Symphony." These works of art speak directly to the senses and are apprehended at once without the mediation of language. Indeed, an attempt to interpose language at the moment of apprehension is likely to distort the message of the painter, sculptor, or composer. This is not to say that the experiential impact of plastic or musical art is not to be talked about in _ the conceptualizing process but rather to stress that visual and aural presentations can rarely be translated successfully into language.

> The meanings given through language are successively understood, and gathered into a whole by the process called discourse; the meanings of all other symbolic elements that compose a larger, articulate symbol are understood only through the meaning of the whole, through their relations within the total structure. Their very functioning as symbols depends on the fact that they are involved in a simultaneous integral presentation. This kind of semantic may be called "presentational symbolism" to characterize its essential distinction from discursive symbolism, or "language" proper. (Langer, 1956, p. 78)

"Presentational symbolism" has a syntax of its own: the structured balance of sensuous forms in rhythm, in line, in color, and in space. Language, although usually used in a discursive manner, can be molded in this way in poetry. On the other hand, pictures can be discursive (literal exposition); for example, in a series of pictograms, graphs, hieroglyphics, or literal picture stories. The difference between the discursive idiom and the nondiscursive idiom is that the latter speaks with directness and immediacy in its totality. The nondiscursive idiom, or symbolic presentation, can present concepts involving emotional overtones and significant particulars more effectively than can lines of discourse.

The fact that the arts are presentational symbols of ideas is the reason for their inclusion in the school program and especially for their integration into study of the content areas such as social studies. They are not just activities to be added to make classroom studies more fun or to teach appreciation of "classy" culture, as was common in their earlier introduction into the curriculum. The arts are substantive in themselves and they add substance to study in other areas. Along with humanistic and scientific literature, they represent the highest ideations of humanity in all the world cultures and are as much a part of the heritage of knowledge as are the others.

Visual Presentation of Form: The Literature of Pictures

For many children, the illustrations in picture books are their first experience with the art world. Illustrations in children's books should be visual presentations by which the discursive text is illuminated and extended in richness of meaning. They should not dominate a book and rob the text of its vitality, nor should they be so subsidiary to the words that they merely decorate. On the other hand, a neutral position wherein the picture literally repeats the text is wasteful. Such illustrations are pictograms and should stand alone as they do in wordless comic strips. In basal readers, pictures are placed in the text to give children a pictorial context even though their usefulness for that purpose is limited. "Picture clues" may be a distraction from the main task of comprehending the printed form of the language. The pictures in the readers might better be true illustrations, bringing aesthetic extension to the text, rather than being dull repetitions of dull discourse.

Early reading can draw on books that use a combination of language and pictures created by a skillful artist-writer team that judiciously combines the elements that can best be told in words or in pictures. The story is twice told and the pictures are artful illustrations to give substance and create a context for a story.

Marcia Brown's Caldecott winner, *Once a Mouse,* is a good example of a strong but lean folktale text enriched by illustrations that highlight in blocked greens and sepias the mystery and surprise in the telling of a good folktale. In Robert McCloskey's *Time of Wonder,* alliterative and fast-paced language join with active and colorful illustrations to project, among other Maine coast happenings, a hurricane in all its terror and splendor. Lynd Ward's *The Biggest Bear* has become a classic among picture books because both the reading text and the illustrations are substantive and artistic. A child who is still learning to read is not overwhelmed by the text; the pictures fill out the story, the background, and the mood. *The Little House* by Virginia Lee Burton achieves the same complementarity in text and picture in its building of historical and social concepts through a story of sentiment.

The art of many picture books appeals also to older children. For example, M.B. Goffstein's *An Artist* is a quiet and spiritually full picture book that examines the role of art and artist in our society. The delicate watercolors and poetic text combine to make an abstract subject appealing to middle-grade children. Also, there are books like *Castle, Cathedral, Unbuilding and Pyramid*—all by David Macaulay. This author-illustrator's satiric style, wry sense of humor, and immensely detailed pen-and-ink drawings, which expertly depict the unique structural perspectives and cross-sections of various types of architecture, can be appreciated by children in the upper elementary and middle grades.

Picture essays such as *Life Magazine's History of the United States* present concepts of the ways of life in various epochs that, if left to words alone, would require volumes and might still miss the essence of an age. For example, George Caleb Bingham's paintings present the adventure and robustness of the frontier as only a sensitive participant in the experience could. Art photography has become in the twentieth century a highly expressive form that is as applicable as other media. The work of Ansel Adams in his Sierra Club posters has done much toward making Americans apprehend their wonderful natural surroundings and, incidentally, to feel deeply the need to preserve them.

Film has become another effectively expressive medium that has had an artistic impact that began with silent film in the early part of the century and continues through movies and television. Chaplin's "Modern Times" is as stunning a commentary on modern dilemmas as any social novel or tract, and the ideation is entirely conveyed through cinematic means.

The ancient Greeks' desire for the golden mean can be sensed in the sculpture and architecture of the time as well as in the writings of the philosophers. The Middle Ages are not understood until the massiveness and loftiness of the cathedrals and intricacies of the stone carvings are seen. Painters, sculptors, and architects around the world presently and in ages past have presented the ideas and the feeling of their cultures in intense and focused forms. Their works can be viewed and studied as reflections of the relationship of people to the world about them.

Strategies for Teaching Application of the Visual Arts

Teachers who believe that the visual arts are important complements to language arts for the communication of ideas will make every possible use of them in their own right. However, use of the pictorial arts can encourage language users and even be the stepping-stone to language. One of the authors observed a most effective use of the picture essay with a group of under-achieving junior high school youngsters from a black and Puerto Rican neighborhood school. They were given simple cameras and sent around their neighborhood to take pictures of the life of the people there. Then, involved in learning how to print their pictures, they were next asked to make a story from selected ones if they had not already conceived of a story when they took the pictures. The photographs were mounted in a thematic series. Although they told a story by themselves, the teacher then asked the students to develop captions and a narrative to accompany the pictures. Similar activities can be done with 8mm film or videotape.

Youngsters are usually eager to illustrate stories that they have written. In such an activity the teacher can work with them in thinking through what kind of illustrations would complement the story and not merely repeat aspects of it. A painted mural or a series of pictures, comic-book style, can be made by young people to summarize concepts learned in social studies or science.

Teachers can use the folk art and fine arts of local or distant cultures to assist students in conveying the varied ways cultures express ideas and feelings. It is also possible to study the arts themselves as symbolic representations of ideas, encouraging youngsters to respond to them and try out the various media themselves as conveyors of their ideas. It is possible to have a small museum in the classroom as one of the learning centers, where graphic arts in print form or in books are displayed and where different materials are available from time to time for expressive exploration. Instruction in the way to use them is often necessary, but copying adult works or presented patterns should be avoided. The variety of materials available and the wide range of art ideas, drawing upon the past, the present, and the world's many cultures, make myriad possibilities for presentations in art forms.

Music

Another direct idiom of presentation is music artfully made from the harmony of sound, in which composers state their ideas about the world musically. Although much of music is linear in time, impressions are created by a piling up of notes and rhythms in harmony and in counterpoint. A Bach fugue conveys a religious sense of awe; a Schubert song can illuminate the concept of human love. Program music like Beethoven's "Pastoral Symphony," Vivaldi's "Four Seasons," or Debussy's "La Mer" paints an aural picture; a Haydn symphony ("The Miracle") or a Stravinsky chamber piece (for example, "Dumbarton Oaks Concerto") presents abstractly human delight in being alive.

Children respond directly to musical forms. Their ability to apprehend music has not yet been thwarted by cultural pressure for conformity that has labeled classical music as "highbrow," or rock music as "trashy." Some music teaching of the past has abetted this conformity by placing an aura of difficulty and sophistication around some music, in contrast with the natural introduction to music that children were given in earlier times. Today's interpretation of music has almost become a cult open to only those who have had courses in so-called appreciation. The result of this approach to the teaching of music is the separation of the child's natural sensitivity to rhythm and harmonious sound from the messages of the musical composition. Some jazz and rock-and-roll forms are the folk music of today and can be the entry-way to musical understanding. Most music in the modern Western tradition was written for adults, and therefore much of the musical literature is no more accessible to children than the writings of modern literature. However, as with literature, some musical compositions, such as Saint-Saens' "Carnival of Animals," for example, have universal appeal. Also, there have been some remarkable compositions written expressly for children; for example, Prokofiev's "A Summer Day" suite and Mozart's "Toy Symphony."

Folk Music

Most folk music from the various cultural groups of the world can become meaningful to children because it is composed in a family or a total community setting. Children are as much a part of the rituals, festivities, and occasions where music is used as are the adults, except for special religious rites involving only the priests or elders. The best introductions to the musical idiom for children are the folksong and dance literature from family and community occasions. Black jazz and blues, Scottish and Irish airs, American Indian ceremonial dances, African drum music, English folk carols, and Haitian carnival tunes are but a few examples.

Folk music has in it all the basic elements of the musical idiom; therefore, the step from the folk heritage to composed music is not as difficult as some imagine, provided highly complex musical forms and overlong compositions are not stressed. Listening to Bach's "Air for the G String" can easily follow singing of the "Londonderry Air." The learning of a Hungarian folksong can be precursor to the hearing of Bartok's "Music for Children." The dancing of a Russian folk dance can lead to some of the music of early Stravinsky or Prokofiev. Aaron Copland and Roy Harris in the United States have created music that can have meaning for American children because it has roots in the folk tradition of the frontier and of the age of jazz. Scott Joplin's ragtime music for piano or small band combines folk and classical qualities that have an appeal for children similar to that of the highly original Sousa marches; they both represent American cultural ages in musical form.

Composed Music

A few of the great composers have written expressly for children. Bach wrote a substantial body of music for his many talented sons to use in practice and in the study of musical invention. Some of these were collected in the "Anna Magdalena

Notebook" and the "Two and Three Part Inventions." Schumann wrote four major piano works for the young, including "Children's Ball" and "Album for the Young." In our time Bartok composed "Music for Children." Almost all these pieces are suitable for children's listening and some for performing. Their particular advantage is that they introduce the child to the fundamentals of music, for usually each piece develops a musical idea with only one or two musical inventions, a particular rhythmic pattern, harmonic device, or contrapuntal line. Didactics are not required as children experience directly the building blocks of the musical art. The mode of electronic music is perhaps closer in comprehension to the children of this generation than it is to adults.

Making Music
Modern musical education theory suggests that children can learn the art of music making by experiencing their own composition of musical ideas. They can create music just as they create written language composition or their own paintings. Children are quite capable of inventing melodies, rhythms, and even harmonies to present a feeling about some situation or experience. They can use their singing voices and various rhythmic and simple melody-carrying or rhythm instruments to set forth their musical ideas. Children of the slums are seen making very exciting music on oil drums, bottles, and tin cans, but this music is hardly ever brought into the school and made the base for further musical study and performance, as it should be.

Carl Orff, the modern composer, has devised for children a structured program of activities for the creation of music. Benjamin Britten, the modern English composer, in addition to writing the most successful educational musical film for children, "The Young Person's Guide to the Orchestra," has composed several works in which children can participate. Among them are "Let's Make an Opera" and Noye's "Fludde." Prokofiev has been perhaps the most successful composer for children. The popularity of "Peter and the Wolf" placed it in the "classic" category not long after its composition. He has also written a delightful suite of piano pieces for children. Children are surely deprived if they are not given the opportunity to learn how to "read" musical literature.

Dramatic and Dance Literature

The modes of drama and dance are among the first that the child uses and enjoys. Young children delight in dancing to a tune or some rhythmic beat, musical or otherwise. In the preschool years, playing house and dressing up are natural diversions in which young children rehearse their concepts of adult societal roles. During the middle years of childhood, group theatricals are neighborhood entertainments studiously planned although not always persuasively acted by adult standards. Their content usually expresses a child's view of adult happenings or fragments of the child's fantasy. Children respond readily to chants and rhythms that are the essence of choral dancing and speaking.

Froebel, in his recommendations for childhood education, included eurhythmics as part of his proposal to present children with the unities of the world. Plato, in his curriculum for Athenian children, stressed the importance of music and choral dance, for teaching balance and control to bring harmony to the emotions:

> The whole choral art is also in our view the whole of education; and in this art rhythm and harmonies form that part which has to do with the voice. . . . The movement of the body has rhythm in common with the movement of the voice. . . . The sound of the voice readies and educates the soul. (All these) we have ventured to call music. (Plato; Jowett translation, 1892, p. 672)

In modern times the dance and dramatic arts have been included in the school curriculum mainly as activities that would bring enjoyment and in time would permit release of the emotions in a "respectable" form. Creative play was seen as an opportunity for appropriate expression of aggressions and untutored emotions. Children were permitted to express themselves freely but within limits imposed by dance and dramatic forms. This was a modern psychological rationale for accomplishing ends not too dissimilar from those proposed by Plato.

But dances and dramas are not composed just for fun or for psychic release. They are made for the presentation of ideas and archetypal patterns. They convey human knowledge as surely as do books.

The Modes of Dance and Drama

The forms of dance are made in space and in time and by bodily movement. Choreography is the art of planning a dance presentation. Effects are created by the rhythmic movements of the dancer's limbs, torso, and head, alone or in concert with the patterned movements of other dancers. Gestures may be used to emphasize or highlight a meaning. In some cultures, particular gestures convey particular agreed-upon meanings, while in modern dance or ballet, although movements may be conventionalized to some extent, the meanings depend more directly on the dynamics of tension and release expressible in the body as it moves.

The dramatic arts are extensions of miming that sometimes incorporate all the other presentational forms: the literary language of dialogue, the painting and sculpture of scenery, the visual effects of light and costume, music either as background or as an integral part of the performance, and sometimes elements of the dance. Children understand the theater's essential means of presentation when they watch a pantomime or when they enact one.

Children need to learn how to "read" the presentations of dance and theater in order to gain meaning from them directly without a roundabout explanation of them through discursive means. They must become accustomed to their special cues for communication. One way to learn the syntax and rhetoric of these special arts is to create one's own forms, much as children practice creative writing or painting. In "rhythms" young people can build whole dance forms from stories that deal with emotions. A kindergarten teacher used a story made up by the children as the base for a class opera: a music-dance-drama presentation. After hearing the story read aloud and discussing its content, the children plotted several episodes to enact. The class composed songs and dances, and prepared the scenery. They performed for parents and other classes. Newspaper publicity brought them an invitation to do a special performance at the local "Friends of the Opera."

Youngsters should experience the aesthetic presentations of all cultures. The folk-dance literature can convey directly the attitudes of peoples toward certain aspects of life. An Indian rain dance or an African hunting dance tells of these peoples' dependence on the vagaries of nature far more immediately than verbal explanation. The "Second Shepherd's Play," from one of the medieval cycles of religious plays, captures the rude humor of those times and the mystery of a people's religion. A dance from the Japanese Kabuki cycle gives a picture of medieval life and thought in Asian culture.

Motion Picture and Television

The motion picture and television can be purely visual presentations when they deal with natural phenomena, but when they present human situations they use dialogue as well as movement and miming. The child learns early how to "read" visual drama because of its availability on television and at local theaters.

Films used in the school for social studies and science should, of course, be authentic, but they should also be artful. Just as good books are preferred over poor ones in teaching, so there should be the same discrimination regarding choice of films. Robert Flaherty's classic "Louisiana Story" not only pictures oilwell drilling on the Gulf coast but also conveys the human drama of people and machines through the sensitive eyes of a curious boy—much in the vein of Walt Whitman's "Out of the Cradle Endlessly Rocking." The movements of the pumping shafts in the derricks are contrasted with the quiet shoreline; the sparse but pungent dialogue stands out against the mingling of harmonica music with sounds of the pumps and the softly lapping water. The total presentation is an artistic masterpiece. Movies of the caliber of "Louisiana Story" can tell children much about their world, and there are many more available since Flaherty showed the way.

Some informational films are very well made, and teachers need to search for them. The better the film, the better the message will be communicated. After seeing the powerful film on preserving wildlife, "Say Goodbye," one class developed petitions to be signed and sent to local, state, and national officers.

Many educators have lamented the preoccupation of people, particularly children, with television. Such laments are unfortunate. Television will not go away by wishing it to or by preaching against its evils. Rather, teachers need to consider its positive aspects and how to help students get the most of their experiences with it.

Television offers a world of varied experiences, particularly with the advent of satellite transmission and cable access to multiple program channels. Schools can help pupils develop personal taste and criteria for making choices in what they will watch.

Many television experiences can lead to reading and school experiences if teachers are aware of what is available for pupils to watch. It's a fact of modern life that for many pupils their "sense of story" and ability to predict plot in literature develops first in watching television dramas.

Situation comedies may be repetitious and trite, but they use the same themes and situations that playwrights from Shakespeare to modern times have used. Sports events, political happenings, space shuttles, news coverage—all provide the basis for school experiences. Many programs, in fact, are followed by suggestions for follow-up reading. Schools need to build media literacy, but they also need to accept and expand on media experience in school.

It has been said that the whole curriculum could simply be youngsters' responses to the television programs and movies that they see or could see every day. Ideas of all sorts, including many misconceptions, are conveyed to them in this manner. One regular topic for class meetings might be response to television programs of the night before. With the availability of color videotaping, teachers and young people can devise their own programs for presenting their ideas to others. Videotape and tape recorders are becoming relatively cheap and widely available. Many school systems can transmit their own programs on public access cable channels.

Multimedia presentations utilizing slides with two or three projectors and a synchronized sound tape can be very useful for presenting contrasting or complementary concepts and themes. Youngsters at the sixth-grade level have composed, for example, a slide-sound show called "Picture Our World," combining their own color slides of children and adults in nature settings of various kinds with a music tape of children singing the verses of the song. Pictures and music create an essay on ecology that is moving and significant.[2]

Cognitive and Affective Impact   The dramatic forms of theater, movies, and television can at their best integrate the several symbolic forms (including language) and create a cognitive and emotional impact impossible in the separate forms. Some critics of our "wordbound" culture feel that the Gutenberg era is over and that mixed media will dominate communication in the near future. Written language will undoubtedly continue in usefulness, however, but children will increasingly need to learn how to use the visual, aural, and terpsichorean modes for coming to know about their world of the future.

References

Susan Cooper, "Escaping into Ourselves," in B. Hearne and M. Kay, *Celebrating Children's Books* (New York: Lothrop, Lee, and Shepard, 1981).

Virginia Haviland, "The Artist as Author: The Strength of Double Vision," in Margaret Meek, A. Warlow, and G. Barton, *The Cool Web: The Pattern of Children's Reading* (New York: Atheneum, 1978).

Suzanne Langer, *Philosophy in a New Key* (Cambridge, MA: Harvard University Press, 1956).

[2]Douglas Cooper, Teacher, Brookside School, Bloomfield Hills, Michigan.

John Lomax and Alan Lomax, *Folk Song USA* (New York: Duell, Sloan, and Pearce-Meredith Press, 1947).

Margaret Meek, *Learning to Read* (London: The Bodley Head, 1982).

Iona Opie and Peter Opie, *The Puffin Book of Nursery Rhymes* (Baltimore: Penguin Books, 1963).

Philip Phenix, *Realms of Meaning* (New York: McGraw-Hill, 1964).

Plato, "The Laws," in Jowett, *Dialogues of Plato,* vol. IIB (London: Oxford University Press, 1892).

Louise Rosenblatt, *Literature as Exploration* (New York: Noble and Noble, 1976); (First Edition, 1938).

Selected Bibliography of Children's Books

Richard Adams, *Watership Down* (New York: Macmillan, 1974).

Lloyd Alexander, *The Black Cauldron* (New York: Holt, Rinehart and Winston, 1965).

————, *The Kestrel* (New York: Dutton, 1973).

————, *Westmark* (New York: Dutton, 1982).

Joan Anglund, *A Friend Is Someone Who Likes You* (New York: Harcourt, Brace, Jovanovich, 1968).

Mitsumasa Anno, *Anno's Alphabet* (New York: Crowell, 1975).

————, *Anno's Counting Book* (New York, Crowell, 1977).

Judy Blume, *Are You There God? It's Me, Margaret* (New York: Bradbury, 1970).

————, *Superfudge* (New York: Dutton, 1981).

N. M. Bodecker, *Hurry, Hurry Mary Dear! And Other Nonsense Poems* (New York: Atheneum, 1973).

Michael Bond, *A Bear Called Paddington* (London: Houghton, Mifflin, 1962).

L.M. Boston, *The Children of Green Knowe* (New York: Harcourt, Brace, Jovanovich, 1955).

John Burningham, *Come Away from the Water, Shirley* (New York: Crowell, 1977).

Eleanor Cameron, *The Court of the Stone Children* (New York: Dutton, 1973).

Eric Carle, *The Grouchy Ladybug* (New York: Crowell, 1977).

Rachel Carson, *The Sea Around Us* (New York: Golden Press, 1958).

Rebecca Caudill, *A Pocketful of Cricket* (New York: Holt, Rinehart and Winston, 1964).

John Christopher, *The City of Gold and Lead* (New York: Macmillan, 1967).

John Ciardi, *I Met a Man* (Boston: Houghton, Mifflin, 1961).

Beverly Cleary, *Ramona and Her Father* (New York: Morrow, 1977).

Susan Cooper, *The Dark Is Rising* (New York: Atheneum, 1973).

Robert Cormier, *The Chocolate War* (New York: Pantheon, 1974).

Tomi DePaola, *The Popcorn Book* (New York: Holiday House, 1978).

————, *Pancakes for Breakfast* (New York: Harcourt Brace Jovanovich, 1978).

Emily Dickinson. *I'm Nobody! Who Are You?* (Boston: Stemmer House, 1978).

Sylvia Engdahl, *Enchantress from the Stars* (New York: Atheneum, 1970).

Aileen Fisher, *Out in the Dark and Daylight* (Chicago: Harper and Row, 1980).

Louise Fitzhugh, *Harriet the Spy* (New York: Dell, 1964).

————, *The Long Secret* (New York: Dell, 1965).

Edith Fowke, *Sally Go Round the Sun: 300 Children's Songs, Rhymes, and Games* (New York: Doubleday, 1970).

Jean Fritz, *Where Do You Think You're Going, Christopher Columbus?* (New York: Putnam, 1980).

John S. Goodall, *Creepy Castle* (New York: Atheneum, 1975).

The Brothers Grimm, *Snow White and the Seven Dwarfs* (New York: Farrar, Strauss, 1977).

Eric Haugaard, *Hakon of Rogen's Saga* (Boston: Houghton, Mifflin, 1963).

Esther Hautzig, *Cool Cooking: 16 Recipes Without a Stove* (New York: Lothrop, 1973).

Russell Hoban, *A Baby Sister for Francis* (New York: Harper and Row, 1974).

Holling C. Holling, *Paddle-to-the-Sea* (Boston: Houghton, Mifflin, 1941).

Tobias Hosea, *Hosie's Alphabet* (New York: Viking, 1972).

Mollie Hunter, *A Stranger Came Ashore* (New York: Harper and Row, 1975).

Pat Hutchins. *Rosie's Walk* (New York: Macmillan, 1968).

Ezra Jack Keats, *The Snowy Day* (New York: Viking, 1962).

Dorothy Kunhardt, *Pat the Bunny* (Golden Press, 1962).

Fernando Krahn, *April Fools* (New York: Dutton, 1974).

Karla Kuskin, *Dogs and Dragons, Trees and Dreams* (New York: Harper and Row, 1980).

Jane Langton, *The Fledgling* (New York: Harper and Row, 1980).

Ursula LeGuin, *The Farthest Shore* (New York: Atheneum, 1976).

Madeleine L'Engle, *A Wrinkle in Time* (New York: Farrar, Strauss, 1978).

C.S. Lewis, *The Lion, the Witch and the Wardrobe* (New York: Macmillan, 1961).

Leo Lionni, *Frederick* (New York: Pantheon, 1967).

Myra Cohn Livingston, *Four-Way Stop and Other Poems* (New York: Atheneum, 1976).

Arnold Lobel, *Frog and Toad Together* (New York: Harper and Row, 1972).

David Macaulay, *Castle* (Boston: Houghton, Mifflin, 1977).

Robert McCloskey, *Homer Price* (New York: Viking, 1943).

David McCord, *One at a Time* (Boston: Little, Brown, 1977).

Eve Merriam, *The Inner-City Mother Goose* (New York: Simon and Schuster, 1969).

A.A. Milne, *Winnie-the-Pooh* (London: Dutton, 1926).

Lillian Morrison, *Overheard in a Bubble Chamber and Other Science Poems* (New York: Lothrop, Lee and Shepard, 1981).

Shirley Murphy, *Silver Woven in My Hair* (New York: Atheneum, 1977).

Helen Oxenbury, *Pig Tale* (New York: Morrow, 1973).

A.B. Paterson, *Waltzing Matilda* (New York: Holt, Rinehart and Winston, 1972).

Katherine Paterson, *Bridge to Terabithia* (New York: Crowell, 1977).

————, *Jacob Have I Loved* (New York: Crowell, 1980).

————, *The Master Puppeteer* (New York: Crowell, 1975).

Johanna Reiss, *The Upstairs Room* (New York: Crowell, 1972).

Hans Peter Richter, *Friedrich* (New York, Holt, Rinehart and Winston, 1970).

Michael Rosen, *You Can't Catch Me* (London: Puffin, 1981).

Antoine de Saint-Exupery, *The Little Prince* (New York: Harcourt, Brace, Jovanovich, 1960).

Carl Sandburg, *Wind Song* (New York: Harcourt, Brace, Jovanovich, 1960).

Alvin Schwartz, *A Twister of Twists, a Tangler of Tongues* (Philadelphia: Lippincott, 1972).

George Selden, *The Cricket in Times Square* (New York: Farrar, Strauss, 1960).

Maurice Sendak, *Where the Wild Things Are* (New York: Harper and Row, 1963).

Shel Silverstein, *A Light in the Attic* (New York: Harper and Row, 1981).

Gloria Skurzynski, *What Happened in Hamelin* (Boston: Houghton/Clarion, 1981).

E. Brooks Smith and Robert Meredith, *The Coming of the Pilgrims* (Boston: Little, Brown, 1964).

————, *Pligrim Courage* (Boston: Little, Brown, 1962).

Peter Spier, *Crash! Bang! Boom!* (New York: Doubleday, 1972).

Flora Annie Steel, *Tattercoats* (London: Bradbury, 1976).

William Steig, *Abel's Island* (New York: Farrar, Strauss, 1976).

Jorg Steiner, *Rabbit Island* (New York: Harcourt, Brace, Jovanovich, 1977).

John Steptoe, *Stevie,* 1970.

Robert Louis Stevenson, *A Child's Garden of Verses* (Oxford, 1895, 1947).

Rosemary Sutcliff, *Scarlet Warrior* Walck, 1958.

Mildred Taylor, *Roll of Thunder, Hear My Cry* (New York: Dial, 1976).

J. R. R. Tolkein, *The Hobbit* (Boston: Houghton, Mifflin, 1938).

Alvin Tresselt and Leonard Weisgard, *Rain Drop Splash* (New York: Lothrop, 1946).

E. B. White, *Charlotte's Web* (New York: Harper and Row, 1952).

Thomas Whitney, *Vasilisa the Beautiful* (New York: Macmillan, 1970).

Brian Wildsmith, *Brian Wildsmith's ABC* (New York: Franklin Watts, 1963).

Paul Zindel, *My Darling, My Hamburger* (New York, Bantam, 1971).

Charlotte Zolotow, *Say It!* (Greenwillow, 1980).

15

Language and Thinking:
Strategies in Teaching

But the curriculum is a microcosm of the culture—condensed, distilled, a little rarefied perhaps; but not a different order of reality. The school is part of the community, and the language of education is part of the community's linguistic resources. The continuity between the curriculum and the rest of the culture is thus again a linguistic continuity: it is expressed through language—through the use of language, in parent-teacher discussions, in public debates, in letters to the press and so on; but also through the forms of language—including the ways that the registers of education infiltrate into ordinary discourse. . . . Our technical educational knowledge is now so far removed from everyday, common-sense knowledge that only a common language can keep them in touch.

(Michael Halliday, 1986)

Great teachers are artists in presenting their views of the world to their students in the context of experiences and in moving them to think and feel deeply about their existence and their relationship to the world about them. They create in the media of language, mime, sound, and picture to effect a thoughtful response to the world in other persons. As artists, teachers must develop the crafts of their art.

Language is the prime vehicle of expression and thought transactions in the classroom. It is the medium for that "mental play" that should distinguish the school from the natural play of the street or the backyard. Teachers, Dewey said, need to be able to "keep track of this mental play, to recognize the signs of its presence or absence, and to know how it is initiated and maintained." (Dewey, 1964)

Teaching can be viewed logically as a "task word," and the action it describes is a "system" somewhat discrete from learning. To learn is seen as a "paralleling" and corresponding "achievement." (Smith, 1961)

Teaching and learning relate through dynamic transactions of language-thought, resulting in students' expanded achievement in knowing and teachers' extended knowledge of their art. This transaction (or as an existentialist would describe it, this "engagement") requires artful strategies of presenting. These include the teachers' logical organization of concepts around appropriate themes and their psychological reorganization for presentation to youngsters, the subtle framing of questions that will create dialogue, the careful preparation of resource materials, displays, and demonstrations to provoke questions and encourage self-study activities. Finally, teachers set means for evaluating not only accomplishments by students but also their own teaching effectiveness. These are the crafts of teaching, which, at their finest, create epiphanies, little revelations of life, for students and teachers alike.

As teachers plan to use these strategies in their teaching, they need to organize classroom curriculum and instruction within a framework of transactions based on the phases of knowing—perceiving, ideating, and presenting.

Developing a General Strategy
for Curriculum and Instruction

Many general strategies for instruction could be developed, each based on a particular view of the educative process. For example, one of the instructional strategies developed from Dewey's emphasis on "experiences" was Kilpatrick's "project method." When a personal knowing cycle of perceiving, ideating, and presenting is postulated, then there should be a similar cycle in the general teaching strategy for helping children to know; Thelen, Woodruff, Taba, and others have projected possible process cycles. (Thelen, 1963, pp. 19–31; Woodruff, 1964, pp. 81–99; Taba, 1962, ch. 17–19) The following discussion is freely adapted from their statements and incorporates additional ideas of the present authors.

Premise: A Transactional Theory of Education

A cycle of process can be built on a metatheory of transactions between individuals and their physical and social environment; the organism sends messages into the environment through feelings toward it and actions in it, many of which are conveyed by language. (Thelen, 1963, pp. 20–26) The environment sends back messages in the form of perceptions, which are then reorganized by the organism through assimilation and accommodation into ideations, and are then sent out again in new forms. The crucial factor is the reorganizing. If individuals merely react to their perceptions impulsively, little is learned; they simply shield themselves as best they can. If they react in terms of the socially accepted manners, they become conditioned to the environment but do not know anything more about it than they did before. They adjust and conform. But if they stop to inquire with an open-minded value-orientation and then to reorganize the new perceptions in relation to previous knowledge, involving their egos in coming to terms with novelty, then they are becoming educated.

The actual curriculum is the set of transactions between the teachers' planned curriculum interpreted through teaching and the students' personal responses of knowing to that teaching.

Main Pedagogical Strategies for Phases of Coming to Know

Perceiving Phase

Confronting   The attention of the learner is arrested by some novelty in the situation. Feelings are aroused; curiosity is engendered.

Students are confronted with new events, challenging questions, seemingly unusual occurrences that will cause bafflement and will stir speculation. Field trips, demonstrations, and audiovisual materials, as well as books or challenging questions, can be used to produce confrontation. Students are encouraged to meet the new event with all their senses open.

Heightening Awareness   If the new event is not rejected because of lack of concern or suppressed because it stirs anxious feelings, individuals will let their preconscious reactions emerge. They will permit vague ideas, memories, speculations, and feelings to be expressed to themselves. The mind wanders freely in and around the subject, sometimes holding an imaginary conversation with a friend or an opponent. It is called in popular parlance "mulling over an idea." The language belonging to the idea is expressed.

This process of allowing the imagination full play should be encouraged in the classroom through informal conversations and thinking out loud immediately after a confrontation. Students begin to get feedback from their peers that further stimulates their curiosity and thinking mechanisms. Time for each pupil to ruminate should be permitted if the classroom talks suggest that imagining is taking place.

Ideating Phase

Problem Finding   Learners begin to search their memories for principles or generalizations that might apply to the new event. They try out categories into which the new event might fit. Conflicting assumptions are brought to the fore as a problem, a question, or a hypothesis is developed. The goal of the search becomes clear.

Clarifying questions are raised by teachers as consideration of past experience is encouraged. Students present hunches regarding relationships to other ideas and hypotheses that might be tested.

Building Dialogue Between Personal Knowledge and Established Knowledge   Students are helped to become aware of alternatives and matters of value, truth, and justice as their personal views and ideas transact with those of educated adults who can interpret integrated and cumulative concepts from scholarship. Eternal questions are raised, and general principles are considered. The student's concepts are placed in dialogue with the common wisdom of humanity. The structure of the individual's knowing is placed in communication with the structures of the disciplines as a process of problem finding is further refined.

Teachers, by participating in class discussion, interject their interpretations of established knowledge at the point at which the students' concepts can be related to and extended by the universal concept. Books, films, and materials can be presented at the same time that the learners are gaining their own concepts from experience. Sometimes the process can be reversed by presenting the adult constructs first, followed by the students finding their own experiential support. The dialogue between personal and established knowledge needs to be interspersed with questions that will define the issues, locate the significant problems or questions, and lead to the mutual forming of objectives for the search and application of findings.

Problem Solving   After finding and describing particular situations in which the issues or questions are present in the perceptual world, a procedure is adopted for finding solutions. The givens are stated and the criteria for solutions are set up. The paths to solutions or processes to be used may involve trial and error, analogy, hypothesizing, or abductive, inductive and deductive reasoning. Concepts become realized as they are put to work in actual situations.

Questions are raised that will focus attention on defining and limiting problems. The teacher challenges the assumptions and helps students clarify the givens. Problem instances have to be chosen in which feedback can be readily perceived by students, more or less instantaneously. As relationships are discovered, tentative generalizations are drawn.

Presenting Phase

Demonstrating and Rehearsing   The concepts and generalizations gained from the instances in problem solving are encoded into language. The original issues are reorganized in light of the experimentation, and language means are used to show the new results. Individual findings are pooled, and concepts are reorganized as different views are considered. The final and composite concepts and generalizations of this investigation are stated in summary.

Students need opportunities to present their own reconstructed concepts in an appropriate manner. Writing down conclusions and summarizing the new ideas in oral or written reports with diagrams or pictograms for further illustration are encouraged. Group discussions and culminating activities, including creative dramatics, murals, videotaped programs, and panels are planned and executed by the children and teacher.

Assessing and Applying   New issues and questions are raised as a result of the study and are set down for future consideration. Projections into future similar situations are surmised as an application of newly learned ideas is attempted in slightly different contexts. Procedures are critically analyzed, and recommendations are made for the next study as objectives are reviewed and reconsidered.

An evaluating session should begin with a look back to the initial question and issues while the class criticizes its own procedures, noting what was effective and what was inefficient. The teacher posits other situations in different contexts that would involve similar concepts and generalizations. The learners apply their knowledge in the new situations. As they confront the new context, new questions arise because the old learnings do not quite fit the new situations. The cycle of perceiving, ideating, presenting, reperceiving is pressed to completion in the classroom by a corresponding cycle of instructional strategies: confronting, building dialogue, rehearsing in new contexts, and then back to new confrontations.

Curriculum-Making Process

The dual curriculum design we have proposed is most suitable for paralleling the knowing cycle; it involves a spiral, thematic curriculum in which designated "focusing ideas" (related concepts and generalizations) are explored in different contexts and at different levels of perception. Cognate increments (ideations) are proposed for developing, enriching, and extending concepts and generalizations, while more complex contexts are suggested for study. Thought-process goals are set with specifically designated intermediate levels that will encourage the cultivation of such scholarly processes of inquiry as classification, substantiation, verification, evaluation, and application. General teaching strategies appropriate to the selected contexts, to the chosen process goals, and to the general capabilities of an age group of learners are recommended. For example, the case-study method is especially appropriate for studying social interactions. Evaluated bibliographies of resource materials for the teacher and students are developed.

In formulating spiral, thematic curricula, scholars from appropriate disciplines, educators with input from the community, and pupil representatives work in concert to prepare generalized key themes of knowledge that interrelate; they then suggest contexts in which the themes can best be developed and describe the general educational goals they would meet. These thematic clusters and possible contexts can be disciplinary or interdisciplinary in nature; in terms of scope for any schoolwide curriculum, they must include themes from the sciences, social sciences, humanities, and literature. Consideration of broad educational goals to be met by study raises the questions of relevance to the lives of young people and of significance in terms of the social and intellectual goals of the local and larger community. Citizens and student representatives can be appropriately involved at the goal-making and theme-generating stage of curriculum development. A most appropriate theme, for example, for study in America's sprawling urban and industrialized megalopolises would be the impact of a technological invention like the computer on the people and their environment. Educational goals involved would include career and work orientation, socioeconomic efficiency, and application of the rational process to sociopolitical judgment questions.

The development and choice of themes and goals should be a constant and open inquiry, and school groups should have open options for both adapting curricular themes to their use and participating in the development of new themes and contexts. A model of open-ended curriculum development through widely representative studies in regions and communities is preferable to any government dictated scheme. The "focusing theme" basis for curriculum planning replaces the old "subject covering" method, which is inappropriate in this age of knowledge explosion.

Once public decisions have been made about the themes and goals, then the scholars, educational strategists, and representative practicing teachers prepare a series of sample curricula around the themes. They follow a process of (1) refining the themes, by defining the concepts involved and proposing the generalizations from interrelating the concepts; (2) proposing general instructional objectives in both expressive and/or activity terms as appropriate; (3) exploring through field-testing sites the feasibility of various instructional strategies and materials development; (4) recommending general instructional strategies and preparing field-tested resource materials and advisories on means for preparing teacher-made materials; and (5) proposing evaluating mechanisms for assessment of the potential ideational gains in both expressive and action terms where appropriate.

The cooperating scholars make certain that themes are based on valid premises and that they may be logically expanded according to modern scholarship. They also recommend contexts that have been previously studied and about which there is suffcient information. In social studies, the recommended context may be an early society or, in biology, a species of butterflies that is well known because scholars have gathered data and tested hypotheses. The scholar will also know whether a particular context can be practically studied in school settings. For example, the life-cycle of certain butterflies is very difficult to follow within a reasonable school schedule, whereas that of other species may be so studied. Scholars can also recommend appropriate types of investigation, such as the grid-mapping procedures followed in an archeological dig, whether it be in a town dump or an ancient ruin.

Education specialists working on a curriculum-planning team contribute the psychological decisions about general instructional strategies; they answer the questions of what levels of generalization children can comprehend at various stages and the questions of which contexts will be most involving for learners. Teachers recommend possible educational tactics that will most likely engage the pupils in study. They also propose the instructional objectives and the means by which progress toward them will be evaluated. Together, the educators, scholars, and teachers screen the literature and available audiovisual presentations for accuracy and for educational soundness. They can prepare several ideational structures and sample contexts in the form of resource studies. The concept of water use, for example, can be studied in the context of either suburban lawn watering or the agricultural output of the Sacramento Valley or the scarcity of water in the Arizona-Sonoran desert. The individual classroom teacher or team of teachers can decide which context or contexts will carry the most meaning for a particular group of students and in which context relationships will be most easily made manifest to them. The teacher, then, prepares the tactical instructional plans, including operational objectives and materials needed.

Sample Curricula Formed on Conceptual Schemes

Attempts have been made to develop curricula for social studies, science, and humanities based on focusing themes; such a method would structure the conceptual schemes that students need to derive in their own ways and in their own language.

Cognitive Schemes Interacting with Values Through Intellectual Processes

Brandwein, in his introduction to an elementary school curriculum, says that concepts are effective not only in ordering a curriculum but also in being the basis for student understanding. "Concepts isolate the common attributes of social behavior and social events. . . .Values permeate a curriculum based on concepts. For understanding is basic to valuing." The "methods of intelligence" used by social scientists are the process goals of a curriculum that attempts to develop conceptual and valuative thinking. (Brandwein, 1970, pp. 2–3)

The "cognitive schemes" of the curriculum for six levels of expansion and sophistication are built around five broad conceptual themes, each from a different discipline of the social sciences. (Center for the Study of Instruction, 1970)

1. People are the product of heredity and environment. (Anthropology)
2. Human behavior is shaped by the social environment. (Sociology)
3. The geographic features of the earth affect people's behavior. (Geography)
4. Economic behavior depends on the utilization of resources. (Economics)
5. Political organization resolves conflicts and makes interaction easier among people. (History, Government, Political Science)

Subsumed under the conceptual themes are six cognitive schemes of varying levels of expansion and sophistication, depending on age. Scheme A (Beginning Level) follows: (1) Individuals resemble each other; (2) members of the family group are alike because of heredity and environment; (3) community groups adapt to the environment; (4) people inherit and learn patterns of behavior; (5) interaction of biological and cultural inheritance results in the adaptation of people to their environment; and (6) biological and cultural inheritance result in variation in the people of the earth.

In another textbook series the content is also clustered around themes of related concepts; for example, one book is devoted to inquiry about cities. (Fielder, 1971). The recommended teaching plans are built around three operations used in dealing with data.

1. Data-gathering operations: observing, counting and quantifying, interviewing, and experimenting
2. Data-organizing operations: classifying, comparing-contrasting, mapping, modeling, graphing, and charting statistics
3. Data-using operations: inferring, deducing, generalizing, explaining, predicting, and hypothesizing

Pictures as well as text and questions are used in interesting ways for setting the stage for the operations. One section, for example, deals with "City as Art" and includes reproductions of paintings by such renowned artist-recorders of city life as Ben Shahn, Raphael Soyer, John Sloan, and Fernand Léger. Responses are then solicited.

Teacher Advisory Books

A group of Canadian educators has developed a series of teacher advisory books, each focusing on a topic of importance in teaching the social sciences and sciences in the elementary and middle grades. An instructional approach gives basic design to this curriculum built loosely around the general theme, "Examining Your Environment." Each concept scheme that is needed for understanding such topics as "Pollution," "Mini-climates," and "Mapping Small Places" is stated, and then the authors describe specific learning activities that will involve the learners in deriving the concepts and putting them to work. The activities include simple construction of instruments and other means for gathering and assessing data gained from the environment; the exercises are presented in sequences that deal with: (1) raising questions, (2) digging deeper, and (3) branching out. Given the essentials with regard to concept and sample instructional activities, teachers are expected "to take it from there," depending on their situations. The topics may be set into any large school system curricular design, but the advantage of this approach is the directness of these teacher manuals in giving functional advice without hamstringing the teacher into some particular format. (Wentworth, et al., 1971, 1972)

The instructional ideas are highly imaginative, while being practical and soundly based in modern science and social science concepts. In "Mapping Small Places," for example, the concept of contour mapping is presented and several activities for making such maps are demonstrated, beginning with the tracing of the edges of evaporating puddles on an uneven asphalt playground and leading to surveying hills and valleys.

Use of Focusing Ideas for Lifting Thinking

The social studies curriculum planned in Contra Costa County, California, under the guidance of the late Hilda Taba, is an example of a curriculum planned around focusing ideas. These are developed and extended with children through comparative studies of different types of social communities, modern and early, in contrasting settings: African jungles, the Swiss Alps, or a Chinese river. The ways of living, the customs, and the traditions of a regional community are the contexts in which such ideas as the following are developed:

> Some people make their own homes and secure their food and clothing from the immediate environment. Some people live a very simple life even though they may be part of an ancient civilization from which came many things we use today. Many activities of primitive people are carried on through the family and/or tribe; a more modern community provides for these activities through organized institutions. All people teach their children the things they think are important for them to learn. They teach them in different ways. (Taba 1962, pp. 373–374)

Taba selected basic concepts (for example, cultural change, interdependence, cooperation, differences, and causality) essential to understanding all sociocultural phenomena as the foundation for the program's ideation structure. They can be dealt with at different levels of complexity, abstraction, and generality, depending on the learner's level of life experience and thinking capabilities.

Interdependence can be studied at the primary school level in terms of relationships between community specialized workers and family members in terms of needs and services. Later it can be treated in terms of relationships between industries and government and between governments. The content to be studied can be selected in terms of opportunities to demonstrate the concepts at work, availability of materials, and connections (relevance) to the learners. Old curricula need not be discarded but merely revised by developing some aspects in greater depth and by abandoning less relevant, less thought-provoking parts. For example, old studies of South America can be revamped to focus on comparing and contrasting just two countries environmentally different but similar in racial and national backgrounds. When this comparative study is completed, two other countries could be selected that are opposite in setting and different in European national influences.

As teachers build such curricula in spirals based on increased sophistication of the "focusing ideas," they need to be concerned with the following criteria for selecting "main ideas":

> Validity: Do they adequately represent ideas of the discipline(s) from which they are drawn?
>
> Significance: Can they explain important segments of the world today?
>
> Appropriateness: Are they suited to needs, interests, and maturational levels of students?
>
> Durability: Are they of lasting importance?
>
> Balance: Do they permit development in both scope and depth? (Taba, 1967, pp. 13-26)

Specific facts change and eventually alter concepts and generalizations; therefore, it is more economical for teachers and learners to deal with concepts and generalizations provided that the teacher keeps abreast of conceptual changes through scholarship. At the second-grade level the concept of interdependence can be developed through the main idea that each worker provides a service someone else needs. The concept can deal with the gas station, the supermarket, or drugstore until those "factual" agencies disappear or become transformed into some other community reality, such as the shopping center.

The "learning experiences" suggested by Taba for implementing each "main idea" are divided into three main instructional episodes: an opener, a development, and a conclusion. In the opener, students are confronted in a dramatic way with a novel situation and new ideas or arrangement of ideas. In the development stage episodes focus around several means for "lifting the levels of thinking" about the idea from factual listing through classifying, categorizing, and labeling to inferring, hypothesizing, and generalizing. The last stage, conclusion, deals with generalizing and applying or testing the generalizations in new but similar situations (comparative study).

Generalized Themes Illustrated in Contexts

In order for children to form generalizations, they must understand certain concepts. Grannis feels that the teacher must be secure in a full understanding of the concepts and the interrelationships that make the generalizations manifest in the context. For example, in a study of the Navaho people the following generalizations and concepts need to be clear:

Generalization: people, animals, plants—all living things need water
Concepts: People, animals, plants, life, need, water, scarcity

If children do not have a fairly complete concept of what constitutes life or the sustenance of life, then they will have difficulty in drawing the proper conclusions. In the context of Navaho life, facts become pertinent for developing the generalization. Navahos live apart partly because water and vegetation are scarce. In winter they may melt snow for their sheep to drink and they save water by using a sweathouse for cleansing their bodies.

The chart below shows the breakdown of the above generalization into its conceptual parts and combinations of subgeneralizations, including the applications in the context of Navaho life. For completing the curriculum design, further charts are developed in which each generalization states as a hypothesis is explored in terms of suggested learning activities for the teacher to set up, major questions that need to be asked and answered, the work and study skills that need to be used and refined, actual activities for evaluation, the equipment and materials needed, and the printed references for teachers and learners.

In strategic long-range planning and tactical daily planning of classroom activity, the teachers need to have well in mind the concepts and generalizations derived from the structure of the pertinent disciplines. They need also to choose contexts for study in which these concepts and generalizations will clearly apply. The chose context should have the potential for relating to the student's personal experience. If the selected context is one with which the student is not acquainted, then ample concrete data must be made available. It should be an interesting context to explore, so that students can transpose and extend ideas from their own situation. For example, refer to the generalizations applied to the context of Navaho life in Table 15.1.

Mankind's Development: A Focus for Study

An interesting social science curriculum plan for the grades has been prepared by the Education Development Center under the guidance of Jerome Bruner, entitled "Man—A Course of Study." (Bruner, 1965) The underlying thematic questions of the course are: What is human about human beings? How did they get that way? How can they be made more so?

The concept themes for the study are instinctual and social learning in animals and the five great humanizing forces: toolmaking, language, social organization, the management of our prolonged childhood, and our urge to explain our world. (Bruner, pp. 74, 75). These are studied in the contexts of salmon-herring-gull life-cycles, babboon troops, the Netsitik Eskimos and their life in land, camp, and on the sea ice.

The main pedagogical strategies are the juxtaposing of contexts to encourage classifying and categorizing processes; the stimulation and use of informed guessing, hypothesis making, and conjectural procedures; and the "use of games that

TABLE 15.1 Breakdown of a Sample Generalization Into Conceptual Parts, Subgeneralizations, and Applications

CONCEPTS	People	Animals	Plants	Life	Need	Water	Scarcity
People	Makers of speech, tools, and art.	Navahos herd sheep and goats.	Navahos grow corn.	Navaho life is relatively hard.	Navahos may have less food than is needed for survival.	Navahos save water by use of sweathouses.	Navahos separate households where water and grass are scarce.
Animals	People domesticate animals.	Life, movement, and feeling.	Sheep eat grass.	Sheep may die of hunger.	Sheep's wool protects from weather.	Navahos melt snow for sheep to drink in winter.	There is not much game to hunt in the Navaho nation.
Plants	People cultivate plants.	Animals depend on plants.	Life, not movement or feeling.	Plants living on Navaho land are very different from those in other places.	Corn needs at least a 90-day growing season.	Absence of leaves on cactus slows loss of water.	Ground cover is thinner in the Navaho nation.
Life	Life may be very hard or easy.	The life of animals is in continual danger.	Plants live by adjustment to environment.	Birth, growth, and death.	The Navahos and the sheep have some needs in common.	In the Navaho nation there is different water life, dry streams, etc.	Navahos regulate the use of scarce resources like grass and wood.

Need	People need food, water, and shelter.	Animals need protection from weather extremes.	Some plants need a long growing season.	All living things function to fulfill basic needs.	For well-being, survival, and functioning.	Water is needed in making some wool products.	Navahos need fewer furnishings, etc. for their way of life.
Water	People need water and conserve it.	Animals need water to drink.	Plants conserve water.	Much life occurs in bodies of water.	Water is needed in many simple and complex industries.	Snow, rain, washes, river, etc.	There is little rainfall on high Navaho land. The land is desert.
Scarcity	Fewer people live where basic resources are scarce.	Where water and plant life are scarce, there are relatively few wild animals.	There are fewer plants where water is scarce.	People can increase the amount of life where resources are scarce.	People acquire fewer needs where resources are scarce.	Water is scarce in some regions.	Not many, not plentiful.

incorporate the formal properties of the phenomenon for which the game is an analogue."

The master units include statements of the ideas to be developed, the contextual contrasts that will provoke queries, and devices that have the quality of puzzles. Highly artistic and dramatic film loops have been prepared of the contrasting situations with the intention of "asking questions and posing riddles." One unusual feature of the plan is the supplying of documentary videotapes showing teachers with groups of children working through the educational problems of the unit. (Bruner, pp. 92, 98, 100.)

Assessment

Unique among many published curricula (both in text and in "packaged" forms of related readings, film strips, and manipulative materials), "Man—A Course of Study" has been evaluated quite extensively. The evaluation pattern is one that can be applied to assess the impact of substantive textbooks or teacher-made curricula if their aims are similar to those of this course. The evaluation was built upon implementation of the seven instrumental or pedagogical aims of the course and five questions about the implementation. (Education Development Center, 1970) The aims and questions are prototypic of modern substantive curricula and can serve as a basis for evaluating curricular programs that strive for the expansion of language and thinking in school.

The pedagogical aims are actually process goals:

1. To initiate and develop in youngsters a process of question posing (the inquiry method)
2. To teach a research methodology where children can look for information to answer questions they have raised and use the framework developed in the course (for example, the concept of life cycle) and apply it to new areas
3. To help youngsters develop the ability to use a variety of first-hand sources as evidence from which to develop hypotheses and draw conclusions
4. To conduct classroom discussions in which youngsters learn to listen to others as well as to express their own views
5. To legitimize the search; that is, to give sanction and support to open-ended discussions where definitive answers to many questions are not found[1]
6. To encourage children to reflect on their own experiences
7. To create a new role for the teacher, who becomes a resource rather than an authority. (Education Development Center, p. 5)

The evaluation questions deal with pupil gains in soundly based knowledge on the specific topics and the ability to go beyond the knowledge and apply it. They also focus on any changes teachers may have made in their teaching styles and on ways the course has impacted on youngsters of differing backgrounds and abilities. The mechanisms for gathering assessment data include child and teacher interview guides, classroom environment checklists, creative writing production, and content questionnaires that pose situations similar to those studied.

[1]It is this aspect of the "Man–A Course of Study" curricuium that seems to have generated opposition to the program among fundamentalists.. They find the concept of deailng with central questions of human existence without absolute right answers a disturbing one.

The Future: A Focus for Study

Since the appearance of Alvin Toffler's provocative book *Future Shock* (1970), many educators have stressed the need to prepare curricula with a futuristic orientation. (Toffler, 1974; Shane, 1973)

The argument for such programs emphasizes the need for education to keep pace with the tumultuous social, political, and economic changes of this current era of technological revolution, not to mention the need for education to absorb the knowledge explosion by some means. Even educated people today can merely react to events as they pass by; they are not prepared to cope with them, much less mold them. Schools have until now educated children in the experience and knowledge of the past with reference to present human situations and predicaments. Preparation for the future, even though it is unpredictable, can be accomplished by educating youngsters to look for alternatives, consider them, and practice making judgments about them; such findings must be based on a humane value system and upon as sound a prognostication of the future as can be seen through present trends and historical patterns of human reactions to events. History can become a basic study for future living if it is used as a study of both our actions in various described situations and the alternatives that might have been taken. Crises such as those in energy, political trust, and pollution can be studied in terms of their causes, the means to meet them, and alternative actions to avoid them in the future. Value decisions can be analyzed as to rationale and effects upon all segments of society and upon the environment. The automobile may or may not be a technological system of the future, but study of that system's impact on the mores, economics, and value orientations of different cultures across the world and upon various environments can be valuable; such work can prepare youngsters to meet the impact of tomorrow's technological systems and to deal with them more intelligently than does the present generation. It is also possible that wiser decisions will be made as new conditions arise in the world and that people can learn to shape the forces released by fast-changing conditions.

Curricula based on such themes require a reflective mode of study and an action form of instruction, with teachers and students learning together as they prepare to take actions that will, if only in small ways, have impact upon changing events.

Relating Curricula to Stages of Educational Development

Many of the British curriculum projects developed by the Schools Council in its extensive program of teacher-oriented curriculum development were based on the stages of child thought and language development proposed by Piaget and his colleagues. At the least they offer suggested instructional activities that suit the various conceptual and thought-process stages of youngsters. Rooted in the belief that teachers make the ultimate decisions regarding their classroom curriculum, regardless of established texts, materials, or packaged plans, the Schools Council teacher-dominated Governing Board set the general format for their projects in terms of curriculum guides for teachers.

The project teams are generally composed of experts in the particular fields of study, educational psychologists and evaluators, and a majority of classroom teachers. As they propose objectives and learning processes, they also suggest many tried and tested instructional activities for use with young people at various stages of educational development, and provide economical materials and resources and/or recommended ways for making suitable materials. Each program is served by an evaluator who makes certain from the beginning of the project that evaluation and assessment procedures are used and then are made available to teachers. The resulting programs of many interrelated instruction units are disseminated through the local education authorities and the teachers' centers. School faculties with their "head" teacher, which are quite autonomous in Britain, may choose to adapt the program to their local setting or disregard it for another program or for a program of their own. Sometimes interesting local curriculum programs are considered for national development by the Schools Council. (Schools Council, 1970) For example, faculties can develop their own set of work or activity cards and accompanying packages of reading and pictured materials. Teachers become the curriculum innovators in a real sense.

For the Science 5–13 curriculum the Schools Council Project Team developed over 20 units for teachers for the different levels of educational development. (Schools Council, 1971–1973) A sample of the topics gives an idea of the range and imagination incorporated into these units: Minibeasts," "Working with Wood," "Children and Plastics," "Coloured Things," "Science from Toys," "Holes, Gaps, and Cavities," and so on. Also, for the teacher there are background publications such as *With Objectives in Mind, Evaluation and Science 5–15,* and *Investigations.*

Forming Objectives

A useful chart of objectives is developed by taking each broad aim that deals with an aspect of the scientific process and subsuming the appropriate learning objectives for each stage of thought development. For example, under the broad aim of "Posing questions and devising experiments or investigations to answer them," the following sample educational objectives are subsumed: For the intuitive stage, "Make comparisons in terms of one property or variable"; for the stage of concrete operations, "Select a suitable degree of approximation and work to it"; for the abstract thinking stage, "Visualize a hypothetical situation . . . construct scale models for investigation. (p. 78)

Evaluation

With objectives like these in mind, evaluation strategies were developed that not only assess learner outcomes but also look at influences on the learning environment and on ways teachers perform. Some achievement testing was done in the form of film loops of an incomplete science manipulative demonstration with follow-up questions. Instrumented Teacher Style Preference Forms and Diagnostic Record Sheets of actual learner responses to materials were developed and used.

Scheduled visitor observations and interviews with teachers and learners were devised to check written data and to add information to the evaluation system.

Teachers can adapt some of this evaluation methodology to aid them in assessing the effectiveness of their studies with children in terms of concept development and use of inquiry processes. Piaget-type interviewing of individuals or small groups of learners is an effective means for sampling the concepts and generalized learning of students who are trying to meet expressive objectives in a substantive curriculum area. The interviewer-teacher sets up a manipulatory situation with pertinent objects and then asks learners to do the task and explain what they are doing and why. For example, after instructing children in the attraction capabilities of magnets the teacher can present learners with a box of materials similar but not exactly the same as those used in instruction. Children are asked to hypothesize about the attraction and give reasons for it.

References

Paul Brandwein, *Notes on Teaching the Social Sciences: Concepts and Values* (New York: Harcourt, Brace, Jovanovich 1970).

Mary Brown and Norman Precious, *The Integrated Day in the Primary School* (London: Ward Lock, 1968).

Jerome Bruner, *Toward a Theory of Instruction* (Cambridge, MA: Harvard University Press, 1965).

Center for the Study of Instruction, *The Social Sciences: Concepts and Values* (New York: Harcourt, Brace, Jovanovich, 1970).

John Dewey, *The Relation of Theory to Practice in Education* (republished in 1964 by Association for Student Teaching, Washington, D.C.).

Education Development Center, "Man–A Course of Study: An Evaluation and Evaluation Strategies" (Cambridge, MA: Education Development Center, 1970); D. Whitla, J. Hanley, E. Moo, and A. Walter, evaluators.

W. Fielder (Ed.), *Teachers Guide, Inquiry about Cities* (New York: Holt, Rinehart and Winston, 1971).

"Language Across the Culture," in *Language in Learning,* Makhan Tickoo (Ed.) (Singapore: SEAMEO Regional Language Centre, 1986).

Schools Council Publications, London 165 Great Portland St., 1970.

Schools Council, *Science 5-13,* Len Ennever. (Director) (London: Macdonald Ltd., 1971–1973).

Harold Shane, *The Educational Significance of the Future* (Bloomington, IN: Phi Delta Kappa Educational Foundation, 1973).

B. Othanel Smith, "A Concept of Teaching," in B. O. Smith and R. H. Ennis (Eds.), *Language and Concepts in Education* (Skokie, IL: Rand McNally, 1961).

Hilda Taba, *Curriculum Development* (New York: Harcourt, Brace, Jovanovich, 1962).

————, *Teachers' Handbook for Elementary Social Studies* (Palo Alto, CA: Addison-Wesley, 1967).

Herbert Thelen, "Insight for Teaching from a Theory of Interaction," in *The Nature of Teaching* (Milwaukee, WI: University of Wisconsin-Milwaukee, 1963).

Alvin Toffler, *Future Shock* (New York: Random House, 1970).

Alvin Toffler (Ed.), *Learning for Tomorrow* (New York: Vintage Books, 1974).

D. F. Wentworth, J. K. Couchman, J. C. MacBean, and A. Stecher, *Examining Your Environment,* published by Holt, Rinehart and Winston of Canada, and in the United States by Winston Press, Minneapolis, MN.: individual Titles: *Mini-climates* (1971), *Pollution* (1971), and *Mapping Small Place*r (1972).

Asahel Woodruff, "The Use of Concepts in Teaching and Learning," *Journal of Teacher Education,* vol. 15, no. 1 (March 1964), pp. 81–99.

16

Teaching: Tactics and Strategies

The cognitive need is as commanding and constraining, and at times as fulfilling, as any realization of the more primitive organic needs. . . . Does this mean that the teacher simply responds to all which simply stirs response in the child? I think not. It means, rather, that the interpersonal relations of teacher and pupil, and the pupil's potential response to the reality waiting to be discovered, are two aspects of one learning process. . . . The clarifying merges into the electrifying.

(Murphy, 1961)

Devising Pedagogical Tactics

Teachers need to organize their own ideation ahead of classroom presentation through participating in curriculum development and through their own preplanning of resource study units. They then collect or prepare the materials for instruction: books, articles, pictures, filmstrips, films, maps, diagrams, informational scripts, simple bibliographies, guides, and manuals for groups and individual study, and so on. However, once they meet a particular group of students, they must revise the tactics of instruction. Examples will follow.

Teacher-made Curricula

Teachers working by themselves or preferably in teams can develop their own local curricula with some assistance from appropriate consultants. One of the best ways to begin is to collect a cluster of children's books at various reading levels around a topic and build a long-range plan from the ideas developed in those books. For example, there is an attractive series on careers called *The You Can Work Books*. (Deitz, 1970) These and other books on the same topic could become the basic materials for a local career-education curriculum in the middle grades. There are many children's books available on the theme of "building your own thing." These books include many involving activities that teachers can adapt for instruction. Certainly one of the main roles of a teacher is the making of the curriculum; if teachers are to be accountable with other school personnel for the accomplishments and achievements of learners, they need to know how to build curricula and devise the operational plans to implement them.

There is no single cycle of generalizations and concepts, nor one set of thought process goals, nor any particular contexts that would make the ideal curriculum in any of the content areas or in a combination of them. The spiral-curriculum concept depends on the imagination and ingenuity of the school, university faculties, and specialists assigned to the curriculum-making task. They can select viable themes and prethink the ideation and suggest instructional strategies with materials. However, teachers and pupils are the actual curriculum makers in the classroom, and they need to be involved in the curriculum process at all stages. Resource studies can be composed in a variety of formats, but they will not upgrade the intellectual component of thematic units unless their composers tackle the development of ideation in some disciplined form. Organizing ideation for teaching is a laborious task, but the rewards for doing it are high. When teachers involve themselves in formulating curriculum, they advance their own learning and also gain intellectual excitement about what they will teach and how they will teach it.

Concept Survey Tactic

First, teachers need to take an immediate check on the level and character of their pupils' ideation about the planned subject of study. They can check the class for their conceptual sophistication by making a concept survey of the class. This can be done by individual and group interviews and discussions. The following example of a group interview is from a low fourth-grade situation.[1]

This was done in preparation for a study of prejudice against a white minority. Contemporary life in one of the European countries from which many immigrants came to the United States was to be the context of the study. This immigrant group is making its way in the American system, but they still find prejudice against them.

Question:	Where did the people come from who live in this country?
Children's Answers:	People came from different countries, all over the world. Some from France, Italy, Germany, and lots of other places. Some people came from uncharted islands, from Italy, and most came from the East and the Indians lived here first.
Question:	Where is Italy?
Children's Answers:	It's in the United States. It's not in the United States. It's far from here. It's in the eastern part of our country. Part in Africa, from the other side of the world.
Question:	Do the people who came to this country from another country live the same way here as they did in the old country?
Children's Answers:	No, in the old country they might have a well, while here we have water faucets. No, because in the other place, women wear long dresses and there is no television, no cars; they use horses. I don't think so because I don't think any other countries have to make their own stuff but when they are here they buy the stuff. They don't have stores like we do, and when they come here they go shopping and buy things instead of making them. Their food is different than ours because we have many things in cans and they make theirs a different way. They wouldn't be used to our writing because they have different writing than ours, They have different money than ours.

[1] Haig Derderian, collected as part of a master's thesis, Wayne State University, Detroit, Michigan, 1967, Adapted version.

Question:	What kind of people are the Italians?
Children's Answers:	People who like spicy foods and they dress in different costumes and they are not free. They like to do things old-fashioned. They don't like to be called "dagos" and they make good bread. Italians just wouldn't understand us because we do a lot of things that they don't, such as we eat different foods, dress differently, live in different kinds of houses. Sometimes they got different names. They have an Italian look on their faces, sorta dark faces. Most of them don't have automobiles, they have donkeys and carts and things like that, and cars are different. They like to eat spaghetti and pizza.
Question:	Do they speak the same way as Americans who have been here a long time?
Children's Answers:	No, because they have a real accent when they talk. If they just got here they wouldn't because they have to learn English. They could learn English and sometimes they talk Italian but not all the time. If they are together in a family they talk Italian when they get together.
Question:	What kinds of jobs do they look for when they get here?
Children's Answers:	A bakery. Fixing cars. It depends which job they want. Work for a steel company. Work in a pizza place. They work at restaurants, but they cook and serve.

With this kind of data on the students' preconceptions, the teachers are able to build classroom plans for developing ideation from where the students are in concept development rather than from where they vaguely thought they might be. Teachers know that they must correct some misconceptions and clarify vagueness before they can begin building the planned concepts and attitudes.

The Discovery Tactic

Once teachers have made judgments about the level and nature of the students' thinking and have made some operational plans, they will then want to use tactics that will encourage students to discover new concepts and generalizations or to extend those they already know.

Appropriate variations of those processes used by the scholars in the related disciplines should be considered. Taba says the act of discovery occurs

> at the point in the learner's efforts at which he gets hold of the organizing princi
> ple imbedded in any concrete instance, can see the relationship of facts before
> him, understands the why of the phenomenon, and can relate what he sees to his
> previous knowledge. (Taba, 1961)

Children will discover the concepts and the generalizations in the instances of the context by inductively deriving them from a series of instances or by deductively making a hypothesis and looking for working examples of it. For example, a fourth-grade class studying the mobility of families in their community devised a sociological kind of questionnaire and interview that the children used in house-to-house canvassing. They found the rate of families moving in and out of the community, the general class of employment of the parents, and the reasons for the moves. From their data they generalized that theirs was a "bedroom" community that was transient, since the parents moved upward in job placement in national businesses. The class made a film that showed the typical housing in the community and the method of their interviewing. The discoveries came as they put their data together and began to reflect upon the results.

Discoveries are made as students find clues while observing and manipulating particular materials placed in the environment by the teacher. The discovery tactic is actually a holding tactic on the part of the teachers. The teachers set the stage for the discovery but refrain from demonstrating the discovery themselves.

"Lifting of Thinking" Tactics

The chief instructional tactic for developing concept formation and generalizing in the Taba program is the lifting of thinking by moving learners from the level of information gathering and categorizing through explaining phenomena to generalizing about it. (Taba, 1967)

The process is started by encouraging learners to develop categories and category clusters under differing themes through a process of comparing and contrasting in at least two different socioenvironmental situations. As an opener the teacher presents an open-ended question that leads the youngsters to list and enumerate what they have observed or previously known through a process of differentiating one event or fact from another. For example, in a study of "wood products" the teacher might display a table, a breadboard, a block of fire starter, a newspaper, a pressed-wood block, charcoal, a toothbrush, an Indian woven basket, and a nylon stocking; the teacher would then ask the youngsters to submit their hunches on a slip of paper as to which objects are wood products and which are not by placing them in a slotted box. These hunches would be tallied and presented to the class, leaving the disagreements unresolved at that moment. Then the teacher would ask the group to list on the board or on big sheets of paper everything they can think of regarding "wood." All responses are accepted.

Next, in a development part of the teacher's plan, the question of "what belongs together" is raised as learners group the items by identifying common relationships. They categorize by finding and labeling superordinates and then deciding what belongs under what. In the "wood" example many categories might emerge to be labeled, such as soft woods, hard woods, wood processing, woodworking tools, old uses of wood, new uses, and so on.

Another part of the lifting of thinking strategy is the interpretation of data. Again, a differentiating process is employed as students identify the main points of what they observed, collected, and categorized. The differentiating begins when items are found in two or three categories and the question "Why?" is asked. Then students have to debate rationales and make decisions about relabeling classes and then seeing what other items would fit in the new category. Some questions would certainly arise in the wood episode about why wood was used differently in olden times. Why are some items that were made of wood in olden times or in other cultures not made of wood now? The question of "Why did these things happen?" is asked to encourage the relating of one point to another and raise the issue of cause and effect in an explaining activity.

The mental processes of extrapolating and making implications help teachers and students make inferences that can then be developed into hypotheses to be tested and problems to be solved by asking the question: "What might happen if _____?" In the wood study the following problem question might emerge: "What would happen if there were a great blight and most of the world's fir trees died?"

The concluding stage is the application of principles by finding support for predictions and hypotheses, and finding causal links through asking the question, "Why do you think this would happen?" An example of an application question about wood could be: "Given the facts of the reforestation cycle of soft woods and hard woods and modern needs for wood, what would you advise legislators in heavily forested states to recommend for laws governing the exploitation of forests?"

Finally, there is a verification activity that asks the question: "What would it take to make this proposition probably or generally true?" Sufficient conditions would need to be found. For instance, is it generally true that all wood products burn at a certain degree of heat? The lifting of thinking is advanced mainly through asking the key questions at the crucial points in the study or picking up cues from the students that will advance the thinking. In a class discussion about forests and the use modern people make of wood products, a teacher tried to deepen the reiteration of numbers of wood products by posting the following question, "If you were cavemen and you lived in forest land, what good would the trees be to you?" The responses came quickly, "wood for fires, branches for lean-tos, sticks for digging," and so on. Then the teacher asked, "Does that suggest anything that we use wood for today?" The comparisons were being made when one child interrupted, "but the cavemen didn't have education," and a whole new level of thinking was generated that could take the group into the effects of formalized education on tool making, shelter construction, and so on. New inferences could be made and tested, and so the thinking process would be continually expanded as it was lifted.

Picture-Card Sequences

One of the most convenient tactics for initiating the lifting of thinking is the device of picture-card sequences. Although there are commercial sets prepared around various topics such as urban life and rural life, pictures can be collected, pasted on index cards or larger pieces of cardboard, and laminated so that children may handle them as frequently as they would playing cards. Large pictures in portfolios can be used as the focus for small and large group discussions that take off from the interpretations of what various members see in the pictures. The discussions can lead to value clarification and to problem finding for social science studies. They can also be used for pretesting conceptual levels about a particular topic. In any event, the pictures need to be provoking in the sense that they reveal incidents that have ambiguities in them which allow for raising questions and making inferences. For example, in the picture series *People in Action* (Shaftel and Shaftel, 1970, p. 2), there is a picture that shows three children on the steps of a public library in San Francisco. One of them is holding a torn book, and they all look worried as they peer through the large library window at the reflection of a busy adult. All sorts of responses can emerge if the teacher is accepting of everyone,s comment about what is happening. A questioning sequence is advised following the encouragement by the teacher for the children to act out the situation. What do you think will happen now? Are there other ways to solve the problem? How would you decide? What do you think would really happen? The teacher moves from soliciting facts to having the students suggest inferences and then make value judgments as they explore the incident together through role playing and the sharing of feelings.

Through such pictured episodes youngsters are provided with opportunities to talk with a sympathetic adult, to share responses with their peers about universal problems, to explore alternative solutions, and to build better selfimages. Racial and cultural differences can be faced and talked about. Substantive questions may also be treated. This library picture can lead learners into questions about the need for public institutions, such as libraries, and citizen responsibilities toward them. The library as a service institution can make a fascinating study.

Small picture-card sequences provide another approach to the lifting of thinking. They are sequenced in broad and then narrowing categories with an ambiguous, contrasting, or wild card thrown in here and there. For example, a curriculum consultant[2] developed several sets of picturecard sequences around the themes of "artifacts," "environments," and "animals." The artifacts sequence was subcategorized into art objects and manufactured products. Some interesting and useful cards were pictures of barbed wire that looked like modern objective art, of dated coins, of a Victorian grandfather clock, and of a frieze of an Egyptian pharaoh's household at work. Already it is obvious how much interplay of ideas could be generated by involving children with this set of picture-cards. They can be used in several ways, depending on the teacher's objectives, by posing different task questions. For example, the teacher can ask students to sequence them according to the oldest and the newest. Questions of why they place a card here or there inevitably result in important discussions that involve evidence and good or bad hunches. Another fruitful question could be "Pick out those that have similarities." In one instance, students picked all the artifacts that had wheels, including wheels used as gears. The resultant discussion about gears added insights for the students and the teacher. The gear, of course, is a beautiful tool extension of the wheel.

Picture-card sequences can be used in the opening confrontation state of a learning episode, but they can be used as well in developing the dialogue of ideas, such as investigating the invention of barbed wire and then deciding where it fits in an historical sequence. In some instances, it could be used for testing a student's

[2]Richard Snell, Macomb Intermediate School District, Michigan.

understanding of concepts. Can he or she file the artifact pictures in an historical sequence and give a rationale for doing so? Certainly this performance objective would help reveal a student's comprehension of generalizations about the evolution of tools, machines, and technological systems in history.

The Game Tactic to Encourage Ideas in Dialogues

The teacher's classroom tactics need to be in tune with the "knowing cycle," and they must support the general strategy planned in the curriculum recommendations. For example, the teacher is responsible for making sure that the concepts are clear. The fifth-grade theme in a social studies curriculum was "Our attempts to cope with our world led to our ventures of the spirit." One of the contexts for this study was the travels of Marco Polo. An essential concept to be developed was "trade." One of the teachers found that her group of children were very vague about this term. They certainly had heard it, but they did not seem to be sufficiently aware of its ramifications. The following account describes one teacher's tactics for building meanings of the concept "trade."[3]

> One day I brought a cardboard box with candy to school and carefully kept it high so that the children could not see what it contained. I said that we were going to play. Everyone had eight M and M's of different colors with the hope that some might prefer ones of all the same color and trade accordingly. Some had one or two chocolate squares, two had two-inch paper-covered chocolate Easter eggs, which, I felt, would be the most desired objects and of most value to the children. A few had Life Savers of different colors and three had lollipops. Of the thirteen children in the study group, everyone had at least three types of candy.
>
> I split the group in half. The number-one rule was everyone had to trade, and the number-two rule was that before the candy could be eaten a problem met while trading had to be presented to me. Then for five minutes everyone traded seriously, naturally, and eagerly.
>
> They took their seats after five minutes and we spent the remaining part of the period discussing the problems they had met in trading. In only two cases were the problems entirely similar ones. Their answers:
>
> 1. People may not like the goods you are selling; therefore you have a hard time getting rid of your goods and sometimes don't get as much for them as you feel they are worth. This led into a discussion of the fact that when there was a demand for a certain product its price went way up. The child who ran into this problem had wanted a chocolate egg and had found that all her goods were not enough to buy it. The chocolate eggs were a perfect example to prove this fact.
> 2. Dirty goods are not as desirable as clean ones. One boy with dirty hands had been holding his candy and it had begun to melt. He had a hard time selling his goods for this reason.
> 3. The seller is disagreeable and won't reach an agreement that you are willing to go along with.

[3]Ann Crile, "Trading as a Concept," mimeographed material, Wayne State University, Detroit, Michigan.

4. No one wants to buy your goods. In this case the boy was not able to sell any of his goods. The class suggested the reason for this was perhaps the fact that he was not a good salesman. This led into the idea that a good salesman might sell goods for more than they were worth.
5. Exchange of goods of different value: One thing is worth more than another so that perhaps you have to sell eight little things to get one big thing. In this case, the boy had traded eight M and M's and two chocolate squares for one chocolate Easter egg.
6. If a seller has poor quality goods then you don't want to buy. Someone felt that because the other person's lollipop was broken it wasn't good. This brought up the idea of whether that person should have sold his lollipop for less or not. It was decided in the case of the lollipop that the value of it had not really been changed by the crack.
7. Some people put different value than others on different goods. This question of the problems connected with the value seemed to make the biggest impression on the group as a whole. One girl loved the cinnamon Life Savers and was willing to trade two chocolate squares for one Life Saver. She ended up with just Life Savers. Someone suggested that if certain goods are not highly valued (the M and M's because they were so common) then their price goes down, and if they are valued their price is high. The idea that value is relative to the goods and to the need for the goods was clearly established.
8. How can you decide what the equal worth of different types of goods is? After quite a lengthy discussion the children decided this was a question of judgment between seller and buyer. Most of them had trouble in pricing their goods and all gained a real appreciation of the difficulty in putting a set price to one's goods. Whether three M and M's were worth one Life Saver or two they finally discovered varied with the value the seller or buyer put on his goods.

The game tactic is only one of many that teachers can use to clarify concepts and generate reasoning. Detective games can be arranged by placing clues in a classroom environment in such a way that a search is begun. One teacher set up a mock camping site in her classroom that included clues as to how some campers might have upset nature's cycles by leaving the site somewhat despoiled. Another teacher took his class to an old cellar hole to make some guesses about how the people had lived from assessing the artifacts found in and near the cellar. Many imaginative simulation games have been commercially prepared. However, they are particularly effective when the teacher and groups of students develop their own games to be played by fellow students. Games that veer too far away from life situations may replace intrinsic concept reinforcement with an extrinsic goal of winning.

Open-Inquiry Education: Fostering Personal Knowing in School

The general concept of open-inquiry education (Silberman, 1973) incorporates such ideas as child-centered learning, individualized and self-directed instruction, team or paired learning activity, and discovery learning that encourage students in their inevitable and constant search for meaning in their environment through the manipulation of materials and confrontation with real experience. Although the movement for open-inquiry education has roots in the "life-experiencing activity" programs of the progressive period, it was given new impetus by educational application of the findings ofJean Piaget and his colleagues in their vast studies of children's thinking and valuing, or developmental epistemology as Piaget terms it. Indirect approaches to teaching and learning have been explored extensively by teachers who have been developing the instructional techniques for advancing open-inquiry education. Materials and resources have to be prepared and organized for independent study by children with the guidance of teachers. Convenient resource and study areas are designated for use by individuals and teams of learners to support the open-inquiry approach.

The British Experience in Child-Centered Education

Models for open-inquiry education are well advanced in Britain, and adaptations of them have been made possible in other cultural settings. Although the open-inquiry approach is most evident in the infant and primary school (nursery school through sixth grade), there are programs under way in many junior and secondary schools that continue the approach through adaptations. Even the older buildings have been found adaptable to a more open organization and to team work since many have an assembly area with classrooms opening on to it that can be used for a common resource and study center.

British youngsters do exhibit some different cultural traits from those of American children, but the similarities between the English-speaking children of England and North America are very evident.

Earmarks of the Open-Inquiry Approach in British Primary Schools

The following earmarks are presented to suggest adaptations that teachers can make in their school settings that will foster open-inquiry by attempting to meet the youngsters' personal thinking and language systems head-on and by developing instructional means for extending and enriching thought and language in school.

A mixture of informal and formal teaching is an outgrowth of the British pragmatic sense of a need for mixing idealogies in real life.

The formal part may be scheduled by the teacher or scheduled in time blocks by the head teachers. These periods are mainly set aside for practice in language and mathematics. The time allotted to these formal periods is never more than one-third of the total day. Individualized and small-group work prevails even in these formal periods. Another formal characteristic is the unwritten assumption that every child, every day will do some reading and some writing (composition and this work will be evaluated by the teacher. The daily writing, and usually the math, are done in an "exercise book," a special notebook that children have used in England for many years. The content of the writing in the new programs is likely to be creative or applied to some project in which the child is involved.

The informal part of the day's schedule and of the teaching and learning activities occupies about two-thirds of the time. These activities may occur in a room with a teacher or in a section of a school involving a team of two to four teachers, sometimes with a helper. If the program is room-organized, there will be several learning centers with teacher-made and commercial materials. If it is a school organization, these learning centers will be in different rooms with one of the generalist teachers of the formal periods serving as a specialist teacher in the informal part of the program. Resources and materials around certain content areas are available in these rooms and in the general assembly area outside the rooms. Some schools combine these organizational patterns in their own ways depending on the talents and "likes" of its staff. In all cases the staff, with the head, behave as a team and share responsibilities for maintaining materials and resources in the various content areas as well as for serving as resource consultants to the other teachers. Sometimes the whole staff or several members are using Schools Council or other nationally developed programs. All rooms are full of books, other printed matter, and manipulative materials. They are stored and catalogued for the convenience of the child workers. Teachers use everything for storing from cartons to cheap see-through plastic boxes.

The chief curriculum posture taken by the staff—remembering that the school head and staff are quite autonomous—is that studies for children must be relevant and interdisciplinary. By "relevant," as used here, we mean child-focused study that deals with scientific and social-cultural phenomena that children have experienced or to which they can relate. "Interdisciplinary" refers to employing all the disciplines of study that are appropriate to the child's question, problem, or concern being studied. This point of view toward curriculum may have given rise to the term "integrated day" or "integrated curriculum" that has been used to describe the English primary-school program by some authors. (Brown and Precious, 1968)

The main teaching-learning methods in the informal part of the program revolve around the concept of self-selection of work through child interest and concern. The teacher serves as a guide and as a resource. Teachers behave as if they are tutors, mainly. They ask leading questions to get at the interest or concern, they lead the children toward formulating questions or problems, and they suggest resources. An inquiry attitude is sought in every "teacher-pupil encounter." One of the thrusts of the instructional improvement programs has been to help teachers find their own ways for developing inquiry teaching skills. Some teachers manifest this approach as they study along with the children. Frequently, teachers talk about how much they are learning about science, for example, as they develop new clusters of materials and resources around science themes.

Another key method used is the individualizing of instruction through materials by which pupils can keep track of their own progress. Their problems, questions, and successes are recorded as they sense when they are able to move on to the next level of work. Most of the reading instruction is done this way. Teachers adapt the "reading schemes" (British basals) to the program. The books are made available to children at all levels. They become the basis for classroom libraries to which many trade books are added from purchases and local library collections.

Closely allied to this method is the wide use of team learning. Children do a great deal of their work in pairs or triads, rarely more than four in a work group. Children pair off with different children for different tasks, usually with the guidance of the teacher. The "family grouping" (mixed-age) structure in each room helps in this situation when it is used. Sometimes older children help younger ones, or more advanced children in a content area help less advanced children or even slow learners. Team learning is used from the earliest age levels to the top of the school, often in the same way as the rural schoolteacher uses this method but with many more materials available. Sometimes pairs or triads of children work together over long periods on a subject or a project while the teacher keeps an eye constantly on their productivity. When attentiveness and productivity begin to decline, new materials are presented, new questions are raised, or the work group is redeployed after some summarizing of what has been done so far. Individual records of progress, problems, and suggestions are kept on each child even though he or she is working in these small groups. All children keep individual folders of their work as well as their "exercise books." The teacher writes comments on everything.

Even though children may work in pairs or triads, each child prepares his or her own report of the work done, and the teacher examines it and makes recommendations for improvement or accepts it as the accomplished task. The pupils can work independently because they are very accustomed to reading and writing every day. In writing they are usually allowed to prepare a first draft as best they can. Then they bring it to the teacher, and usually through an inquiry-type process the editing is done and a final copy is presented. In reading, the children tend to work independently, asking their teammate or teacher for help when they need it. Reading and writing activities are very frequently interrelated. Young children learn to write while they learn to read, and very often this is well under way at 5 years of age. It might even be said that a sequence of reading, writing, and then reading again is one of the main methods for teaching reading. With this rich language-learning background, independent work becomes possible at quite an early age. Some examples are quoted by Rosen and Rosen. (Rosen and Rosen, 1973)

The most practical method for permitting the teachers to organize individualized, paired and small-group study based on child interests and concerns is the "work card." The work card, when properly prepared using an inquiry approach, not only assists the teacher in tailoring work for individuals or small groups but also actually puts an inquiry burden and responsibility on the student. Each card is tied to available materials or ones that can be constructed easily. This method encourages the development of child-made materials that can then be used by the next group of students. The making of work cards brings focus to the teacher's own curriculum development. The informal part of British schooling could not function without this device. Teachers prepare interdisciplinary resource study units of all kinds, often based upon the national curricular programs, and then they develop their own work cards to meet the aims of these units with their groups of youngsters. The result of the application of these methods in the new organizational patterns is a busy school with children working all over the school on all sorts of learning tasks and educational questions. An interdisciplinary approach is used, and the language tools of reading and writing as well as the creative arts are employed.

The teacher who wishes to move into open-inquiry education needs to develop over several years a system of independent study tactics for individual learners, pairs, and triads of learners. The open-inquiry programs with their self-selecting and self-directing study formats can only be held together by strands of focused and thematic learning that students can tie into at various levels and interest points. Since the economy would not bear the expense of a one-to-one tutorial system in public schools, a plan of instruction needs to be devised whereby students can work as independently as possible, learning from cleverly arranged materials for self-teaching, from each other through peer interaction, and from teacher guidance at the most crucial point of a learning episode.

A methodology and classroom management structure base for fostering open-inquiry education evolved as an outgrowth of experimental teaching in several areas: the curriculum reform projects of the 1960's, the team-teaching experiments, and British efforts to accomplish an "integrated day" in the primary school program.

An individualized approach to instruction has evolved based upon intrinsic motivation through self-discovery of meaning and upon an intrinsic human desire to explore and become competent in one's world. This approach is in tune with a psychobiological process of thought-feeling-value generation through the process of "assimilation" and "accommodation."

Learning Centers
Open-inquiry education is best advanced through the learning center with its collections of materials and resources and accompanying work or activities for short learning episodes, and unit sequences for longer-ranged study. Learning centers focusing on science, social studies, language arts, literature and reading, mathematics, and the arts may be organized in areas of a classroom or located in different classrooms or in clustered areas of a building (minischools at the primary and middle grade levels) or in sections of a large school resource center. In any event, they need to have the materials conveniently available that are needed for studying a focused problem or theme. The tasks at the centers must be manageable and clear in direction, and foster an inquiry approach.

Unit plans concentrate on guiding students through learning tasks that have focus and contribute to extending and enriching a learner's concept-value schema and related skills. They need to include not only the search tasks usually posed by inquiry questions and the materials needed, but also methods for recording results and sharing them with others. A summarizing activity that can be evaluated for conceptual understanding and skill attainment needs to be included. When there are several tasks involved and the activities can extend over several days or weeks, a contract is a convenient device. A contract in a suburban school setting might read as follows:

Confronting and gathering data: Next time you go with your parents to your neigh
borhood shopping center, (1) draw a map in scale of the center, including each
store, its approximate size, the parking areas, the walking areas, and the delivery
areas; (2) list for each store the categories of products it sells; (3) look at a filmstrip of
a country store in a small town at the turn of the century (prepared by the teacher
from photos taken at a historical reconstruction site); and (4) list the products it sold
and diagram their placement in the store.

Inferring and hypothesizing: (1) Share your data with a classmate who has collected
similar data; (2) ask yourselves the questions: What are the similarities and differences
between the shopping center and the country store? What are the reasons for the
differences and similarities?

Problem finding: (1) together write down a question or two that you would like to
investigate; (2) list the materials, resources, and techniques you need in order to get
at the answers; (3) choose the question for investigation that you could accomplish in
school and/or in the neighborhood in a reasonable length of time.

Problem solving: (1) Write down an hour-by-hour and day-by-day plan and schedule of work; discuss this with the teacher and get approval to go ahead; (2) do your
investigation and gather new data.

Summarizing and reporting: (1) Put your findings together into charts, graphs, pictures, and story form; (2) prepare a presentation to other members of the class.

Evaluating: Write in your own study record book a summary of what you learned and
what questions you did not answer and would like to investigate later on. (The
teacher uses the report and the account in the study record book as bases for
assessing the Learning gains from the accomplishment of the activity card. The
materials prepared by the students and the study record book are available for
parents to see on visiting day.)

Briefer plans can be devised for less elaborate activities for shorter time
blocks and for younger children. For example, the teacher can prepare a packet (in
a see-through bag or container so that the youngsters can easily locate materials)
which will include a metric ruler, a simple fulcrum made of a small triangular block
of wood, and three pennies. The instructions would include the following: (1) Find
as many ways as you can for balancing the ruler on the triangular block with the
pennies on top of it; (2) draw little pictures of the ways you tried; (3) explain to a
classmate in talk or in writing why you think it balanced each time when it did.
Another independent work aid for student and teacher is the retrieval chart, in
which together they list the references in texts, trade books, filmstrips, and so on
for discussions of certain key concepts.

The structure that holds together an open-inquiry classroom is composed of
such pedagogical mechanisms, which allow students to accomplish their learning
goals somewhat independently of each other. These devices absorb the attention of
the youngsters and set the pattern for their concentrated learning activity. This is an
orderly educational program that involves students in more self-selected and
directed learning activity than is possible in conventionally organized classrooms.
Success in these endeavors depends largely on the ingenuity, imagination, and

thoroughness of the teacher's preplanned, independent instruction devices and routines. When this system works, the teacher is freed to become an adult learner along with the students, as well as a true guide for helping them advance their learning.

The Open "Classroom Meeting" Technique: An Instructional Model for Encouraging Personal Knowing

A major technique for personalizing inquiry, outlined in William Glasser's *Schools Without Failure* (Glasser, 1968), is the classroom meeting—a class discussion with the teacher and students seated in a circle. What distinguishes Glasser's class meeting from the typical class discussion is not that children are seated in a circle (how much better it is to respond to people when you can see their faces) but that a change occurs in the roles of the teacher and the student. In the circle, conversation should primarily be between student and student. The teacher is there to stimulate thinking and student talk, not to correct responses or dominate the discussion. The teacher should be listening. Children should be learning to converse with each other, to argue or to disagree with peer opinions, and to listen before responding or asking for clarification. Traditionally, teachers have viewed discussions as another way to deliver some information, to lead students to asking the "right questions" in the pursuit of more knowledge. Glasser stresses that teacher talk should be minimal; student talk is maximized as students "try out" their ideas with their peers. For young children, opportunities for decentering their points of view are increased as they listen to others respond to their ideas and experiences. The role of the teacher is most important in getting meetings started and sustaining them by stimulating children's thinking with open-ended, divergent questioning strategies. Once children proceed with a topic, the teacher's role is to ensure equal participation and a reasonable focus for discussion.

An additional difference between traditional discussions and "class meetings" is that class meetings usually focus on one topic. The teacher may find it necessary to intervene to help students refocus if they stray from the topic too far. At times this may be desirable if the new topic engenders more interest, although too many topics under discussion will limit opportunities for in-depth discussion and resolution of thinking. Class meetings should not be freewheeling, off-the-cuff discussions about anything and everything. They demand careful teacher planning. The questions to be used must be carefully thought out in advance. The success and length of any meeting is dependent upon student age, student and teacher experience with class meetings, and the amount of interest the topic may have for the students.

In the end, Glasser feels class meetings help youngsters develop a sense of success and worthiness. It is most reasonable here, however, to examine how class meetings might enhance the ability of children to present their ideas, concepts, and experiences to their teachers and classmates within an organized structure for discussion.

Glasser outlines three types of class meetings. One is the social problem-solving meeting, in which individual and social-educational problems are discussed. The second type is the open-ended meeting in which learners' out-of-school experiences and interests are discussed. The third type, the educational-diagnostic meeting, provides teachers with the opportunity to evaluate student success in the attainment of concepts taught in classroom learning activities. Discussion is always focused on how the learnings relate to student interests, experiences, and concerns. The teacher remains nonjudgmental of student responses and does not evaluate children in the traditional sense. Students must feel free to participate and express themselves without fear of being corrected.

Glasser illustrates the diagnostic meeting by describing an experience he conducted with an eighth-grade class that had just completed a study of a unit of the American Constitution. (Glasser, pp. 139–141) He surmised that the students had learned about the Constitution individually, had not individually internalized its meaning. His first question led the students to an examination of the Bill of Rights. He asked, "Do these rights pertain to you?" There was heated discussion, which illustrated a real lack of confrontation with this question in their regular study. Glasser felt his next question was the key to testing the students' understanding: "What happens if you do something on your own property that is against the law? For example, may you drive a car on your own property even though you don't have a driver's license and are too young to drive?" This question did generate a lively discussion, one which led to issues related to the Constitution and allowed the teacher, who was present, to judge the effectiveness of his unit of study. Based on the student responses to this meeting, Glasser concluded that during their study the students would have profited from a more relevant look at the Constitution and its meaning to their life situations. In effect, the meeting had enabled the teacher to evaluate his learning activities. Student responses in the meeting suggested to the teacher the need for new learning activities that would assist his students in arriving at a more complete understanding of the concepts related to the Constitution.

Glasser's class meetings provide the opportunity for students to learn the social and intellectual skills of discussing within a structure of minimum teacher talk or interference. Teachers need to be listeners, for much can be learned by listening to children—how they think, what they think, and what is meaningful to them. The suspension of teacher judgment, as suggested by Glasser, supplies the added benefit of encouraging all students to gain confidence in their ability to verbalize: to present their ideas and concerns freely. For many students oral presentation may be the primary means of success for presentation of their knowledge.

The Rehearsing Tactic: A Means for Summarizing and Assessing Ideational Gains

Child conceptions that are confused, too narrow, or disparate can become better delineated and then reinforced through the classroom procedure of rehearsal. (Frank, 1960) This is a means for presenting to children the opportunity to use and redefine a concept in a context that is different from the one in which the concept was initially developed but that is similar enough to reveal pertinence.

Both Taba and Grannis recommend strategies very like "rehearsal" in their experimental programs for developing concepts in the social sciences. Taba suggests that after "confronting" children with a social situation that causes "bafflement" and that in turn encourages "discovery" of the underlying concept, the teacher can "rotate" from this inductive process to a deductive procedure. In the deductive phase children are confronted with a comparable situation in which they are expected to apply the concept previously discovered. (Taba, 1962) Concepts are rehearsed as different settings are introduced. Grannis, in his curriculum planning, builds a cyclical series of social contexts in which an expanding cluster of interrelated concepts and generalizations are developed in complexity over time as children study in each new context. Previously learned concepts are rehearsed while extensions and modifications of them are developed. (Grannis, 1963)

Frank suggests that more use should be made in the classroom of miniature toys, such as plastic models of farms or frontier towns, to give the children the opportunity to rehearse or play out the concepts they have been gaining about farming or life on the frontier. He refers to this learning activity as analogical operations. Abductive learning involves such operations. (Frank, pp. 31–37) The toys in combination become analogues of life situations. This type of learning is in contrast with digital operations, which deal with discrete logical steps as seen in arithmetical computation. The analogue is something felt, seen, or heard in its whole and is applicable at all age levels of learning. It is a model toy, a picture, a film, a sculpture, a play, or it can be a model of atomic structure or a diagram of mathematical combinations. The learner can manipulate it or see it over and over again or dramatize with it.

The analogical operation is a means for rehearsing concepts. Language is integral to the manipulation rehearsal. The learners talk about it while they are doing it. The conceptions are repeated, reformed, and encoded in language during a rehearsal operation. Communication is set up between classmates as they play out their conceptions with toys or other analogues. The language is repeated and restated as the teacher plans for a "calculated redundancy" that will ensure that pupils with various views and abilities will build the conception as different approaches develop through the natural expansiveness of children's play. (Frank, p. 25.)

Since Froebel discovered the learning potential in children's play, educators have known that a chief mode of children's learning is play. Yet how often is this essential instrument for children's cognitive development used beyond the kindergarten program? Older boys and girls to the age of at least 12 continue to play with miniature toys of all kinds, from toy space creatures to trains and dollhouses. The play world is the real world of childhood, and it should be tapped for educational purposes in the school setting without robbing children of the spontaneity of out-of-school play that is so essential to their psychic and cognitive development.

Play episodes can be the contexts for concept rehearsal when the teacher accepts play as a learning situation. Sand table models, miniature dioramas of historical or social events, or small-scale constructions of buildings can serve as the instruments of rehearsal if the children are allowed to talk as they play. Puppet plays, creative dramatics, and role playing can also serve the purpose of concept rehearsal when the teacher sets the stage and the limits but leaves the children to play out the substance of the event. Corinne Seeds working at the UCLA demonstration school developed sociodrama into a classroom learning device in which the entire classroom is transformed and pupils play out roles. For example, in a transportation unit various sections of the room become trucking centers, shipping rooms, raw material suppliers, factories, and stores, and pupils assume the pertinent roles.

At upper-school levels simulation games serve as an excellent means for rehearsal. A commonly used one is a mock international situation involving several small countries that have special environmental and socioeconomic problems creating shortages and/or overproduction of certain materials and goods. The game is played by setting up delegations from each country who must work out the conflicts caused by the disparities. The delegations receive message cards from time to time about changing political situations, and, while trying to keep peace, they must decide what their representatives will say at the international confrontation meetings. Other kinds of simulation games, about response to polluting factors in a community or to changing real estate patterns, can be patterned after games like Monopoly. However, in any educational game the enlightening discussion that occurs while playing is more important than the winning. Microcomputers have opened up new ways of making these simulations available.

Rehearsing can serve as a clarifying process, because concepts of one child are tested against those of other children and against knowledge from the disciplines as presented by the teacher. The process of trying out the idea by writing it down is another form of rehearsing concepts that aids clarification. To think out loud on paper or on a typewriter is a playful act, especially when the pupil-author starts developing a story that becomes a variation on an original context. New life is fused into conceptions as they are put to work by being rehearsed in changing contexts and situations.

Matching educative strategies and teaching tactics to the children's "knowing cycle" and their individual patterns of coming to know is the greatest challenge to the educator who makes curricula and to the teacher who devises instructional plans. Thus can education become knowing.

Utilizing Language Strategies

Bellack, in his investigations of classroom teaching, found it convenient to view teaching and learning as episodes of "language games" between teacher and students.

> In his (Wittgenstein's) view, "The speaking of language is part of an activity, or of a form of life. . . ." Wittgenstein referred to these activities as "language games," a metaphor used to point up the fact that linguistic activities assume different forms

and structures according to the functions they come to serve in different contexts. . . . Learning the language rules that govern the use of words in these activities (is necessary for) successful communication. (Bellack and Davitz, 1963)

Language of Soliciting and Structuring

The teacher's questions and comments about events presented to students tend to solicit from them certain kinds of responses or replies, and particular language forms are expected and used. (Bellack and Davitz, 1963, pp. 4-9)

If teachers are searching for propositions, they will formulate their comments in such a way as to solicit a hypothetical statement from the students. The teacher will ask, "What do you think is happening here and how could we be sure?" And the students will make reasonable guesses in the form of conditional statements.

The structuring strategy is used when the teacher is organizing the pupils' work for a period of time in relation to accomplishing tasks. The teacher might say, "This morning we are going to take out our arithmetic books and do the review examples of subtracting numbers having zeros in them." The students would react dutifully by opening to the page, but one student might ask, "Do we have to do all of them?" Instead of answering, the teacher might place the burden of structuring on the students by saying, "Some of you had trouble with the handling of zero in subtraction yesterday. What might be our plan for today in attacking this problem?" Such various language games invoke different cognitive patterns. The quality of the classroom discourse is lifted when the teacher's soliciting and structuring abilities are such that they provoke independent thinking and study planning on the part of the children.

The following example is taken from a discussion in a first-grade class that was studying animal fur as insulation. It shows the teacher soliciting responses and structuring the situation with the intent of having the children plan their own structure of investigation.

A caged hamster had been brought into the room. It was being handed around as the teacher asked for observations. The children noted that it was furry and when asked if it felt warm, they all agreed.

Teacher (Soliciting):	I'll ask you another question. How many think that hamsters would feel warm in winter when it is cold?
Pupil (Responding):	Just like a cat doesn't (feel cold). Some things are furry so that when they go out in the cold they don't feel cold.
Teacher (Structuring):	I am going to get you something. (She brings over a picnic cooler with ice cubes in it. The children show excitement.)
Pupils (Reacting):	An animal in there! On ice? Must be.
Teacher (Soliciting and Structuring):	One thing is whether a hamster would be warm or cold when outside in the winter. In the box we have something to help us find out.

Pupils (Reacting):	I didn't see. Ice. Ice cold. Ice cubes. I knew it was ice.
Teacher (Structuring):	The hamster, when not in a room, lives where it is cold. When it goes outside, what does it do, how does it feel? How can we find out?
Pupil (Structuring):	We could put it in the box of ice.[4]

Imaginative soliciting and clever structuring of the situation that foster causal, relational, and hypothetical thinking in students are the teaching strategies that Taba calls "lifting" the level of cognitive activity among the pupils. (Taba, 1964)

Language of Managing and Evaluating Pupil Performance

Marie Hughes's studies highlighted the importance of language in all aspects of teaching. (Hughes, 1964, pp. 11–13) Even giving directions and admonishing children in management of the classroom can be either destructive or constructive depending on the language used. Children were found to respond negatively to the little language subterfuges that teachers often use to keep children in line. Typical are "Look how nicely Johnny is working this morning" or "Let's remember that we are all going to behave like the grown-up second-graders that we are when we go to assembly." These directional admonishments either set one child against another or suggest that the children are not going to meet the standard. The language of directions should be direct; admonishments should be straightforward.

The language a teacher uses to evaluate children's work has an effect upon their attitude toward study. The offhand statement of mild praise does not have the educational effect of a thoughtful comment about a child's work that includes an assessment of strengths and weaknesses to be improved in terms of a problem to be faced. Instead of "That's nice, Mary," the teacher should say, "I like your ideas here, but they seem a little repetitious. Can you think of some way of saying them so that all your sentences don't start in the same way?" Admonitions that make a student look foolish and deter her from exploring alternatives should be avoided. (Bruner, 1963, p. 526) The crowning result of invoking artful language strategy in the classroom is the releasing of students to become their own problem solvers or "self-sufficient learners." The goal is to have students "participate in the process that makes possible the establishment of knowledge. . . . Knowing is a process, not a product." (Bruner, 1963, pp. 319, 335)

Questioning in Teaching[5]

The most common language strategy used by teachers in the classroom is questioning. Unfortunately, the type of question most frequently used is one that

---

[4]From protocols gathered at the Summer School Elementary Science Study, Summer 1963.
[5]This section was written in collaboration with Lawrence Gagnon. (Gagnon, 1965)

refers to a specific phrase in a text and requires the recitation of the phrase as an answer. (Board, 1984)

Teachers need to consider a wider range of interrogation strategies. Questioning has been considered a method of teaching since Socrates asked, "What is good?" The recitation format with a question followed by a memorized response is as old as ritualistic teachings, like the catechism. The two main conventions of instructional interrogation are based on the logic-probing strategy of the Socratic dialogue and on the fact-questioning format of the recitation. To these two ancient customs of instruction a third has been added in modern times—the nondirective question developed in psychotherapy for encouraging free-associative thinking. From these older interlocutory conventions, the modern educator has devised three kinds of strategies for instructional questioning, which, when placed in artful interplay, will foster divergent or open-ended thinking when appropriate and will encourage convergent or step-by-step thinking when that is advantageous. In these ways the teacher can stimulate and direct the "mental play" of the classroom.

Inquisitive Quentioning

The Socratic dialogue is a method of inquiry. Students and teachers become involved in a search for truth. The teacher is a co-inquirer with the student. (Jordan, 1953, pp. 97–98; Broudy, 1965, pp. 8–17) But the Socratic method is useful to build the spirit of inquiry in search of truth in pupils. Children can inquire at their own level and can find reason and purpose within the limits of their capabilities. Teachers' questions should serve as catalysts for the inquiring process among the students. They should also contribute their experience to the discussion when it seems appropriate.

> (Socratic method) is a method of inquiry in which one seeks to determine what the true nature of things is. The object of the inquiry is a definition that captures the very essence of a thing. Definitions are tested by seeking their consequences for different cases. . . . It is not an inquiry into things that have not been experienced but an inquiry into the meanings of experience as it is presently held. . . . The first principle of the method is to begin with a trial definition and to test the definition against the combined wits of those engaged in the discussion. The procedure is necessarily unstructured because the direction of the inquiry de pends on the trial definition.
>
> If one learns anything from the Socratic method, he probably learns to bring forth counter-instances. He learns that what one does with a definition is test it by examples from his experience and imagination. (Jordan, pp. 102–103)

Inquisitive questioning in the spirit of the Socratic method can be used when common experiences have been gained and their meaning in life is to be considered. After an eighth-grade class has visited a juvenile court with their teacher, made observations of the neighborhood where the court sits, and read something of judicial procedures, they cannot turn from the questions: What is delinquency? What is lawful? and What is just? This is the time when the teacher should help the students propose trial definitions and ask the kinds of questions that encourage checking instances from their observations and from their own experience with limits and approbations imposed by society.

Scientific Inquiry

There is another kind of inquiry that probes toward discovery of unknown and possible new combinations. This type of inquiry is exemplified by the part of the scientific method in which the scientists play with possibilities suggested by given data. They follow hunches and let their minds wander over the probabilities of finding a clue if they turn their attention this way or that. Like the Socratic method, the inquiry in scientific method is an occupation of sophisticated adults. Even granting their limitations in experience and thinking, however, the spirit of the open-ended, intuitive inquiry can be encouraged in children. They will inquire in their own manner and in their own world.

The climate for discussion must be permissive and accepting, allowing for both the wild guess and the critical challenge. The questions asked by the teacher need to be of the open-ended variety: What would happen if we tried it this way? Can you think of any other ways we could do it? Inquisitive questioning suits both an open and exploring activity in the mode of scientific discovery and a closing-in activity in the mode of scientific validation.

Examples of Special Questioning Strategies That Encourage Dialogue

Language strategies in teaching can contribute as much to the process of knowing as does the strategic manipulation of materials for discovery. For example, Suchman's special science-teaching strategies for "learning through inquiry" create a language game of dialogue. He requires children to talk as they explore a scientific phenomenon, so that the teacher gets a picture of their thinking. (Suchman, 1963 setting up the classroom dialogue in such a way that the children are always asking questions about an observed film clip of a physical phenomenon, Suchman emphasizes "that the direction and control of the data flow are mostly in the hands of the child. Students are in this way helped to develop a set of skills and a broad schema for the investigation of causal relationships."

Suchman divides an inquiry episode into three stages through which the teacher guides the questioning after the children have witnessed a filmed episode of natural phenomena (for example, the bending of two thin metal strips under heat and in cold water).

Stage I. A verification of facts as the child identifies the objects and the conditions under which they have been placed.
Stage II. A determination of relevance as the child manipulates one variable at a time while the others are controlled, and an identification of conditions that produce the outcome.
Stage III. A discovery of physical principles and relationships that govern change.

The children are restricted to asking questions of the teacher that have a "yes" or "no" answer, very much like the game "Twenty Questions." This forces the children to talk out their thinking about the general question, "Why?" Suchman found in his experimentation with this particular language strategy that it "had a marked effect on the motivation, autonomy and question-asking fluency of children. . . . They clearly enjoyed having the freedom and power to gather their own data in their quest for assimilation." (Suchman, 1963, p. 81)

In another of the experimental science programs (the Elementary Science Study), an open-ended approach is used. Instead of building question sequences around a structured episode, the children were confronted with materials strategically chosen for the conceptualizing potential in the relationships that can be made among them. Then the students were permitted to manipulate the materials freely, to talk among themselves and with the teacher about the relationships, and to hypothesize possible explanations and ways of finding causes. "Enlightened opportunism" describes this methodology, which allows the children to meet events in their own way, assuring that they build preconceptual backgrounds of identification with the feel, the look, and the smell of objects as they appear in space and time before they conceptualize the relationships that begin to have meaning for them. The teachers, after having set the stage for this kind of exploration, respond to the manipulation they observe and the talk they hear by summing up the children's findings and by reviewing the situation at which they have arrived. They use a questioning voice as if to say, "What does that mean?" and "How could we find out if that would happen again?" The ideation and the process for investigation are "discovered" by the children as they work and talk together.

Sometimes a concept which has already been discovered in the classroom can be extended to a generalization by proposing a novel occurrence and by inviting talk about other possible novel situations.

In a seventh grade which was studying light and shadow, the teacher said, "Last night I had dinner at an outdoor restaurant. It was raining, but I ate under a rain shadow."
The students were pleased with the new situation and recalled sun shadows under beach umbrellas. They were then divided into teams and asked to write down as many other kinds of shadows as they could construe. Some of the responses were as follows:

A space ship makes a radiation shadow.
The nose cone of a space capsule makes a heat shadow.
A diving bell makes a water shadow.
A bullet-proof vest makes an energy shadow.

The teacher asked, "What is a shadow then?"
    Pupil: Blocking out something.
    Pupil: A shadow is the absence of something, a light shadow is the absence of light.

The artfulness of the teacher who uses "enlightened opportunism" is found both in the proper timing of the questions or reflections on the student's comment and in the phrasing, so that the children carry on the dialogue and make the discoveries their own.

The skillful teacher uses open-ended questions or nondirective comments that reflect the pupil's statement, to encourage divergent thinking in combination with closure questions, which bring about convergent thinking. A rhythm of expansive exploration and narrowing specificity promotes a progressive flow of constructive thinking as the discipline of education takes place.

The Clarifying Question

There is an objectivity about inquiry that does not always touch personal conceptualizing and commitment. A type of questioning is needed to strike at personal involvement—the clarifying question. The neo-Freudians were concerned with helping psychologically disoriented individuals clarify their value orientation to life; from this approach a format of questioning has been developed that permits free association of ideas and feelings. Psychologists have proposed that individuals can incorporate only the ideas, feelings, and concepts into their personalities that can be brought to personal awareness and can be freely accepted by them. A nondirective approach is the only way to place the burden of acceptance upon them.

Rogers emphasizes the need for client-centered therapy. In his clinical process, the therapist mirrors the client's reactions with such questions as:

You feel that (he repeats the client's statement)?
What are your reactions?
You would feel thus and so (he summarizes the client's reactions)? (Rogers, 1951)

This strategy of nondirective questioning in a permissive interview situation, when no judgments of actions or feelings were made by the therapist, served well the purpose of forcing clients to work out their own value judgments in emotionally charged situations. Later, Rogers and others suggested that the therapist might participate more in the interview beyond reflective questioning by sharing with the client similar experiences the interviewer had had or had heard about. The decisions made by others could be mentioned, but the therapist is always careful not to tell the client what to do or to challenge him with direct questions that require direct conventional answers.

Rogers extended his theories and procedures to the teaching situation, noting that teachers are not concerned with intricacies of personality adjustments in psychotherapeutic situations but, rather, are concerned with normal personality development in which personal valuing decisions are involved. The nondirective approach and the open-ended nonevaluative question become strategies of the classroom teacher to encourage independence in decision making. This technique places upon students the burden of thinking about value judgments and about the significance of what they are learning. If, as stated earlier in the chapter on coming to know, the acquisition of knowledge is a personal process of conceptualizing, then a nondirective approach in teaching would seem to be most appropriate at certain crucial stages in the teaching-learning process. Louis Raths and his followers have taken this approach in attempting to develop a teaching strategy of questioning that will encourage pupils to examine and clarify their values as they deal with subjects that have personal and social implications. (Raths, 1963; Raths, et al., 1966; Simon et al., 1972)

Some activities helpful in value clarification are (1) question-and-answer discussion periods involving moot questions for the class to consider (for example: Are athletes better than scholars?); (2) role-playing situations where questions of value are raised and then acted out; and (3) discussion of a classroom social incident. The teacher needs to inject the clarifying question into these situations. Most teachers tend to ask questions only when they possess the answers.

The key criterion for selecting clarifying questions is that they must be questions for which only the student knows the answer. Teachers who have worked with this level of questioning suggest that the questions are more effective when asked in a nonjudgmental manner. The following types of clarifying questions have been used in the classroom:

Reflect back what the student has said and add, "Is that what you mean?"
Reflect back what the student has said with distortion and add, "Is that what you
  mean?"
"How long have you felt (acted) that way?"
"Are you glad you think (act) that way?"
"In what way is that a good idea?"
"What is the source of your idea?"
"Should everyone believe that?"
"Have you thought of some alternatives?"
"What are some things you have done that reflect this idea of yours?"
"Why do you think so?"
"Is this what you really think?"
"Did you do this on purpose?"
Ask for definitions of key words.
Ask for examples.
Ask if this position is consistent with a previous one he or she has taken. (Raths,1966
  p. 513)

A questioning attitude among students needs to be implemented within the classroom environment. The dignity and acceptance of any question asked by a student as one that is worthy of an answer is an idea that needs to be encouraged by teachers. If teachers brush aside questions, they can deter the questioning process of students. Teachers should ask some clarifying questions of students that show the teachers are in agreement with them, as well as some that show that they are not. The development of skill in questioning techniques by both students and teachers will depend, to a degree, on the ability of individuals to maintain open minds during classroom interaction.

Another technique for encouraging the clarifying process is the coding of written work. Coding can be used to clarify values and to sharpen the students' insights into their own thinking. A "V" for a positive value and a "V-" for a negative value are symbols that can be marked in the margin of a student's paper whenever the teacher sees an indication of attitudes, feelings, beliefs, aspirations, and the like. The student learns to identify these symbols as representing two questions that the teacher is asking. They are: "Do you believe this?" and "Do you want to change it?" As the student reflects and responds to the questions, he or she is thinking and valuing. The clarifying question can serve to raise the level of the "mental play" in the classroom, ensuring to some degree the personalization of concepts and the commitment of students to a value orientation. In the social studies and science areas, questions about "segregation," "peace and war," or the "uses of nuclear power" need to be explored in this manner by interweaving clarifying questions with inquiry and fact finding. Thought-provoking pictures showing racial, ethnic, or socioeconomic conflicts can set the stage for a values clarification discussion.

Questioning Levels

Saunders, in his book *Classroom Questions*, presents a hierarchy of types of questions based on classifications of educational objectives related to the advancing levels of the higher thinking process. He encourages teachers to frame questions at the appropriate moment of thought development in a teaching episode that will lift the level of the students' thinking. (Saunders, 1966)

Hunkins, in a useful book on the techniques of questioning, focuses his attention particularly on their use in inquiry-oriented curricula. (Hunkins, 1972) He sets some criteria for the framing of questions, such as: Is it clear what is expected both cognitively and affectively of the student? Does the wording allow students to respond with optimal productivity? Does it give them adequate direction and permit them freedom to interrelate ideas? Hunkins recommends a simple Teacher-Pupil Question Inventory Form that teachers can use with student teachers or among themselves for looking at the levels of questioning they use and the levels of response they get from pupils. The observer can simply indicate the level of each question and response by teacher and pupils as a learning activity proceeds. The code is based on the cognitive levels from the Bloom taxonomy: (1) memory, (2) comprehension, (3) application, (4) analysis, (5) synthesis, and (6) evaluation. A matrix can be formed of the pattern, and this becomes a basis for discussion of questioning strategies. An audio- or videotape recording taken at the same time would be useful for an analysis of the different types of questions and the responses from the children.

Expert searching with questions by the teacher-scholar can imbue students with a love of investigation. Inquiry and clarification can electrify learning and make moments of teaching exciting.

Exposition in Teaching

The art of questioning is crucial in the teaching act, but the communicative arts of presenting and explaining information and ideas are equally pivotal. Not much work has been done on this latter aspect of teaching at any school level, because most theoretical positions about school teaching recognized that beginning teachers do too much lecturing in a style learned from hours of listening in college classes. As a result, many new teachers leave the teacher-education institution with the impression that they should never talk to the students but rather should always be soliciting talk from them. They are drilled on the adage, "When tempted to tell, think of a question instead." This is good advice for checking teacher talk and forcing a focus on the child's language and thought. However, when the importance of language interchange and the dialogue between the child conception and the adult scientific and public concepts are stressed, then teachers' language presentations to children become crucial.

Teachers need to consider ways to present information and ideas both effectively and artfully. The presentations of the teacher must be prepared in such a way as to follow the psycho-logic and socio-logic of the content from the point of view of the learners as well as the natural logic of the subject matter. Children's experience of seeing puddles evaporate fast on a sunny, windy day (psycho-logic) must be woven into the logical, scientific explanation of evaporation. Means for involving the child directly in participation and indirectly in silent parallel thinking activity are a problem of teaching tactics. When no further questions can be raised or considered until the pupils have more information, or when added information is needed to provoke further questions or to challenge premature judgments, teachers must plan their own presentations.

The temptation to translate the material to be presented into childish language should be avoided. As in the making of good informational books for children, simplification is not the main task. Rather, the main task is the presentation of the material in a mode that children will comprehend. Operational descriptions and imagery-evoking presentations are preferable to logical argumentation for explaining events to most elementary school children. Building sequences of concrete examples that lead to an inductively derived generalization for the pupils to locate and express are effective in science or social science presentations by the teacher. The opposite, deductive structure, beginning with a restated generalization just learned, could be used as a challenge for the pupils to locate examples in other settings. The teacher might in another instance present an overview of a subject to be studied to give a total frame of reference in which learners would investigate the specifics that would lead them to some principles. Geographical studies, for example, can be approached in this way, with the teachers using pictures, films, and recordings as well as exposition in their initial presentation. Such introductions to a study should not present the generalizations or the conclusions, for then there would be no reason to study. Instead, they should present impressions, descriptive statements, and feelings about the subject from which learners can draw their own generalizations through questioning.

After learners have investigated, framed some propositions, and raised some questions, there will be need for more information and explanation. Teachers need to be wary of giving out too much unstructured, diffuse, and unrelated information unless the strategy calls for the pupils to assemble and structure the facts on their own in a kind of mental game. Usually, the teachers need to think of themselves as organizing the information for presentation. With some kinds of content, such as the explanation of a computational process in mathematics after a concept has been built, a step-by-step logical structure might be effective. With other sorts of content (for example, an exploration of a scientific concept) the teacher might move through successively more complex examples.

Repetition, a studied redundancy, may be necessary, and points should be summarized at regular intervals. The technique of class response can be useful as explanations proceed. The teacher should call for restatement and for questions that will focus on elements that still need explanation. Whatever the teacher's presentation is, it should provoke pupil questions and statements for further investigation. In this way the dialogue of the classroom occurs.

As Huebner (1962) suggests, teachers can be conceived of as composers. Sometimes their compositions are prepared ahead of time, but they are always flexibly planned for the turn of events that will come from pupil involvement. At other times, the teachers' compositions are improvised on the occasion. They are composers in all the arts of presentation and communication. As composers in the literary arts, they may use the poignant story to good effect, as did the teachers of biblical times. They may use the extended metaphor or the rhetorical question to the advancement of learning, as did Socrates. Or they may use exposition and argument with the directness and simplicity of a Francis Bacon. The whole rich fabric of the English language can be at their command.

In the visual arts they can compose imaginative collages and scenarios of pictures for bulletin boards or classroom presentations. With miming and gesturing, teachers can dramatize a point or create impressions of attitude. There are worlds of language, of illustration, and of imitation at the teacher's beck and call. From these treasure troves of human ingenuity they can compose "letters to the world" that speak to the generations of students and lead them in their knowing.

References

Arno Bellack and J. Davitz, "The Language of the Classroom," USOE Project 1487, Washington, D.C., 1963.

Peter Board, "Toward a Theory of Instructional Influence: Aspects of the Instructional Environment and Their Influence on Children's Acquisition of Reading," unpublished doctoral dissertation, University of Toronto, 1984.

Harry Broudy, "Two Exemplars of Teaching Method," in *Theories of Instruction* (Washington, D.C.: Association for Supervision and Curriculum Development, 1965).

Mary Brown and Norman Precious, *The Integrated Day in the Primary School* (London: Ward Lock, 1968).

Jerome Bruner, "Needed: A Theory of Instruction," *Educational Leadership* (May 1963, pp. 523–532).

—,"Some Theories on Instruction Illustrated with Reference to Mathematics," *Theories of Learning and Instruction, NSSE Yearbook 63,* Part 1 (Chicago: University of Chicago Press, 1964).

Betty Warner Deitz, *The You Can Work Books* (New York: John Day, 1970).

Lawrence K. Frank, *The School as Agent for Cultural Renewal* (Cambridge, MA: Harvard University Press, 1960).

Lawrence Gagnon, "An Analysis of an Experimental Methodology in Teaching Thinking and Clarifying Values," unpublished doctoral dissertation, Wayne State University, Detroit, 1965

William Glasser, *Schools Without Failure* (New York: Harper & Row, 1968).

Joseph Grannis, "The Framework of the Social Studies Curriculum," *The National Elementary Principal* (1963), pp. 20–26.

Dwayne Huebner, "The Art of Teaching," mimeograph, Teachers College, Columbia University, 1962.

Marie Hughes, "What Teachers Do and the Way They Do It," *NEA Journal* (September, 1964) pp. 11–13.

Francis Hunkins, *Questioning Strategies and Techniques* (Boston: Allyn and Bacon, 1972).

James Jordan Jr., "Socratic Teaching," *Harvard Educational Review,* vol. 33, no. 1 (Winter 1953), pp. 97–98.

Gardner Murphy, *Freeing Intelligence Through Teaching* (New York: Harper & Row, 1961).

Louis E. Raths, "Clarifying Values," in Robert S. Fleming (Ed.), *Curriculum for Today's Boys and Girls* (Columbus, OH: Merrill, 1963).

Louis Raths, Merrill Harmin, and Sidney Simon, *Values and Teaching* (Columbus, OH: Merrill, 1966).

Carl Rogers, *Client Centered Therapy* (Boston: Houghton Mifflin, 1951).

Harold Rosen and Connie Rosen, *The Language of Primary School Children* (London: Penguin, 1973).

Norris Saunders, *Classroom Questions: What Kinds* (New York: Harper & Row, 1966).

Fannie Shaftel and George Shaftel, *People in Action: Role-playing and Discussion Photography for Elementary School Social Studies* (New York: Holt, Rinehart and Winston, 1970), Teachers Guide.

Sidney Simon, et al., *Values Clarification: A Handbook of Practical Strategies for Teachers and Students* (New York: Hart Publishing, 1972).

Charles Silberman (Ed.), *The Open Classroom Reader* (New York: Vintage Books, 1973).

J. Richard Suchman, "Learning Through Inquiry," *NEA Journal* (March 1963).

——, The Elementary School Training Program in Scientific Inquiry (Urbana: University of Illinois, 1962).

Hilda Taba, "Learning by Discovery," lecture delivered at San Francisco State College, 1961.

——, *Curriculum Development* (New York: Harcourt, Brace, Jovanovich, 1962).

——, "Thinking in Elementary School Children," USOE Project No. 1574, 1964.

——, *Teachers' Handbook for Elementary Social Studies* (Palo Alto, CA: Addison Wesley, 1967).

17

Building Whole-Language Programs

I play it cool and dig all jive.
That's the reason I stay alive.
My motto, as I live and learn,
Is dig and be dug in return.

Langston Hughes

In Chapter 1 and throughout this book we've presented the case for a dual school curriculum centered around the expansion of language and thinking. A key premise is that development of language and thought are interdependent: language is the medium of thought, learning, and communication, and it is learned best in the process of its use.

In Chapter 16 we dealt with transactional teaching and curriculum to develop thinking and knowing. In this final chapter we'll focus on implementing curriculum designed to promote language development. We'll consider the realities of current school programs; we'll examine some existing school policies and programs that are designed to promote language and thinking and that are consistent with concepts we've presented; we'll consider some of the essentials of such whole-language programs and the problems involved in implementing them; and we'll make some optimistic predictions for the future.

Where the Schools Are

If schools existed in a completely rational world, useful new ideas and theories would be the basis for a continuous, innovative process in our schools as teachers, administrators, and decision makers sought to improve the effectiveness of teaching and learning. To some extent, even in the less than rational world that schools exist in, that really does happen, but it is sometimes hard to see, particularly in the United States, against the background of irrational demands for accountability based on standardized test scores, fundamentalist pressures for narrowed curricula, and "back to basics" movements.

Schools in the United States have a tradition of local political control. That's one reason for the slow spread of innovative ideas in American schools. It also, however, explains the resilience of some school reform movements in the face of public criticism. In any case, American schools have always presented an uneven pattern of response to reforms and innovations. In his extensive study of American elementary and secondary schools, Goodlad found a "monstrous hypocrisy"—he found a ". . . gap between the rhetoric of individual flexibility, originality and creativity in our educational goals and the cultivation of these goals in our schools. . . ." (Goodlad, 1984, p. 241) School experiences, he found, are focused on conditioning students to conform, to seek right answers, and to stay closely to what is known. He concluded that "the emphasis on individual performance and achievement would be more conducive to cheating than to development of moral integrity." (Goodlad, 1984 pp. 241–242)

Much of the demands for reform of schools in the 1980's have focused on demands for schools and teachers to "get back to basics," yet Goodlad concludes that "back to basics is where we've always been." (Goodlad, 1983, p. 6)

"For years," he says, "schools and teachers have been criticized for neglecting the fundamentals. But . . . it appears teachers are very preoccupied with trying to teach children and youth precisely what we blame them for not teaching." (Goodlad, 1984, p. 243)

Goodlad found far more emphasis on usage in English classes than on literature and concern for human personal and social problems. In reading he found an overwhelming focus on textbooks and workbooks.

In the schools he studied he found that the focus in the first nine grades and in the lower tracks beyond was on language arts and mathematics but only as facts and skills. In these "basic" subjects, the schools were not "developing all those qualities listed under 'intellectual development': the ability to think rationally, the ability to use, evaluate, and accumulate knowledge, a desire for further learning." (Goodlad, 1984, p. 236) He found that surprisingly little time in school is spent on reading and writing and that the time decreases from elementary to junior high school and then to senior high schools. Around 30 percent of elementary school time is spent on written work, but much of this involves filling in the blanks and answering questions in workbooks. He found the state of reading ". . . quite dismal. Exclusive of the common practice of students taking turns reading orally from a common text, reading occupied only about 6% of class time at the elementary level and then dropped off to 3% and 2% for junior and senior highs. . . ." (Goodlad, 1984, pp. 106–107)

He found heavy use of methodology in all subjects largely confined to "lecturing, questioning, monitoring seatwork, and testing." (Goodlad, 1984, p. 244)

This portrayal of the state of American schools in the early 1980's is probably true for other English-speaking countries to a considerable extent. But there are some differences in the recent history of education in schools in the United States as compared to Britain, Canada, New Zealand, and Australia that have led to some markedly different trends and to a more rapid use of recent research and theory on language and thinking in the policies and curricula in these other countries. American teachers have found themselves more and more hedged in by highly structured mastery learning schemes, by pressures to teach standardized tests, and by arbitrary policies on grading, methodology, and discipline. It has become very hard in many American schools for teachers to function as decision makers. This has not totally prevented innovation on classroom, school, and district levels, but it has greatly increased the risks involved.

One important influence on school curriculum throughout the English-speaking world, but least in the United States, was the report of the Bullock Committee in Great Britain titled, "A Language for Life." This report drew on insights into the relationships of language, thinking, and learning to propose the basis for major changes in the objectives, curricula, and methodology of education. It stressed that "the link between language and thought is one that must be acknowledged." (Bullock Committee, 1975, p. 49) The report did not so much start a process as raise it to the level of policy. Its widespread discussion among school decision makers facilitated important innovations.

In any case, the trends toward whole-language school programs focusing on expanding language and thinking are more widespread and visible in other English-speaking countries than they are in the United States. In the United States there are many classrooms and occasional schools committed to whole-language concepts, but in other countries there is widespread commitment to whole-language programs, and basic policies for schools are based on the centrality of language and thinking and on holistic views of teaching and learning.

Programs, Frameworks, and Policies for Promoting Language and Thinking

To illustrate these widespread programs we'll summarize a few school language policy documents from different countries developed in the last decade.

Edmonton, Alberta, Canada

A team from the Language Arts Services developed a Language Arts Working paper (Edmonton Public Schools, 1982). The key premises of this document are:

Language arts must be integrated based on the interdependence of listening, speaking, reading, and writing and the need for people to have language to communicate with others and understand and control their daily experiences.

Language and thought develop together, and subject area concepts develop at the same time as pupils' ability to express their understandings through reading and writing.

Language is an active process learned through its use. "Teaching about language without opportunity for meaningful use of language will not develop students' skill with language."

Evaluation should emphasize actual language use in a variety of contexts for a variety of purposes and should specify both strengths and weaknesses.

Finally, "concern for the development and use of language is a whole school responsibility, since language and thought are the common denominators of all school subjects. An understanding of the process and direction of language and learning can assist schools in planning effective instruction. School objectives and decisions relating to curriculum, instruction, and evaluation should all reflect this understanding."

The Edmonton working paper stresses its theoretical premises and provides foundational information for teachers. It relates to detailed "Language Arts Outcomes," which are broad enough and specific enough to give direction to teachers and planners but not trivialized as so many so-called behavioral objectives become. They classify their objectives as attitudes, knowledge, and skills. Here are a few examples.

Students can and will read, listen, and view for recreation and information.
Students are able to use language to discuss language when constructing their own messages and when analyzing the message of others.
Students can express thoughts, feelings, and experience in extended discourse.

This working paper clearly presupposes that teachers must be informed professionals and that the program will not support learning unless teachers understand it and are there to facilitate it.

The Edmonton schools recognize the need for parent understanding and support. They provide a leaflet for parents in which these simple objectives are stated:

The Language Arts program incorporates all aspects of language and aims to:

Motivate and help children to read for enjoyment and knowledge
Introduce children to the pleasures and experiences presented in traditional literature
Help children read and write stories and poems to learn about themselves and the world around them
Develop children's ability to express thoughts and feelings orally and in writing
Help children understand and judge new experiences
Help children anticipate and question ideas encountered in reading and listening
Guide children in adjusting their language to suit particular situations
Develop children's ability to talk about language when planning their work and when analyzing messages of others

The leaflet encourages the parents to support the program with these kinds of activities in the home:

Talk with your children, listening to their experiences and sharing your own.
If your children watch television, spend time watching with them. Talk about the shows together.
Read to and with your children. When they read react and ask questions that will encourage them to think about what they read.
Take your children to the library.
Make sure writing materials are available at home. Encourage children to write to relatives or friends.
Engage in language play by making up rhymes and sharing jokes. (Edmonton Public Schools, 1985)

Province of Quebec, Canada

The program, "English Language Arts I–VI," is the official policy document of the Direction Generale du Developement Pedagogique, Ministere de L'Education, for the Province of Quebec. (Gouvernement du Quebec, 1983) This program is described as a "whole language, child centered, integrated approach." Theoretical assumptions and instructional principles spell out the basis of this whole-language approach (see Table 17.1).

TABLE 17.1 Language Arts Program of the Province of Quebec

Theoretical Assumptions	Instructional Principles
1. Language learning is an active developmental process which occurs over a period of time.	1. Children need time to internalize the process by actively engaging in the process of speaking, listening, reading and writing.
2. Speaking, listening, reading and writing are processes of making meaning rather than product-oriented practice exercises.	2. Children need to make sense of their learning and need to focus on making meaning rather than product-oriented practice exercises.
3. The language arts must occur in meaningful contexts for some purpose, in some situation, for some intended audience.	3. Children need to experience meaningful contexts for listening, speaking, reading, and writing.
4. The language arts must occur and do flourish in literate environments where language users are free to discover and to realize their intentions in trial and error fashion with varied opportunities for language use.	4. Children need to be encouraged to take risks and need to experience varied opportunities for language use.
5. Language use is not independent of function and meaning. Language use is meaningful when it is functional, personally based for the language user.	5. Children need to experience an environment which encourages a wide range of language uses, where language use is not independent of function and meaning.

Source: Reproduced with permission from "English Language Arts I-VI", Gouvernement du Quebec, 1983, p. 12.

Like all programs dedicated to promoting language and thinking, the Quebec program sees the teacher as playing a crucial but supportive role creating a meaningful context for learning. The teacher creates "invitational, emulative environments" with three goals in mind:

1. To provide integrated experiences with the language arts
2. To influence the children's attitudes toward language while promoting development through appropriate, varied opportunities for language use
3. To support the natural process of learning, building language, and extending knowledge, shaping meaning, and shaping the world through language. (Gouvernement du Quebec, p 14)

Goals in this whole-language program are quite differently stated than the behavioral objectives that have become common in the United States. They begin with a global objective:

The elementary language arts program will lead students to appreciate and use the English language as a means of shaping and communicating their ideas and feelings clearly, effectively, and imaginatively and of understanding the ideas and feelings of others.

From this global objective four goals are derived:

Fostering positive attitudes toward use of the English language
Fostering knowledge and enjoyment of cultural and literary heritage
Fostering abilities in using language-thinking strategies appropriately and efficiently

Fostering engagement in language interactions that are purposeful and meaningful from the students' viewpoints

From these goals a series of general objectives are derived, which in turn are further specified as terminal objectives. The general objective answers the question: "What is the expected outcome?" An example is: The student will view English as a dynamic and living language. The terminal objectives answer the question, "How will the student accomplish this?" The answers for speaking, listening, reading and writing become the terminal objectives. In reading, for example, the student is expected to respond "to a wide variety of print in meaningful contexts."

The program then specifies "related content" for each terminal objective. For this reading objective, the related content is reading experiences with stories, poems, plays, nonfiction, content material, magazines, and newspapers. "Indicators" are then specified for this related content and for monitoring the achievement of the objectives. "Response" and "value" indicators are specified. Here are those for the reading objective we've taken as an example:

Response
Reads every day
Recreates stories
Recognizes and responds to important incidents
Responds to ideas and concepts expressed in print
Relates personal experiencs to ideas and concepts
Expresses personal viewpoints about ideas and concepts
Makes judgments

Value
Reads every day
Shows an interest in books and other print material
Enjoys the different uses of language by authors

These objectives, related content, and indicators are broad enough to be specified across a range of grades and specific enough to be useful in planning for a particular group of children with a particular range of background and abilities in a particular grade in a particular community. As specific as this set of goals and objectives become, they never lose their holistic, functional, contextual qualities.

Evaluation is treated, in the Quebec Language Arts Program, as "an integral part of the teaching/learning process." (p 55) The program divides evaluation into formative (that which takes place almost daily in the classroom) and summative (that which evaluates the attainment of objectives at regular intervals).

The formative evaluation has as its purpose immediate response to the needs of the students. Both teachers and students need to know: (1) the extent to which particular language arts objectives are being met; (2) what must still be learned—how is the student developing? (3) how effective is the program, and how appropriate are the materials, activities and procedures? Each learning activity is subject to this formative evaluation. Self-evaluation, peer-evaluation, and teacher evaluation are all involved.

Summative evaluation has similar concerns, but its focus is more global: What has been learned and needs to be learned? How well are the students developing? How effective is the teaching/learning process and what changes are needed? This form of evaluation is used not only by students and teachers but also by administrators, planners, and decision makers.

In this program the evaluation is designed to be holistic and consistent with the program's philosophy and objectives. It involves real situations requiring language use. It uses concepts of development rather than absolute or adult standards. Expectations are relative to the students' background and growth patterns rather than being based on comparisons to others. Monitoring over time gives a frame of reference for judging progress and growth. Parents, students, teachers, and administrators all need to be involved in evaluation and in communicating to each other progress and what changes need to be made.

Holistic evaluation requires a variety of evaluatory techniques. The Quebec program suggests observation, informal and formal tests, parent and student conferences, school records, checklists, questionnaires, and tapes of oral language. A key is that the student is involved in the process and is helped to achieve an honest self-evaluation.

The Quebec program is explicit about why it has chosen the whole-language/personal growth model over others. The authors reject two other models. They reject the skills model:

> Proponents of this model believe that language is learned in a prescribed manner, by building from the smallest unit of language to the largest units and that language learning is the sum of learned skills.

> The adequacy of this model for teaching the language arts is highly questionable because of its false assumptions about language learning, the nature of language use in general and its tendency to proliferate the language arts classroom with "dummy runs" personified in senseless drills and workbook exercises. . . .

> Language learning is not the buildup and step-by-step sequencing of learned skills in isolation. Children do not learn about language on one level of organization (letters, words) before they can manipulate units (meaning) at higher levels.

They also reject what they label as the cultural heritage model, one common in their region, the focus of which is on:

> literature as a moral and spiritual influence on children. . . . The language arts are viewed as the vehicle for the transmission of "culture" and classics to children and the training of children by intelligent, knowledgeable adults in relation to social, religious, moral, ethical, time honored values. The assumptions underlying this model are:
>
> 1. that the child is a passive recipient to whom culture and knowledge is given.
> 2. that the most valuable experience is second-hand experience.
> 3. that the way to acquire competence in the language arts is to surrender to something or someone larger than oneself: i.e., culture, traditions, knowledgeable adults.

> This model is questionable . . . because it does not recognize the value of children's experiences in the learning process, the validity of their world or their roles as unique persons and creative language users; and it has a tendency to separate language, composition and literature into discrete subjects to be studied and taught.

Eclecticism, drawing on several different approaches and methodologies, is popular among teachers and curriculum planners, but the planners of the Quebec language arts program chose not to be eclectic; they recognized that the principles, research, and theory they had built their program on were also the basis for rejecting other approaches that were inconsistent with their criteria.

New Zealand English Syllabus

New Zealand is a small country (3 million people) that operates as a single administrative unit in education. So the "Statement of Aims" developed by the National English Syllabus Committee for secondary English is policy for all New Zealand secondary schools. Like the other whole-language programs that we have cited, it is neither a prescription nor a set of absolutes. Its purpose is "to provide a philosophical base for the development of language programmes in New Zealand secondary schools. It has been written to indicate to teachers how language development may be based on the individual student's language within the context of the classroom." (National English Syllabus Committee, 1976, p. 1)

The overall purpose of secondary education in New Zealand is "to help young people develop fully as individuals and members of society by encouraging growth of concern for others; the urge to enquire; the desire for self-respect." (p. 5)

The New Zealand document states these beliefs about learning and about language:

Learning:

1. Students are more important than subject matter.
2. Students learn best when programmes satisfy their personal and social needs.
3. A co-operative learning atmosphere encourages learning, and enjoyment increases students' willingness and ability to learn.
4. Learning is likely to occur as a response to the challenge of ideas.

Language:

1. Language is a form of human behavior.
2. Language development is central to personal growth. . . .
3. Students explore and extend language through speaking and listening; these modes are basic to development of literacy.

The New Zealand program provides no single structure or sequence. Rather, schools must suit the program to the particular needs of their students and the local circumstances. The program is school wide. It recognizes that:

> Students acquire language habits through all their school experiences, structured and unstructured, as well as in specific English periods. Therefore, schools will

need to consider not only the nature of their language courses, but also their total policy for aiding their students' language development across the curriculum. (p. 13)

The concept of "language across the curriculum" is one central to many secondary programs in Great Britain, Canada, and Australia, as well as in New Zealand. It recognizes the interdependence of language and learning. In a departmentalized secondary school it recognizes that there must be a unified language policy, that all teachers must know about and be concerned about language development, and that success in content fields will be strongly related to language development. Some program documents are now using the phrase "language and learning," rather than "language across the curriculum," to emphasize to subject teachers the interdependence of the development of language and concepts.

The New Zealand secondary language aims are:

1. To increase the students' ability to understand language and use it effectively.
2. To extend their imaginative and emotional responsiveness to and through language.
3. To extend their awareness of ideas and values through language. (p. 15)

Each classroom is expected to develop a program within the school program based on the language and learning objectives. In this classroom program teachers are urged to use all language modes, written and oral. Teachers and students should plan together "an appropriate range of language situations arising from and widening the students' own experience" with concern for expanding the range of language situations in which students are confident and competent. Language activities should be relevant based on the everyday lives, widening interests, and developmental needs of the pupils. Students need to be encouraged to reflect on their own language and that of others. There should be many chances to use and respond to language sensitively and imaginatively. The purpose and direction of the school language program should be made clear to students. (p 24)

The New Zealand program also makes evaluation an essential component of the teaching/learning process based on the language aims and undertaken for the benefit of students, teachers, parents, and interested members of the community.

For students, the purposes of evaluation include showing concern and appreciation for their work, identifying both strengths and weaknesses, judging growth, assessing changes in interests and attitudes, and considering the present and future values of their learning and the directions that learning might take.

For teachers the purposes include gathering information to use with students in planning and modifying programs and methods to better serve the development of each student, determining the consistency and balance of the language program in relation to the language aims, and providing a basis, objective and subjective, for reporting student achievement.

Reports of evaluation should be understood by parents, teachers, pupils, and the community. They should be the result of continuous monitoring. They should reflect the full range of the student's language achievements, and they should include useful, helpful statements. (p. 31) The New Zealand policy rejects the single mark that "disguises developmental levels students have achieved within the different language modes. . . . it provides a limited assessment of a narrow range of reading and writing skills." Linguistic effectiveness and appropriateness can only be judged in terms of the purpose and audience for whom it is intended, so evaluation must be based on a wide range of language use from different situations rather than tests. Furthermore, the policy calls attention to the need to consider growth over a considerable period of time rather than being confined to short-term measures. (p. 32)

Like the Quebec program, the New Zealand policy calls for a variety of assessment techniques:

The keeping of logs, folders, and tapes of work produced for comment
Records of teacher/student conferences about the work
Careful and continued observation and comment by the teacher and peers on
     activities, such as role playing, group discussion, and making collages and
     sound pictures
Informal tests
Assessment by an audience of class plays, debates, and other such language
     activities

The policy encourages student self-evaluation. It also stresses that teachers and classes should jointly set their goals and evaluation criteria.

The Kendall Program Guide
One common myth is that curricula and methodology that are appropriate for learners who are physically and mentally normal are not suitable for special populations with particular handicaps, because such learners can't learn like normal learners or because they need more highly structured programs. Considered carefully, such belief implies that there is more than one kind of human mind—that normal human minds learn with language and thinking developing interdependently in the context of experience, whereas handicapped learners learn less like normal humans than like laboratory animals through sequences of conditioned responses to isolated stimuli.

Teachers of handicapped children over the years have had to fight the stereotypes that because children are abnormal in one or more respects, they are abnormal in all respects, particularly in how they learn and how their minds work. What special education teachers have come to realize is that human beings have a remarkable ability to overcome handicaps and that a holistic curriculum with language learning strongly rooted in functional experiences is essential to providing handicapped learners the full range of cues for them to draw on.

"The Language Arts Program Guide" of the Kendall Demonstration Elementary School was developed for a population of hearing-impaired pupils. Kendall Demonstration Elementary School is an affiliate of Gallaudet College.

The program is described as:

whole-language, meaning-centered, and a pragmatic approach. These terms reflect Kendall's recognition of the importance of understanding and encouraging the process by which students acquire language in its written, spoken, and signed forms. . . . a whole language approach focuses on providing sufficient context for the task. Meaning-centered emphasizes the concern with students' construction of meaning, while pragmatic approach emphasizes the concern with the many and varied functions of language. (Kendall, Demonstration School, undated, p. 3)

The Kendall program emphasizes "through the air" language forms, which include various forms of signed languages as well as oral/auditory modes. Their concern is that their hearing-impaired pupils should have access to language in every possible form available to them. They stress that these must be developed in the context of opportunities for the students to experience the various functions of language. Experiencing language in situational contexts helps them to develop the pragmatics of particular situations and build language competence while attempting to accomplish something important to the student. Hearing-impaired students need the support and encouragement of teachers so that they will take the risks of using language, even if they're not sure it's right. Even becoming confident enough to say "I didn't understand" or "Say that again, please" involves being willing to take risks.

Written language development, in the Kendall program, also involves functional use and risk taking. The focus is on comprehension and expression in the context of functional use. Teachers are encouraged to accept growth and not to expect perfection as written language develops.

> The theoretical base of this guide is that reading and writing are language processes. Since language is used in a social context for particular purposes, language is not learned in a vacuum. It comes from a need to relate to other human beings and to communicate with them for a variety of reasons. It must also be stated that the word language as used in this guide does not refer to English alone, but to any symbol system which effectively conveys meaning. (Kendall, Demonstration School, p. 13)

The Kendall guide recognizes that ASL, American Sign Language, is not a representation of the English language but a separate language, with its own spatial grammar, which represents meaning. Hearing-impaired users of ASL who are learning to read English are much like other pupils learning to read English as a second language. Teachers are encouraged to expect and accept ASL-like features in the reading of their subjects. In the guide, reading, writing, and oral/manual listening and speaking activities are keyed to language functions as delineated by Michael Halliday. (Halliday, 1975) Objectives are classified as awareness, learning, and review.

Evaluation in the Kendall Program is a continuous process strongly emphasizing the intuition and sensitivity of the teacher gained from close and repeated interaction with the student. Evaluation by the teacher is in a natural setting as the student is pursuing meaning.

Whole Language in the Language-Thinking Centered Curriculum

We've previously illustrated some school policies that focus on promoting language through its use in communicating, learning, and developing knowledge and thinking. In North America there has been a grass-roots movement among teachers which is generally labeled the whole-language movement. In Canada this movement has reached such proportions that it has led to some of the official curriculum policies previously described and even to publishers labeling their basal reading programs as whole language. Implementing a curriculum for development of language and thinking in areas where the teachers and the school policies support each other is relatively easy and there is abundant evidence where this happy circumstance exists of the success of such programs.

Because of the political and educational climate in the United States in recent years, there has been an emphasis on technology on the one hand and back-to-basics fundamentalism on the other in schools. Some school systems or regions in larger systems in the United States have been moving toward holistic programs. To some extent, the popularity of whole-language programs among American teachers has been a reaction against atomistic and mechanistic school programs. Many teachers have found it necessary to think through what they believe in as professionals and develop their own support system to teach transactionally and holistically.

Because this whole-language movement is a grass-roots movement, it has come to mean different things to different people. It may help for us to summarize here, on the basis of the views we have developed in this book, what the essential commonalities of successful whole-language programs are.

Essentials of Whole Language

One teacher[1] asked a group of fourth-grade pupils how they learned to ride a bike. There were some differences of opinions among the pupils, but they were agreed on three things:

1. You've got to really want to.
2. You've got to keep trying even when you aren't successful.
3. You've got to be willing to fall down a lot.

These are essentials of learning any process, and they illustrate the need for risk taking and functional practice. To learn to ride a bike you have to be on a bicycle trying to make it go someplace. You've got to do it a lot to get really good at it, and you've got to be willing to make the mistakes that make you fall off but eventually get you to the point at which you're an effective, efficient bike rider who only falls when you take new risks.

[1]We're indebted to Debra Goodman, Detroit Public Schools, for this anecdote.

Language learning has all these same elements, but it has one thing going for it that bike riding doesn't. Not everyone needs to ride a bicycle, but everyone needs language. So children, given opportunities, keep trying to learn language until they succeed. And human interaction provides all children with many, many opportunities for language to be learned in the context of its use. However, just as bicycle riding requires getting on a bike and trying to go someplace, language learning requires trying to communicate, trying to comprehend, and trying to make oneself understood. It has to be whole language in the context of real, human, communicative transactions. Oral language is learned holistically in the context of speech acts; written language is learned holistically in the context of literacy events.

Whole-part relationships must be eventually learned in any area of knowledge, but the learning is not facilitated by freezing dynamic processes, chopping the whole up, and dissecting it. The whole is a lot more than the sum of its parts. The whole speech act or literacy event involves the intrinsic learning motivation that comes from wanting to "dig and be dug," as Langston Hughes put it.

One reason that whole-language programs are necessary, then, is that they relate to the view of the learner as a whole person with the human need to make sense of the world and communicate with others. They treat the learner as actively seeking to understand and organize the world, using everything already known to support further learning and to organize new experience. Whole-language programs thus always expand on what the learners already know, on current needs, on intrinsic motivation. They take an optimistic, positive view of the learners, even when the learners are handicapped, and they build on strength rather than isolate weaknesses.

Learning in a holistic program is seen as making sense of the real world, finding order in it, and solving the problems of coping with it. Thus, learning involves no sequence of parts adding up to wholes—no string of skills and subskills to be mastered before productive reading and writing may take place. It is functional in the sense that languge is a means to an end and not an end in itself. Whole-language programs assume that form will follow function and develop as the means of serving the function. Thus we learn to use print-sound relationships in the context of trying to make sense of print.

Learning is thus contextual—processes develop best in the context of their use: real speech acts and literacy events. Learning in a whole-language program is seen as developmental—growth toward increased proficiency in making sense of and through language. The language mistakes and miscues are signs both of strengths and weaknesses in the course of this development. Whole-language teachers expect these miscues and use them as indicators of development. Mastery never really exists; rather, there is a continuum of development with proficiency continuously increasing. Even highly proficient readers and writers, however, will make miscues, and even the most effective language users will be continuing to grow and develop proficiency.

Language learning in whole-language programs is seen as both personal and social. It is personal in the Piagetian sense in which the learner is changed through assimilation and accommodation, through alternatives of disequilibrium and equilibration as new experiences are encountered. It is social in the sense that language is learned in the context of learning how to mean—understanding others and being understood by them. Such social learning never simply happens in the head of one person. Language makes it possible for people to link their minds into a social mind capable of much greater learning than any single mind. Thus, language is the means by which we come to share what others have learned and by which others help us learn from our own experiences.

So whole-language programs are concerned both with language as sociolinguistic and psycholinguistic. They are holistic in being concerned with language as a means of social communication, as the medium of personal thought, and as the means of personal and social learning.

At several points in this text we cited the view of Michael Halliday that there are three kinds of language learning that must happen together if any one of the three are to occur: learning language, learning about language, and learning through language. All three occur simultaneously; none are dependent on any of the others, but rather each is dependent on the whole speech act or literacy event.

A language curriculum concerned about all three forms of language learning must therefore be a whole-language program. It cannot artificially isolate and sequence each form of language learning or arbitrarily make one dependent on another. Pupils do not learn language by first learning about it. They do not learn language first and then use it to learn. Rather, they learn language and learn about language while they use language to learn.

What all this adds up to is that school experiences must be real speech acts and literacy events much like nonschool experiences that contribute to language development. The role of the curriculum planner and of the teacher is to create in the classroom whole, real speech acts and literacy events that will involve the learners as real participants with their own purposes and functions. Planning for learning thus involves assuring that all the elements of these speech acts/literacy events are present for the learners.

These elements include:

1. *Real roles for the learners.* In a speech act/literacy event each participant has a productive or a receptive role or alternates roles (as in dialogue). These roles must be self-chosen and self-motivated in the situational context. Thus, the teachers and planners cannot simply assign roles; they must create and take advantage of situational contexts in which the learners will choose roles.
2. *Real purposes for the learners.* If people choose to engage in speech acts/literacy events, they have purposes that will guide their participation, their choice of language form (written or oral, formal or informal, narrative or expository, for example). They will also evaluate their success on the basis of their purposes.
3. *Real messages and content.* People engage in language because they have something to say or because they really want to know what is being said to them. Many other animal species seem to have the ability to produce sounds as complex as any that human language uses. What they lack is the ability to think complex thoughts and share them with others of their species.

4. *Real situational contexts.* People learn oral language as they find themselves in situational contexts in which speech acts naturally occur as people interact. Reading and writing, as we have shown, also begin to develop in the course of naturally occurring literacy events in situational contexts in which children find themselves. We've spoken of the classroom as a literate environment, one in which literacy events will naturally occur and in which situational contexts will stimulate pupils to be active participants. Involving pupils in transacting with an attendance chart in the process of taking attendance is a simple example. A more complex example is a group of fourth-grade children composing a question-naire and accompanying letter to send to local or national candidates for office to find out their positions on matters of importance to the children.

Whole-language programs are whole, then, in the sense that they are com-posed of whole speech acts and literacy events. But they are whole also in the sense that they don't separate the language processes from each other or language from its use, particularly in learning. The whole-language program is thus an integrated program in both senses: speaking, listening, reading, and writing are all integrated, and learning language is merged with learning through language. Development in each involves development in all, and the choice of which to use in particular speech acts/literacy events depends on the particular functions, purposes, content, and context of a situation. The letter and questionnaire just mentioned are appro-priate in the situation in which the candidates are not personally available. Consid-er, however, a school career-week program in which a local politician has come to talk about his job with the same fourth-grade group. In preparing for the career week the class may discuss who they want to invite, write letters, make phone calls or issue personal invitations, read to get background, discuss what to ask the person on the day of the visit, prepare questions, take notes, summarize and report the presentation, and write thank you notes afterward. There are a series of speech acts/literacy events, and the pupils and teacher will decide which language process is most appropriate for each event.

Thematic units, as discussed in Chapter 6, came about as a means of integrat-ing development in the language arts with conceptual development and problem solving around a particular theme or series of related questions. They provide rich opportunities for speech acts/literacy events in which language competence can be built while conceptual schemas are being built.

Whole-language programs are holistic in yet another sense. They broaden the curriculum to include the fullest range possible of oral and written language forms and functions. As important as literature is, it represents only a small portion of the range of functions for oral and written language. Schools have tended to neglect the very areas of language use that are most common in the outside-of-school experiences of children. These include what we called in the chapters on reading and writing "environmental print": signs on streets, stores, and walls, as well as product packaging. Schools pay too little attention to newspapers and magazines (including comics), to informational sources such as television guides, phone books, mail-order catalogues and other directories, and to directions for assem-bling models or playing games.

There is too little concern for informal note writing, for games involving reading and writing (not games to teach phonics skills), and in general for the mundane but very frequent and functional experiences children and young people have with written language. Perhaps that's why there is little concern in school with speech and even less with listening.

In whole-language programs the whole of language is the concern of the teacher and planners; pupils learn to appreciate and build on the full range of language experiences they have.

Planning the curriculum in broad outline and in detail is governed by the need to involve the pupils in real speech acts/literacy events that are part of integrated studies. Use of materials, including texts, needs to be geared to these integrated studies rather than building the curriculum around the texts. Texts would be used as resource materials and, in fact, if whole-language programs spread, eventually new kinds of texts would appear that deal with single concepts, themes, or a series of single concepts or themes.

As the specific programs cited above show, evaluation in whole-language programs tends to be ongoing. It's not a separate event that takes place after and sometimes before learning but a continual process that is part of the whole-language program. That's because whole-language teachers and planners recognize that development can only be accurately observed and monitored in the full context of events. Tests become reduced and distorted speech acts/literacy events. They produce unusual performance in unusual situations, which are not at all representative of the real contexts in which real language occurs.

This ongoing evaluation is not difficult for a professional teacher with a strong sense of how language develops a strong set of criteria for judging proficiency. It is not time consuming for the pupils, since it seldom involves special times set aside for testing or evaluation—that's part of the regular day's activities. It takes some time from the teacher because the teacher will save papers and other products, observe children reading, writing, speaking, and listening, keep anecdotal records of these observations and any other notable events; but these will be used by the teacher in planning and reporting to parents and administrators, so it is not really extra time.

Implementing Whole-Language Programs

What we have said in this book applies to the individual learner as well as to larger groups of learners. Thus, it can be applied on a classroom level, a school level, a district level, or on a state or provincial policy level. We've just provided some examples of whole-language policies. Ultimately successful implementation of holistic programs that expand language and thinking must reach that point at which a teacher is transacting with a learner. So the major problem where whole language is the policy of the school or the local educational authority is helping teachers to translate policy into practice in their classrooms. Conversely, many teachers, particularly in the United States, find that to implement whole language they must overcome administrative or policy obstacles. They find themselves at odds with the prescribed practice. Sometimes they are the only teachers in their schools bucking the system and trying to apply what they know for the good of their pupils.

Helping Teachers Move

No policy or curriculum guide can accomplish change unless it is understood, accepted, and enthusiastically supported by the teachers. That means in planning for innovative, holistic programs there must be continuous staff development. Unlike mechanistic, materials-based programs, this staff development can't simply tell teachers "what to do on Monday." The teachers must know why they are doing what they are doing. In this book we've built a theoretical base for the dual curriculum that builds language through knowledge and builds cognition through language. Teachers must develop a sound understanding of the reason why these dual curricula must be integrated and why language can't be taught piece by piece in isolation from its use. They must develop their own criteria for suitable classroom activities so that they can liberate themselves and their pupils from dependence on textbooks.

This staff development requires patience and strong support. Teachers, like students, take risks when they attempt new things. They need to plan and be in control of their own transitions. They need to be prepared to fall down and then pick themselves up with the help of others and try again. Whole-language teaching is less predictable then mechanistic approaches and appears harder to evaluate on a day-by-day basis.

It will help in staff development if teachers confront the reality of what their pupils are reading, writing, saying, and understanding as they listen. Just moving from group tests to close examination of real language use will help teachers to revalue their teaching and their pupils' learning.

Since change can't be mandated anyway, it is best to work with those teachers who volunteer to shift toward whole language. As they gain confidence and build successful curricula in their classes, they will be able to influence their peers. It ought not to be necessary for reluctant teachers to bootleg phonics into their classrooms to avoid the wrath of whole-language consultants and administrators. Rather, it should be legitimate for them to do what they believe in as long as they are willing to take responsibility for the effect on their pupils. Eventually, they can be helped to plan their own transitions with the help of colleagues who already have paved the way.

In essence, what whole-language programs are trying to do is to support the natural development of language and thinking in authentic speech acts and literacy events. That's why the programs are successful in the hands of teachers who understand this natural development. That's why advocates can afford to be patient in helping teachers to implement the concepts of whole language.

Building a Whole-Language Program in One Classroom

Clearly, it is more pleasant for a teacher to move toward a whole-language program in a supportive environment with sympathetic colleagues and supervisors, but many teachers in the United States have built whole-language classrooms without such support and even in the face of strong opposition.

On the positive side, these teachers draw strength from the sound base from which they operate. They know what they want to do and why. They have theoretically based criteria for the choices that they make in methods, materials, and activities. They are able and willing to take the responsibility for what happens in their classrooms. They have the basis for evaluating their successes and failures and learning from them. They will need to be able to explain what they are doing and why, particularly as it involves changes from what has been conventional practice in their schools. Parents, colleagues, administrators, and the pupils themselves will need to understand the reasons for the changes.

On the negative side, there are risks involved in innovating without administrative support. If teachers are successful, administrators are often quite willing to permit them to continue what they are doing. But if success is narrowly judged by acievement test gain scores. Or if the administrators are unwilling or unable to recognize the evidence of success in learning, then teachers may indeed be at risk.

Compromise is a characteristic of most human endeavor. In a classroom with a strong holistic, integrated focus on the development of language and thinking, children will not be harmed nor their development strongly interfered with by some experiences or materials that are not ideal. But there are some conditions that make it impossible to achieve even minimal integration of the learning. Some American schools have mandated highly structured mastery learning programs that lock both the teacher and the learner into so rigid and tight a sequence that there is no possibility of movement or even compromise. When teachers as a group recognize such an intolerable condition, they can act together, perhaps through their unions. An individual may only be able to respond by leaving and looking for another job. Doctors, at least in theory, will not practice under conditions that endanger their patients. Teachers must also refuse to practice under conditions that are harmful to their pupils.

Support Groups

Partly because whole language is a grass-roots movement among teachers, a number of support groups have sprung up. These groups vary greatly from place to place. Their common characteristic is that teachers who find themselves isolated in what they are trying to do in their schools band together with like-minded others. They provide their own staff development; they also serve a group-therapy function as they share their successes, their failures, and their strategies for dealing with hostile principals, suspicious parents, or jealous colleagues.

School systems attempting to implement whole language have encouraged teachers to form support groups so that they can learn from each other in nonthreatening settings.

The support group helps a great deal to eliminate the sense of'isolation. It also makes it possible for teachers to gain perspective on how well their innovation is going. They get a sense of the experiences other teachers have trying to shift toward language-thinking centered programs (Hood, in press).

Self-Planned Transitions

Teachers shifting toward whole language shouldn't feel that they must make the transition in a single leap. They can plan small steps, perhaps strengthening what they are most pleased with in their teaching or eliminating first what they are least pleased with. For example, a teacher who already uses thematic units might expand their scope and include more and more of the reading and writing within the unit. Or a teacher who has had little writing going on might introduce a process writing program. A teacher who has relied heavily on basal readers might stop using the skill exercises and begin to vary the way stories and reading selections are used to put a heavier emphasis on reading for meaning.

Teachers who don't quite know where to begin might plan to visit the classroom of a whole-language teacher or invite a colleague into their classrooms to offer suggestions on how to plan a transition.

Authenticity

The key is to move toward authenticity in all the experiences the pupils have in the classroom that involve using language. That means eliminating exercises to practice reading, handwriting, spelling, composition, and grammar. So eventually special materials for developing language must go. Spelling is given the importance it deserves by involving pupils in actual writing—not sentences to practice the spelling. Handwriting is developed during real writing so that the influence of legibility on the success of being understood can be judged by the writer. When the pupils talk, it's because they have something to say to someone; when they listen, they have a personal purpose that isn't totally bound within a school assignment. The questions they ask—and seek answers to—are their questions.

The whole-language teacher needs to shift so that texts support the learning and teaching rather than controlling it. When pupils write, it should be because that's the best way to say what they need to say, whether its a letter to the world—a poem, story, personal narrative, or essay—or a note to the kid across the aisle.

Largely, for the teacher, the transition is in point of view—how the teacher defines himself or herself in relation to the learners. The American teacher has been in danger of becoming a technician who administers a sequenced and impersonal program to passively defined learners. All teachers need to become guides, supports, and monitors of learning. They need to take back the power in their classrooms from the textbooks and the tests so they can help their pupils to expand their power to use language and to think.

References

Bullock Committee, "A Language for Life," Report of the Committee of Inquiry appointed by the Secretary of State for Education and Science, Department of Education and Science (London: Her Majesty's Stationery Office, 1975).

John I. Goodlad, *A Place Called School* (New York: McGraw-Hill, 1984).

————, "Where are School Goals Beyond the Basics?" *Education Digest* (November, 1983), p. 6.

Edmonton (Alberta) Public Schools, "Language Arts Working Paper," unpublished, October 1982.

Edmonton Public Schools, Language Arts Program, "The Elementary Language Arts Program," Edmonton, Alberta, September, 1985.

Gouvernement du Quebec, "English Language Arts I–VI," Direction Generale du Developement Pedagogique, Ministere de L'Education, Province of Quebec, July 1, 1983.

Kendall Demonstration School, "Goals of Language Arts Program Guide," Washington, D.C., undated.

Michael Halliday, *Learning How to Mean* (London: Edward Arnold, 1975).

Wendy Hood, "How to Build a TAWL Group," *Learning 87* (in press).

National English Syllabus Committee, "Statement of Aims," New Zealand Department of Education (Government Printer: Wellington, New Zealand, 1976).

Index